Second Workshop on Document-grounded Dialogue and Conversational Question Answering (DialDoc 2022)

Dublin, Ireland
26 May 2022

ISBN: 978-1-7138-6734-0

Printed from e-media with permission by:

Curran Associates, Inc.
57 Morehouse Lane
Red Hook, NY 12571

Some format issues inherent in the e-media version may also appear in this print version.

Printed with permission by Curran Associates, Inc. (2023)

Association for Computational Linguistics
209 N. Eighth Street
Stroudsburg, Pennsylvania 18360

Phone: 1-570-476-8006
Fax: 1-570-476-0860

acl@aclweb.org

Additional copies of this publication are available from:

Curran Associates, Inc.
57 Morehouse Lane
Red Hook, NY 12571 USA
Phone: 845-758-0400
Fax: 845-758-2633
Email: curran@proceedings.com
Web: www.proceedings.com

DialDoc 2022

Proceedings of the Second DialDoc Workshop on Document-grounded Dialogue and Conversational Question Answering

Proceedings of the Workshop

May 26, 2022

The DialDoc organizers gratefully acknowledge the support from the following sponsors.

Gold

IBM **Research** AI

Introduction

Welcome to the Second Workshop on Document-grounded Dialogue and Conversational Question Answering (DialDoc) co-located with ACL 2022.

Following the exiting outcome for the First DialDoc Workshop co-located at ACL-IJCNLP 2021, we continue the goal and effort to explore document knowledge for information-seeking goal-oriented dialogue systems. There is a vast amount of document content created every day by human writers to communicate with human readers for sharing knowledge, ranging from encyclopedias to customer service FAQs. Making the document content accessible to users via conversational systems and scaling it to various domains could be a meaningful yet challenging task. There are significant individual research threads that show promise in handling heterogeous knowledge embedded in documents for building conversational systems, including (1) unstructured content, such as text passages; (2) semi-structured content, such as tables or lists; (3) multi-modal content, such as images and videos along with text descriptions, and so on. The purpose of the workshop is to invite researchers and practitioners to bring their individual perspectives on the subject of document-grounded dialogue and conversational question answering to advance the field in a community-wise joint effort.

Different than the First DialDoc Workshop, we highlight the challenge of the scalability on building information-seeking goal-oriented dialogue systems in this workshop. We also propose a special theme on on scaling up document-grounded dialogue systems especially for *low-resource* domains, such as minority language support and emerging and unforeseen situations such as COVID-19 pandemic. In addition, for the Shared Task on modeling goal-oriented information-seeking dialogues, one of the tasks is based on the low-resource setting.

For the Shared Task competition, it mainly focuses on building open-book goal-oriented information-seeking conversation systems. The task are to generate agent responses based on dialogue history and domain documents, where each dialogue could correspond to multiple grounding documents. It includes two leaderbards based on different settings: the first one (*SEEN* leaderboard) is that all dialogues in the test data are grounded in the documents from the same domains as the training data; the second one (*UNSEEN* leaderboard) is that all dialogues in the test data are grounded in the documents from an unseen domain. There are a total of 22 teams that participated in the Dev Phase. For the final Test Phase, 10 teams submitted to the leaderboards. Many submissions outperform baseline significantly. On the *SEEN* leaderboard, the best-performing system achieved 52.2 F1 comparing to 35.95 by the baseline. On the *UNSEEN* leaderboard, the best-performing system achieved 34.65 F1 comparing to 19.26 by the baseline.

In this workshop, we have the research track and technical system track for Shared Task. There are a total 21 submissions. There are 14 accepted papers in the research track, including 12 long papers and 2 short papers. There are 6 accepted papers in the technical system track. The workshop program features 18 paper presentations either as a poster or oral presentation. We are also fortunate to have invited talks from Jeff Dalton, Michel Galley, Mari Ostendorf, Siva Reddy and Zhou Yu.

Finally, we would like thank all people who contributed to this workshop: the authors for their paper submissions, the teams for participating the Shared Task, the program committee members for their fundamental contributions, ACL workshop co-chair for the guidance and the amazing invited speakers. Special thanks to IBM Research for sponsoring the rewards for the Shared Task competition.

Song, Chengguang, Ellen, Hui, Caixia, Svitlana

Organizing Committee

Organizers

Song Feng, Amazon AWS AI
Chengguang Tang, Alibaba DAMO Research
Ellen (Zeqiu) Wu, University of Washington
Hui Wan, IBM Research AI
Caixia Yuan, Beijing University of Posts and Telecommunication
Svitlana Vakulenko, Amazon

Program Committee

Program Chairs

Amanda Buddemeyer, University of Pittsburgh
Asli Celikyilmaz, Meta AI Research
Bowen Yu, Chinese Academy of Sciences
Chen Henry Wu, Carnegie Mellon University
Chulaka Gunasekara, IBM Research AI
Chun Gan, JD Research
Cunxiang Wang, Westlake University
Danish Contractor, IBM Research
Dian Yu, Tencent
Diane Litman, University of Pittsburgh
Ehud Reiter, University of Aberdeen
Elizabeth Clark, University of Washington
Fanghua Ye, University College London
Tao Feng, Monash University
Guanyi Chen, Utrecht University
Hanjie Chen, University of Virginia
Hao Zhou, Tencent
Haotian Cui, Toronto University
Haochen Liu, Michigan State University
Houyu Zhang, Amazon
Ioannis Konstas, Heriot-Watt University
Jingjing Xu, Peking University
Jia-Chen Gu, USTC
Jinfeng Xiao, UIUC
Jian Wang, The Hong Kong Polytechnic University
Jingyang Li, Alibaba DAMO Academy
Jiwei Li, SHANNON.AI
Jun Xu, Baidu
Kai Song, ByteDance
Ke Shi, Tencent
Kun Qian, Columbia University
Kaixuan Zhang, Northwestern University
Libo Qin, MLNLP
Michael Johnston, Interactions
Meng Qu, MILA
Minjoon Seo, KAIST
Pei Ke, Tsinghua University
Peng Qi, Stanford University
Ravneet Singh, University of Pittsburgh
Ryuichi Takanobu, Tsinghua University
Rongxing Zhu, The University of Melbourne
Seokhwan Kim, Amazon Alexa AI
Shehzaad Dhuliawala, Microsoft Research Montreal
Srinivas Bangalore, Interactions
Zejiang Shen, AllenAI
Vaibhav Adlakha, MCGill and MILA

Wanjun Zhong, MSRA
Xi Chen, Tencent
Yifan Gao, The Chinese University of Hong Kong
Yekun Chai, Baidu
Yinhe Zheng, Alibaba DAMO Academy
Yiwei Jiang, Ghent University
Yajing Sun, Chinese Academy of Sciences
Yunqi Qiu, Chinese Academy of Sciences
Yosi Mass, IBM Research
Yutao Zhu, University of Montreal
Zheng Zhang, Tsinghua University
Zhenyu Zhang, Chinese Academy of Sciences
Zhenzhong Lan, Westlake University
Zhixing Tian, JD

Keynote Talk: How grounded is document-grounded conversational AI?

Siva Reddy
McGill University, Facebook CIFAR AI, Mila Quebec AI

Bio: Siva Reddy is an Assistant Professor in the School of Computer Science and Linguistics at McGill University. He is a Facebook CIFAR AI Chair and a core faculty member of Mila Quebec AI Institute. Before McGill, he was a postdoctoral researcher at Stanford University. He received his PhD from the University of Edinburgh in 2017, where he was a Google PhD Fellow. His research focuses on representation learning for language that facilitates systematic generalization, reasoning and conversational modeling. He received the 2020 VentureBeat AI Innovation Award in NLP, and the best paper award at EMNLP 2021.

Keynote Talk: Knowledge-Grounded Conversation Search and Understanding: Current Progress and Future Directions

Jeff Dalton
University of Glasgow

Bio: Dr. Jeff Dalton is an Assistant Professor in the School of Computing Science at the University of Glasgow where he leads the Glasgow Representation and Information Learning Lab (GRILL) (https://grilllab.ai). His research focuses on text understanding and conversational information seeking. He completed his Ph.D. at the University of Massachusetts Amherst in the Center for Intelligent Information Retrieval. Later in Google Research, he worked on Information Extraction as part of the Knowledge Discovery Team (Knowledge Vault) and on language understanding in the Assistant Response Ranking team. He is the lead organizer for the TREC Conversational Assistance Track (CAsT) (http://treccast.ai) and previously helped organize the Complex Answer Retrieval track. He is the recipient of a prestigious UKRI Turing AI Acceleration Fellowship on Neural Conversational Assistants and received research awards from Google, Amazon, and Bloomberg. He is the faculty advisor for the 2021/2022 Alexa Prize Taskbot challenge team, GRILLBot. He holds multiple patents in retrieval, information extraction, and question answering.

Keynote Talk: Knowledge-infused dialog systems

Zhou Yu
Columbia University

Bio: Zhou Yu joined the CS department at Columbia University in Jan 2021 as an Assistant Professor (http://www.cs.columbia.edu/ zhouyu/). Before that, she was an Assistant Professor at UC Davis. She obtained her Ph.D. from Carnegie Mellon University in 2017. Zhou has built various dialog systems that have a real impact, such as a job interview training system, a depression screening system, and a second language learning system. Her research interests include dialog systems, language understanding and generation, vision and language, human-computer interaction, and social robots. Zhou received an ACL 2019 best paper nomination, featured in Forbes 2018 30 under 30 in Science, and won the 2018 Amazon Alexa Prize.

Keynote Talk: Interactive Document Generation

Michel Galley
Microsoft Research

Bio: Michel Galley is a Senior Principal Researcher at Microsoft Research. His research interests are in the areas of natural language processing and machine learning, with a particular focus on conversational AI, text generation, statistical machine translation, and summarization. He obtained his M.S. and Ph.D. from Columbia University and his B.S. from EPFL, all in Computer Science. Before joining Microsoft Research, he was a Research Associate in the CS department at Stanford University. He co-authored more than 70 scientific papers, many of which appeared at top NLP, AI, and ML conferences.

Keynote Talk: Understanding conversation context is central to conversational AI

Mari Ostendorf
University of Washington

Bio: Mari Ostendorf is an Endowed Professor of System Design Methodologies in the Electrical Computer Engineering Department at the University of Washington and currently serves as UW's Vice Provost for Research. She is a Fellow of the IEEE, ISCA and ACL, a former Australian-American Fulbright Scholar, a member of the Washington State Academy of Sciences, a Corresponding Fellow of the Royal Society of Edinburgh, and a member of the National Academy of Engineering. For her contributions in spoken language processing, she was awarded the 2018 IEEE James L. Flanagan Speech and Audio Processing Award. In 2017, she served as a faculty advisor for the student team winning the inaugural AlexaPrize competition to build a socialbot, and conversational AI is a focus of her current work. Her research explores dynamic models for understanding and generating speech and text, particularly in multi-party contexts, and it contributes to a variety of applications, including call center analytics, information seeking dialogues, equitable assessments in education, and clinical information extraction.

Table of Contents

Program

Thursday, May 26, 2022

09:00 - 09:05 *Opening Remark*

09:05 - 09:40 *Invited talk I by Siva Reddy*

09:40 - 10:25 *Paper presentation*

Conversation- and Tree-Structure Losses for Dialogue Disentanglement
Tianda Li, Jia-Chen Gu, Zhen-Hua Ling and Quan Liu

Construction of Hierarchical Structured Knowledge-based Recommendation Dialogue Dataset and Dialogue System
Takashi Kodama, Ribeka Tanaka and Sadao Kurohashi

Retrieval-Free Knowledge-Grounded Dialogue Response Generation with Adapters
Yan Xu, Etsuko Ishii, Samuel Cahyawijaya, Zihan Liu, Genta Indra Winata, Andrea Madotto, Dan SU and Pascale Fung

10:25 - 10:40 *Coffee break*

10:40 - 11:15 *Invited talk II by Jeff Dalton*

11:15 - 11:55 *Paper lightning talk I*

TRUE: Re-evaluating Factual Consistency Evaluation
Or Honovich, Roee Aharoni, Jonathan Herzig, Hagai Taitelbaum, Doron Kukliansy, Vered Cohen, Thomas Scialom, Idan Szpektor, Avinatan Hassidim and Yossi Matias

Pseudo Ambiguous and Clarifying Questions Based on Sentence Structures Toward Clarifying Question Answering System
Yuya Nakano, Seiya Kawano, Koichiro Yoshino, Katsuhito Sudoh and Satoshi Nakamura

Parameter-Efficient Abstractive Question Answering over Tables or Text
Vaishali Pal, Evangelos Kanoulas and Maarten de Rijke

Conversational Search with Mixed-Initiative - Asking Good Clarification Questions backed-up by Passage Retrieval
Yosi Mass, Doron Cohen, Asaf Yehudai and David Konopnicki

Graph-combined Coreference Resolution Methods on Conversational Machine Reading Comprehension with Pre-trained Language Model
Zhaodong Wang and Kazunori Komatani

Thursday, May 26, 2022 (continued)

	G4: Grounding-guided Goal-oriented Dialogues Generation with Multiple Documents Shiwei Zhang, Yiyang Du, Guanzhong Liu, Zhao Yan and Yunbo Cao
	UniDS: A Unified Dialogue System for Chit-Chat and Task-oriented Dialogues Xinyan Zhao, Bin He, Yasheng Wang, Yitong Li, Fei Mi, Yajiao Liu, Xin Jiang, Qun Liu and Huanhuan Chen
	MSAMSum: Towards Benchmarking Multi-lingual Dialogue Summarization Xiachong Feng, Xiaocheng Feng and Bing Qin
11:55 - 12:55	*Poster session*
12:55 - 14:00	*Lunch break*
14:00 - 14:35	*Invited talk III by Zhou Yu*
15:05 - 14:35	*Paper presentation*
	Low-Resource Adaptation of Open-Domain Generative Chatbots Greyson Gerhard-Young, Raviteja Anantha, Srinivas Chappidi and Bjorn Hoffmeister
	Task2Dial: A Novel Task and Dataset for Commonsense-enhanced Task-based Dialogue Grounded in Documents Carl Strathearn and Dimitra Gkatzia
15:05 - 15:20	*Coffee break*
15:20 - 15:35	*DialDoc 2022 Shared Task*
15:35 - 15:50	*Shared Task Prizes and Best Paper Awards presented by Luis Lastras*
15:50 - 16:25	*Invited talk IV by Michel Galley*
16:25 - 17:00	*Invited talk V by Mari Ostendorf*
17:00 - 17:05	*Ending Remark*

Thursday, May 26, 2022 (continued)

MSAMSum: Towards Benchmarking Multi-lingual Dialogue Summarization

Xiachong Feng, Xiaocheng Feng, Bing Qin
Harbin Institute of Technology, China
{xiachongfeng,xcfeng,bqin}@ir.hit.edu.cn

Abstract

Dialogue summarization helps users capture salient information from various types of dialogues has received much attention recently. However, current works mainly focus on English dialogue summarization, leaving other languages less well explored. Therefore, we present a multi-lingual dialogue summarization dataset, namely MSAMSum, which covers dialogue-summary pairs in six languages. Specifically, we derive MSAMSum from the standard SAMSum (Gliwa et al., 2019) using sophisticated translation techniques and further employ two methods to ensure the integral translation quality and summary factual consistency. Given the proposed MSAMum, we systematically set up five multi-lingual settings for this task, including a novel mix-lingual dialogue summarization setting. To illustrate the utility of our dataset, we benchmark various experiments with pre-trained models under different settings and report results in both supervised and zero-shot manners. We also discuss some future works towards this task to motivate future researches[1].

Figure 1: A multi-lingual meeting scenario, in which multinational people participate in one meeting concurrently. It is valuable to provide them with summaries in a preferred language.

1 Introduction

Recent years have witnessed increasing interest in dialogue summarization (Feng et al., 2021a; Tuggener et al., 2021). It aims to distill the most important information from various types of dialogues, which can alleviate the problem of communication data overload. Towards this research direction, various datasets have been proposed to promote this task.

The AMI (Carletta et al., 2005) and ICSI (Janin et al., 2003) datasets provide the initial opportunity for meeting summarization. With the advent of data-hungry neural models and pre-trained language models, Gliwa et al. (2019) come up with the first high quality large-scale dialogue summarization dataset, namely SAMSum, which resurges this task. Then, various datasets are proposed to meet different needs and scenarios (Chen et al., 2021a; Malykh et al., 2020; Rameshkumar and Bailey, 2020; Zhong et al., 2021; Zhu et al., 2021; Chen et al., 2021b; Zhang et al., 2021; Fabbri et al., 2021). Despite the encouraging progresses achieved, current works overwhelmingly focused on English. Meanwhile, with the help of instantaneous translation systems[2], a dialogue involving multinational participants becomes more and more common and frequent. Therefore, it is valuable to provide them with dialogue summaries in a preferred language.

To this end, we propose a *multi-lingual dialogue summarization task*. The practical benefits of this task are twofold: it not only provides rapid access to the salient content, but also enables the dissemination of relevant content across participants of other languages. Intuitively, to achieve this goal, we need to answer two key questions, one is *Where do we get data resources for this multi-lingual research?* the other is *How do we perform various multi-lingual settings?*

[1] https://github.com/xcfcode/MSAMSum

[2] https://translatebyhumans.com/en/services/interpretation/zoom/

Proceedings of the Second DialDoc Workshop on Document-grounded Dialogue and Conversational Question Answering, pages 1 - 12
May 26, 2022

For the first question, we seek for potential available resources that can support our multi-lingual research. Although creating English datasets has proven feasible, the need for dialogues and summary-written experts in different languages makes the collection of multi-lingual datasets highly costing or even intractable. To mitigate this challenge, we devote our efforts to constructing the multi-lingual dataset via sophisticated translation techniques following Zhu et al. (2019). Firstly, we select SAMSum (Gliwa et al., 2019) as our source English dataset because of its large scale and wide domain coverage. Then, we translate it into five other official languages of the United Nations via high-performance translation API, including Chinese, French, Arabic, Russian and Spanish. Furthermore, We employ two methods: *round-trip translation* and *textual entailment* to filter out low-quality translations and ensure the factual consistency at both the dialogue-level and summary-level. Finally, *we obtain our MSAMSum dataset as the data resource for this multi-lingual research.*

For the second question, given the well-constructed MSAMsum dataset, we set up various settings for our multi-lingual dialogue summarization task, including ONE-TO-ONE, MANY-TO-ONE, ONE-TO-MANY and MANY-TO-MANY. The ONE-TO-ONE setting can be further divided into *Mono-lingual* and *Cross-lingual* settings. To further boost the research on multi-lingual dialogue summarization, we creatively propose one new setting, namely MIX-TO-MANY, which takes a mix-lingual dialogue as input and produce summaries in different languages. This setting is in line with the real world scenario that multinational participants can use their mother tongue to communicate with each other by means of instantaneous translation systems (depicted in Figure 1). To sum up, *we set up five settings for the research on the whole scene of multi-lingual dialogue summarization.*

To illustrate the utility of our MSAMSum, we conduct extensive experiments under five multi-lingual settings based on the current multi-lingual pre-trained model mBART-50 (Tang et al., 2020), and evaluate it in both supervised and zero-shot manners. The results reveal the feasibility of multi-lingual dialogue summarization task. The case study also shows that the multi-lingual model is able to produce fluent and factual consistency summaries in different languages. We further conclude several future works to prompt future researches.

2 Related Work

2.1 Multi-lingual Summarization

Multi-lingual summarization is a valuable research direction, which can benefit users from various countries (Cao et al., 2020; Wang et al., 2022). Especially, cross-lingual summarization, which receives a document in a source language and produces a summary in a another language, has attracted lots of research attentions (Wan et al., 2010). For a long time, pipeline systems combining both machine translation and summarization tools are used to solve this problem (Ouyang et al., 2019). However, pipeline systems do have their own drawbacks, like error propagation and system latency. Therefore, researchers turn to end-to-end neural methods. Zhu et al. (2019) first propose two cross-lingual summarization datasets using machine translation techniques. Afterwards, various models (Zhu et al., 2020b; Xu et al., 2020; Wang et al., 2021) and datasets (Ladhak et al., 2020; Hasan et al., 2021; Varab and Schluter, 2021) are proposed for this task. These works have achieved great progresses and have proved the feasibility of end-to-end multi-lingual summarization. In this paper, for the first time, we study the dialogue summarization task under various multi-lingual settings.

2.2 Dialogue Summarization

The earlier publicly available meeting datasets AMI (Carletta et al., 2005) and ICSI (Janin et al., 2003) have prompted dialogue summarization for a long time. Recently, the introduction of SAMSum dataset has resurged this direction. Researchers propose various methods to tackle this problem by incorporating auxiliary information, modeling the interaction and dealing with long input sequences (Chen and Yang, 2020; Feng et al., 2021b; Zhu et al., 2020a; Feng et al., 2021c). Additionally, various valuable datasets are carried out to meet different needs, which further accelerate the development of dialogue summarization (Zhong et al., 2021; Zhu et al., 2021; Zhang et al., 2021). What is more, Mehnaz et al. (2021) study dialogue summarization under the Hindi-English code-switched setting and get the best performance based on multi-lingual pre-trained language models. Nonetheless, the current datasets and models are mainly tailored for English, which leave other languages less well explored. To mitigate this challenge, we propose the MSAMSum to study the multi-lingual dialogue summarization task.

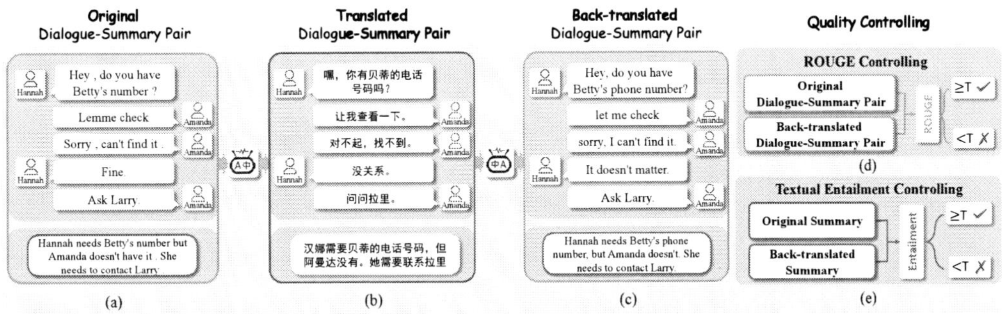

Figure 2: Illustration of our data construction process. (a) Given the original English data in the SAMSum (Gliwa et al., 2019), we translate it into another language (e.g., Chinese). Furthermore, we employ two quality controlling methods: *round-trip translation* and *textual entailment*. (c) For the first method, we back-translate the Chinese data into English and (d) calculate the ROUGE score between the original one and the back-translated one. (e) For the second one, we calculate the entailment score between back-translated summary and the original summary. If both scores exceed the pre-defined threshold, the translated dialogue-summary pair is retained.

3 The MSAMSum Dataset

In this section, we introduce our MSAMSum dataset, including (1) Why we choose SAMSum dataset? (2) How we translate the original SAMSum dataset? (3) How we control the translation quality? and (4) Statistics for the newly created MSAMSum dataset. The whole dataset construction process is shown in Figure 2.

3.1 Dataset Selection

Current dialogue summarization datasets are mainly tailored for English (Gliwa et al., 2019; Chen et al., 2021a,b; Zhang et al., 2021), resulting in existing works not centring on other languages. In order to support our multi-lingual research, we follow Zhu et al. (2019), which uses state-of-the-art machine translation techniques to construct datasets in different languages.

Before launching the translation of the current dataset, we first need to choose a suitable dataset. After carefully comparing several datasets, we finally choose SAMSum (Gliwa et al., 2019) as our source English dataset according to the following two reasons: (1) it is a human-labeled large-scale dataset; (2) it covers a wide range of domains.

3.2 Machine Translation

For each dialogue-summary pair in the selected English SAMSum dataset (shown in Figure 2(a)), we translate the utterances and the summary to the target language (shown in Figure 2(b)) via high-performance machine translation service[3]. To make our work more representative and generalized, we choose five other official languages of the United Nations as our translation target languages[4]. Note that for each dialogue, we perform the translation at the utterance-level since machine translation can achieve good results with utterances of moderate length. After this process, we can get dialogue-summary pairs in Chinese (Zh), French (Fr), Arabic (Ar), Russian (Ru), Spanish(ES) and also original English (En).

3.3 Quality Controlling

To ensure the data quality, we further leverage two quality controlling methods. First, we employ *round-trip translation* strategy at both dialogue and summary level to filter out low-quality translations. Second, at the summary level, we use *textual entailment* strategy to verify factual consistency.

3.3.1 Round-trip Translation

Round-trip translation is the process of translating a text into another language (forward translation), then translating the result back into the original language (back translation), using MT service. Given the translated dialogue-summary pair in target language (shown in Figure 2(b)), we back-translate it into the original English version (shown in Figure 2(c)). Afterward, we follow Zhu et al. (2019) and calculate the ROUGE-1 score (Lin, 2004) between the original dialogue-summary pair and the back-translated dialogue-summary pair (shown in Figure 2(d)). In detail, we first calculate the ROUGE-1 score for the corresponding utterances and the sum-

[3]https://cloud.google.com/translate

[4]https://www.un.org/en/our-work/official-languages

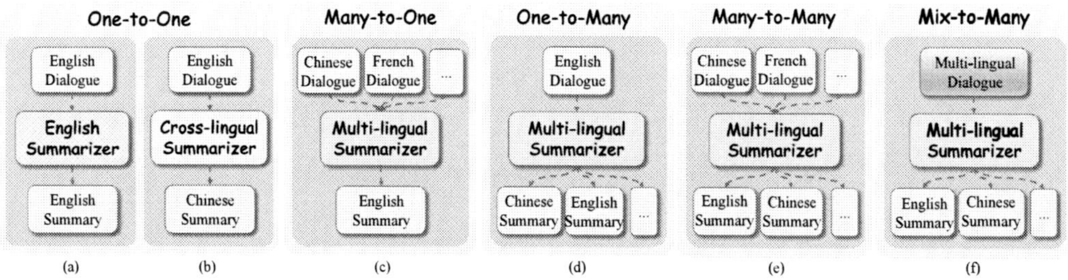

Figure 3: Illustration of different multi-lingual settings. We set up five settings in total, according to the number of input and output languages the model can handle. Concretely, the ONE-TO-ONE is the basic setting, the MANY-TO-ONE model encodes N languages and decodes to English, while the ONE-TO-MANY model encodes English and decodes into N languages, the MANY-TO-MANY model encodes and decodes N languages. Besides, we originally explore one new MIX-TO-MANY setting, where the model takes a mix-lingual dialogue (utterances in a dialogue belongs to different languages) as input and outputs summaries in different languages.

mary respectively, and then get the final ROUGE-1 score by averaging all scores. If the final ROUGE-1 score exceeds the pre-defined threshold, the translated dialogue-summary pair (shown in Figure 2(b)) is retained. Otherwise, the pair will be filtered[5].

3.3.2 Textual Entailment

Since the summary serves as the core part of dialogue summarization, it not only needs coarse-grained surface-level high quality but also fine-grained factual consistency (Huang et al., 2021). To this end, we adopt the textual entailment method to access whether the translated summary is consistent with the original summary. Specifically, we obtain the entailment score for the translated English summary and the original English summary via state-of-the-art entailment model[6], as shown in Figure 2(e). If the entailment score exceeds the pre-defined threshold, the translated dialogue-summary pair is retained. Otherwise, the pair will be filtered.

3.4 Datasets Alignment and Statistics

Following the above steps, we can get translated and pure datasets in different languages. Note that these datasets are of different sizes, which is caused by the quality controlling process. To unify our experiments, we get the intersection of these datasets in six languages, resulting in the final MSAMSum dataset (statistics in Table 1)[7].

		Train	Valid	Test
	#	5307	302	320
	Avg.Turns	11.01	10.48	11.15
En	Avg.Tokens	115.72	115.19	118.21
En	Avg.Sum	22.18	22.33	22.06
Zh	Avg.Chars	242.08	237.39	246.95
Zh	Avg.Sum	34.65	35.36	35.08
Fr	Avg.Tokens	99.33	99.01	102.5
Fr	Avg.Sum	19.30	19.47	19.16
Ar	Avg.Tokens	57.17	55.85	56.63
Ar	Avg.Sum	18.81	18.71	18.80
Ru	Avg.Tokens	89.00	88.53	91.11
Ru	Avg.Sum	15.99	16.07	16.11
Es	Avg.Tokens	89.83	89.35	92.08
Es	Avg.Sum	18.67	18.60	18.68

Table 1: Statistics for MSAMSum dataset. "#" means the number of dialogue-summary pairs, "Avg.Turns", "Avg.Tokens", "Avg.Chars" and "Avg.Sum" mean the average number of turns of dialogues, tokens of dialogues, characters of dialogues and tokens of summaries respectively. Note that sentences in Arabic tend to be shorter than those in other languages[8].

4 Multi-lingual Settings

In this section, we introduce various multi-lingual dialogue summarization settings, including a newly proposed MIX-TO-MANY setting. All settings are depicted in Figure 3.

4.1 ONE-TO-ONE

The ONE-TO-ONE setting can be viewed as a specific type of multi-lingual setting, where the model can merely handle the input of one language and the output of one language. According to whether the

[5] We show detailed round-trip translation ROUGE scores in the supplementary file.

[6] https://github.com/pytorch/fairseq/blob/main/examples/roberta/README.md

[7] We show the statistics for different parts before alignment in the supplementary file.

[8] https://forum.wordreference.com/threads/english-to-arabic-length-change.1495268/

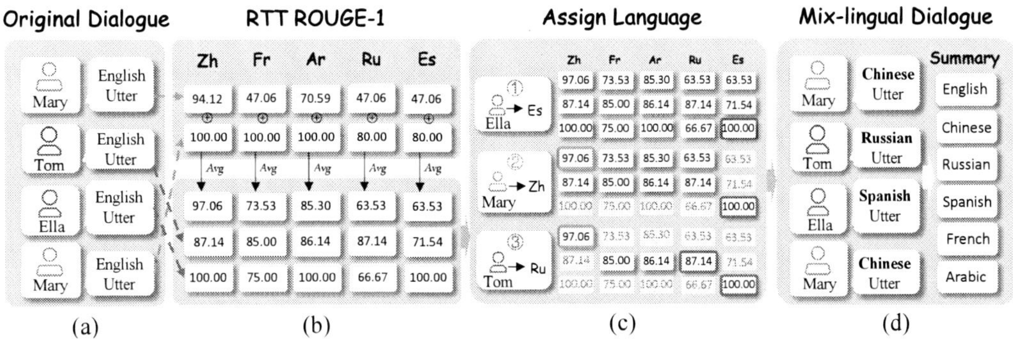

Figure 4: Illustration of the mix-lingual dialogue construction process. Given one English dialogue, we first group utterances for the same participant and get the averaged round-trip translation ROUGE-1 score for each language. Then, we adopt a greedy search strategy to assign each participant a language. Finally, we can get the mix-lingual dialogue associated with summaries in different languages.

input and output belong to the same language, this setting can be further divided into *Mono-lingual* setting (shown in Figure 3(a)) and *Cross-lingual* setting (shown in Figure 3(b)).

Experimental Setting: For *mono-lingual* experiments, we train six models based on {En→En}, {Zh→Zh}, {Fr→Fr}, {Ar→Ar}, {Ru→Ru} and {Es→Es} mono-lingual pairs respectively. For *cross-lingual* experiments, we train two models based on {En→Zh} and {Zh→En} cross-lingual pairs respectively. All eight models are tested in supervised manner.

4.2 MANY-TO-ONE and ONE-TO-MANY

MANY-TO-ONE models are able to process dia logues in various languages and output the summary in one language, as shown in Figure 3(c). On the contrary, ONE-TO-MANY models have the ability to produce summaries in various languages given a fixed language input, as shown in Figure 3(d). Both settings require models with multilingual capabilities.

Experimental Setting: For MANY-TO-ONE experiments, we train one model based on all {En→En, Zh→En, Fr→En, Ar→En, Ru→En, Es→En} pairs. For ONE-TO-MANY experiments, we train one model based on all {En→En, En→Zh, En→Fr, En→Ar, En→Ru, En→Es} pairs. These two models are tested in supervised manner.

4.3 MANY-TO-MANY

As shown in Figure 3(e), MANY-TO-MANY models can take dialogues in various languages as inputs and produce summaries in various languages. Thanks to the pre-trained multi-lingual language models (Liu et al., 2020; Tang et al., 2020), based on which, MANY-TO-MANY models can perform zero-shot summarization even though the input-output language pair is not seen during the training process.

Experimental Setting: For MANY-TO-MANY experiments, we train one model based on all {En→En, Zh→Zh, Fr→Fr, Ar→Ar, Ru→Ru, Es→Es} pairs and test it in both supervised and zero-shot manners.

4.4 MIX-TO-MANY

Nowadays, dialogue participants from different countries can use their mother tongue to communicate with each other based on instantaneous translation systems. To investigate the possibility of generating summaries directly from mix-lingual dialogues (utterances in different languages), we come up with an innovative new setting: MIX-TO-MANY, as shown in Figure 3(f).

To this end, we first simulate the real scenario and construct mix-lingual dialogue-summary pairs, the whole construction process is shown in Figure 4. Given each English dialogue in MSAMSum (shown in Figure 4(a)), we first group utterances by participants, which results in several groups for different participants (shown in Figure 4(b)). Then, for each group, we calculate the average round-trip translation ROUGE-1 score for each language (shown in Figure 4(c)). Afterward, we adopt a greedy search strategy to assign each participant a language (shown in Figure 4(d)). The goal of our strategy is twofold: choose as many languages as possible and as high-quality translations as possi-

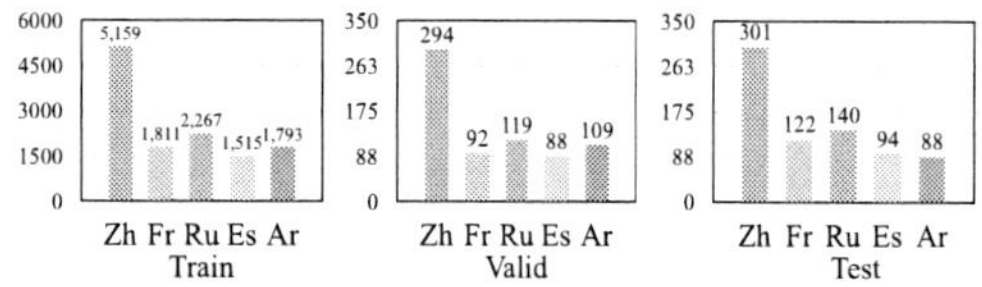

(a) The number of dialogues that contain L language, L=*Zh, Fr, Ru, Es, Ar.*

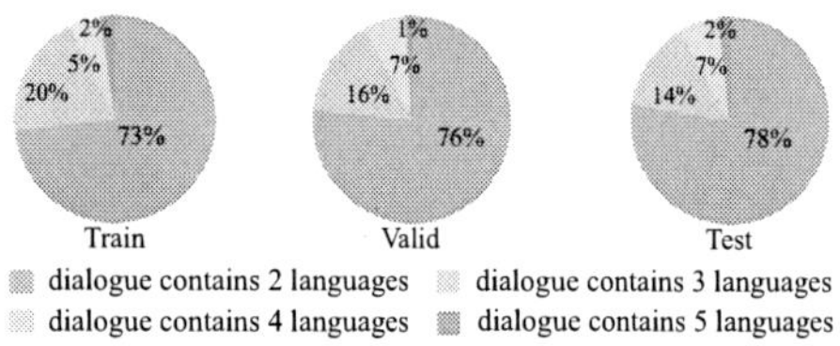

(b) The percentage of dialogues that contain N language. N=*2,3,4,5.*

Figure 5: Statistics for mix-lingual dialogues. (a) We show the language distribution by calculating the number of dialogues containing one specific language; (b) We provide the distribution of the number of languages included in the dialogue.

ble. Finally, we can get the mix-lingual dialogue, in which utterances are in different languages. The number of mix-lingual dialogues is in line with MSAMSum. The statistics for mix-lingual dialogues are shown in Figure 5. Finally, we pair the mix-lingual dialogue with summaries in different languages (shown in Figure 4(e)).

Experimental Setting: For MIX-TO-MANY experiments, we train one model based on all {Mix→En, Mix→Zh, Mix→Fr, Mix→Ar, Mix→Ru, Mix→Es} pairs and test it in supervised manner.

5 Experiments

In this section, we first introduce our model mBART-50. After, we describe the evaluation metrics. Finally, we show the implementation details.

5.1 Backbone Model

We employ mBART-50 (Tang et al., 2020) as our multi-lingual summarizer, which is a Transformer-based model and pre-trained on a huge volume of multi-lingual data. It is derived from mBART (Liu et al., 2020) and extends the language processing capabilities from 25 languages to 50 languages in total. The architecture of mBART-50 is based on the BART (Lewis et al., 2020), which adopts position-wise feed-forward network, multi-head attention (Vaswani et al., 2017), residual connection (He et al., 2016) and layer normalization (Ba et al., 2016) modules to map the source dialogue into distributed representations and further generate the target summary.

To handle various input and output languages, mBART-50 needs to receive inputs with language identifiers (e.g., En, Zh) at both the encoder and the decoder side. According to the practical experience, we set both the source language identifier and target language identifier at the start of the source and target sequences respectively.

5.2 Evaluation Metrics

The most widely used metrics for summarization are ROUGE scores (Lin, 2004). However, the original ROUGE is specifically designed for English. To make this metric suitable for our experiments, we employ the multi-lingual ROUGE (Hasan et al., 2021) as our evaluation metrics, which takes segmentation and popular stemming algorithms for various languages into consideration[9].

5.3 Implementation Details

For MSAMSum construction, we set round-trip translation ROUGE-1 threshold to 80.00 and the textual entailment threshold to 0.9. For experiments, we use the standard mBART-50 implementation provided by Huggingface/transformers[10]. For fine-tuning process, the learning rate is set to 5e-06, the dropout rate is 0.1, the warmup is set to 2000 and the batch size is 4. In the test process, beam size is 5, the minimum decoded length is 10 and the maximum length is 150. All our experiments are conducted based on the Tesla-V100-32GB GPU.

6 Results

In this section, we describe experimental results and show our analyses for different settings.

6.1 ONE-TO-ONE Results

Table 2 shows the results for ONE-TO-ONE setting, including both the *mono-lingual* and the *cross-lingual* experiments. According to the 52.98 ROUGE-1 score achieved by fine-tuning BART-large on full English SAMSum dataset (Chen and Yang, 2020), we can see that our experiments achieve impressive results. For *mono-lingual* experiments, Ar→Ar results perform worse than others to some extent, we attribute this to the fact that the Arabic language processing capability of the

[9]https://github.com/csebuetnlp/xl-sum/tree/master/multilingual_rouge_scoring

[10]https://huggingface.co/facebook/mbart-large-50-many-to-many-mmt

ONE-TO-ONE			
Src→Tgt	R-1	R-2	R-L
Mono-lingual			
En→En	49.16	24.18	40.15
Es→Es	43.95	20.01	35.87
Zh→Zh	40.11	16.93	33.48
Fr→Fr	41.77	19.20	34.47
Ru→Ru	37.95	15.74	31.76
Ar→Ar	28.66	6.61	23.07
Cross-lingual			
Zh→En	45.75	20.18	36.90
En→Zh	42.62	17.43	34.88

Table 2: Test set results on the different language pairs of MSAMSum dataset by fine-tuning mBART-50 under the ONE-TO-ONE setting, where "R" is short for "ROUGE".

MANY-TO-ONE			
Src→Tgt	R-1	R-2	R-L
En→En	48.18	22.43	38.63
Zh→En	45.01	17.76	35.49
Fr→En	44.22	18.49	35.30
Ar→En	31.09	08.00	24.18
Ru→En	44.20	17.53	35.06
Es→En	44.50	17.97	35.56

Table 3: Test set results on the different language pairs of MSAMSum dataset by fine-tuning mBART-50 under the MANY-TO-ONE setting.

pre-trained mBART-50 is relatively weak, which is in line with the size of original pre-training corpus (Lewis et al., 2020). For *cross-lingual* experiments, surprisingly, we find that En→Zh get better results compared with Zh→Zh, which may due to the model's strong English comprehension ability.

6.2 MANY-TO-ONE and ONE-TO-MANY Results

Table 3 and table 4 show results for MANY-TO-ONE and ONE-TO-MANY settings respectively. For both settings, we find that the results of the multi-lingual model varied less between pairs compared with ONE-TO-ONE models. For the MANY-TO-ONE model, the results of En→En and Zh→En are slightly worse than results of corresponding single ONE-TO-ONE models. This is because the MANY-TO-ONE model needs to handle multiple languages, which may cause the parameters interference problem (Lin et al., 2021), and is therefore inferior to a single expert model. In contrast, the

ONE-TO-MANY			
Src→Tgt	R-1	R-2	R-L
En→En	49.84	24.73	40.67
En→Es	47.27	21.82	37.87
En→Zh	43.86	18.25	35.56
En→Fr	44.33	19.58	35.20
En→Ru	41.26	15.76	33.00
En→Ar	39.71	14.96	32.82

Table 4: Test set results on the different language pairs of MSAMSum dataset by fine-tuning mBART-50 under the ONE-TO-MANY setting.

MANY-TO-MANY						
Src→Tgt	En	Zh	Fr	Ar	Ru	Es
En	**36.79**	*30.83*	*30.76*	*20.93*	*28.35*	*34.51*
Zh	*18.46*	**35.56**	*30.65*	*25.93*	*30.03*	*33.01*
Fr	*22.90*	*31.77*	**36.25**	*26.25*	*29.94*	*34.01*
Ar	*14.64*	*20.69*	*20.72*	**23.47**	*19.74*	*22.94*
Ru	*22.57*	*32.02*	*30.08*	*25.27*	**33.28**	*32.58*
Es	*27.74*	*32.09*	*31.97*	*25.75*	*30.11*	**37.21**

Table 5: Test set R-L results on the different language pairs of MSAMSum dataset by fine-tuning mBART-50 under the MANY-TO-MANY setting. Results in **bold** are achieved by supervised summarization. Results in *italics* are achieved by zero-shot summarization.

ONE-TO-MANY model improves the performance of both En→En and En→Zh results, which shows the ONE-TO-MANY training setting enhances the model's English understanding ability. Additionally, both Ar→En and En→Ar get relatively lower results, which coincide with the findings in ONE-TO-ONE experiments.

6.3 MANY-TO-MANY Results

Table 5 shows ROUGE-L results for the MANY-TO-MANY setting[11]. We test each language pair in the cartesian product of six languages, which results in two types of manners: supervised and zero-shot summarization. For the supervised manner (results in **bold**), almost all results show the best performance. For the zero-shot manner (results in *italics*), we find that despite the model is fine-tuned based on mono-lingual dialogue-summary pairs, it still has the strong ability to perform summarization across different languages. In line with previous experiments, we find the MANY-TO-MANY model that balances across various languages inevitably loses some performances compared with the ONE-TO-ONE model. Nonetheless, the MANY-

[11]We show all ROUGE-1, ROUGE-2 and ROUGE-L scores in the supplementary file.

MIX-TO-MANY			
Src→Tgt	R-1	R-2	R-L
Mix→En	44.68	17.78	35.17
Mix→Es	43.51	18.08	34.75
Mix→Zh	40.76	15.76	33.14
Mix→Fr	41.50	17.04	32.76
Mix→Ru	38.26	13.38	30.75
Mix→Ar	36.06	12.09	29.60

Table 6: Test set results on the different language pairs of MSAMSum dataset by fine-tuning mBART-50 under the MIX-TO-MANY setting.

TO-MANY model, which greatly reduces the deployment cost while preserving the performance, is an important research direction in the future.

6.4 MIX-TO-MANY Results

Table 6 shows the results for the MIX-TO-MANY setting. As the first step towards this direction, we find that current multi-lingual pre-trained models can obtain encouraging results. The Mix→Es, Mix→Zh, Mix→Fr and Mix→Ru models achieve comparable results with respect to the corresponding ONE-TO-ONE model. These results verify that despite the multi-lingual model only deals with one language at a time in the pre-training progress, after fine-tuning, it can handle mix-lingual inputs concurrently. Surprisingly, the Mix→Ar results even surpass the performance of singe Ar→Ar model. We think this is due to the mix-lingual dialogue essentially acts as an utterance-level code-switching data, which helps the representation space of the low-resource language align with other languages. This also inspire us that it would be better to generate the low-resource language summary directly from the mix-lingual dialogue.

6.5 Case Study

Figure 6 shows summaries in different languages generated by the ONE-TO-MANY model for an example English dialogue. We can see that all the generated summaries achieve good ROUGE performance, with English being the highest. We find that the multi-lingual model can generate fluent summaries while preserving the important information of the dialogue. Besides, the model also has the ability to accurately express participants information (e.g., Elliot, Jordan) and keep entities' factual consistency (e.g., 8 pm) across different languages.

English Dialogue	
Elliot : I can't talk rn , I'm rly busy. Elliot : Can I call u back in about 2 hours? Jordan : Not really , I'm going to a funeral. Jordan : I'll call you tonight , ok? Elliot : Sure Elliot : Whose funeral is it? Jordan : My colleague's , Brad. Jordan : I told you about him , he had a liver cancer. Elliot : I'm so sorry man , I hope u're ok. Elliot : I'll call u at 8 pm.	
Generated Summaries (*One-to-many*)	
English	Elliot can't talk because he's busy. Jordan is going to a funeral for his colleague, Brad, who had a liver cancer. Elliot will call him at 8 pm. [71.19-42.11-50.85]
Chinese	乔丹要去参加他的同事布拉德的葬礼。他得了肝癌。埃利奥特将在晚上8点给乔丹打电话[66.67-40.00-35.09]
Russian	Джордан собирается на похороны своего коллегы Брэда, у него рак печени.Элиот позвонит Джордана в 20: 00. [58.38-30.00-38.10]
French	Elliot ne peut pas parler parce qu'il est occupé.Jordan va au funeral de son collègue, Brad, qui a un cancer du foie.Il appellera Elliot à 20 h. [68.97-42.86-55.17]
Arabic	جوردن هو الذهاب إلى جنازة زميلها براد لديه سرطان الكبد.إيليت سوف ندعو له في الساعة الثامنة مساء. [57.78-27.91-31.11]
Spanish	Elliot no puede hablar porque está ocupado.Jordan va a un funeral de su colega, Brad, que tuvo un cáncer de hepática.Eliot llamará a Jordan a las 8 p.m. [60.71-29.63-39.29]

Figure 6: Example English dialogue in the MSAMSum dataset and summaries in different languages generated by the ONE-TO-MANY model. The scores in square brackets are R-1, R-2 and R-L respectively.

7 Conclusion and Future Work

In this paper, we innovatively explore the multi-lingual dialogue summarization task. To this end, we carefully create MSAMSum as our testbed, which covers dialogue-summary pairs in six languages, including English, Chinese, Russian, French, Arabic and Spanish. Furthermore, we systematically set up five multi-lingual settings to benchmark extensive experiments. Our results indicate that various models can achieve impressive performance based on pre-trained models. Besides, the newly proposed MIX-TO-MANY setting also shows its effectiveness in low-resource scenarios.

In the future, we think several concerns need to be addressed for this task. Firstly, multi-lingual models tend to underperform mono-lingual models; Secondly, low-resource languages tend to perform poorly; Thirdly, the difficulty of aligning fine-grained information in different languages. Future works should pay particular attention to these concerns to facilitate this multi-lingual dialogue summarization research direction.

8 Acknowledgments

We thank the anonymous reviewers for their insightful comments. This work was supported by the National Key RD Program of China via grant 2020AAA0106502, National Natural Science Foundation of China (NSFC) via grant 61976073 and Shenzhen Foundational Research Funding (JCYJ20200109113441941).

References

Jimmy Lei Ba, Jamie Ryan Kiros, and Geoffrey E Hinton. 2016. Layer normalization. *In arXiv*.

Yue Cao, Xiaojun Wan, Jin-ge Yao, and Dian Yu. 2020. Multisumm: Towards a unified model for multilingual abstractive summarization. In *The Thirty-Fourth AAAI Conference on Artificial Intelligence, AAAI 2020, The Thirty-Second Innovative Applications of Artificial Intelligence Conference, IAAI 2020*. AAAI Press.

Jean Carletta, Simone Ashby, Sebastien Bourban, Mike Flynn, Mael Guillemot, Thomas Hain, Jaroslav Kadlec, Vasilis Karaiskos, Wessel Kraaij, Melissa Kronenthal, et al. 2005. The ami meeting corpus: A pre-announcement. In *International workshop on machine learning for multimodal interaction*. Springer.

Jiaao Chen and Diyi Yang. 2020. Multi-view sequence-to-sequence models with conversational structure for abstractive dialogue summarization. In *Proceedings of the 2020 Conference on Empirical Methods in Natural Language Processing (EMNLP)*, Online. Association for Computational Linguistics.

Mingda Chen, Zewei Chu, Sam Wiseman, and Kevin Gimpel. 2021a. Summscreen: A dataset for abstractive screenplay summarization. *arXiv preprint arXiv:2104.07091*.

Yulong Chen, Yang Liu, Liang Chen, and Yue Zhang. 2021b. Dialsumm: A real-life scenario dialogue summarization dataset. *arXiv preprint arXiv:2105.06762*.

Alexander Fabbri, Faiaz Rahman, Imad Rizvi, Borui Wang, Haoran Li, Yashar Mehdad, and Dragomir Radev. 2021. ConvoSumm: Conversation summarization benchmark and improved abstractive summarization with argument mining. In *Proceedings of the 59th Annual Meeting of the Association for Computational Linguistics and the 11th International Joint Conference on Natural Language Processing (Volume 1: Long Papers)*, pages 6866–6880, Online. Association for Computational Linguistics.

Xiachong Feng, Xiaocheng Feng, and Bing Qin. 2021a. A survey on dialogue summarization: Recent advances and new frontiers. *ArXiv*, abs/2107.03175.

Xiachong Feng, Xiaocheng Feng, Bing Qin, and Xinwei Geng. 2021b. Dialogue discourse-aware graph model and data augmentation for meeting summarization. In *Proceedings of the Thirtieth International Joint Conference on Artificial Intelligence, IJCAI-21*. International Joint Conferences on Artificial Intelligence Organization. Main Track.

Xiachong Feng, Xiaocheng Feng, Libo Qin, Bing Qin, and Ting Liu. 2021c. Language model as an annotator: Exploring DialoGPT for dialogue summarization. In *Proceedings of the 59th Annual Meeting of the Association for Computational Linguistics and the 11th International Joint Conference on Natural Language Processing (Volume 1: Long Papers)*, Online. Association for Computational Linguistics.

Bogdan Gliwa, Iwona Mochol, Maciej Biesek, and Aleksander Wawer. 2019. SAMSum corpus: A human-annotated dialogue dataset for abstractive summarization. In *Proceedings of the 2nd Workshop on New Frontiers in Summarization*, Hong Kong, China. Association for Computational Linguistics.

Tahmid Hasan, Abhik Bhattacharjee, Md. Saiful Islam, Kazi Mubasshir, Yuan-Fang Li, Yong-Bin Kang, M. Sohel Rahman, and Rifat Shahriyar. 2021. XL-sum: Large-scale multilingual abstractive summarization for 44 languages. In *Findings of the Association for Computational Linguistics: ACL-IJCNLP 2021*, Online.

Kaiming He, Xiangyu Zhang, Shaoqing Ren, and Jian Sun. 2016. Deep residual learning for image recognition. In *2016 IEEE Conference on Computer Vision and Pattern Recognition, CVPR 2016, Las Vegas, NV, USA, June 27-30, 2016*. IEEE Computer Society.

Yichong Huang, Xiachong Feng, Xiaocheng Feng, and Bing Qin. 2021. The factual inconsistency problem in abstractive text summarization: A survey. *arXiv preprint arXiv:2104.14839*.

Adam Janin, Don Baron, Jane Edwards, Dan Ellis, David Gelbart, Nelson Morgan, Barbara Peskin, Thilo Pfau, Elizabeth Shriberg, Andreas Stolcke, et al. 2003. The icsi meeting corpus. In *ICASSP*. IEEE.

Faisal Ladhak, Esin Durmus, Claire Cardie, and Kathleen McKeown. 2020. Wikilingua: A new benchmark dataset for multilingual abstractive summarization. In *Proceedings of the 2020 Conference on Empirical Methods in Natural Language Processing: Findings*.

Mike Lewis, Yinhan Liu, Naman Goyal, Marjan Ghazvininejad, Abdelrahman Mohamed, Omer Levy, Veselin Stoyanov, and Luke Zettlemoyer. 2020. BART: Denoising sequence-to-sequence pre-training for natural language generation, translation, and comprehension. In *Proceedings of the 58th Annual Meeting of the Association for Computational Linguistics*, Online. Association for Computational Linguistics.

Chin-Yew Lin. 2004. ROUGE: A package for automatic evaluation of summaries. In *Text Summarization Branches Out*, Barcelona, Spain. Association for Computational Linguistics.

Zehui Lin, Liwei Wu, Mingxuan Wang, and Lei Li. 2021. Learning language specific sub-network for multilingual machine translation. In *Proceedings of the 59th Annual Meeting of the Association for Computational Linguistics and the 11th International Joint Conference on Natural Language Processing (Volume 1: Long Papers)*, Online. Association for Computational Linguistics.

Yinhan Liu, Jiatao Gu, Naman Goyal, Xian Li, Sergey Edunov, Marjan Ghazvininejad, Mike Lewis, and Luke Zettlemoyer. 2020. Multilingual denoising pre-training for neural machine translation. *Transactions of the Association for Computational Linguistics*, 8.

Valentin Malykh, Konstantin Chernis, Ekaterina Artemova, and Irina Piontkovskaya. 2020. SumTitles: a summarization dataset with low extractiveness. In *Proceedings of the 28th International Conference on Computational Linguistics*, Barcelona, Spain (Online).

Laiba Mehnaz, Debanjan Mahata, Rakesh Gosangi, Uma Sushmitha Gunturi, Riya Jain, Gauri Gupta, Amardeep Kumar, Isabelle Lee, Anish Acharya, and Rajiv Ratn Shah. 2021. Gupshup: An annotated corpus for abstractive summarization of open-domain code-switched conversations. *arXiv preprint arXiv:2104.08578*.

Jessica Ouyang, Boya Song, and Kathy McKeown. 2019. A robust abstractive system for cross-lingual summarization. In *Proceedings of the 2019 Conference of the North American Chapter of the Association for Computational Linguistics: Human Language Technologies, Volume 1 (Long and Short Papers)*, Minneapolis, Minnesota. Association for Computational Linguistics.

Revanth Rameshkumar and Peter Bailey. 2020. Storytelling with dialogue: A Critical Role Dungeons and Dragons Dataset. In *Proceedings of the 58th Annual Meeting of the Association for Computational Linguistics*, Online. Association for Computational Linguistics.

Yuqing Tang, Chau Tran, Xian Li, Peng-Jen Chen, Naman Goyal, Vishrav Chaudhary, Jiatao Gu, and Angela Fan. 2020. Multilingual translation with extensible multilingual pretraining and finetuning. *arXiv preprint arXiv:2008.00401*.

Don Tuggener, Margot Mieskes, Jan Deriu, and Mark Cieliebak. 2021. Are we summarizing the right way? a survey of dialogue summarization data sets. In *Proceedings of the Third Workshop on New Frontiers in Summarization*, Online and in Dominican Republic. Association for Computational Linguistics.

Daniel Varab and Natalie Schluter. 2021. MassiveSumm: a very large-scale, very multilingual, news summarisation dataset. In *Proceedings of the 2021 Conference on Empirical Methods in Natural Language Processing*, Online and Punta Cana, Dominican Republic.

Ashish Vaswani, Noam Shazeer, Niki Parmar, Jakob Uszkoreit, Llion Jones, Aidan N. Gomez, Lukasz Kaiser, and Illia Polosukhin. 2017. Attention is all you need. In *Advances in Neural Information Processing Systems 30: Annual Conference on Neural Information Processing Systems 2017, December 4-9, 2017, Long Beach, CA, USA*.

Xiaojun Wan, Huiying Li, and Jianguo Xiao. 2010. Cross-language document summarization based on machine translation quality prediction. In *Proceedings of the 48th Annual Meeting of the Association for Computational Linguistics*, Uppsala, Sweden. Association for Computational Linguistics.

Danqing Wang, Jiaze Chen, Hao Zhou, Xipeng Qiu, and Lei Li. 2021. Contrastive aligned joint learning for multilingual summarization. In *Findings of the Association for Computational Linguistics: ACL-IJCNLP 2021*, Online. Association for Computational Linguistics.

Jiaan Wang, Fandong Meng, Duo Zheng, Yunlong Liang, Zhixu Li, Jianfeng Qu, and Jie Zhou. 2022. A survey on cross-lingual summarization. *arXiv preprint arXiv:2203.12515*.

Ruochen Xu, Chenguang Zhu, Yu Shi, Michael Zeng, and Xuedong Huang. 2020. Mixed-lingual pre-training for cross-lingual summarization. In *Proceedings of the 1st Conference of the Asia-Pacific Chapter of the Association for Computational Linguistics and the 10th International Joint Conference on Natural Language Processing*, Suzhou, China. Association for Computational Linguistics.

Shiyue Zhang, Asli Celikyilmaz, Jianfeng Gao, and Mohit Bansal. 2021. EmailSum: Abstractive email thread summarization. In *Proceedings of the 59th Annual Meeting of the Association for Computational Linguistics and the 11th International Joint Conference on Natural Language Processing (Volume 1: Long Papers)*, Online. Association for Computational Linguistics.

Ming Zhong, Da Yin, Tao Yu, Ahmad Zaidi, Mutethia Mutuma, Rahul Jha, Ahmed Hassan Awadallah, Asli Celikyilmaz, Yang Liu, Xipeng Qiu, and Dragomir Radev. 2021. QMSum: A new benchmark for query-based multi-domain meeting summarization. In *Proceedings of the 2021 Conference of the North American Chapter of the Association for Computational Linguistics: Human Language Technologies*, Online. Association for Computational Linguistics.

Chenguang Zhu, Yang Liu, Jie Mei, and Michael Zeng. 2021. MediaSum: A large-scale media interview dataset for dialogue summarization. In *Proceedings* of the 2021 Conference of the North American Chapter of the Association for Computational Linguistics: Human Language Technologies, Online. Association for Computational Linguistics.

Chenguang Zhu, Ruochen Xu, Michael Zeng, and Xuedong Huang. 2020a. A hierarchical network for abstractive meeting summarization with cross-domain pretraining. In *Findings of the Association for Computational Linguistics: EMNLP 2020*, Online. Association for Computational Linguistics.

Junnan Zhu, Qian Wang, Yining Wang, Yu Zhou, Jiajun Zhang, Shaonan Wang, and Chengqing Zong. 2019. NCLS: Neural cross-lingual summarization. In *Proceedings of the 2019 Conference on Empirical Methods in Natural Language Processing and the 9th International Joint Conference on Natural Language Processing (EMNLP-IJCNLP)*, Hong Kong, China. Association for Computational Linguistics.

Junnan Zhu, Yu Zhou, Jiajun Zhang, and Chengqing Zong. 2020b. Attend, translate and summarize: An efficient method for neural cross-lingual summarization. In *Proceedings of the 58th Annual Meeting of the Association for Computational Linguistics*, Online. Association for Computational Linguistics.

A Ethical Considerations

As we propose a new multi-lingual dialogue summarization dataset and conduct experiments based on large pre-trained language models, we make several clarifications to address potential concerns:

- **Dataset:** Since our MSAMSum is derived from the SAMSum (Gliwa et al., 2019), which is a well-constructed and human-labelled dataset. Therefore, our dataset inherits the contents of SAMSum and does not contain toxic information.
- **Model:** The experiments described in this paper are based on the mBART-50-large (Tang et al., 2020) and make use of V100 GPUs. Despite we run dozens of experiments, our results could help reduce parameter searches for future works. We also consider to alleviate such resource-hungry challenge by exploring light-weight distilled models.

B Round-trip Translation ROUGE Scores

Table 7 shows the average ROUGE scores between the English data in SAMSum (Gliwa et al., 2019) and the round-trip translated English data. These results indicate the overall translation quality.

		R-1	**R-2**	**R-L**
Train	Zh	84.57	60.87	86.77
	Ru	75.97	47.70	78.91
	Es	75.05	46.43	78.19
	Ar	76.09	48.13	79.02
	Fr	75.53	47.02	78.68
Valid	Zh	84.47	60.80	86.69
	Ru	75.57	46.81	78.56
	Es	74.85	46.19	77.99
	Ar	75.97	48.09	78.93
	Fr	75.24	46.74	78.40
Test	Zh	84.11	59.91	86.32
	Ru	75.74	47.18	78.67
	Es	74.68	45.63	77.84
	Ar	75.56	47.24	78.48
	Fr	75.15	46.39	78.33

Table 7: The average ROUGE scores between each original English data in the SAMSum (Gliwa et al., 2019) and corresponding round-trip translated English data for five languages.

	Train	**Valid**	**Test**
Original			
SAMSum	14732	818	819
Before alignment			
Zh	11738	658	660
Ru	6089	329	354
Es	6697	369	370
Ar	6341	340	337
Fr	7523	426	417
After alignment			
Final	5307	302	320

Table 8: The size of datasets at different stages.

C The Changing of Data Size

Table 8 shows how the data size changes. After quality controlling process, we can get different data size for different languages (before alignment). After taking the intersection of different languages, we get our final MSAMSum (after alignment).

D Detailed MANY-TO-MANY Results

Table 9 shows detailed ROUGE-1, ROUGE-2 and ROUGE-L results for MANY-TO-MANY experiments in both supervised and zero-shot manners, as a supplement to Table 5.

	Many-to-Many					
Src→Tgt	En	Zh	Fr	Ar	Ru	Es
En	**48.00/22.29/36.79**	*37.51/13.82/30.83*	*38.81/14.56/30.76*	*24.48/8.16/20.93*	*34.50/11.49/28.35*	*42.86/17.38/34.51*
Zh	*24.24/8.37/18.46*	**43.75/19.14/35.56**	*39.80/13.96/30.65*	*32.28/10.10/25.93*	*37.82/12.87/30.03*	*41.97/16.08/33.01*
Fr	*29.71/08.69/22.90*	*39.53/13.73/31.77*	**45.26/21.60/36.25**	*31.92/10.34/26.25*	*37.11/12.17/29.94*	*42.59/16.59/34.01*
Ar	*18.75/3.74/14.64*	*25.27/6.36/20.69*	*26.46/6.30/20.72*	**29.15/7.76/23.47**	*24.48/5.04/19.74*	*29.24/6.89/22.94*
Ru	*30.88/9.99/22.57*	*39.80/14.46/32.02*	*38.29/13.84/30.08*	*30.72/9.49/25.27*	**41.50/15.95/33.28**	*41.53/15.18/32.58*
Es	*37.18/12.14/27.74*	*39.79/15.05/32.09*	*41.04/15.91/31.97*	*31.41/10.18/25.75*	*37.34/12.02/30.11*	**46.40/21.53/37.21**

Table 9: Test set ROUGE-1/ROUGE-2/ROUGE-L results on the different language pairs of MSAMSum dataset by fine-tuning mBART-50 under the Many-to-Many setting. Results in **bold** are achieved by supervised summarization. Results in *italics* are achieved by zero-shot summarization.

UniDS: A Unified Dialogue System for Chit-Chat and Task-oriented Dialogues

Xinyan Zhao[1]*, Bin He[2], Yasheng Wang[2], Yitong Li[2], Fei Mi[2], Yajiao Liu[2], Xin Jiang[2], Qun Liu[2], Huanhuan Chen[1]

[1] University of Science and Technology of China
[2] Huawei Noah's Ark Lab
sa516458@mail.ustc.edu.cn,
{hebin.nlp, wangyasheng, liyitong3, mifei2, yajiao.liu, Jiang.Xin, qun.liu}@huawei.com,
hchen@ustc.edu.cn

Abstract

With the advances in deep learning, tremendous progress has been made with chit-chat dialogue systems and task-oriented dialogue systems. However, these two systems are often tackled separately in current methods. To achieve more natural interaction with humans, dialogue systems need to be capable of both chatting and accomplishing tasks. To this end, we propose a **uni**fied **d**ialogue **s**ystem (**UniDS**) with the two aforementioned skills. In particular, we design a unified dialogue data schema, compatible for both chit-chat and task-oriented dialogues. Besides, we propose a two-stage training method to train UniDS based on the unified dialogue data schema. UniDS does not need to adding extra parameters to existing chit-chat dialogue systems. Experimental results demonstrate that the proposed UniDS works comparably well as the state-of-the-art chit-chat dialogue systems and task-oriented dialogue systems. More importantly, UniDS achieves better robustness than pure dialogue systems and satisfactory switch ability between two types of dialogues. This work demonstrates the feasibility and potential of building a general dialogue system.

1 Introduction

Dialogue system is an important tool to achieve intelligent user interaction, and it is actively studied by NLP and other communities. Current research of dialogue systems focus on task-oriented dialogue (TOD) systems (Hosseini-Asl et al., 2020; Peng et al., 2020; Yang et al., 2021), achieving functional goals, and chit-chat dialogue systems aiming at entertainment (Zhou et al., 2018; Zhang et al., 2020; Zhao et al., 2020; Roller et al., 2021). Different methods are devised for these two types of dialogue systems separately. However, a more suitable way for users would be to have one dialogue agent that is able to handle both chit-chat and TOD in one conversation. As illustrated in Figure 1, users may have communication-oriented needs (e.g. chatting about money and happiness) and task-oriented needs (e.g. hotel reservation) when interacting with a dialogue agent. Furthermore, inputs of dialogue systems are often interfered by background noise, such as voice from other people or devices, collected by the preceding automatic speech recognition (ASR) module. Therefore, the chit-chat ability may also improve the robustness of a task-oriented dialog system (Zhao et al., 2017).

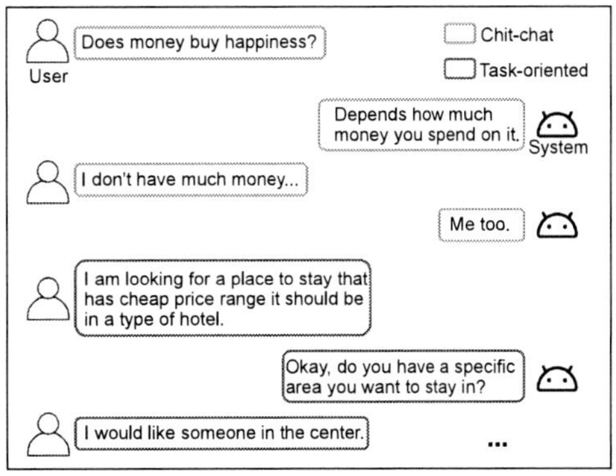

Figure 1: Illustration of users being interested to chit-chat with the dialogue system before booking a hotel.

As shown in Table1, there are many differences between chit-chat and task-oriented dialogues. Creating a single model for different tasks without performance degradation is challenging (Kaiser et al., 2017). Some works attempt to model different dialogue skills via different experts or adapters (Madotto et al., 2020; Lin et al., 2021). However, these methods increase the number of parameters and hard to achieve satisfactory performance on both types of dialogues. Besides, previous work lack the exploration of the ability to switch between different types of dialogues.

This work proposes a auto-regressive language model based dialogue system to handle chit-chat

*This work was done during an internship at Huawei Noah's Ark Lab.

Proceedings of the Second DialDoc Workshop on Document-grounded Dialogue and Conversational Question Answering, pages 13 - 22
May 26, 2022 ©2022 Association for Computational Linguistics

	Diversity	Purpose	Turns	Mainstream method
Chit-chat	Strong	Entertainment	Long	End-to-end method
Task-oriented dialogue	Weak	Completing tasks	Short	Pipeline method*

Table 1: Differences between chit-chat and task-oriented dialogues. *: The model will predict belief state and system act before giving a response, to this end, the training set needs to be annotated with belief state and system act.

and TOD in a unified framework (UniDS). Specifically, since chit-chat data do not have explicit belief state and agent action, to unify chit-chat and task-oriented dialogues format, we device belief state and agent act for chit-chat dialogues as task-oriented dialogues. On the other hand, because of the diversity of chit-chat, chit-chat dialogue systems need more training data than task-oriented dialogue systems, e.g., 147,116,725 dialogues for DialoGPT (Radford et al., 2019) and 8,438 dialogues for UBAR (Yang et al., 2021). To overcome this difference, we propose to train UniDS in a two-stage way. A chit-chat model is first trained with huge chit-chat dialogues, and then we train UniDS from the chit-chat dialogue system with mixed dialogues based on our proposed unified dialogue data schema.

We evaluate UniDS using a public task-oriented dialogue dataset MultiWOZ and a chit-chat dataset extracted from Reddit[1] through both automatic and human evaluations. UniDS achieves comparable performance compared to the state-of-the-art chit-chat dialogue system DialoGPT, and TOD system UBAR. In addition, we empirically show that UniDS is more robust to noise in task-oriented dialogues, and UniDS shows a desirable ability to switch between the two types of dialogues.

The contributions of this work are summarised as follows:

- To the best of our knowledge, this is the first work presenting a unified dialogue system to jointly handle chit-chat and task-oriented dialogues in an end-to-end way.
- We design a *unified dialogue data schema* for chit-chat and TOD, allowing the training and inference of dialogue systems to be performed in a unified manner.
- To tackle the gap between chit-chat dialogue systems and task-oriented dialogue systems in the requirement of training data, a two-stage training method is proposed to train UniDS.
- Extensive empirical results show that UniDS performs comparably to state-of-the-art chit-chat dialogue systems and task-oriented dialogue systems. Moreover, UniDS achieves better robustness to dialog noise and satisfactory switch ability between two types of dialogues.

[1]https://www.reddit.com/

2 Related Work

With the development of large-scale language models, chit-chat dialogue systems achieve remarkable success. Based on GPT-2 (Radford et al., 2019), DialoGPT (Zhang et al., 2020) is further trained on large-scale dialogues extracted from Reddit. DialoGPT could generate more relevant, contentful, and fluent responses than previous methods. Afterwards, larger pre-train LM based chit-chat dialogue systems (Adiwardana et al., 2020; Bao et al., 2020; Roller et al., 2021) are proposed and achieve even better performance. In the area of task-oriented dialogue systems, recent research (Hosseini-Asl et al., 2020; Peng et al., 2020; Yang et al., 2021) concatenated elements in a dialogue into one sequence and utilized pre-train LM to generate the belief state, system act, and response in an end-to-end way and achieved promising results.

There are several works related to the unified dialogue system. Zhao et al. (2017) insert one turn chit-chat dialogue into task-oriented dialogues to train a model with better out-of-domain recovery ability. Attention over Parameters (AoP) (Madotto et al., 2020) utilizes different decoders for different dialogue skills (e.g., hotel booking, restaurant booking, chit). However, the performance of AoP can be improved and it largely increases parameters comparing with models that handle a single type of dialogues. ACCENTOR (Sun et al., 2021) adds chit-chat utterance at the beginning or end of task-oriented responses to make the conversation more engaging, but ACCENTOR is unable to have a chit-chat with users. Unlike the above works, UniDS does not add extra parameters to existing dialogue models, and UniDS could alternatively handle chit-chat and task-oriented dialogues in a seamless way.

3 Unified Dialogue System

3.1 Architecture of UniDS

As illustrated in Figure 2, we formulate unified dialogue system as an auto-regressive language model. A dialogue session at turn t has the following components: user input U_t, belief state B_t, database search result D_t, system act A_t, and response R_t. Each component consists of tokens from a fixed vocabulary. For turn t, the dialogue context C_t is the concatenation of all the components of the previous dialogues as well as the user input at turn t: $C_t = [U_0, B_0, D_0, A_0, R_0, \cdots, R_{t-1}, U_t]$. Given the dialogue context C_t, UniDS first generates the belief state B_t:

$$B_t = \mathrm{UniDS}(C_t)\,, \tag{1}$$

and use it to search the database to get the search result D_t. Then, UniDS generates the system act A_t conditioned on the updated context by extending C_t with B_t and D_t:

$$A_t = \mathrm{UniDS}([C_t, B_t, D_t])\,. \tag{2}$$

Lastly, the response R_t is generated conditioned on the concatenation of all previous components:

$$R_t = \mathrm{UniDS}([C_t, B_t, D_t, A_t])\,. \tag{3}$$

3.2 Unified Dialogue Data Schema

In the widely adopted task-oriented dialogue system pipeline, a dialogue session consists of a user input utterance, a belief state that represents the user intention, a database search result, a system act, and a system response (Young et al., 2013; Yang et al., 2021). However, due to the diversity of chit-chat and the cost of manual annotation, chit-chat dialogue systems do not assume the existence of the belief state nor system act (Bao et al., 2020; Zhang et al., 2020). The inconsistency of data format between chit-chat and TOD hinders the implementation of a unified model. To tackle this problem, we design a data schema with belief state, database result representation and system act for chit-chat. Table 2 illustrates such unified data schema with examples. The following sections explain each component in detail.

3.2.1 Belief state

The unified belief state is represented in the form of "<domain> slot [value]". A belief state could have several domains, each containing several slot-value pairs. As we can observe, extracting belief state of TOD may need to copy some words from the user utterance. To make UniDS keep this copy mechanism, for chit-chat, nouns in the user utterance U_t are extracted as the slot or value of belief state.

3.2.2 DB result

We use a special token to represent the number of matched entities under the constraints of the belief state in the current turn.

3.2.3 System act

System acts are represented as "<domain> <act> [slot]" for TOD. The meaning of "<domain>" is the same as in belief states. "[act]" denotes the type of action the system needs to perform. Following the "domain-act" pair, slots are optional. For chit-chat, token "<chit_act>" denotes the dialogue system will chat with the user.

Therefore, a processed dialogue sequence X_t at turn t for either TOD or chit-chat can be both represented as:

$$X_t = [C_t, B_t, D_t, A_t, R_t]. \tag{4}$$

3.3 Two-stage training method

Since the diversity of chit-chat in topics and terms, chit-chat dialogue systems need much larger training data than task-oriented dialogue systems. If directly training UniDS with the unified dialogue data which contains much more chit-chat dialogues than task-oriented dialogues, the trained model may ignore the ability to complete task-oriented dialogues. Therefore, this work proposes a two-stage method for training UniDS. As illustrated in Figure 3, we propose to first train a chit-chat dialogue model with huge chit-chat dialogues, and then we train UniDS from the chit-chat dialogue system with mixed dialogues. The mixed dialogue data is obtained by mixing chit-chat and TOD data which are pre-processed by the proposed unified data schema in the ratio of 1:1. Motivated by the recent success of applying GPT-2 for task-oriented dialogue systems (Hosseini-Asl et al., 2020; Peng et al., 2020; Yang et al., 2021) and chit-chat dialogue systems (Zhang et al., 2020), we use DialoGPT(Zhang et al., 2020) as our chit-chat model, and train UniDS from DialoGPT.

The training objective for UniDS is to maximize the joint probability of all tokens in X_t computed

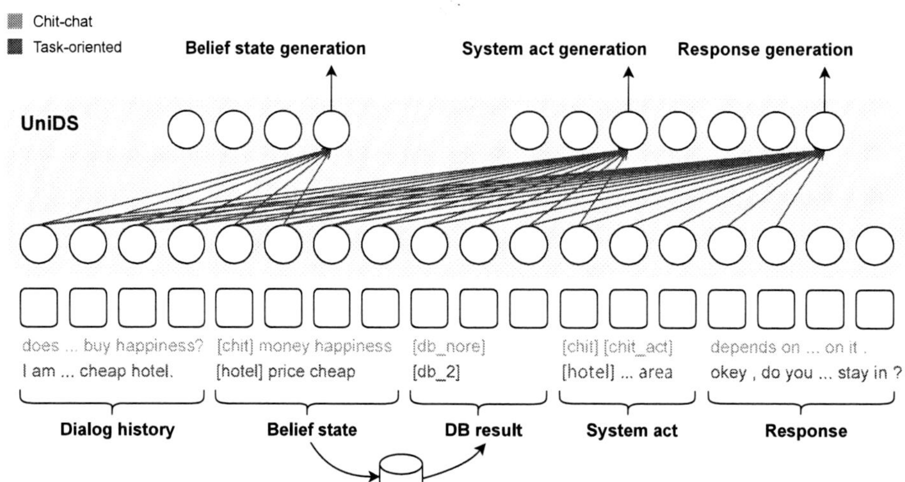

Figure 2: The architecture of UniDS.

	Unified dialogue data schema	Chit-chat example	Task-oriented example
User input	Tokenized utterance	does money buy happiness ?	i am looking for a cheap hotel .
Belief state	<domain> slot [value]	<chit> money happiness	<hotel> price cheap
DB result	A token indicated the number of candidate entities	<db_nore>	<db_2>
Act	<domain> <act> [slot]	<chit> <chit_act>	<hotel> <request> area
Response	Tokenized utterance	depends on how much money you spend on it .	do you have a specific area you want to stay in ?

Table 2: Unified dialogue data schema (where tokens inside the square bracket are optional) and examples.

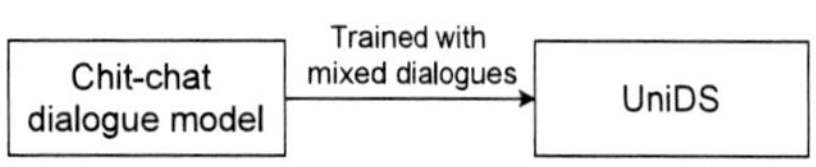

Figure 3: Training process of UniDS.

in an auto-regressive manner as:

$$\mathcal{L} = \sum_{i=1}^{N} -\log P(\boldsymbol{x}_i|\boldsymbol{x}_{<i}), \quad (5)$$

where $\boldsymbol{x}_i$ is a token of X_t, and $\boldsymbol{x}_{<i}$ are the preceding tokens.

4 Experiment

4.1 Datasets

4.1.1 Task-oriented Dialogue Dataset

For task-oriented dialogues, we adopt the publicly multi-domain task-oriented MultiWOZ (Budzianowski et al., 2018), which consists of $10,438$ dialogues spinning over seven domains (*taxi, attraction, police, restaurant, train, hotel, hospital*).[2] The train/validation/test sets of MultiWOZ have $8438/1000/1000$ dialogues, respectively. Each dialogue contains 1 to 3 domains.

4.1.2 Chit-chat Dataset

We derived open-domain chit-chat dialogue from Reddit dump[3]. To avoid overlapping, the chit-chat training set and test set are extracted from the Reddit posts in 2017 and 2018 respectively. To ensure the generation quality, we conduct a careful data cleaning. A conversation will be filtered when (1) there is a URL in the utterance; (2) there is an utterance longer than 200 words or less than 2 words; (3) the dialogue contains "[removed]" or "[deleted]" tokens; (4) the number of utterances in the dialogue is less than 4; (5) the dialogue contains offensive words. Finally, we sample $8,438$ dialogues for training which is the same size as the training set of MultiWOZ. The validation set and test set contain $6,000$ dialogues and $8,320$ dialogues, respectively.

4.2 Baselines

For chit-chat dialogue, we compare UniDS with **DialoGPT** (Zhang et al., 2020). For fair comparisons,

[2]We use MultiWOZ 2.0.

[3]https://files.pushshift.io/reddit/comments/

Model	# of para.	Task-oriented Dialogue				Chit-chat			
		Inform	Success	BLEU	Combined	BLEU	Dist-1	Dist-2	AvgLen
UBAR*	82M	91.5	77.4	17.0	101.5	-	-	-	-
PPTOD	~220M	89.20	79.40	18.62	102.92	-	-	-	-
UBAR-12L	117M	**89.40**	75.10	16.93	99.18	-	-	-	-
DialoGPT-12L	117M	-	-	-	-	0.27	**6**	**32**	14.00
UniDS-12L	117M	87.10	**77.00**	**18.01**	**100.06**	**0.35**	**6**	30	12.00
UBAR-24L	345M	89.40	75.50	16.86	99.31	-	-	-	-
DialoGPT-24L	345M	-	-	-	-	0.43	**7**	**36**	12.28
UniDS-24L	345M	**90.30**	**80.50**	**18.72**	**104.12**	**0.45**	6	35	14.62

Table 3: Automatic evaluations of UniDS with two model sizes over two types of dialogue datasets. All results are reported in percentage, except Combined and AvgLen. Best results are in **bold**. *: Results reported in original paper (Yang et al., 2021) is not obtained by end-to-end evaluation. This result is reported by authors of UBAR in https://github.com/TonyNemo/UBAR-MultiWOZ/issues/3.

we further fine-tune a 12-layer DialoGPT and a 24-layer DialoGPT with our chit-chat dialogue training set, which we refer to as DialoGPT-12L and DialoGPT-24L, respectively.

For TOD, we consider the state-of-the-art end-to-end TOD system **UBAR** (Yang et al., 2021) and **PPTOD**(Su et al., 2021). For a fair comparison with UniDS, we also fine-tune UBAR from 12 layers DialoGPT and 24 layers DialoGPT with Multi-WOZ dataset, the fine-tuned models are denoted as UBAR-12L and UBAR-24L, respectively.

4.3 Implementation Details

UniDS and other baselines are implemented based on HuggingFace's Transformers (Wolf et al., 2019). The max sequence length is 1024 and sequences longer than 1024 are truncated from the head. We use the AdamW optimizer (Loshchilov and Hutter, 2019) and greedy decoding method for inference. All models are trained on a single Tesla V100, and we perform a hyper-parameter search on batch size and learning rate. The best model and hyper-parameter are selected through the performance on the validation set of MultiWOZ only.

As shown in Table1, chit-chat dialogues need to attract users to talk more, while TOD needs to complete tasks as soon as possible. Therefore, a model trained with the mixed dialogue data tends to talk long turns instead of efficiently completing the task. Since entity recommendation acts are important for dialogue system to complete tasks efficiently, we use a weighted cross-entropy loss as the training objective of UniDS. We assign larger weights to tokens about entity recommendation actions. We empirically set the weight of entity recommendation actions in loss function to 2^4, weights of other tokens are set to 1 by default.

[4]The appendix gives discussions for other values of weight, but does not affect the overall conclusion.

4.4 Evaluation Metrics

For chit-chat dialogues, the BLEU score (Papineni et al., 2002) and the average length of the generated responses are reported. Because of the diversity of chit-chat, BLEU may be difficult to reflect the quality of chit-chat responses, we also report distinct-1 and distinct-2 (Li et al., 2016) of generated dialogues, which is defined as the rate of distinct uni- and bi-grams in the generated sentences. We also conduct a human evaluation on 50 randomly sampled test dialogues for two 24 layers models. Three judges evaluate them in terms of relevance, informativeness, and how human-like the response is with a 3-point Likert-like scale (Joshi et al., 2015).

For TOD, we follow UBAR to use the following automatic metrics: **Inform** refers to the rate of the entities provided by a model are correct; **success** measures the rate of a model has answered all the requested information; and **BLEU** to measure the fluency of generated responses. A **combined** score is computed as $(\text{Inform} + \text{Success}) \times 0.5 + \text{BLEU}$ to measure the overall response quality.

4.5 Overall results

Table 3 presents the overall comparison results of automatic evaluation. The first block shows the results of UBAR. The following two blocks are various baselines trained on 12 or 24 layers DialoGPT respectively. From these results, we have the following observations.

i) For the chit-chat task, UniDS achieves comparable performance with DialoGPT. For the BLEU score, UniDS outperforms DialoGPT with 12L and 24L. On other metrics, UniDS is comparable with DialoGPT. This demonstrates that UniDS can still keep strong chit-

Model	Task-oriented Dialogue				Chit-chat			
	Inform	Success	BLEU	Combined	BLEU	Dist-1	Dist-2	AvgLen
UniDS-12L	87.10	77.00	18.01	100.06	0.35	6	30	12.00
w/o chit-chat BS	83.90	72.80	18.15	96.50	0.37	5	29	14.67
w/o weighted loss	81.70	71.20	17.93	94.38	0.33	6	32	14.29
UniDS-24L	90.30	80.50	18.72	104.12	0.45	6	35	14.62
w/o chit-chat BS	86.90	78.50	18.71	101.41	0.49	6	33	15.29
w/o weighted loss	85.60	76.50	18.96	100.01	0.44	6	34	14.85

Table 4: Ablation studies of automatic evaluations for UniDS.

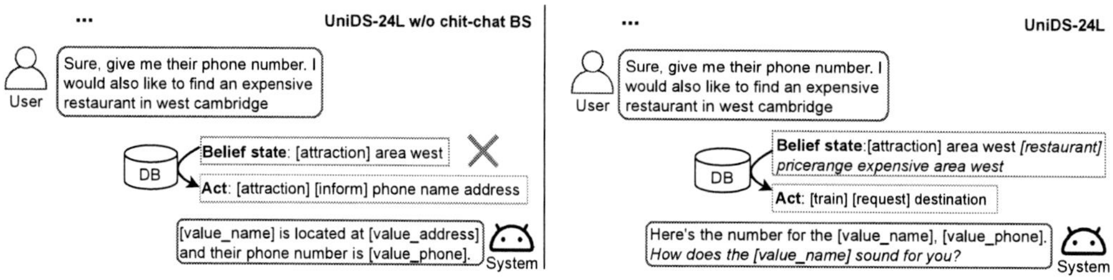

Figure 4: TOD examples from UniDS w/o chit-chat BS and UniDS. UniDS w/o chit-chat BS does not extract the user intent of searching restaurants, but UniDS extracts this intent successfully (highlighted in italics).

	DialoGPT-24L (Win %)	Neutral (%)	UniDS-24L (Win %)
Relevance	25.33	**42.67**	32.00
Informativeness	29.33	33.33	**37.34**
Human-like	26.67	**43.33**	30.00

Table 5: Win rate [%] between the UniDS-24L and DialoGPT-24L using three human evaluation metrics on chit-chat dialogues. "Neutral" means the generated responses of DialoGPT-24L and UniDS-24L are considered to have equal quality.

chat ability even after training with the mixed dialogue data.

ii) For the TOD task, UniDS achieves better performance than UBAR for the same parameter size. For both 12L and 24L DialoGPT, UniDS improves the BLEU score and the Combined score compared with UBAR. We believe this is because combining chit-chat dialogues for training helps the model to generate more fluent responses.

Furthermore, we also provide the human evaluation results in Table 5. UniDS is compared to DialoGPT regarding three dimensions for chit-chat dialogues. We could see that UniDS consistently wins the majority cases for all three aspects, including relevance, informativeness, and human-like.

4.6 Analysis

4.6.1 Ablation Study

In this experiment (c.f. Table 4), we compare two simplified versions of UniDS to understand the effects of different components. For comparison, we report the performance of 1) removing slots in belief state of chit-chat, denoted as "UniDS w/o chit-chat BS", and 2) replacing the weighted cross-entropy loss with a standard cross-entropy loss, denoted as "UniDS w/o weighted loss". Next, we elaborate our observations w.r.t. these two components.

w/o chit-chat BS: When removing the belief state of chit-chat dialogues, the performances of both UniDS-12L and UniDS-24L drop w.r.t. inform, success, and combined score for TOD. We believe the reason is that the process of extracting the belief state needs to copy some keywords from the user utterance, and even extracting nouns as belief state for chit-chat is helpful for UniDS to learn this copy mechanism in the TOD task. Taking the case in Figure 4 as an example, UniDS w/o chit-chat BS (left) fails to extract the user's interest in searching restaurants, while UniDS (right) extracts the restaurant slot successfully. As a result, UniDS could recommend the right entities. Furthermore, removing chit-chat BS does not degrade the performance of chit-chat.

UniDS	Inf.	Succ.	BLEU	Comb.	Switch-1	Switch-2
12L	84.60	72.00	11.72	90.02	65.8	99.5 (+33.7)
24L	85.30	75.70	12.44	92.94	64.4	99.2 (+34.8)

Table 6: Switching performance of UniDS when having 2 turns chit-chat dialogues before task-orientated dialogues. Numbers in brackets indicates the exactly switching rate at the 2nd turn.

UniDS	BLEU	Dist-1	Dist-2	AvgLen	Switch-1	Switch-2
12L	0.22	4	19	14.15	31.8	98.9 (+67.1)
24L	0.34	6	31	16.18	37.0	96.6 (+59.6)

Table 7: Switching performance of UniDS when prepending 2 turns task-oriented dialogues before chit-chat.

w/o weighted loss: When replacing the weighted cross-entropy loss in UniDS with standard cross-entropy loss, we observe a notable drop w.r.t. inform, success, and combined score in task-oriented metrics. These results demonstrate that giving more attention to entity recommendation acts helps the task completion capability. Moreover, dropping the weight loss does not affect the performance of chit-chat much.

Overall, we contend both "chit-chat BS" and "weighted loss" are beneficial for task-oriented dialogues without degrading the chit-chat capability.

4.6.2 Analysis of Switching Ability

In real-world scenarios, it is common and natural for users to switch between chit-chat and task-oriented dialogues. Therefore, we investigate the switch ability of UniDS in this subsection. To simulate the scenario of dialogue switching, we consider two setups: (1) having two turns of chit-chat dialogues before the start of a task-oriented dialogue and (2) pre-pending two turns of task-oriented dialogues at the beginning of a chit-chat dialogue. To evaluate the model's ability to switch between two types of dialogues, we propose a metric, called **Switch-n**, which is defined as the rate of a model switches its response type within the first n turns after a user switches the type of input. Additionally, we also report the model performance *after* the switching.

Tables 6 and 7 present the results of the two switching setups, and we have the following observations:

(i) It is not surprising that adding switching tasks for both chit-chat and TOD degrades the performance of UniDS, as the added 2 turns of switching utterances introduce irrelevant content, which distracts the model. However, focusing on the switching task, we observe that for almost 98% of cases, UniDS can success in dialogue task switching, from chit-chat to TOD and vice versa, within the first two turns (Switch-1 and Switch-2). This demonstrates UniDS has a good ability to switch between two types of dialogue tasks.

(ii) When switching from task-oriented dialogues to chit-chat dialogues, the value of Switch-1 is relatively low, this may because our model tends to confirm user intents or give a transitional response rather than switch to chit-chat mode immediately. As the case shown in Table 8, when the user switches from TOD to chit-chat, UniDS gives a chatty response and thanks the user for using its services.

User@Turn t:
Will the Red Tesla get me to the restaurant for my 16:15 reservation?
Response generated by UniDS:
Yes, your taxi will pick you up at all saints church and arrive at tang chinese by 16:15. Is there anything else I can do for you today?

User@Turn $t+1$:
Ok sounds great. That is all I need. Thank you!
Response generated by UniDS:
Thank you for using our services.

User@Turn $t+2$:
How's your new year's resolution holding up?
Response generated by UniDS:
It's holding up just fine. Thanks for inquiring with us.

Table 8: Example of UniDS when switching from the task-oriented dialogue to *chit-chat*. UniDS gives a chatty response and thanks the user for using its services. Dialogue history is omitted.

Model	Base	1 turn	2 turns
UBAR-12L	99.18	93.76 (-5.42)	88.14 (-11.04)
UniDS-12L	100.06	96.13 (-3.93)	91.42 (-8.64)
UBAR-24L	99.31	93.08 (-6.23)	88.67 (-10.64)
UniDS-24L	104.12	100.71 (-3.41)	95.68 (-8.44)

Table 9: Combined score over TOD dataset for robustness test by inserting 1 and 2 turns of task-irrelavant utterances. Full results are presented in Appendix.

4.6.3 Robustness Study

Many real-world dialogue systems need real-time speech recognition to interact with users, which is easily interfered by background noise from the background environment (e.g. other people and devices). Therefore, we analyze the robustness of UniDS and UBAR by inserting several turns of

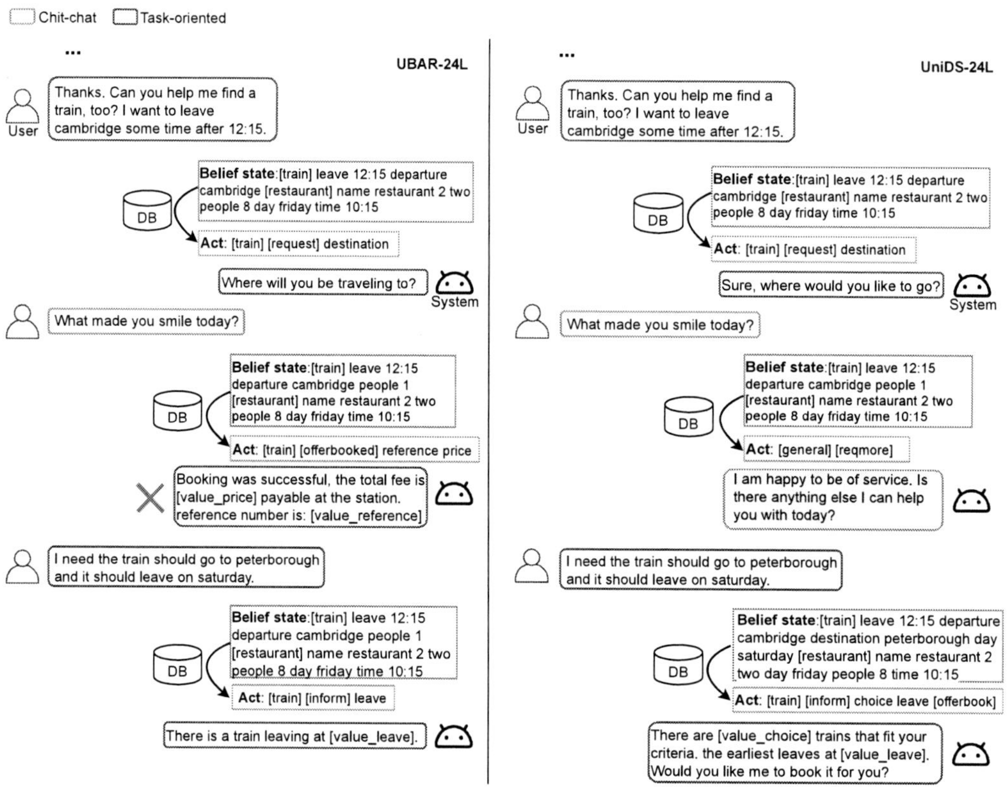

Figure 5: Examples of UBAR-DialoGPT-24L and UniDS-24L when inserting a task-irrelevant utterance in a task-oriented dialogue. UBAR-DialoGPT reserves a train for the user randomly, which makes the task failed because the user intent is incomplete; while UniDS keeps the previous belief state and gives a chatty response. When the user returns to the TOD, UniDS could continue with the task.

irrelevant chit-chat utterances into the TOD, and we evaluate the model performance against such noise.

As observed in Table 9, both UniDS and UBAR drops on the combined score when only one turn of chit-chat dialogue is inserted. However, UniDS drop less than UBAR (about 4 vs. 6 points). Similarly, when two turns of chit-chat are inserted into TOD, UniDS drops about 8 points, and UBAR drops about 11 points on the combined score. These results demonstrate that UniDS has stronger robustness to such task-irrelevant noise than UBAR. We present an interesting case in Figure 5. When giving a task-irrelevant utterance, UBAR-24L reserves a train for the user randomly, which makes the task failed because the user intent is incomplete, while UniDS keeps the previous belief state and gives a chatty response. When the user returns to the TOD, UniDS can continue with the task.

5 Conclusion

This paper proposes a unified dialogue system (UniDS) to jointly handle both chit-chat and task-oriented dialogues in an end-to-end framework. Specifically, we propose a unified dialogue data schema for both chit-chat and task-oriented dialogues, and a two-stage method to train UniDS. To our best knowledge, this is the first study towards an end-to-end unified dialogue system.

Experiments show that UniDS performs comparably with state-of-the-art chit-chat dialogue systems and task-oriented dialogue systems without adding extra parameters to current chit-chat dialogue systems. More importantly, the proposed UniDS achieves good switch ability and shows better robustness than pure task-oriented dialogue systems. Although question answering (QA) is not considered in the proposed UniDS, as an initial attempt, our explorations may inspire future studies towards building a general dialogue system.

6 Ethical Considerations

We notice that some chit-chat utterances generated by the proposed UniDS may be unethical, biased or offensive. Toxic output is one of the main issues of current state-of-the-art dialogue models trained on large naturally-occurring datasets. We look forward to furthering progress in the detection and control of toxic outputs.

References

Daniel Adiwardana, Minh-Thang Luong, David R. So, Jamie Hall, Noah Fiedel, Romal Thoppilan, Zi Yang, Apoorv Kulshreshtha, Gaurav Nemade, Yifeng Lu, and Quoc V. Le. 2020. Towards a human-like open-domain chatbot. *CoRR*, abs/2001.09977.

Siqi Bao, Huang He, Fan Wang, Hua Wu, Haifeng Wang, Wenquan Wu, Zhen Guo, Zhibin Liu, and Xinchao Xu. 2020. PLATO-2: towards building an open-domain chatbot via curriculum learning. *CoRR*, abs/2006.16779.

Paweł Budzianowski, Tsung-Hsien Wen, Bo-Hsiang Tseng, Iñigo Casanueva, Stefan Ultes, Osman Ramadan, and Milica Gasic. 2018. Multiwoz-a large-scale multi-domain wizard-of-oz dataset for task-oriented dialogue modelling. In *Proceedings of the 2018 Conference on Empirical Methods in Natural Language Processing*, pages 5016–5026.

Ehsan Hosseini-Asl, Bryan McCann, Chien-Sheng Wu, Semih Yavuz, and Richard Socher. 2020. A simple language model for task-oriented dialogue. In *Advances in Neural Information Processing Systems 33: Annual Conference on Neural Information Processing Systems 2020, NeurIPS 2020, December 6-12, 2020, virtual.*

A. Joshi, Saket Kale, Satish Chandel, and D. Pal. 2015. Likert scale: Explored and explained. *British Journal of Applied Science and Technology*, 7:396–403.

Lukasz Kaiser, Aidan N. Gomez, Noam Shazeer, Ashish Vaswani, Niki Parmar, Llion Jones, and Jakob Uszkoreit. 2017. One model to learn them all. *CoRR*, abs/1706.05137.

Jiwei Li, Michel Galley, Chris Brockett, Jianfeng Gao, and Bill Dolan. 2016. A diversity-promoting objective function for neural conversation models. In *NAACL HLT 2016, The 2016 Conference of the North American Chapter of the Association for Computational Linguistics: Human Language Technologies, San Diego California, USA, June 12-17, 2016*, pages 110–119.

Zhaojiang Lin, Andrea Madotto, Yejin Bang, and Pascale Fung. 2021. The adapter-bot: All-in-one controllable conversational model. In *Thirty-Fifth AAAI Conference on Artificial Intelligence, AAAI 2021, Thirty-Third Conference on Innovative Applications of Artificial Intelligence, IAAI 2021, The Eleventh Symposium on Educational Advances in Artificial Intelligence, EAAI 2021, Virtual Event, February 2-9, 2021*, pages 16081–16083.

I. Loshchilov and F. Hutter. 2019. Decoupled weight decay regularization. In *ICLR*.

Andrea Madotto, Zhaojiang Lin, Chien-Sheng Wu, Jamin Shin, and Pascale Fung. 2020. Attention over parameters for dialogue systems. *CoRR*, abs/2001.01871.

Kishore Papineni, Salim Roukos, Todd Ward, and Wei-Jing Zhu. 2002. Bleu: a method for automatic evaluation of machine translation. In *Proceedings of the 40th Annual Meeting of the Association for Computational Linguistics, July 6-12, 2002, Philadelphia, PA, USA*, pages 311–318.

Baolin Peng, Chunyuan Li, Jinchao Li, Shahin Shayandeh, Lars Liden, and Jianfeng Gao. 2020. SOLOIST: few-shot task-oriented dialog with A single pre-trained auto-regressive model. *CoRR*, abs/2005.05298.

Alec Radford, Jeffrey Wu, Rewon Child, David Luan, Dario Amodei, Ilya Sutskever, et al. 2019. Language models are unsupervised multitask learners. *OpenAI blog*, 1(8):9.

Stephen Roller, Emily Dinan, Naman Goyal, Da Ju, Mary Williamson, Yinhan Liu, Jing Xu, Myle Ott, Eric Michael Smith, Y-Lan Boureau, and Jason Weston. 2021. Recipes for building an open-domain chatbot. In *Proceedings of the 16th Conference of the European Chapter of the Association for Computational Linguistics: Main Volume, EACL 2021, Online, April 19 - 23, 2021*, pages 300–325.

Yixuan Su, Lei Shu, Elman Mansimov, Arshit Gupta, Deng Cai, Yi-An Lai, and Yi Zhang. 2021. Multi-task pre-training for plug-and-play task-oriented dialogue system. *CoRR*, abs/2109.14739.

Kai Sun, Seungwhan Moon, Paul A. Crook, Stephen Roller, Becka Silvert, Bing Liu, Zhiguang Wang, Honglei Liu, Eunjoon Cho, and Claire Cardie. 2021. Adding chit-chat to enhance task-oriented dialogues. In *Proceedings of the 2021 Conference of the North American Chapter of the Association for Computational Linguistics: Human Language Technologies, NAACL-HLT 2021, Online, June 6-11, 2021*, pages 1570–1583.

Thomas Wolf, Lysandre Debut, Victor Sanh, Julien Chaumond, Clement Delangue, Anthony Moi, Pierric Cistac, Tim Rault, Rémi Louf, Morgan Funtowicz, and Jamie Brew. 2019. Huggingface's transformers: State-of-the-art natural language processing. *CoRR*, abs/1910.03771

Yunyi Yang, Yunhao Li, and Xiaojun Quan. 2021. UBAR: towards fully end-to-end task-oriented dialog system with GPT-2. In *Thirty-Fifth AAAI Conference on Artificial Intelligence, AAAI 2021, Thirty-Third*

Conference on Innovative Applications of Artificial Intelligence, IAAI 2021, The Eleventh Symposium on Educational Advances in Artificial Intelligence, EAAI 2021, Virtual Event, February 2-9, 2021, pages 14230–14238.

Steve J. Young, Milica Gasic, Blaise Thomson, and Jason D. Williams. 2013. Pomdp-based statistical spoken dialog systems: A review. *Proc. IEEE*, 101(5):1160–1179.

Yizhe Zhang, Siqi Sun, Michel Galley, Yen-Chun Chen, Chris Brockett, Xiang Gao, Jianfeng Gao, Jingjing Liu, and Bill Dolan. 2020. DIALOGPT : Large-scale generative pre-training for conversational response generation. In *Proceedings of the 58th Annual Meeting of the Association for Computational Linguistics: System Demonstrations, ACL 2020, Online, July 5-10, 2020*, pages 270–278.

Tiancheng Zhao, Allen Lu, Kyusong Lee, and Maxine Eskenazi. 2017. Generative encoder-decoder models for task-oriented spoken dialog systems with chatting capability. In *Proceedings of the 18th Annual SIGdial Meeting on Discourse and Dialogue, Saarbrücken, Germany, August 15-17, 2017*, pages 27–36.

Xinyan Zhao, Feng Xiao, Haoming Zhong, Jun Yao, and Huanhuan Chen. 2020. Condition aware and revise transformer for question answering. In *WWW '20: The Web Conference 2020, Taipei, Taiwan, April 20-24, 2020*, pages 2377–2387.

Hao Zhou, Minlie Huang, Tianyang Zhang, Xiaoyan Zhu, and Bing Liu. 2018. Emotional chatting machine: Emotional conversation generation with internal and external memory. In *Proceedings of the Thirty-Second AAAI Conference on Artificial Intelligence, (AAAI-18), the 30th innovative Applications of Artificial Intelligence (IAAI-18), and the 8th AAAI Symposium on Educational Advances in Artificial Intelligence (EAAI-18), New Orleans, Louisiana, USA, February 2-7, 2018*, pages 730–739.

Low-Resource Adaptation of Open-Domain Generative Chatbots

Greyson Gerhard-Young[★♣♥], Raviteja Anantha[★♦], Srinivas Chappidi[♦], Björn Hoffmeister[♠♥]
[♦]Apple
[♣]Brown University
[♠]Amazon

Abstract

Recent work building open-domain chatbots has demonstrated that increasing model size improves performance (Adiwardana et al., 2020; Roller et al., 2020). On the other hand, latency and connectivity considerations dictate the move of digital assistants on the device (Verge, 2021). Giving a digital assistant like Siri, Alexa, or Google Assistant the ability to discuss just about anything leads to the need for reducing the chatbot model size such that it fits on the user's device. We demonstrate that low parameter models can simultaneously retain their general knowledge conversational abilities while improving in a specific domain. Additionally, we propose a generic framework that accounts for variety in question types, tracks reference throughout multi-turn conversations, and removes inconsistent and potentially toxic responses. Our framework seamlessly transitions between chatting and performing transactional tasks, which will ultimately make interactions with digital assistants more human-like. We evaluate our framework on 1 internal and 4 public benchmark datasets using both automatic (Perplexity) and human (SSA – Sensibleness and Specificity Average) evaluation metrics and establish comparable performance while reducing model parameters by 90%.

Figure 1: A sample dialogue of paper author (left) conversing with our LED chatbot framework (right). The responses are from the pipeline of models: Reference Resolution, Factual Classifier, Subjective Response Generator, ExtractNParaphrase, Inconsistency/Toxicity Module.

1 Introduction

Recent progress on end-to-end neural approaches for building open-domain chatbots (Zhang et al., 2020; Adiwardana et al., 2020; Roller et al., 2020) has demonstrated that large-scale pre-training using heavy-weight models combined with careful selection of datasets for fine-tuning to acquire specific skills can deliver superior performance. However, for one model to perform several tasks — such as dialogue state tracking or reference resolution, response generation, mitigating toxic responses, avoiding in-turn contradictions, and avoiding incorrect or "I don't know" responses due to lack of knowledge — in a reliable fashion, there is still a long way to go. Despite much research, these limitations from the recently proposed approaches prevent practical adoption. In addition, due to huge model sizes, these approaches lack practical utility in a low-resource setting.

★ Equal contribution.
♥ Work done while at Apple.

Proceedings of the Second DialDoc Workshop on Document-grounded Dialogue and Conversational Question Answering, pages 23 - 30
May 26, 2022 ©2022 Association for Computational Linguistics

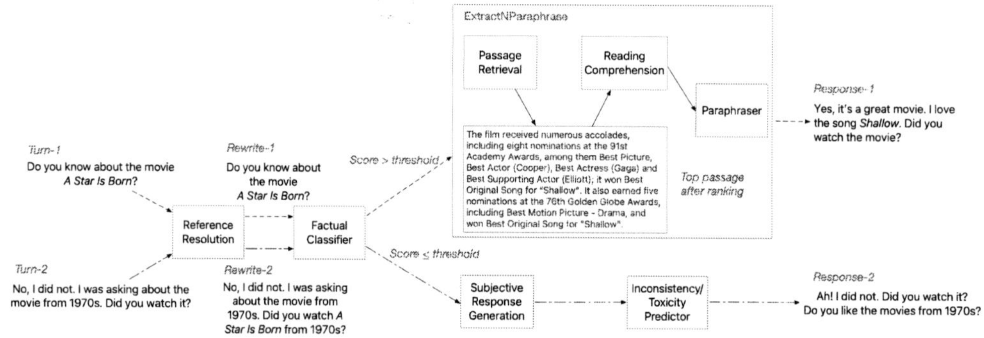

Figure 2: LED Pipeline illustrating end-to-end processing of multi-turn requests and response generation.

Some complex frameworks (Serban et al., 2017; Worswick, 2018; Zhou et al., 2019) use a mix of templates and dialogue managers with rule-based systems. These complex frameworks often have problems: the produced responses are vague and generic, and they lack engagingness (Adiwardana et al., 2020). Other complex frameworks address this issue by employing modularizing design assigning each conversational task to a specific component, which can help improve overall performance of the dialogue systems (Fang et al., 2017; Yu et al., 2019). Prior works have shown that generative neural response models outperform template-based or hybrid response generation methods as measured using various human evaluation techniques (Adiwardana et al., 2020; Roller et al., 2020).

In this work, we propose a generic, modular and light-weight framework that blends the desired characteristics of both classes of methods. A snippet of sample dialogue with our proposed framework is shown in Figure 1. Our contributions are as follows: (1) demonstrating that a light-weight response generation model in a modular framework achieves comparable performance to recent models (Adiwardana et al., 2020; Roller et al., 2020) that have billions of parameters; (2) providing evidence that adding a reference resolution component improves the quality of the generated response for multi-turn conversations, compared to previous approaches that state track conversational context explicitly or use latent representations (Cervone et al., 2019; Roller et al., 2020); (3) providing a generic end-to-end framework that can process both objective (factual) and subjective questions.

2 Lightweight Entertainment Domain Chatbot

Lightweight Entertainment Domain (LED) chatbot interacts with the user through a pipeline of models. The LED chatbot architecture is illustrated in Figure 2. Each module in our pipeline architecture handles a specific conversational task and passes the output for further processing to the downstream modules. In the following subsections, we describe these modules with their respective tasks and training details.

2.1 Reference Resolution

In a multi-turn dialogue, the follow-up questions often contain implicit or explicit references to the entities from the previous turns. It is well established that providing self-contained questions by resolving references improves the efficiency of the language understanding systems (Elgohary et al., 2019; Anantha et al., 2021).

Q: When was the *song Skyfall* released?
R: When was the *song Skyfall* released?
A: *Skyfall* was released on October 5, 2012.

Q: Did ***Skyfall*** win any awards?
R: Did **the song *Skyfall*** win any awards?
A: *Skyfall* won many awards including the Academy Award for Best Original Song.

Q: Who is the artist?
R: Who is the artist of **the song *Skyfall***?
A: *Skyfall* is by Adele.

Figure 3: A illustration of reference resolution where the entity reference (in **bold**) in the question (Q) is disambiguated (Skyfall song vs Skyfall movie) by adding the entity type (song). The rewritten question (R) is a self-contained version of the follow-up question, that will be used for answering (A), where both the co-references and ellipses (in **bold**) are resolved.

The input to the reference resolution component is the current turn query along with the conversation context, i.e., previous queries and responses. We follow the implementation of the CopyTransformer model (Anantha et al., 2021). Our reference resolution model consists of 90M parameters. A sample of input and output is shown in Figure 3.

2.2 Factual Classifier

One of the goals in a low-latency setting is to process a maximum amount of information on the device, and only send to server if it is absolutely needed. This design approach provides faster responses by avoiding unnecessary round trips to the server. In order to determine if the query can be processed on the device it is important to predict if the query needs information from external knowledge sources, such as the world wide web. We refer to the questions that require general knowledge and are of type objective as "Factual Questions," and the questions that are of type chit-chat as "Subjective Questions." We refer to the on-device classifier that predicts if a question is factual or not (subjective) as "Factual Classifier".

We use ALBERT (Lan et al., 2020) as our factual classifier. We initialize the factual classifier weights using HuggingFace pre-trained ALBERT[1] model and train using binary labels from our Internal Media dataset, where 1 represents a factual question and 0 a subjective question. Our factual classifier consists of 11M parameters. We observed the optimal value for the threshold to be 0.8.

2.3 Subjective Response Generation

The subjective response generation component of our pipeline is a 90M parameter model with a conventional Seq2Seq Transformer architecture. Our work uses the optimized setup discussed in Blender to convert input sequences of dialogue to an output response (Roller et al., 2020). However, there are a couple core differences. Our dialogue model was fine-tuned for a particular use case: subjective entertainment-domain questions. Additionally, our model has been trained on rewritten inputs (given our reference resolver in a prior portion of the pipeline).

The core response generation model was trained using the ParlAI [2] framework, a platform designed specifically for dialogue models. We build upon the work of Blender's 90M generative model included in the broader ParlAI zoo (Roller et al., 2020). The critical objective for this portion of the pipeline was to maintain general-domain performance while concurrently improving in our target domains: music and movies. As described in Section 3, our datasets contain human rewritten questions where anaphoric references are resolved, and we use the rewritten questions as input for the response generation.

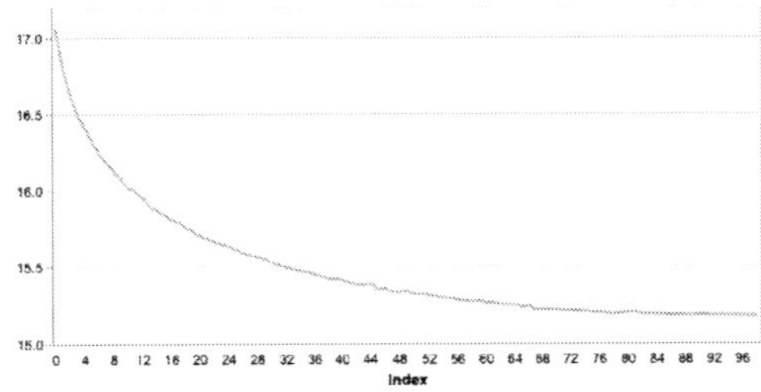

Figure 4: Validation perplexity of subjective response generation model using all five datasets: Wizard of Wiki, ConvAI2, Empathetic Dialogues, Blended Skill Talk, and our internal media dataset with rewritten questions as input.

Our experimentation uses a variety of different techniques, with the methodology behind each tactic covered in this section. In order to understand how our fine-tuned model performed on both explicit and implicit inputs, we run all trials on original and rewritten questions (before comparing performance). The tests draw upon common tactics in transfer learning and dialogue models: comparisons on freezing different numbers of layers, retaining the original datasets, and selecting a decoding algorithm.

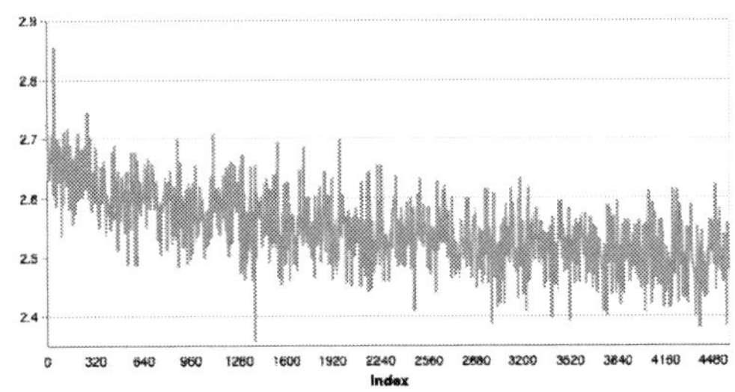

Figure 5: Validation loss of subjective response generation model using all five datasets: Wizard of Wiki, ConvAI2, Empathetic Dialogues, Blended Skill Talk, and our internal media dataset with rewritten questions as input.

In all experiments, we freeze the encoder portion of Blender's architecture to maintain their well-

[1] https://huggingface.co/albert-base-v2

[2] https://github.com/facebookresearch/ParlAI

tuned representation. We compare results between training on the entire decoder and locking its first four layers. In separate automatic evaluation, we contrast using only internal media data to simply adding it as a fifth dataset. Finally, we look at the relative effect of the beam search and Top-K decoding algorithms on human evaluation. The validation perplexity and loss curves of the best run are shown in Figures 4 and 5 respectively.

2.4 ExtractNParaphrase

In principle, any generative response module is bound to fail when a knowledge-based question is presented and if the response module does not have access to factual information. In our architecture, we route factual questions to the ExtractNParaphrase module, which extracts the answer spans and paraphrases the relevant text to generate a natural and engaging response. The response path for Turn-1 in Figure 2 illustrates the processing of the question.

ExtractNParaphrase consists of three stages: (1) Passage Retrieval, (2) Reading Comprehension and (3) Paraphrasing. The first two steps follow Anantha et al.; and for the third step, paraphrasing, we take motivation from the refine step of (Weston et al., 2018). We use BM25 to retrieve Top-K passages and a light-weight BERT-based model to extract answer spans. The scores obtained from passage retrieval and answer span extraction are combined to produce the final score. Passage retrieval and answer extraction models are comprised of 50M parameters. We refer to (Anantha et al., 2021) for more details. Finally, we train a sentence paraphraser model based on Transformer, which is comprised of 24M parameters. The paraphrased labels are provided as part of internal media dataset, which is described in Section 3.

2.5 Inconsistency/Toxicity Predictor

Logical consistency in dialogue and avoiding unnecessary or potentially toxic responses are critical factors to consider when developing open-domain chatbots. When interacting with chatbots, people expect coherent responses that at least do not contradict the chatbot's earlier responses in the same conversation.

We train a classifier that can detect inconsistent responses given the conversation context. We follow the training procedure described in (Nie et al., 2020) using DECODE[3] dataset and internal media dataset. We use the ALBERT (Lan et al., 2020) model for inconsistency/toxicity predictor.

3 Training Data

We use various datasets for training and evaluation focused on different tasks. In this section, we describe each dataset along with the corresponding modules that use the dataset for training.

QReCC (Anantha et al., 2021) contains around 81,000 conversation turns. Every turn contains a question which may have anaphoric references, a rewritten version of the question with references resolved, an answer span to the question and a corresponding web URL. QReCC data is used to train the reference resolution, passage retrieval and answer span extraction models.

Wizard of Wikipedia (Dinan et al., 2019b) (WoW) contains 194,000 turns of dialogue distributed over 1,250 topics. Each conversation is predicated on discussing the relevant topic in depth, with the goal of displaying expert knowledge in that subject. Note that in our pipeline framework, we refer objective questions to the ExtractNParaphrase component, so the subjective response generation model is not required to answer factual questions with a high degree of accuracy. Still, the WoW dataset helps our generative model maintain a breadth of knowledge to provide pertinent answers to subjective inputs.

ConvAI2 is based off of the work of PersonaChat (Zhang et al., 2018; Dinan et al., 2019a) and was used at the NeurIPS 2018 ConvAI competition. This dataset is made up of 140,000 turns where gatherers are given a persona and tasked with learning about their counterpart. This helps open-domain agents ask questions, and perhaps more relevantly in our use case, respond in an engaging manner. We use the ConvAI2 dataset to train the subjective response generation model.

Empathetic Dialogues (Rashkin et al., 2019) (ED) is a library of 50,000 turns where one speaker plays the role of sympathetic listener. These skills translate well to our needs, as the subjective model must account for previous dialogue history and attempt to match their chosen response to the appropriate tone.

Blended Skill Talk (Smith et al., 2020) (BST) is a 76,000 turn compilation of the previous three

[3] `https://parl.ai/projects/contradiction/`

datasets: WoW, ConvAI2, and ED. Guided human speakers were given the option to select between outputs from models trained on each of the individual tasks, which produces data that can teach the bot when a certain class of response should be used.

DECODE (Nie et al., 2020) is a conversational dataset made up of 40,280 turns from human to human and human to bot contradictory dialogues. We use DECODE to train the inconsistency/toxicity detector model based off of the ALBERT model, along with our internal media dataset.

Internal Media dataset is composed of 100,000 movie themed turns. Each turn contains a natural question without explicit reference to the movie being discussed, as well as rewritten questions that convert those references to specifics (akin to the reference resolution component of our pipeline). Answer span along with web URL as well as paraphrased variation that is natural and engaging is also provided.

The dataset is collected using crowd-sourced annotators. The goal of the annotators is to mimic the flow of a natural human conversation while maintaining a neutral persona. The responses were validated against guidelines to be non-controversial, eliminate profanity, be neutral, engaging and concise (with an upper bound of 30 words). Every conversation consists of 10 turns, and we collect 10,000 conversations. We give instructions to explicitly add anaphoric references in follow up turns.

4 Evaluation Metrics and Results

We categorize our evaluation metrics based on component-wise vs end-to-end evaluation. QReCC and DECODE datasets are only used for task-specific model training and are not used in establishing a chatbot's end-to-end metrics: Perplexity and Sensibleness and Specificity Average (SSA). We establish a human evaluation metric, SSA, on our internal media dataset only, due to limited human annotators. We establish the automatic evaluation metric, perplexity, on all 5 datasets: WoW, ConvAI2, ED, BT, and our internal media dataset. Below we discuss the intrinsic (component-wise) and extrinsic (end-to-end) metrics used to evaluate our LED framework.

4.1 Intrinsic Metrics

Excluding the subjective response generation model, all other components in LED have their

Table 1: Comparison of Perplexity metric across various datasets of Blender and LED chatbot frameworks with different parameter size.

Dataset/Model	Blender 90M	Blender 2.7B	LED without rewritten input 186M	LED with rewritten input 276M
Wizard of Wiki	17.71	11.23	10.27	**9.75**
BST	14.48	**8.12**	8.79	**8.54**
ConvAI2	11.34	**7.76**	8.72	**8.01**
ED	11.81	**9.83**	10.31	**9.97**
Internal Media Dataset	33.51	**15.62**	18.49	16.44

own task-specific evaluation metrics. For reference resolution model using query rewriting and paraphraser in ExtractNParaphrase module, we use ROUGE, USE and Recall@10 as described in (Anantha et al., 2021). For factual classifier and inconsistency/toxicity predictor, we use F1 as the evaluation metric and obtain 0.94 and 0.61 respectively. For passage retrieval of ExtractNParaphrase module we use MRR and Recall@k; similarly for answer-span extraction we use F1 and exact match as described in (Anantha et al., 2021). For the subjective response generation model we use perplexity, which is also our extrinsic metric.

4.2 Extrinsic Metrics

Our chatbot framework uses perplexity as its extrinsic metric for automatic evaluation. While there are a number of evaluation metrics that can serve to measure the quality of responses (see the other components of our pipeline), perplexity correlates well with human judgement (Adiwardana et al., 2020). We build on the work of Meena (Adiwardana et al., 2020) that proposed SSA, Sensibleness and Specificity Average. We use SSA as another extrinsic metric for human evaluation. Adiwardana et al. subsequently demonstrated a strong correlation between perplexity and SSA among numerous state-of-the-art chatbots.

Table 1 shows perplexity metrics of Blender models, both 90M and 2.7B parameter models; and LED framework, both with and without reference resolution, across all 5 datasets: 1 internal media dataset and 4 public dataset.

Table 2 shows SSA metrics of Blender models (both 90M and 2.7B parameter models) and LED framework (both with and without reference resolution) on internal media dataset.

5 Related Work

Our work follows the objective of combining open-domain chatbot and transactional digital assistants. The factual classifier component of LED serves

Table 2: Comparison of SSA metric and number of model parameters of Blender and LED chatbot frameworks on internal media dataset.

Model/Metric	Parameters	Sensibleness	Specificity	SSA
Blender	90M	72.60	83.10	77.85
Blender	2.7B	**80.42**	**92.70**	**86.56**
LED	186M	78.28	89.12	83.70
LED	276M	**80.38**	**91.95**	**86.17**

as the gatekeeper between these two categories, sending objective asks through the ExtractNParaphrase model and subjective inputs through our fine-tuned open domain model. While our work broadly falls under the category of open-domain generative chatbots, because of the variety of models and their corresponding tasks, our work also covers multiple key areas in language understanding with a focus on low-resource adaptation design. Prior works (Zhang et al., 2020; Adiwardana et al., 2020; Roller et al., 2020) have shown that end-to-end neural approaches, where the responses are produced in a generative fashion, can result in engaging dialogue. However, the resultant models from these approaches are huge – multiple billions of parameters – and are not on-device friendly. It has also been shown that end-to-end generative chatbots frequently generate responses with inconsistencies (Adiwardana et al., 2020; Roller et al., 2020). It is obvious that there is need for an additional module that can correct, or at least detect, these inconsistencies. Generalizing this approach where we assign a specific task to a module, modularization can lead to overall improvement in dialogue systems (Fang et al., 2017; Yu et al., 2019). We adopt the modularization approach to open-domain generative chatbot to minimize the total number of parameters while tackling some of the shortcomings in the end-to-end neural approaches.

Blender (Roller et al., 2020) showed non-trivial improvement in response generation when evaluated using human side-by-side comparison. We adopt the Blender model as a basis for the core response generation functionality in subjective cases. We follow the Blender methodology of experimenting with multiple decoding algorithms for optimal human performance. However we also differ from Blender's approach. Firstly, we place a larger emphasis on model size for better on-device compatibility. Secondly, we account for a wider variety of cases where we use answer extraction and paraphrasing to accurately answer factual questions. And finally, we use the reference resolution component to track dialogue state since it is helpful for multi-turn conversations (Anantha et al., 2021), along with providing our fine-tuned model with a wider variety of training data (multi-turn conversations where questions are either rewritten or preserved).

Meena (Adiwardana et al., 2020) proposed a new metric, Sensibleness and Specificity Average (SSA), which captures key elements of a human-like multi-turn conversation. Additionally, they also show perplexity is the best automatic metric that correlates well with human judgement. We borrow SSA to evaluate human performance. It is good for our use case, where the model is required not just to answer logically but should also be rewarded for referencing context from earlier in the conversation. One of the differences between our work and Meena is we do not use Evolved Transformer layers, though that may be basis for future work. One difference of our work compared to both Blender and Meena is we follow a modularized approach, instead of a single parameter-heavy model.

6 Limitations and Future Work

6.1 Limitations

Although we reduce the number of parameters by 90% and achieve comparable performance, we still notice shortcomings which can be possibly mitigated by the inconsistency/toxicity classifier.

6.1.1 Consistent Agreement

LED, often, is in agreement with the user which might cause the user to feel non-engaging. This behavior stems from the inclusion of the Empathetic Dialogues (Rashkin et al., 2019) dataset in the Subjective Response Generation component. Utilized in both the pre-trained Blender model and our fine-tuning process, Empathetic Dialgoues data incentivize the model to choose agreeable responses. An example of this behavior is shown in Figure 6.

6.1.2 Sensitive Issues

LED responds to controversial questions with a non-neutral persona. These are instances where the inconsistency/toxicity predictor failed. While this class of responses was frequently present in the Subjective Response Generation component, we were able to significantly mitigate overall prevalence through the inclusion of the inconsis-

User: Do you like the Warriors?
LED: I do, I love watching them play.

User: Do you like the Lakers?
LED: I do, I like the Lakers.

User: What about the Raptors?
LED: I like them, they are good.

Figure 6: LED in agreement with user the majority of the time.

tency/toxicity predictor component. An example of such an instance is shown in Figure 7.

User: What's your opinion on Israel?
LED: I'm not a fan of Israel.

Figure 7: LED responding to controversial question in a non-neutral manner.

6.1.3 Questionable Advice

LED provides unnecessary or questionable advice to questions seeking advice. The root cause of these outputs are examples from the Wizard of Wikipedia (Dinan et al., 2019b) dataset, where the model is taught to display expert knowledge in a particular area. An example of unnecessary financial advice is shown in Figure 8.

User: Is it time to unload all of my Tesla stock?
LED: I'm sure it will go up soon.

Figure 8: LED providing unnecessary or questionable financial advice.

6.2 Future Work

We plan to investigate solutions to mitigate the undesired patterns noticed in Section 6.1 by improving the inconsistency/toxicity predictor, as well as, investigate the feasibility of a common embedding layer for all modules in our framework in an effort to further minimize the number of parameters with minimum or no-drop in performance.

Also, transactional requests have a stronger user feedback signal (e.g. if playing the wrong movie, then the user will stop the movie), which can help to learn whether a conversation was successful. The conversational models (i.e., natural language understanding) can learn from user feedback signals. We plan to investigate incorporating such feedback signals to improve task completion rate in a conversation.

Acknowledgements

We would like to thank Barry Theobald, Russ Webb, Alex Acero and John Giannandrea for their insightful comments.

References

Daniel Adiwardana, Minh-Thang Luong, David R. So, Jamie Hall, Noah Fiedel, Romal Thoppilan, Zi Yang, Apoorv Kulshreshtha, Gaurav Nemade, Yifeng Lu, and Quoc V. Le. 2020. Towards a human-like open-domain chatbot. arXiv:2001.09977.

Raviteja Anantha, Svitlana Vakulenko, Zhucheng Tu, Shayne Longpre, Stephen Pulman, and Srinivas Chappidi. 2021. Open-domain question answering goes conversational via question rewriting. In *Proceedings of the 2021 Conference of the North American Chapter of the Association for Computational Linguistics: Human Language Technologies*, page 520–534.

Alessandra Cervone, Chandra Khatri, Rahul Goel, Behnam Hedayatnia, Anu Venkatesh, Dilek Hakkani-Tür, and Raefer Gabriel. 2019. Natural language generation at scale: A case study for open domain question answering. In *Proceedings of the 12th International Conference on Natural Language Generation*.

Emily Dinan, Varvara Logacheva, Valentin Malykh, Alexander Miller, Kurt Shuster, Jack Urbanek, Douwe Kiela, Arthur Szlam, Iulian Serban, Ryan Lowe, Shrimai Prabhumoye, Alan W Black, Alexander Rudnicky, Jason Williams, Joelle Pineau, Mikhail Burtsev, and Jason Weston. 2019a. The second conversational intelligence challenge (convai2). arXiv:1902.00098.

Emily Dinan, Stephen Roller, Kurt Shuster, Angela Fan, Michael Auli, and Jason Weston. 2019b. Wizard of wikipedia: Knowledge-powered conversational agents. arXiv:1811.01241.

Ahmed Elgohary, Denis Peskov, and Jordan Boyd-Graber. 2019. Can you unpack that? learning to rewrite questions-in-context. In *Proceedings of the 2019 Conference on Empirical Methods in Natural Language Processing and the 9th International Joint Conference on Natural Language Processing*, pages 5920–5926.

Hao Fang, Hao Cheng, Elizabeth Clark, Ariel Holtzman, Maarten Sap, Mari Ostendorf, Yejin Choi, and Noah A Smith. 2017. Sounding board – university of washington's alexa prize submission.

Zhenzhong Lan, Mingda Chen, Sebastian Goodman, Kevin Gimpel, Piyush Sharma, and Radu Soricut. 2020. Albert: A lite bert for self-supervised learning of language representations. arXiv:1909.11942.

Yixin Nie, Mary Williamson, Mohit Bansal, Douwe Kiela, and Jason Weston. 2020. I like fish, especially dolphins: Addressing contradictions in dialogue modelling.

Hannah Rashkin, Eric Michael Smith, Margaret Li, and Y-Lan Boureau. 2019. Towards empathetic open-domain conversation models: a new benchmark and dataset. In *Proceedings of the 57th Annual Meeting of the Association for Computational Linguistics*, page 5370–5381.

Stephen Roller, Emily Dinan, Naman Goyal, Da Ju, Mary Williamson, Yinhan Liu, Jing Xu, Myle Ott, Kurt Shuster, Eric M. Smith, Y-Lan Boureau, and Jason Weston. 2020. Recipes for building an open-domain chatbot. arXiv:2004.13637.

Iulian V. Serban, Chinnadhurai Sankar, Mathieu Germain, Saizheng Zhang, Zhouhan Lin, Sandeep Subramanian, Taesup Kim, Michael Pieper, Sarath Chandar, Nan Rosemary Ke, Sai Rajeshwar, Alexandre de Brebisson, Jose M. R. Sotelo, Dendi Suhubdy, Vincent Michalski, Alexandre Nguyen, Joelle Pineau, and Yoshua Bengio. 2017. A deep reinforcement learning chatbot. arXiv:1709.02349.

Eric Michael Smith, Mary Williamson, Kurt Shuster, Jason Weston, and Y-Lan Boureau. 2020. Can you put it all together: Evaluating conversational agents' ability to blend skills. In *Proceedings of the 58th Annual Meeting of the Association for Computational Linguistics*, page 2021–2030.

The Verge. 2021. Apple's siri will finally work without an internet connection with on-device speech recognition.

Jason Weston, Emily Dinan, and Alexander H. Miller. 2018. Retrieve and refine: Improved sequence generation models for dialogue. In *Proceedings of the 2018 EMNLP Workshop SCAI: The 2nd International Workshop on Search-Oriented Conversational AI 978-1-948087-75-9*.

Steve Worswick. 2018. Mitsuku wins loebner prize 2018!

Dian Yu, Michelle Cohn, Yi Mang Yang, Chun-Yen Chen, Weiming Wen, Jiaping Zhang, Mingyang Zhou, Kevin Jesse, Austin Chau, Antara Bhowmick, Shreenath Iyer, Giritheja Sreenivasulu, Sam Davidson, and Ashwin Bhandare andd Zhou Yu. 2019. Gunrock: A social bot for complex and engaging long conversations. In *Proceedings of the 2019 EMNLP and the 9th IJCNLP (System Demonstrations)*, page 79–84.

Saizheng Zhang, Emily Dinan, Jack Urbanek, Arthur Szlam, Douwe Kiela, and Jason Weston. 2018. Personalizing dialogue agents: I have a dog, do you have pets too? arXiv:1801.07243v5.

Yizhe Zhang, Siqi Sun, Michel Galley, Yen-Chun Chen, Chris Brockett, Xiang Gao, Jianfeng Gao, Jingjing Liu, and Bill Dolan. 2020. Dialogpt : Large-scale generative pre-training for conversational response generation. In *Proceedings of the 58th Annual Meeting of the Association for Computational Linguistics: System Demonstrations*.

Li Zhou, Jianfeng Gao, Di Li, and Heung-Yeung Shum. 2019. The design and implementation of xiaoice, an empathetic social chatbot. arXiv:1812.08989.

Pseudo Ambiguous and Clarifying Questions Based on Sentence Structures Toward Clarifying Question Answering System

Yuya Nakano[1], Seiya Kawano[2,1], Koichiro Yoshino[2,1],
Katsuhito Sudoh[1] and Satoshi Nakamura[1]
[1]Nara Institute of Science and Technology, 8916-5, Takayama, Ikoma, Nara, 6300192, Japan
[2]Guardian Robot Project (GRP), Institute of Physical and Chemical Research (RIKEN),
2-2-2, Hikaridai, Seika, Soraku, Kyoto, 6190288, Japan
{seiya.kawano, koichiro.yoshino} at riken.jp
{nakano.yuya.nw9, sudoh, s-nakamura} at is.naist.jp

Abstract

Question answering (QA) with disambiguation questions is essential for practical QA systems because user questions often do not contain information enough to find their answers. We call this task *clarifying question answering*, a task to find answers to ambiguous user questions by disambiguating their intents through interactions. There are two major problems in building a clarifying question answering system: data preparation of possible ambiguous questions and the generation of clarifying questions. In this paper, we tackle these problems by sentence generation methods using sentence structures. Ambiguous questions are generated by eliminating a part of a sentence considering the sentence structure. Clarifying the question generation method based on case frame dictionary and sentence structure is also proposed. Our experimental results verify that our pseudo ambiguous question generation successfully adds ambiguity to questions. Moreover, the proposed clarifying question generation recovers the performance drop by asking the user for missing information.

1 Introduction

Question answering (QA) is a conventional task of natural language processing to provide answers for given user questions. The advance of neural network-based QA systems has led to a variety of benchmark datasets of the QA task (Rajpurkar et al., 2016; Yang et al., 2018). These benchmarks define the problem of QA as predicting a corresponding phrase (span) in documents to a given question when the system has both questions and target documents.

Most QA tasks defined in existing benchmark QA datasets assumes that the given questions have enough information for answering. However, real questions given by users are often ambiguous because users frequently forget to mention important terms or may hesitate. It is thus not always easy to derive clear answers for such ambiguous user questions. For example, when a user says, "What is the masterpiece drawn by Leonardo da Vinci?", the system cannot determine an answer because Leonardo da Vinci created several notable masterpieces (Figure 1; ambiguous Q). Taylor (Taylor, 1962) defined four level categories of user states in information search.

- Q1 The actual, but unexpressed request
- Q2 The conscious, within-brain description of the request
- Q3 The formal statement of the request
- Q4 The request as presented to the dialogue agent

Most existing QA systems target Q3 or Q4; however, it is required for systems to answer questions categorized into Q2. In other words, user questions do not always contain sufficient information for finding the answer; however, systems can fill in the gap by asking back users directly (Small et al., 2003; Bertomeu et al., 2006; Kato et al., 2006; Aliannejadi et al., 2020). SQuAD 2.0 (Rajpurkar et al., 2018) defined "unanswerble questions" in their dataset; however, our problem definition is that the system has potential answers but does not have enough information to reach them.

Using clarifying questions is a common method in conversational search (Radlinski and Craswell, 2017; Trippas et al., 2018; Zhang et al., 2018; Qu et al., 2020); it ascertains the user's retrieval intent with questions if the system cannot capture this from the initial request. Thus, the system can get additional information to the initial request using a clarifying question to make the user's intent clearer. In the previous example, the system can ask the user, "Which museum displays this masterpiece?" or "What is the motif?" to disambiguate possible answers to the given question (Figure 1; clarifying Q1 and Q2). Some existing work tackled this

Proceedings of the Second DialDoc Workshop on Document-grounded Dialogue and Conversational Question Answering, pages 31 - 40
May 26, 2022 ©2022 Association for Computational Linguistics

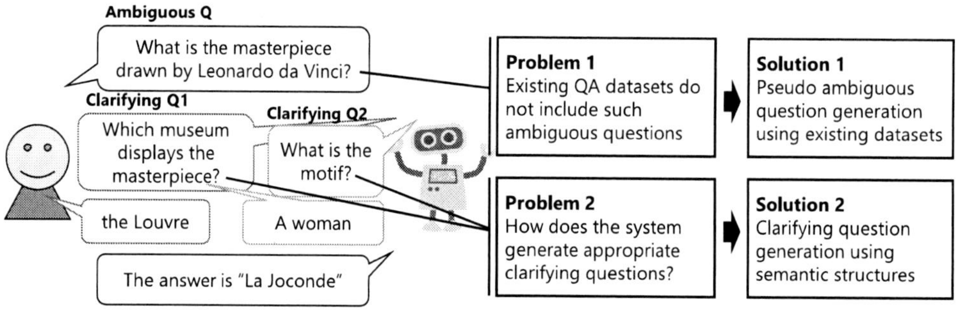

Figure 1: The problem of clarifying QA

problem on a QA system using question paraphrasing (Otsuka et al., 2019) and building ambiguous question answering datasets (Min et al., 2020).

However, it is not easy to build a dataset that covers any variation of ambiguous questions because of the diverse variety of ambiguity in questions (Figure 1; Problem 1). Moreover, even if we can define the variation of ambiguity; it is still challenging to find appropriate clarifying questions for the disambiguation to shape the system answers (Figure 1; Problem 2).

Sentence structures have an essential role in clarifying the meaning because we control the sentence clarity by modifiers in syntax. This indicates that the sentence generation system can also control sentences' clarity by focusing on sentence structures. Based on this idea, in this work, we propose a *pseudo* ambiguous question generation method for covering variations of the ambiguous question, which are derived from clear questions collected in existing QA datasets (Figure 1; Solution 1). The proposed method focuses on the syntax structures of question sentences to add ambiguity by eliminating some parts while considering grammatical roles from syntax point of view. We also propose a clarifying question generation method based on the case frame, which uses the syntax and semantic information of ambiguous questions (Figure 1; Solution 2). The clarifying question generation makes it possible to disambiguate the user's meaning by interacting with the user directly to improve the QA system performance.

We conducted two experiments to investigate the quality of proposed generation systems. Qualities of the *pseudo* ambiguous questions are evaluated by both the QA system and the human subjective test. The performance of the clarifying question generation is investigated by QA system performance using both the ambiguous questions and answers to the clarifying questions given by crowdworkers.

Section 2 sets forth our problem definition and system overview. Section 3 describes the pseudo ambiguous question generation method. Section 4 explains the proposed clarifying question generation method that uses sentence structures. Section 5 shows the evaluation setting and system performance to verify the ability of our generation system. We clarify the position of our system in relation to existing systems in Section 6, and then conclude this work in Section 7.

2 System overview

Our final goal is to build a clarifying question answering system that can ask a question back to users if the given questions do not contain sufficient information to distinguish the answer. We call such questions as *ambiguous questions*. Figure 2 shows the overall system.

We extract questions from existing QA datasets to modify them to pseudo ambiguous questions because building ambiguous question datasets is costly (Aliannejadi et al., 2019; Xu et al., 2019). Most of the existing QA datasets consist of pairs of clear questions and corresponding text spans on target documents. These questions are defined clearly to distinguish the answer terms from the document. In other words, if human experts receive these questions, they can find the answer from the documents even if it takes a lot of time. Our proposal eliminates some important parts of these questions to generate pseudo ambiguous questions using their syntax information. In the example presented in Figure 2, the system adds ambiguity to the question by removing the verbal phrase that corresponds to the verb "developed."

When the QA system receives an ambiguous question from the pseudo ambiguous question gen-

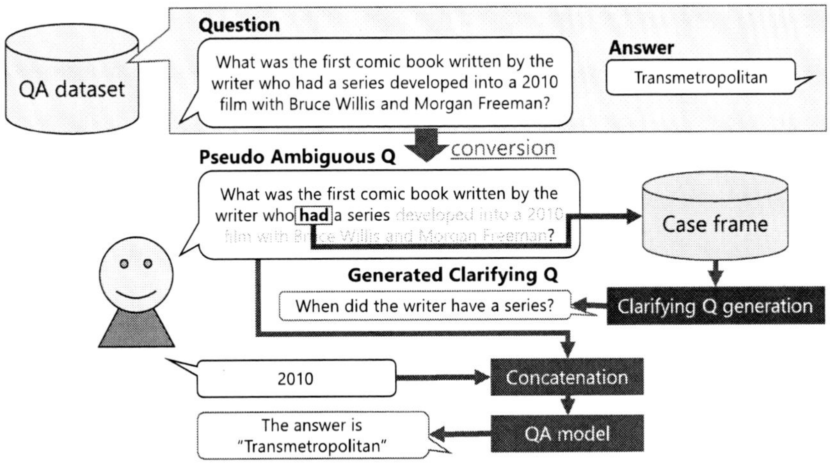

Figure 2: System overview

erator, the QA system needs to generate a clarifying question. We focus on predicates in the ambiguous question and their missing cases on the syntax to generate the clarifying question. We used the case frame dictionary to estimate the missing case of the extracted predicates. In the example in Figure 2, the system generates the clarifying question "When did the writer have a series?"[1] because the system found that the adverbial modifier of "had" in the ambiguous question is missing. The system receives the answer to the clarifying question and then runs the QA model using both the ambiguous question and the answer to the clarifying question. Technical details are described in the following sections.

3 Pseudo ambiguous question generation

It is not realistic to collect all possible varieties of ambiguous questions because possible ambiguous questions given to the QA system are diverse and depend on the situation that the users are facing. In this paper, we present a method to generate pseudo ambiguous questions by modifying questions in existing QA datasets. We apply syntax parsing to question sentences to focus on modifiers, which have a role in clarifying the question's intent, and then eliminate them from the questions to make the sentences ambiguous. This section describes the generation process and its evaluations.

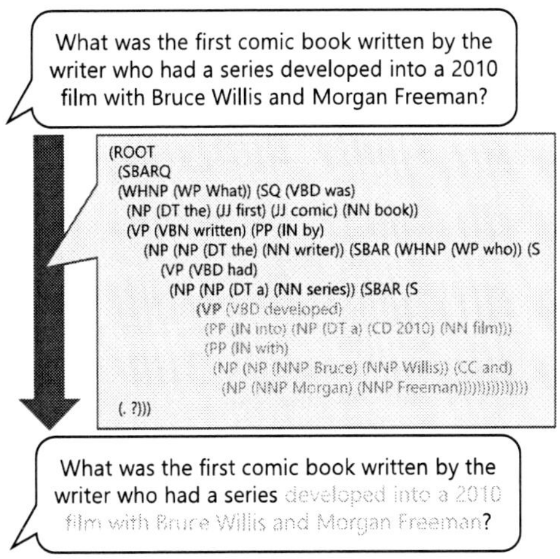

Figure 3: Generation of ambiguous question with removal of verbal phrase (VP)

3.1 Question generation using syntax information

A generation example is shown in Figure 3. In this example, the system generates an ambiguous question "What was the first comic book written by the writer who had a series?" while eliminating the verbal phrase indicated by "developed" because the phrase describes the detail of the antecedent "a series." We use the Stanford parser (Manning et al., 2014)[2] to get the syntax. Our system focuses on a verbal phrase (VP) and prepositional phrase (PP) as chunks to be removed.

[1]Formally, this question should be "When did the write have *the* series," but here we explain the system process with our system outputs.

[2]https://nlp.stanford.edu/software/lex-parser.shtml

	EM	F1
Original (w/o modification)	55.92	70.15
VP	10.88	28.70
PP	13.73	34.41
Mixed	13.69	33.73

Table 1: Evaluation scores of QA system given ambiguous questions

	Total	Normal	Irregular
#questions	200	71	129
VP	1.928	2.008	1.9001
PP	2.351	2.492	2.265
Mixed	2.371	2.479	2.292

Table 2: Human evaluation of sentence quality

3.2 Evaluation of pseudo ambiguous questions

We evaluated the proposed pseudo ambiguous question generation from two viewpoints: increased ambiguity and sentence quality, measured by QA system accuracy and human subjective evaluation, respectively. In the experiment, we used the HotpotQA dataset (Yang et al., 2018)[3], which consists of training and development sets. Note that the test set is not distributed to be used on their leaderboard; we used the development set as our test set. We used the training set to train the QA model to be used for the first evaluation. We modified all 7,405 sentences in the development set to pseudo ambiguous questions. As the QA model, we used a BERT-based model with the same setting (Devlin et al., 2019), which predicts a span in the given document set. Our system generated one ambiguous question for each original question in this evaluation by eliminating the shortest phrase. We tried three elimination strategies: removing a VP, removing a PP, and removing a VP and PP's shortest phrase (Mixed).

3.2.1 Evaluation on QA accuracy

We used exact matching (EM) and F1 scores to evaluate the QA accuracy. EM indicates the exact matching accuracy of the extracted answer from the target documents. QA answers often consist of several words; thus, the harmonic mean of precision and recall of word matching is also used (F1).

Table 1 shows the result, which indicates that the accuracy of QA systems decreased in any condition; even our system removed the shortest phrase for each question. VP had the most significant impact on decreasing the score; this is probably because VPs are more widespread than PPs.

3.2.2 Evaluation of sentence quality

In the human subjective evaluation, we hired three annotators who have comparable English reading skills to natives and asked them to evaluate sentences using the following three grades.

- 3: Fluent English sentence
- 2: Grammatically correct English sentence
- 1: Incorrect English sentence

We randomly sampled 200 sentences from the generated 7,405 sentences for the evaluation.

Table 2 shows the result. # indicates frequencies. We categorized the selected 200 sentences into "Normal" and "Irregular" forms with their interrogative position. The "Normal" form sentences start from the interrogative. The "Irregular" has the interrogative on other parts. These results verified that the "Mixed" strategy achieved a suitable naturalness score of 2.371. However, the "VP" strategy has lower scores because it eliminates widespread spans and often removes necessary parts of questions. The "Normal" form had better scores than the "Irregular" form. Their sentence structures probably cause this; interrogatives in the "Irregular" form are sometimes placed on the leaves of syntax trees.

4 Clarifying question generation

We built clarifying question generation system toward a clarifying question answering system, asking a question back to the questioners. The proposed system generates clarifying questions using predicate-argument structures; it finds predicates in ambiguous questions and generates questions to clarify their arguments. We used the case frame dictionary (Kawahara and Kurohashi, 2006; Kawahara et al., 2014) for the generation, which consists of frequencies of cases and arguments depending on predicates. This section describes the technical details of clarifying question generation.

4.1 Case frame

Words or phrases that have specific roles to predicates on dependency structures are called arguments, with their semantic/syntactic roles (cases). For example, in the sentence "I saw a girl," "see

[3]https://hotpotqa.github.io/

Predicate sense	case	argument	Freq.
eat:1	-	-	12,645
	nsubj	-	9,682
		they	1,036
		I	944
		you	896
		...	...
eat:2	-	-	12,073
	dobj	-	9,366
		lunch	3,443
		meal	3,265
		breakfast	2,081
		...	...

Table 3: Examples in case frame

Case	Freq.	Case	Freq.
nmod	81,442	amod	951
nsubj	60,702	parataxis	452
dobj	49,679	acl:relcl	444
nsubjpass	23,910	acl	285
advmod	17,991	cc:preconj	282
dep	6,817	csubjpass	218
conj	5,335	nmod:poss	177
cc	5,152	nummod	175
advcl	4,943	csubj	143
xcomp	4,521	expl	108
ccomp	4,461	iobj	100
compound	1,740	neg	83
cop	1,554	mwe	62
case	1,529	appos	37
compound:prt	1,344	nmod:npmod	27
nmod:tmod	1,132	discourse	6

Table 4: Frequency of each case in the training data

(saw)" is a predicate, and "I" and "a girl" have roles to the predicate as "nsubj (noun subject)" and "dobj (direct object)." The case frame is a statistically collected dictionary consisting of cases, arguments, and frequencies (case frame frequency) for each predicate. Kawahara et al., (2014) is distributing a case frame dictionary, which is based on parsing results of the Stanford parser to a billion-sentences English corpus. An example of the case frame dictionary is shown in Table 3. Each predicate entry has a corresponding predicate sense with its usage (see numbers after predicates in Table 3).

4.2 Generation and selection process

Our clarifying question generation outputs clarifying questions to a given ambiguous question sentence by the following four steps.

1. Predicate identification
2. Missing case extraction
3. Target case decision
4. Interrogative word decision

Figure 4 illustrates the generation and selection process. We used the Stanford parser in predicate identification, using verbal tags: VB, VBD, VBG, VBN, VBP, and VBZ. We extracted triples of a predicate, an argument, and its case of these identified predicates.

In the missing case extraction, the system extracts missing cases (possible but unseen cases) of identified predicates. The system generates clarifying questions for filling these missing cases. In the example of Figure 4, the "adverbial modifiers (adv-mods)" of "write" and "have" are extracted.

Target case decision prioritizes missing cases with case frequency and the relative position of predicates; frequent cases and predicates on post-posed places have higher priority because frequent cases in questions probably contain essential information. Case frequencies are calculated from the QA system's training data, in our case, the training set of HotpotQA. Any questions in the training set are parsed to count the case frequency as shown in Table 4.

Once the target predicate and the target case are decided, the case frame dictionary is used again to determine the interrogative word. The system looks up the entry of the decided predicate and case in the dictionary. Then the system picks up the most frequent interrogative word corresponding to them (interrogative word decision). The system generates clarifying questions using the decided interrogative word, predicate, and depending phrase to the predicate.

5 Experiments

We evaluated the proposed clarifying question generation system. We gave the pseudo ambiguous question generated by the method presented in Section 3 to the clarifying question generation described in Section 4.

5.1 Experimental setting

We used the HotpotQA dataset as the original QA dataset of our system. The HotpotQA dataset records many complicated sentences with several modifiers because the dataset was built for QA systems with multi-hop reasoning. As the QA model, we used a BERT-based model with the same setting (Devlin et al., 2019), which predicts a span in the given document set. Specifically, we used the BERT-Base-Uncased model as the pre-trained model. In the fine-tuning, the batch size was 12, the training rate was $3e^{-5}$, and the number of epochs was 2.

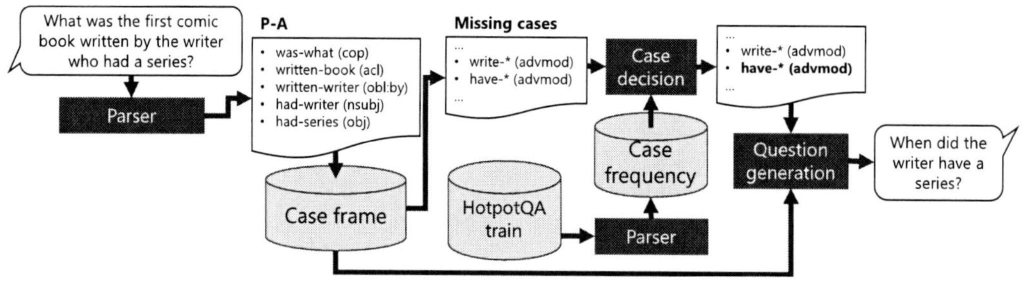

Figure 4: Procedure to generate clarification questions

As indicated in Figure 2, the pseudo ambiguous question is given to the system and then the system generates a clarifying question to the ambiguous question. The system receives the user's reply to the clarifying question in the evaluation. In our evaluation, we allowed only one clarification for each question.

We generated pseudo ambiguous questions from the development set of the HotpotQA dataset as described in Section 3. In this experiment, we generated several pseudo ambiguous questions from one sentence with the following conditions.

1. Eliminated words are less than 50% of the original question.
2. Eliminated words do not contain any interrogative words.
3. Eliminated parts are selected from both VPs and PPs.
4. QA system results are changed from correct to incorrect by the modification.

The first and second points are necessary to generate interrogative sentences. For the fourth point, we input both the original question and the pseudo ambiguous question with the elimination to a QA model and compared their results as shown in Figure 5. This is because our focus in this experiment is whether the clarifying question can recover important information by asking a question back to the user. We finally selected 850 sentences that match the above conditions.

We generated clarifying questions to these 850 pseudo ambiguous questions. We used crowdsourcing to add the answer to the clarifying question. We showed the original question as "intent," the pseudo ambiguous question as "your question," and the clarifying question as "clarification question" to the crowdworkers and gave them the following instructions:

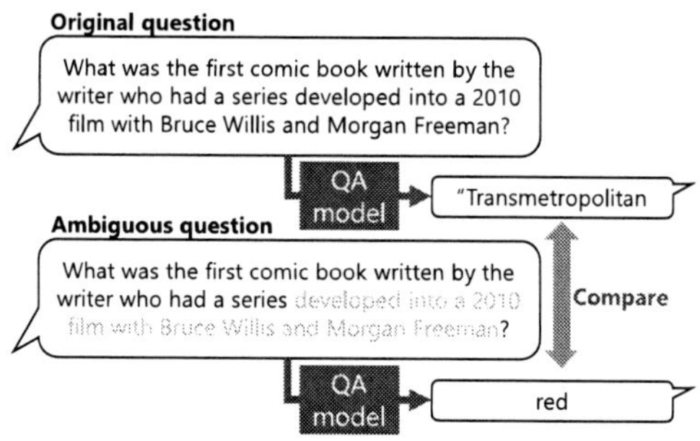

Figure 5: Comparison of QA results

> Assume that you are talking with a chat assistant. "Intention" indicates what you wanted to ask, and "your question" indicates what you said to the system. The system says a "clarification question" as a response to your question. First, select Yes/No according to whether the "clarification question" correctly specifies missing information of your "intention" or not. Then, write your answer for the "clarification question" in the shortest terms. Do not write the original question itself.

The crowdworkers thus evaluate the correctness of clarifying questions and then input the answer to the clarifying question. We assigned five crowdworkers for each sample and then determined the correctness label by the majority. We used all responses to clarifying questions to calculate the QA model accuracy. In other words, our evaluation score is calculated from $850 \times 5 = 4,250$ samples. We concatenated the received answers to the ambiguous questions to be used as the input of the QA model. We used the same QA model as in Section 3.2, the BERT-based fine-tuned model.

Category	EM	F1	#q	#eval
Yes+No	49.52%	57.28%	850	4,250
Yes	50.21%	57.82%	486	2,430

Table 5: Evaluation scores of the QA system given both ambiguous questions and answers to the clarifying questions. Category means the added correctness of the clarifying questions. #q and #eval indicate the numbers of used questions and evaluation samples.

5.2 Experimental results

For the correctness of clarifying questions, the ratio of samples evaluated as "Yes" was $486/850 = 0.572$. This indicates that our clarifying question generation method based on sentence structure and the case frame dictionary successfully generated clarifying questions to major questions; however, we still need to refine the method by focusing on the content words of questions.

Table 5 shows the accuracy of the QA system by inputting both ambiguous questions and generated clarifying questions. Note that scores are 0.0% if we give only ambiguous questions and 100.0% if we give the original question before adding the ambiguity. These results show that our clarifying question recovers 50% of lost information through interactions, which is lost in the modification process of a pseudo ambiguous question.

5.3 Analysis

Table 6 shows examples from the evaluation. In example 1, the pseudo ambiguous question generation removed the term "Jerry Goldsmith" and the clarifying question successfully got the word to recover the information. In example 2, the system also succeeded in recovering the removed information, but the QA system failed to output the correct answer by a small difference. In examples 3 and 7, the system's clarifying question is not appropriate, but the system output the correct answer. In examples 6 and 7, users may misunderstand their task and put a new question to clarify their original question. Recent search system interfaces probably cause this; the users usually give a new query to the system if their first search fails. We can improve the clarification quality in some cases; however, the system could get additional information to recover the information, even if the system failed to ask questions back to the users correctly. In general, when the ambiguous question was generated by eliminating PPs, our clarifying question successfully worked in many cases to ask back the phrase. Recovering VPs was more difficult for the system.

6 Related works

We built a generation system that clarifies user's requests by clarifying questions when the user's questions are ambiguous. There are two major approaches for building a QA system that can withdraw additional information to the initial ambiguous user query. One approach is based on paraphrasing, which paraphrases ambiguous sentences to clear sentences. The other major approach is using clarifying or confirmation questions, which is similar to our system. This section describes relationships to these works.

6.1 Paraphrasing approach

The paraphrasing approach's critical idea is converting given user questions to other forms (McKeown, 1983; Buck et al., 2017; Dong et al., 2017). This idea is similar to query expansion, which is used in the information retrieval area. It is often difficult for users to express their questions in clear language. This difficulty often causes ambiguous questions. This kind of works tackled this problem by presenting possible paraphrases of the given ambiguous question with their answers. However, such approaches do not work well if paraphrased questions do not contain the appropriate question for the user. Moreover, the system needs paraphrasing datasets to learn the paraphrasing models, which requires enormous annotation costs in the open domain (Min et al., 2020).

Otsuka et al., (2019) used syntactic structures to generate pseudo training examples for the paraphrasing approach. Our approach is similar to their works; however, we also used statistical information from the case frame to distinguish the clarified point to realize a dialogue-based system. The dialogue-based approach has an advantage in decreasing user interaction costs if the system can predict the clarifying point appropriately.

6.2 Clarifying approach

The second approach is giving clarifying questions to users, which is closer to our approach. The clarifying strategy has been used widely in conventional spoken dialogue systems because the systems sometimes fail the task by ambiguity caused by speech recognition or natural language understanding errors (Misu and Kawahara, 2006; Stoy-

#	Methods	sentence
	(O) original	What is the name of the executive producer of the film that has a score composed by Jerry Goldsmith?
	(A) ambiguous	What is the name of the executive producer of the film that has a score composed?
	(C) clarifying	which composed?
1	**(R)** reply to C	Jerry Goldsmith
	(G) gold	Ronald Shusett
	(QA w/ A)	Jerry Goldsmith
	(QA w/ A+R)	Ronald Shusett
	(O) original	The lamp used in many lighthouses is similiar to this type of lamp patented in 1780 by Aime Argand?
	(A) ambiguous	The lamp used in many lighthouses is similiar to this type?
	(C) clarifying	what was similiar?
2	**(R)** reply to C	lamp patented in 1780 by Aime Argand
	(G) gold	Argand lamp
	(QA w/ A)	oil lamp
	(QA w/ A+R)	Lewis lamp
	(O) original	Lt Col. Stewart Francis Newcombe was a British army officer and associate of a military officerthat was given what title?
	(A) ambiguous	Lt Col. Stewart Francis Newcombe and associate of a military officerthat was given what title?
	(C) clarifying	which was the Newcombe and associate given?
3	**(R)** reply to C	a military officer
	(G) gold	Lawrence of Arabia
	(QA w/ A)	British archaeologist, military officer, diplomat, and writer
	(QA w/ A+R)	Lawrence of Arabia
	(O) original	According to the 2001 census, what was the population of the city in which Kirton End is located?
	(A) ambiguous	According, what was the population of the city in which Kirton End is located?
	(C) clarifying	where was the End located?
4	**(R)** reply to C	population of the city in which Kirton End is located
	(G) gold	35,124
	(QA w/ A)	66,900
	(QA w/ A+R)	66,900
	(O) original	Hatyapuri was a novel by the filmmaker of what nationality?
	(A) ambiguous	Hatyapuri was a novel of what nationality?
	(C) clarifying	what was novel?
5	**(R)** reply to C	Hatyapuri
	(G) gold	Indian
	(QA w/ A)	Bengali
	(QA w/ A+R)	Bengali
	(O) original	Which other Mexican Formula One race car driver has held the podium besides the Force India driver born in
	(A) ambiguous	Which other Mexican Formula One race car driver has held the podium besides the Force India driver?
	(C) clarifying	where did the car hold?
6	**(R)** reply to C	When was the force India driver born?
	(G) gold	Pedro Rodriguez
	(QA w/ A)	1990/1/26
	(QA w/ A+R)	Pedro Rodriguez
	(O) original	What relationship does Fred Gehrke have to the 23rd overall pick in the 2010 Major League Baseball Draft?
	(A) ambiguous	What relationship does Fred Gehrke have overall pick in the 2010 Major League Baseball Draft?
	(C) clarifying	when did the Gehrke have?
7	**(R)** reply to C	What is the number of the overall pick?
	(G) gold	great-grandfather
	(QA w/ A)	Miami Marlin
	(QA w/ A+R)	23rd

Table 6: Examples of clarifying question answering. **O**, **A**, and **C** indicate an original question, ambiguous question generated from the original question, and the generated clarifying question, respectively. Crowdworkers saw these contexts and input "(R) reply to **C**". **G** is the correct answer to question **O** and **QA w/ A** is the output of the QA model given only the ambiguous question. **QA w/ A+R** uses both the ambiguous question and the reply to the clarifying question given by the crowdworkers.

anchev et al., 2014). Our system uses this idea to tackle a problem of question ambiguity in the QA system caused by the user's ability or lack of knowledge. In recent QA systems, there is a study to learn the re-ranking function of clarifying questions by deep neural networks (Rao and Daumé III, 2018). They also proposed a model based on a generative neural network to generate clarifying questions (Rao and Daumé III, 2019). These studies require triples of an ambiguous question, a clarifying question, and a corresponding fact. Building a large dataset to cover open-domain QA is costly. Our system does not require such data preparation cost and uses a general syntactic parser and the case frame dictionary built without specified annotations. The system can work on any QA datasets already developed in the existing work of QA systems.

Question generation is also widely researched by using generative models (Duan et al., 2017; Du et al., 2017; Sasazawa et al., 2019) or syntactic rules (Heilman and Smith, 2010). Our clarifying question generation is motivated by them.

7 Conclusion

In this paper, we worked on building a clarifying question answering system for ambiguous questions, questions with some necessary information dropped. We proposed two-generation methods toward the clarifying question answering system: pseudo ambiguous question generation based on syntax and clarifying question generation based on sentence structures and case frame dictionaries. Our experimental results revealed that these generation methods worked to drop and to regain the important information in the original clear questions. The system used domain-independent syntactic and semantic information of questions; thus, the method can be applied to various QA domains. Moreover, our method does not require data annotation; we can extend existing QA datasets for the clarifying QA task.

As future work, we can integrate our model with other generative models. Another approach is to use pseudo ambiguous questions as training data of QA-related modules such as discriminative systems to predict or score given questions. Improving the model architecture is another issue, for example, network design to feed the whole dialogue history to the QA network.

References

Mohammad Aliannejadi, Julia Kiseleva, Aleksandr Chuklin, Jeff Dalton, and Mikhail Burtsev. 2020. Convai3: Generating clarifying questions for open-domain dialogue systems (clariq). *arXiv preprint arXiv:2009.11352.*

Mohammad Aliannejadi, Hamed Zamani, Fabio Crestani, and W Bruce Croft. 2019. Asking clarifying questions in open-domain information-seeking conversations. In *Proceedings of the 42nd international acm sigir conference on research and development in information retrieval*, pages 475–484.

Núria Bertomeu, Hans Uszkoreit, Anette Frank, Hans-Ulrich Krieger, and Brigitte Jörg. 2006. Contextual phenomena and thematic relations in database qa dialogues: results from a wizard-of-oz experiment. In *Proceedings of the Interactive Question Answering Workshop at HLT-NAACL 2006*, pages 1–8.

Christian Buck, Jannis Bulian, Massimiliano Ciaramita, Wojciech Gajewski, Andrea Gesmundo, Neil Houlsby, and Wei Wang. 2017. Ask the right questions: Active question reformulation with reinforcement learning. *arXiv preprint arXiv:1705.07830.*

Jacob Devlin, Ming-Wei Chang, Kenton Lee, and Kristina Toutanova. 2019. Bert: Pre-training of deep bidirectional transformers for language understanding. In *Proceedings of the 2019 Conference of the North American Chapter of the Association for Computational Linguistics: Human Language Technologies, Volume 1 (Long and Short Papers)*, pages 4171–4186.

Li Dong, Jonathan Mallinson, Siva Reddy, and Mirella Lapata. 2017. Learning to paraphrase for question answering. In *Proceedings of the 2017 Conference on Empirical Methods in Natural Language Processing*, pages 875–886.

Xinya Du, Junru Shao, and Claire Cardie. 2017. Learning to ask: Neural question generation for reading comprehension. In *Proceedings of the 55th Annual Meeting of the Association for Computational Linguistics (Volume 1: Long Papers)*, pages 1342–1352.

Nan Duan, Duyu Tang, Peng Chen, and Ming Zhou. 2017. Question generation for question answering. In *Proceedings of the 2017 Conference on Empirical Methods in Natural Language Processing*, pages 866–874.

Michael Heilman and Noah A. Smith. 2010. Good question! statistical ranking for question generation. In *Human Language Technologies: The 2010 Annual Conference of the North American Chapter of the Association for Computational Linguistics*, pages 609–617, Los Angeles, California. Association for Computational Linguistics.

Tsuneaki Kato, Jun'ichi Fukumoto, Fumito Masui, and Noriko Kando. 2006. Woz simulation of interactive question answering. In *Proceedings of the Interactive Question Answering Workshop at HLT-NAACL 2006*, pages 9–16.

Daisuke Kawahara and Sadao Kurohashi. 2006. Case frame compilation from the web using high-performance computing. In *LREC*, pages 1344–1347.

Daisuke Kawahara, Daniel Peterson, Octavian Popescu, and Martha Palmer. 2014. Inducing example-based semantic frames from a massive amount of verb uses. In *Proceedings of the 14th Conference of the European Chapter of the Association for Computational Linguistics*, pages 58–67.

Christopher D Manning, Mihai Surdeanu, John Bauer, Jenny Rose Finkel, Steven Bethard, and David McClosky. 2014. The stanford corenlp natural language processing toolkit. In *Proceedings of 52nd annual meeting of the association for computational linguistics: system demonstrations*, pages 55–60.

Kathleen McKeown. 1983. Paraphrasing questions using given and new information. *American Journal of Computational Linguistics*, 9(1):1–10.

Sewon Min, Julian Michael, Hannaneh Hajishirzi, and Luke Zettlemoyer. 2020. Ambigqa: Answering ambiguous open-domain questions. In *Proceedings of the 2020 Conference on Empirical Methods in Natural Language Processing (EMNLP)*, pages 5783–5797.

Teruhisa Misu and Tatsuya Kawahara. 2006. Dialogue strategy to clarify user's queries for document retrieval system with speech interface. *Speech Communication*, 48(9):1137–1150.

Atsushi Otsuka, Kyosuke Nishida, Itsumi Saito, Hisako Asano, and Junji Tomita. 2019. Specific question generation for reading comprehension. *Proceedings of the AAAI 2019 Reasoning and Complex QA Workshop*, pages 12–20.

Chen Qu, Liu Yang, Cen Chen, Minghui Qiu, W Bruce Croft, and Mohit Iyyer. 2020. Open-retrieval conversational question answering. In *Proceedings of the 43rd International ACM SIGIR Conference on Research and Development in Information Retrieval*, pages 539–548.

Filip Radlinski and Nick Craswell. 2017. A theoretical framework for conversational search. In *Proceedings of the 2017 conference on conference human information interaction and retrieval*, pages 117–126.

Pranav Rajpurkar, Robin Jia, and Percy Liang. 2018. Know what you don't know: Unanswerable questions for squad. In *Proceedings of the 56th Annual Meeting of the Association for Computational Linguistics (Volume 2: Short Papers)*, pages 784–789.

Pranav Rajpurkar, Jian Zhang, Konstantin Lopyrev, and Percy Liang. 2016. SQuAD: 100,000+ questions for machine comprehension of text. In *Proceedings of the 2016 Conference on Empirical Methods in Natural Language Processing*, pages 2383–2392.

Sudha Rao and Hal Daumé III. 2018. Learning to ask good questions: Ranking clarification questions using neural expected value of perfect information. In *Proceedings of the 56th Annual Meeting of the Association for Computational Linguistics (Volume 1: Long Papers)*, pages 2737–2746.

Sudha Rao and Hal Daumé III. 2019. Answer-based adversarial training for generating clarification questions. In *Proceedings of the 2019 Conference of the North American Chapter of the Association for Computational Linguistics: Human Language Technologies, Volume 1 (Long and Short Papers)*, pages 143–155.

Yuichi Sasazawa, Sho Takase, and Naoaki Okazaki. 2019. Neural question generation using interrogative phrases. In *Proceedings of the 12th International Conference on Natural Language Generation*, pages 106–111.

Sharon G Small, Nobuyuki Shimizu, Tomek Strzalkowski, and Ting Liu. 2003. Hitiqa: A data driven approach to interactive question answering: A preliminary report. In *New Directions in Question Answering*, pages 94–104.

Svetlana Stoyanchev, Alex Liu, and Julia Hirschberg. 2014. Towards natural clarification questions in dialogue systems. In *AISB symposium on questions, discourse and dialogue*, volume 20.

Robert S Taylor. 1962. The process of asking questions. *American documentation*, 13(4):391–396.

Johanne R Trippas, Damiano Spina, Lawrence Cavedon, Hideo Joho, and Mark Sanderson. 2018. Informing the design of spoken conversational search: Perspective paper. In *Proceedings of the 2018 Conference on Human Information Interaction & Retrieval*, pages 32–41.

Jingjing Xu, Yuechen Wang, Duyu Tang, Nan Duan, Pengcheng Yang, Qi Zeng, Ming Zhou, and SUN Xu. 2019. Asking clarification questions in knowledge-based question answering. In *Proceedings of the 2019 Conference on Empirical Methods in Natural Language Processing and the 9th International Joint Conference on Natural Language Processing (EMNLP-IJCNLP)*, pages 1618–1629.

Zhilin Yang, Peng Qi, Saizheng Zhang, Yoshua Bengio, William Cohen, Ruslan Salakhutdinov, and Christopher D Manning. 2018. HotpotQA: A dataset for diverse, explainable multi-hop question answering. In *Proceedings of the 2018 Conference on Empirical Methods in Natural Language Processing*, pages 2369–2380.

Yongfeng Zhang, Xu Chen, Qingyao Ai, Liu Yang, and W Bruce Croft. 2018. Towards conversational search and recommendation: System ask, user respond. In *Proceedings of the 27th acm international conference on information and knowledge management*, pages 177–186.

Parameter-Efficient Abstractive Question Answering over Tables or Text

Vaishali Pal[1] **Evangelos Kanoulas**[2] **Maarten de Rijke**[2]
[1]Discovery Lab, University of Amsterdam [2]University of Amsterdam
v.pal, e.kanoulas, m.derijke@uva.nl

Abstract

A long-term ambition of information seeking question answering (QA) systems is to reason over multi-modal contexts and generate natural answers to user queries. Today, memory intensive pre-trained language models are adapted to downstream tasks such as QA by fine-tuning the model on QA data in a specific modality like unstructured text or structured tables. To avoid training such memory-hungry models while utilizing a uniform architecture for each modality, parameter-efficient adapters add and train small task-specific bottle-neck layers between transformer layers. In this work, we study parameter-efficient abstractive QA in encoder-decoder models over structured tabular data and unstructured textual data using only 1.5% additional parameters for each modality. We also ablate over adapter layers in both encoder and decoder modules to study the efficiency-performance trade-off and demonstrate that reducing additional trainable parameters down to 0.7%–1.0% leads to comparable results. Our models out-perform current state-of-the-art models on tabular QA datasets such as Tablesum and FeTaQA, and achieve comparable performance on a textual QA dataset such as NarrativeQA using significantly less trainable parameters than fine-tuning.

1 Introduction

Information seeking systems over diverse contexts require model capabilities to reason over unstructured and structured data such as free-form text, tables, and images (Agrawal et al., 2016; Vakulenko et al., 2019; Hudson and Manning, 2019; Zhang et al., 2020; Zhu et al., 2021; Deldjoo et al., 2021). Such systems might have the additional requirement of generating natural language responses if deployed as task-oriented conversational agents (Wen et al., 2015; Carnegie and Oh, 2000; Rambow et al., 2001; Ratnaparkhi, 2002). Recent work on open-domain question answering (QA) predominately addresses these challenges by fine-tuning

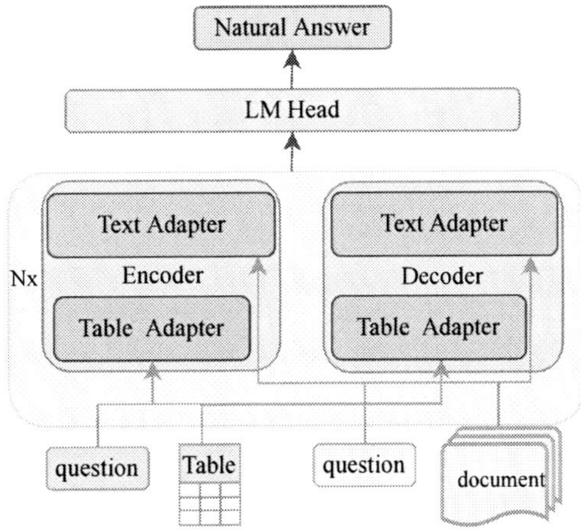

Figure 1: Parameter-efficient transfer learning using modality-specific (table/text) adapters for Abstractive Question Answering

massive pre-trained language models on different modalities such as tables and text (Yin et al., 2020; Herzig et al., 2020, 2021; Katsis et al., 2021; Nan et al., 2021). However, each model trained on a specific input type is incompatible with other modalities and requires modality-specific fine-tuning. For example, in tabular QA (Herzig et al., 2020), the structure of the table is learnt by training additional position embeddings (row and column identifiers) to identify which row and column a table cell belongs to. This renders such modality specific models incompatible with free-form text-based models. Multi-modal models (Zhu et al., 2021) can reason over both tables and text by concatenating the textual context and the flattened table, leading to longer input sequences and limiting the length of the context that can be encoded.

To address these challenges, we study parameter-efficient transfer learning for abstractive QA over tables and over text. We are motivated to use adapter-layers that inject small bottle-neck layers between frozen pre-trained transformer layers as they achieve comparable performance to fine-

Proceedings of the Second DialDoc Workshop on Document-grounded Dialogue and Conversational Question Answering, pages 41 - 53
May 26, 2022 ©2022 Association for Computational Linguistics

tuning on a variety of tasks such as multi-lingual translation (Pfeiffer et al., 2020; Philip et al., 2020; Guo et al., 2020), classification (Houlsby et al., 2019a), text-to-text generation (Lin et al., 2020), domain-adaptation in dialogue state tracking, and response generation (Hung et al., 2021).

Ablation studies on adapter layers (Rucklé et al., 2020) on masked language models such as BERT-base and RoBERTa over the GLUE benchmark demonstrate that removing beginning adapter layers leads to a minimal drop in performance. Extending adapter layer ablation over separate encoder and decoder modules is non-trivial as the conventional approach of sequential pruning of layers does not extend to consecutive encoder and decoder modules. Our work explores the interaction of adapter layers from both modules in the context of abstractive QA.

Lin et al. (2020) explore the impact of the adapter bottle-neck dimension for various language generation tasks over an auto-regressive model such as GPT-2 (Radford et al., 2019). They do not study tabular data nor ablate adapter layers, which is crucial in understanding impact of individual adapters in sequential transformer module architectures such as encoder-decoder. Our analysis is complementary to (Lin et al., 2020) as we ablate adapter layers to study parameter-performance trade-off whereas they only focus on adapter bottleneck size. Also, we generalize beyond the text-to-text setting and explore language generation from structured or unstructured input such as tables and text. This introduces domain-shift in both the *task* and *structure* of the downstream data.

We propose a system, named **P**arameter, **E**fficient, **A**bstractive **Q**uestion **A**nswering (PeaQA), shown in Figure 1, which learns to reason over unstructured and structured input using a *shared* pre-trained language model and modality-specific adapter layers. We automatically transform hierarchical tables to regular tables to have a uniform representation without breaking associations between table cells. In addition, we extend the study of ablating adapter layers over both encoder and decoder modules.

Our main contributions are summarized as:

(1) We perform parameter-efficient abstractive question answering over multi-modal context using only additional 1.5% of trainable parameters for each modality. Our adapter-tuned model outperforms existing work by a large margin on tabular QA datasets and achieves comparable performance on a textual QA dataset.

(2) We study tabular QA as a new modality that introduces massive input domain shift to pre-trained language models. We propose a 2-step transformation of hierarchical tables to sequences, which produces a uniform representation to be used by a single, shared pre-trained language model and modality-specific adapter layers. To the best of our knowledge, this is the first work that explores tabular QA question answering in a parameter-efficient manner.

(3) We ablate adapter layers in both encoder and decoder modules to study their impact and show that beginning layers from both encoder and decoder can be eliminated without significant drop in performance. We also demonstrate that last encoder adapter layers are indispensable and have greater contribution than decoder layers at the same level.

2 Related Work

Tabular question answering. Tabular QA systems aim to answer questions from structured tables, which can be regular or hierarchical. Hierarchical tables can have header cells and body cells spanning across multiple rows and columns (Cheng et al., 2021). In most tabular QA systems (Herzig et al., 2020; Zhu et al., 2021; Katsis et al., 2021), the structure of the table is encoded in the embedding layer of large language models by introducing table specific position information such as row id and column id. Concurrent to our work, abstractive QA over tables (Nan et al., 2021; Cheng et al., 2021) poses additional challenges of generating natural answers by reasoning and aggregating discontinuous facts from the table.

Textual question answering. Question answering over text measures a system's ability to comprehend free-form text in the user question and context passage(s) and predict an answer. The answer predicted can be extractive in nature, where the system identifies short text spans in the context passage to answer the user query (Lee et al., 2016; Seo et al., 2016; Rajpurkar et al., 2016; Pearce et al., 2021), or it can be abstractive, where it is required to generate a free-form answer (Yin et al., 2016; Mitra, 2017; Bauer et al., 2018; Reddy et al., 2019).

Transfer learning. Transfer learning techniques such as fine-tuning pre-trained models for downstream tasks, require a new set of parameters to be learnt for each new task. To avoid such memory intensive transfer learning methods, adapters have been proposed as a parameter-efficient method of adapting to new domains (Houlsby et al., 2019b; Pfeiffer et al., 2020). Adapters have been extended to language generation in a variety of generative tasks such as translation, summarization, multi-turn dialogue, and task-oriented natural language generation (Lin et al., 2020).

Our work combines all the aforementioned aspects to generate abstractive answers from *both* tables and text with only 0.7%–1.0% trainable parameters without compromising performance.

3 Model

We focus on encoder-decoder models for the task of abstractive question answering. We use a BART (Lewis et al., 2019) encoder-decoder architecture which comprises of a bidirectional encoder and an auto-regressive decoder. The input sequence consists of the question, the context title and context sequence preceded with prompts indicating the beginning of the each sub-sequence. Formally, the input sequence is represented as *<question>* $q_0\ q_1 \ldots q_m$ *<title>* $t_1\ t_2 \ldots t_p$ *<context>* $c_0\ c_1 \ldots c_n$, where q_i is the i-th question token, t_j is the j-th title token, and c_k is the k-th context token. The context can either be a text passage or a flattened table. The parameters of the pre-trained BART model are frozen during training. Modality specific adapter layers added to the model are trained on either tabular context or textual context to generate natural answers.

4 Textual Question Answering

To study multi-modal abstractive QA, we first focus on free-form text as context to the system. We train adapter layers for textual context on the NarrativeQA dataset (Kočiský et al., 2018). NarrativeQA is a complex abstractive question answering dataset over stories. The dataset contains $32,747$ samples in the training set, $3,461$ samples in the validation set, and $10,557$ samples in the test set. For our task, we have selected the input context passage to be the human annotated *summary* of each sample which is the Wikipedia page summary of the story and represented as a paragraph. The input to the model is the *question*, *title* and *summary* of each passage and the target is the abstractive answer.

5 Tabular Question Answering

We study tabular QA as a new modality which introduces massive input domain shift to pre-trained language models. Tables enforce structural constraints in their representation which is incompatible with the expected input format of pre-trained language models. To achieve our goal of parameter efficiency by utilizing a uniform pre-trained language model, we only train table specific adapter layers while keeping the pre-trained model frozen. However, this necessitates a uniform input representation for both tables and text. An additional challenge is introduced to maintain uniformity across different table types (regular, hierarchical).

For our task, we explore 2 tabular QA datasets, namely, Tablesum (Zhang et al., 2020) and FeTaQA (Nan et al., 2021). Tablesum consists of 200 unique Wikipedia tables over which questions and abstractive answers are manually annotated; 40% of the samples are questions over hierarchical tables but the tables in their released data are missing information in the hierarchical cells and their work do not handle hierarchies. We address this issue by extracting the wikitables from the respective Wikepedia pages and release a clean version of the dataset.[1]

FeTaQA (Nan et al., 2021) is a larger abstractive tabular QA dataset consisting of question and free-form answers over $10,330$ regular tables. The dataset consists of $7,326$ samples in the training set, $1,001$ in the validation set, and $2,003$ in the test set. FeTaQA consists of human-annotated answers containing explanations involving entities and relations.

5.1 Table Representation

For our work, we choose to represent all tables uniformly in a two-step process: (1) Transformation of a hierarchical table into a regular table; and (2) Linearization of a regular table into a flattened sequence which can be encoded with a language model.

Linearize hierarchical table headers. Hierarchical table headers are linearized into a single row of headers by the following process. A header cell spanning multiple columns is duplicated and split into multiple cells. Next, the cell values over which this header spans are concatenated with the entire split. Repeating this process over all header rows flattens the hierarchical header into a sequential

[1]The cleaned data and code can be found at `https://github.com/kolk/Pea-QA`

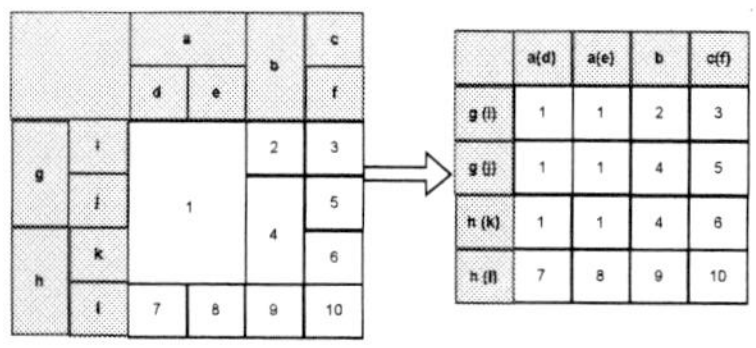

(a) A multi-span table represented as a regular table.

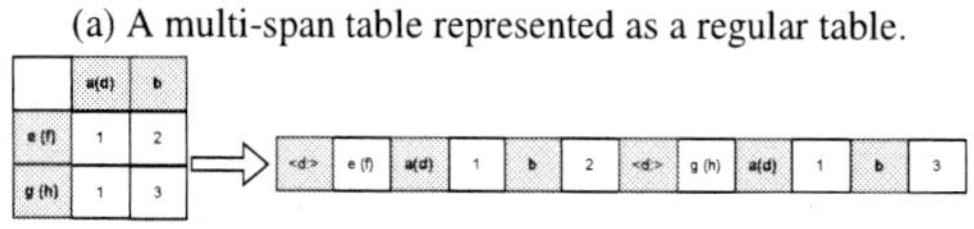

(b) Linearize regular table to a sequence of *key:value* pairs.

Figure 2: Table representation.

one. We depict this process in Figure 2a, which yields a linear header $a(d)$, $a(d)$, b, $e(f)$.

Linearizing table body. Multi-span table body cells are parsed differently than headers. Each table body cell is replicated with one or multiple header cells depending on its span across columns. Cells that span across multiple rows are replicated with all the spanned rows. This process leads to a regular table. We flatten the regular table in row-major form, concatenating rows sequentially. Each row is a sequence of *(key, value)* pairs where a key is a column header and the value is the cell value of that column as depicted in Figure 2b.

6 Experimental Setup

We seek to answer the following research questions with our experiments: (RQ1) How does adapter–tuning perform compared to fine-tuning in the context of multi-modal input? (RQ2) Do all adapter layers across the encoder and decoder contribute equally to performance across tasks/modalities?

6.1 Fine-Tuning

We perform all our experiments on the *large* variant of BART model. We fine-tune the BART-large model over the 3 datasets as the state-of-the-art fine-tuned models utilize different architectures for different datasets making comparison with adapter-tuning difficult. We treat our fine-tuned BART models on the 3 datasets as baselines. We sweep learning rates from $\{8e^{-4}, 6e^{-4}, 3e^{-4}, 1e^{-4}, 5e^{-5}, 4^{e}-5, 3e^{-5}, 2e^{-5}, 1e^{-5}\}$ and select the best performing learning rate for each dataset. We select $4e^{-5}$ for fine-tuning on Tablesum, $8e^{-4}$ on FeTaQA datasets and $2e^{-5}$ to fine-tune NarrativeQA. We use a batch size of 4 and gradient accumulation of 8 to emulate an effective batch size of 32. The maximum target sequence length is set to 200 for tabular QA datasets and to 100 for the textual QA dataset. On the Tablesum dataset, we follow 5-fold cross validation as described in the original work to evaluate our models. On FeTaQA and NarrativeQA, we utilize the test split for evaluating our models. We train the model on each dataset for 15 epochs and evaluate on Rouge-2, Rouge-L and sacreBLEU metrics.

6.2 Adapter-Tuning

We perform adapter-tuning as a parameter-efficient alternative to adapt BART-large model to the abstractive question answering task across different modalities. We first freeze all layers of the pre-trained BART-large model which was trained on text reconstruction as mentioned in the original BART paper (Lewis et al., 2019). We add bottleneck adapter layers from the Houlsby adapter configuration (Houlsby et al., 2019a) which are trained to adapt to the downstream abstractive question answering task and also to modality specific input context. Each adapter layer has a bottle-neck embedding size of 64. As mentioned in Section 6.1, we sweep learning rates and select the best performing learning rate for each dataset. We select $6e^{-4}$ for the tabular QA datasets Tablesum and FeTaQA, and select $1e^{-1}$ to train the textual QA dataset NarrativeQA. We use the same batch size and maximum target sequence length as fine-tuning for effective comparison. A summary of hyper-parameters are mentioned in Table 1.

Dataset	Params	ATune	FTune
All	scheduler	linear	linear
	batch size	32	32
	seed	6	6
	max epochs	15	15
Tablesum	learning rate	6e-4	4e-5
	input length	200	200
FeTaQA	learning rate	6e-4	8e-4
	input length	100	100
NarrativeQA	learning rate	1e-4	2e-5
	input length	50	50

Table 1: Hyper-parameters for training. **ATune** indicates Adapter-tuning, **FTune** indicates Fine-tuning, **All** indicates all 3 datasets.

6.3 Ablation Study: Adapter Pruning

Adapter-layer pruning has been explored on the GLUE benchmark in (Rucklé et al., 2020), which

Dataset	Model	Training	Rouge-1	Rouge-2	Rouge-L	BLEU
Tablesum (Zhang et al., 2020)	GPT2	fine-tune	0.272	0.073	0.200	5.35
	T5		0.362	0.143	0.276	**10.43**
	Ours (Pea-QA)	fine-tune(Baseline)	**0.400**	**0.186**	**0.316**	6.30
		Adapter-tune	0.393	**0.186**	0.312	6.75
FeTaQA (Nan et al., 2021)	T5-small	fine-tune	0.550	0.330	0.470	21.60
	T5-base		0.610	0.390	0.510	28.14
	T5-large		0.630	0.414	0.530	30.54
	Ours (Pea-QA)	fine-tune(Baseline)	0.632	0.415	0.534	30.81
		Adapter-tune	**0.651**	**0.436**	**0.553**	**33.45**
NarrativeQA (Kočiský et al., 2018)	Masque (Nishida et al., 2019)	fine-tune	–	–	**0.547**	–
	Ours (Pea-QA)	fine-tune(Baseline)	0.518	0.268	0.515	21.07
		Adapter-tune	0.510	0.270	0.500	20.08

Table 2: Results: Scores obtained on the Tablesum, FeTaQA and NarrativeQA datasets.

demonstrates that removing adapter layers from the beginning of BERT-base and RoBERTa models leads to minimal performance drop. We extend adapter layer ablation to encoder-decoder architectures and hypothesize that this phenomenon should be observed on both the encoder and decoder modules. However, it is non-trivial how the adapter-layers in the encoder and decoder interact with each other and contribute to performance. Previous studies (Rucklé et al., 2020) on adapter ablation prune consecutive adapter layers in masked language models. This approach does not extend directly to sequential modules of encoder-decoder where intra-module adapters not only contribute to their respective objective of encoding and decoding but also contributes to inter-module interaction and performance. To measure the impact of the adapter layers in different modules, we perform adapter ablation in both the encoder and decoder. First, we uniformly remove adapter layers from both encoder and decoder modules starting from the beginning layers of both modules and finally deleting all layers. This leads to 12 experiments corresponding to eliminating 12 encoder and 12 decoder adapter layers. To study interaction across inter-module adapters at different levels, we conduct 36 experiments of different configurations of adapter elimination from the last 6 levels of encoder and decoder. We analyze the performance by each configuration in Section 7.3.

7 Results

We compare the results of our baseline fine-tuned models with the state-of-the-art fine-tuned models in Section 7.1. We address (RQ1) "How does adapter-tuning perform compared to fine-tuning in the context of multi-modal input?" in Section 7.2 and (RQ2) "Do all adapter layers across the encoder and decoder contribute equally to performance across tasks/modalities?" in 7.3.

7.1 Fine-Tuned Models

We study the results of our baseline fine-tuned models with the state-of-the-art fine-tuned models for the 3 datasets. The results of the experiments are shown in Table 2. We observe that for the Tablesum dataset, our fine-tuned model outperform the best state-of-art T5 model on Rouge-1 by 3.8% , Rouge-2 by 4.3% and Rouge-L score by 4%. This can be attributed to fine-tuning our model on the clean version of the dataset. Our fine-tuned models perform comparably to the state-of-the-art T5-large on FeTaQA dataset, i.e, 0.2% on Rouge-1, 0.01% higher on Rouge-2, and 0.04% higher on Rouge-L. Our fine-tuning results on NarrativeQA are lower than state-of-the-art models trained with sophisticated reasoning architecture. The focus of this work was primarily on comparing fine-tuning and adapter-tuning and hence we leave explicit reasoning as part of future work.

7.2 Adapter-Tuned Models

We address (RQ1) by comparing the performance of adapter-tuned models to our baseline fine-tuned models. For Tablesum, as observed in Table 2 fine-tuning(baseline) marginally outperforms adapter-tuning with 0.7% higher Rouge-1 and 0.4% higher Rouge-L scores while having the same Rouge-2 score. For FeTaQA, adapter-tune shows a larger

Question: What and when were Akhila Kishore's first two films?

Target: akhila kishore made her debut in the kannada film padhe padhe (2013), and appeared in kathai thiraikathai vasanam iyakkam (2014).

Table:

Year	Film	Role	Language
2013	Padhe Padhe	Kanchana	Kannada
2014	Kathai Thiraikathai Vasanam Iyakkam	Daksha	Tamil
2015	Inimey Ippadithaan	Akhila	Tamil
...	...	...	

Adaper-tune: akhila kishore made her debut in the kannada film padhe padhe (2013) and kathai thiraikathai vasanam iyakkam (2014).

Fine-tune: kathai thiraikathai vasanam iyakkam (2014) and inimey ippadithaan (2015) were kannada films.

Question: Who is the starring actor of Aastik?

Target: aastik is a 1956 hindi film starring shahu modak, paro devi and meenakshi.

Table:

Title	Director	Cast
...	...	...
Aastik	S. P. Kalla	Shahu Modak, Paro Devi, Meenakshi, B. M. Vyas, Praveen Paul
Alam Ara	Nanubhai Vakil	Daljeet, Chitra, Tiwari, Niranjan Sharma, Minu Mumtaz,...
...	...	...

Adaper-tune: aastik is a 1956 bollywood film starring shahu modak.

Fine-tune: a directed by s. p. kalla.

Question: What were the three films directed by Yakub and when were they released?

Target: yakub directed three films: sagar ka sher in 1937, uski tamanna in 1939, and, in 1949, aiye.

Table:

Year	Film	Director
...	...	...
1937	Sagar Ka Sher (Lion of Sagar)	Yakub
...	...	...
1939	Uski Tamanna (Her Last Desire)	Yakub
...	...	...
1949	Aiye	Yakub
...	...	...

Adaper-tune: yakub directed three films: sagar ka sher (lion of sagar) in 1937, uski tamanna (her last desire) in 1939 and aiye in 1949.

Fine-tune: y directed by yakub.

Table 3: Samples where adapter-tune outperforms fine-tune

performance gain with 1.9% on Rouge-1 and Rouge-L and 2.1% on Rouge-2 compared to fine-tuning. The insignificant gains of fine-tuning over adapter-tuning in tabular QA can be attributed to catastrophic forgetting (French, 1999; Kirkpatrick et al., 2017; Chen et al., 2020) induced by differences in the distribution of downstream tabular data format from the original text data format of pre-training.

To explore this phenomenon further, we analyse examples from FeTaQA dataset in Table 3 where adapter-tuning outperforms fine-tuning. We observe that the fine-tuned model is unable to disambiguate surface-form similarities from the column semantics in the first example. The intended semantics of the named-entity *Akhila Kishore* in the question is *Actor*. While the surface-form is similar to the column value *Akhila*, the intended semantics is that of the column header *Role*. The fine-tuned model wrongly predicts the second and third row of the tabular context as correct grounding of information while adapter-tuning is able to disambiguate and predicts information from the first 2 rows as answer. We observe that the fine-tuned model also predicts information from the wrong column *Director* instead of *Cast* in the second example. Adapter-tune correctly identifies the column but partially generates the required information in the prediction. The third example depicts both non-factual and non-fluent prediction by the fine-tuned model.

We demonstrate an example of a hierarchical table of Tablesum in Table 4. The question requires aggregation on the table cells and has various summary-like targets associated with it. The hierarchical table mentions *Ed Sheeran* 3 times, but the actual number of occurrence is 10 times, from

Question: how many times was ed sheeran listed as the performer?

Targets:

- Ed Sheeran was listed as a performer twice in the table documenting the top hits of 2014 in Sweden. Other English-Language top performers included Bruce Springsteen, Sam Smith, and Coldplay, implying that English-Language music has significant success in Sweden.
- According to the table, in 2014, Ed Sheeran was only listed as the performer one time. It was for the song that he performed that is called ""I See Fire"", which was out in January and February of 2014

Table:

Week	Date	Song title	Performer	Album title	Performer
1	3 Jan 2014	"Timber"	Pitbull feat. ...	True	Avicii
2	10 Jan 2014				
3	17 Jan 2014	"I See Fire"	Ed Sheeran	High Hopes	Bruce ...
4	24 Jan 2014				
5	31 Jan 2014			True	Avicii
6	7 Feb 2014			Christer Sjögren sjunger Sinatra	Christer Sjögren
7	14 Feb 2014				
8	21 Feb 2014			True	Avicii
9	28 Feb 2014				
...	...	...	...		
31	31 July 2014	Prayer in C...	Lilly Wood &...	X	Ed Sheeran
32	7 Aug 2014			Honky Tonk Rebels	Lasse Stefanz
...	...			...	...
42	16 Oct 2014	"The Days"	Avicii	X	Ed Sheeran
43	23 Oct 2014				
44	30 Oct 2014			Songs for Daddy	Jill Johnson
...	...	...	...		

Adaper-tune: I found a table of the year 2014. It shows the week of the week, the song title, the artist, the title of the song, the album title, and the performer. There are 11 times that Ed Sheeran was listed as the performer in the year. The song title is "Timber" and the album is True.

Fine-tune: I found a table of Ed Sheeran's year in 2014. He was listed as the performer 14 times in the year 2014. The first time he was listed was on 3 January 2014 with the song "Timber" and the last time was on 4 April 2014 with "I See Fire".

Table 4: Example from the Tablesum dataset.

Adapter-tune		
Encoder adapters removed	**Decoder adapters removed**	**#Trainable parameters**
–	–	$6,343,680$ (1.56%)
0–2	12–14	$4,757,760$ (1.17%)
0–4	12–16	$3,700,480$ (0.91%)
0–6	12–18	$2,643,200$ (0.65%)
0–8	12–20	$1,585,920$ (0.39%)
0–10	12–22	$528,640$ (0.13%)
0–11	12–22	$264,320$ (0.07%)
fine-tune		$406,291,456$ (100%)

Table 5: Trainable parameters in the encoder and decoder. Encoder adapter layers are numbered from 0–11 and decoder adapter layers are numbered from 12–22. x–y implies all adapter layers from x to y inclusive.

Week 3 to *Week 9*, *Week 31* and from *Week 42* to *Week 43*. Our table transformation process handles this to produce a regular table with 10 cells containing *Ed Sheeran* as value. The models can simply aggregate over the mentions. As shown in Table 4, both models generates long answers summarizing information from the context table. However, as the models do not explicitly handle cell aggregation, we observe factual mistakes in both adapter-tuned and fine-tuned models. The models find Tablesum samples challenging even though the generated language is fluent and readable.

For textual QA, on the NarrativeQA dataset, adapter-tuning performs comparable to fine-tuning with the adapter-tuned model achieving 0.8% lower Rouge-1, 1.8% higher Rouge-2 and 1.5% lower Rouge-L scores than fine-tuning.

We conclude that adapter-tuning performs better than fine-tuning for out-of-domain tabular data and comparable performance on in-domain text.

7.3 Ablation of adapter layers

We study (RQ2) by ablating adapter layers in both the encoder and decoder modules. We uniformly eliminate successive adapter layers from both encoder and decoder starting from the first layer in both modules and finally deleting all layers. This leads to 12 experiments corresponding to 12 en-

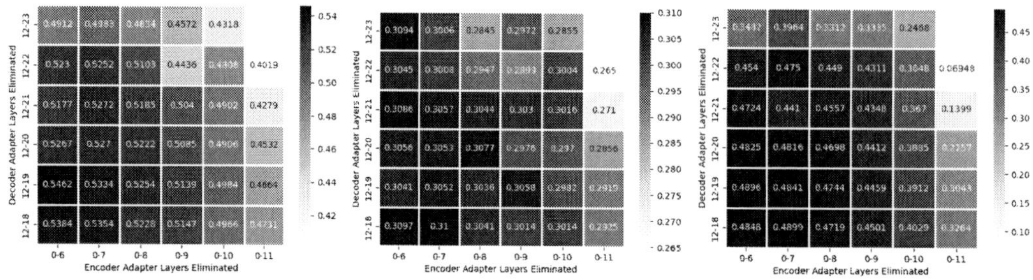

(a) FeTaQA Rouge-L scores (b) Tablesum Rouge-L scores (c) NarrativeQA Rouge-L scores

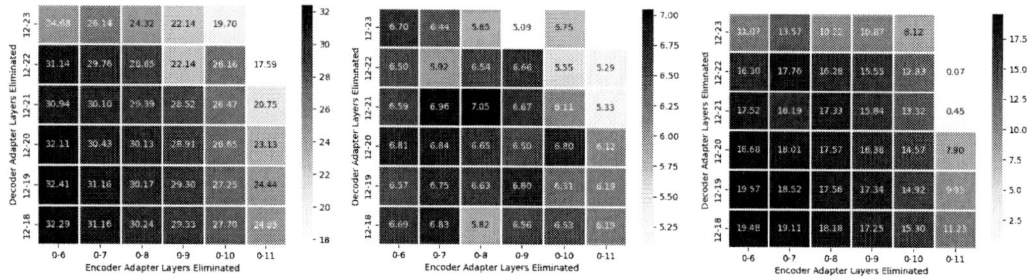

(d) FeTaQA sacreBLEU scores (e) Tablesum sacreBLEU scores (f) NarrativeQA sacreBLEU scores

Figure 3: Adapter layer ablation scores. The X-axis represents range of encoder adapter layers deleted, the Y-Axis represents range of decoder adapter layers deleted. x-y implies all adapter layers from x to y inclusive. There are 36 model ablation configurations displayed. The ablation starts from 0 to 6 encoder adapter layers removal and 12 to 18 decoder adapter layer removal represented by the bottom left cell ((0–6), (12–18)) and progressively increases deletion of encoder adapter layers along the X-axis and decoder adapter layers along the Y-axis.

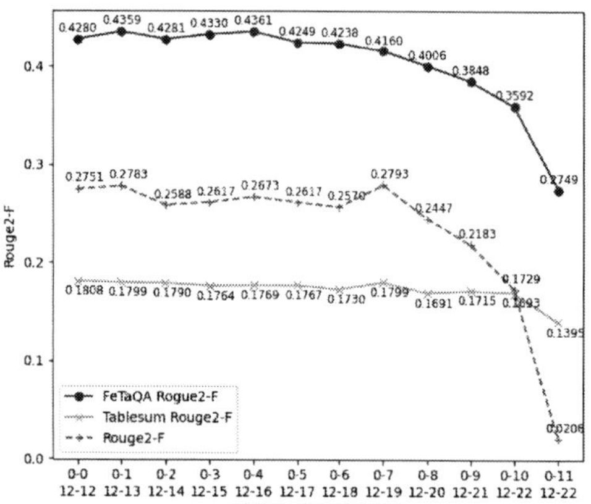

Figure 4: Adapter layer ablation Rouge2 F-scores. The X-axis depicts encoder-adapter layers (0–11) and decoder adapter layers (12–23) deleted progressively. Each $\binom{x-y}{r-s}$ represents F-score with encoder layers p to q deleted and decoder layers r to s deleted.

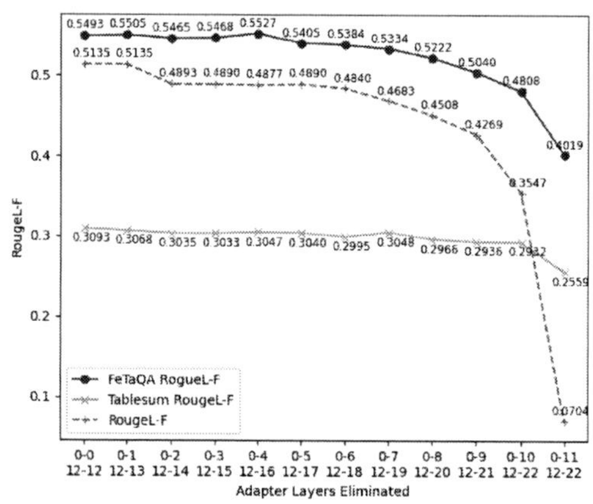

Figure 5: Adapter layer ablation Rouge-L scores. The X-axis depicts encoder-adapter layers (0–11) and decoder adapter layers (12–23) deleted progressively. Each $\binom{x-y}{r-s}$ represents F-score with encoder layers p to q deleted and decoder layers r to s deleted.

coder and 12 decoder adapter layers. We number the encoder adapter layers from 0–11 and the decoder adapter layers from 12–23. We measure the performance of the models using Rouge-2, Rouge-L[2] and sacreBLEU[3] scores. The F-scores for each dataset (NarrativeQA, Tablesum, FeTaQA) are shown in Figure 4, 5 and 6, respectively. We observe that as more adapter layers are eliminated, the performance drops across all datasets. However, the performance drop is minimal until the last adapter layers are also deleted. The inflection point varies across dataset but is limited to the last 2 layers of the encoder and decoder. For the Narra-

[2]https://pypi.org/project/rouge-score/
[3]https://github.com/mjpost/sacreBLEU

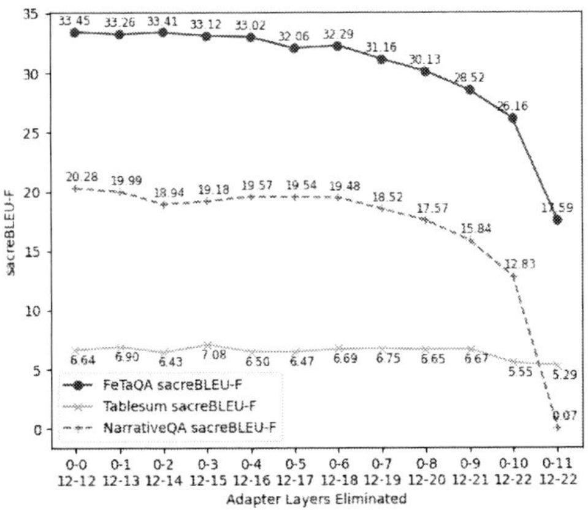

Figure 6: Adapter layer ablation sacreBLEU F-scores. The X-axis depicts encoder-adapter layers (0–11) and decoder adapter layers (12–23) deleted progressively. Each $\binom{x-y}{r-s}$ represents F-score with encoder layers p to q deleted and decoder layers r to s deleted.

tiveQA dataset, this point is when all layers till the second last adapter layer from both the encoder and decoder are deleted. For the FeTaQA and Tablesum datasets, the performance drops sharply only when the last encoder and decoder layers are removed.

To analyze contribution of the i-th adapter layer of encoder and decoder to performance, we perform ablation of adapter layers (0–6), (0–7), ..., (0–11) from encoder and adapter layers (12–18), (12–19), ..., (12–23) from decoder (decoder layers are numbered 12–23). This leads to 36 configurations where a configuration (p–q, r–s) represents removal of all encoder adapters from p-th to q-th layer and all decoder adapters from r-th to s-th. The results are shown in Figure 3. We observe that performance remains comparable as we progressively eliminate adapter layers from encoder and decoder until the last layers. The performance drops steeply when we remove the last encoder and decoder adapter layers depicted towards the top-right corner of RougeL scores in Figures 3a, 3b, and 3c and BLEU scores in Figures 3d, 3e, and 3f. This implies that last adapter layers learns most of the domain information.

We also observe that the last encoder and decoder layers contribute differently to performance. Removing the last encoder layer (column 0–11) leads to substantial score drop across all decoder layers. This indicates that the last encoder layer is indispensable. Keeping only the last decoder adapter (row 12–23) is comparable to keeping last two last encoder layers (column 0–10). We also observe that retaining just the last 50% of adapter layers from both encoder and decoder increases parameter efficiency by 0.7% parameters as summarized in Table 5 without significant compromise to performance.

8 Conclusion

We are the first to study parameter-efficient transfer learning over tables and text for abstractive question answering using adapters. We demonstrate that parameter efficient adapter-tuning outperforms fine-tuning on out-of-domain tabular data and achieves comparable results on in-domain textual data.

We propose a transformation from hierarchical tables to regular ones and further into a sequential form compatible with pre-trained model. We extend an existing ablation study of adapter layers to encoder-decoder setting and demonstrate that adapter layers from the end of the encoder is indispensable to encoding modality specific information than decoder adapter layers at the same level.

Our results are useful for exploring scalability of QA models in memory constrained situations with comparable performance while scaling across modalities using light-weight adapters.

One of the limitations of our work is that our models do not explicitly reason and aggregate over the table cells. This might lead to fluent but factually incorrect answers on challenging Tablesum dataset. Addressing this limitation is left as future work.

9 Acknowledgements

We would like to thank Elsevier for their support throughout this project and funding this work. This work was also supported by the NWO Innovational Research Incentives Scheme Vidi (016.Vidi.189.039), the NWO Smart Culture - Big Data / Digital Humanities (314-99-301), the H2020-EU.3.4. - SOCIETAL CHALLENGES - Smart, Green And Integrated Transport (814961). All content represents the opinion of the authors, which is not necessarily shared or endorsed by their respective employers and/or sponsors.

References

Aishwarya Agrawal, Jiasen Lu, Stanislaw Antol, Margaret Mitchell, C. Lawrence Zitnick, Dhruv Batra, and Devi Parikh. 2016. VQA: Visual question answering. *arXiv preprint arXiv:1505.00468*.

Lisa Bauer, Yicheng Wang, and Mohit Bansal. 2018. Commonsense for generative multi-hop question answering tasks. In *EMNLP*.

Alice Oh Carnegie and Alice H. Oh. 2000. Stochastic language generation for spoken dialogue systems. In *In Proc. of the ANLP/NAACL 2000 Wrkshp. on Conversational Systems*, pages 27–32.

Sanyuan Chen, Yutai Hou, Yiming Cui, Wanxiang Che, Ting Liu, and Xiangzhan Yu. 2020. Recall and learn: Fine-tuning deep pretrained language models with less forgetting. In *Proceedings of the 2020 Conference on Empirical Methods in Natural Language Processing (EMNLP)*, pages 7870–7881, Online. Association for Computational Linguistics.

Zhoujun Cheng, Haoyu Dong, Zhiruo Wang, Ran Jia, Jiaqi Guo, Yan Gao, Shi Han, Jian-Guang Lou, and Dongmei Zhang. 2021. Hitab: A hierarchical table dataset for question answering and natural language generation. *arXiv preprint arXiv:2108.06712*.

Yashar Deldjoo, Johanne R. Trippas, and Hamed Zamani. 2021. Towards multi-modal conversational information seeking. In *SIGIR '21: The 44th International ACM SIGIR Conference on Research and Development in Information Retrieval, Virtual Event, Canada, July 11-15, 2021*, pages 1577–1587. ACM.

Robert M. French. 1999. Catastrophic forgetting in connectionist networks. *Trends in Cognitive Sciences*, 3(4):128–135.

Junliang Guo, Zhirui Zhang, Linli Xu, Hao-Ran Wei, Boxing Chen, and Enhong Chen. 2020. Incorporating bert into parallel sequence decoding with adapters. In *Advances in Neural Information Processing Systems*, volume 33, pages 10843–10854. Curran Associates, Inc.

Jonathan Herzig, Thomas Müller, Syrine Krichene, and Julian Eisenschlos. 2021. Open domain question answering over tables via dense retrieval. *Proceedings of the 2021 Conference of the North American Chapter of the Association for Computational Linguistics: Human Language Technologies*.

Jonathan Herzig, Pawel Krzysztof Nowak, Thomas Müller, Francesco Piccinno, and Julian Eisenschlos. 2020. TaPas: Weakly supervised table parsing via pre-training. In *Proceedings of the 58th Annual Meeting of the Association for Computational Linguistics*, pages 4320–4333, Online. Association for Computational Linguistics.

Neil Houlsby, Andrei Giurgiu, Stanislaw Jastrzebski, Bruna Morrone, Quentin De Laroussilhe, Andrea Gesmundo, Mona Attariyan, and Sylvain Gelly. 2019a. Parameter-efficient transfer learning for NLP. In *Proceedings of the 36th International Conference on Machine Learning*, volume 97 of *Proceedings of Machine Learning Research*, pages 2790–2799. PMLR.

Neil Houlsby, Andrei Giurgiu, Stanislaw Jastrzebski, Bruna Morrone, Quentin de Laroussilhe, Andrea Gesmundo, Mona Attariyan, and Sylvain Gelly. 2019b. Parameter-efficient transfer learning for NLP. *arXiv preprint arXiv:1902.00751*.

Drew A. Hudson and Christopher D. Manning. 2019. GQA: A new dataset for real-world visual reasoning and compositional question answering. *arXiv preprint arXiv:1902.09506*.

Chia-Chien Hung, Anne Lauscher, Simone Paolo Ponzetto, and Goran Glavaš. 2021. DS-TOD: Efficient domain specialization for task oriented dialog. *arXiv preprint arXiv:2110.08395*.

Yannis Katsis, Saneem Chemmengath, Vishwajeet Kumar, Samarth Bharadwaj, Mustafa Canim, Michael Glass, Alfio Gliozzo, Feifei Pan, Jaydeep Sen, Karthik Sankaranarayanan, and Soumen Chakrabarti. 2021. AIT-QA: Question answering dataset over complex tables in the airline industry. *arXiv preprint arXiv:2106.12944*.

James Kirkpatrick, Razvan Pascanu, Neil Rabinowitz, Joel Veness, Guillaume Desjardins, Andrei A. Rusu, Kieran Milan, John Quan, Tiago Ramalho, Agnieszka Grabska-Barwinska, Demis Hassabis, Claudia Clopath, Dharshan Kumaran, and Raia Hadsell. 2017. Overcoming catastrophic forgetting in neural networks. *arXiv preprint arXiv:1612.00796*.

Tomáš Kočiský, Jonathan Schwarz, Phil Blunsom, Chris Dyer, Karl Moritz Hermann, Gábor Melis, and Edward Grefenstette. 2018. The NarrativeQA reading comprehension challenge. *Transactions of the Association for Computational Linguistics*, 6:317–328.

Kenton Lee, Shimi Salant, Tom Kwiatkowski, Ankur Parikh, Dipanjan Das, and Jonathan Berant. 2016. Learning recurrent span representations for extractive question answering. *arXiv preprint arXiv:1611.01436*.

Mike Lewis, Yinhan Liu, Naman Goyal, Marjan Ghazvininejad, Abdelrahman Mohamed, Omer Levy, Ves Stoyanov, and Luke Zettlemoyer. 2019. Bart: Denoising sequence-to-sequence pre-training for natural language generation, translation, and comprehension.

Zhaojiang Lin, Andrea Madotto, and Pascale Fung. 2020. Exploring versatile generative language model via parameter-efficient transfer learning. In *Findings of the Association for Computational Linguistics: EMNLP 2020*, pages 441–459, Online. Association for Computational Linguistics.

Rajarshee Mitra. 2017. A generative approach to question answering. *arXiv preprint arXiv:1711.06238*.

Linyong Nan, Chiachun Hsieh, Ziming Mao, Xi Victoria Lin, Neha Verma, Rui Zhang, Wojciech Kryściński, Nick Schoelkopf, Riley Kong, Xiangru Tang, Murori Mutuma, Ben Rosand, Isabel Trindade, Renusree Bandaru, Jacob Cunningham, Caiming Xiong, and Dragomir Radev. 2021. Fetaqa: Free-form table question answering. *arXiv preprint arXiv:2104.00369*.

Kyosuke Nishida, Itsumi Saito, Kosuke Nishida, Kazutoshi Shinoda, Atsushi Otsuka, Hisako Asano, and Junji Tomita. 2019. Multi-style generative reading comprehension. In *Proceedings of the 57th Annual Meeting of the Association for Computational Linguistics*, pages 2273–2284, Florence, Italy. Association for Computational Linguistics.

Kate Pearce, Tiffany Zhan, Aneesh Komanduri, and Justin Zhan. 2021. A comparative study of transformer-based language models on extractive question answering. *arXiv preprint arXiv:2110.03142*.

Jonas Pfeiffer, Ivan Vulić, Iryna Gurevych, and Sebastian Ruder. 2020. MAD-X: An Adapter-Based Framework for Multi-Task Cross-Lingual Transfer. In *Proceedings of the 2020 Conference on Empirical Methods in Natural Language Processing (EMNLP)*, pages 7654–7673, Online. Association for Computational Linguistics.

Jerin Philip, Alexandre Berard, Matthias Gallé, and Laurent Besacier. 2020. Monolingual adapters for zero-shot neural machine translation. In *Proceedings of the 2020 Conference on Empirical Methods in Natural Language Processing (EMNLP)*, pages 4465–4470, Online. Association for Computational Linguistics.

Alec Radford, Jeff Wu, Rewon Child, David Luan, Dario Amodei, and Ilya Sutskever. 2019. Language models are unsupervised multitask learners. *OpenAI Blog*.

Pranav Rajpurkar, Jian Zhang, Konstantin Lopyrev, and Percy Liang. 2016. Squad: 100,000+ questions for machine comprehension of text. *Proceedings of the 2016 Conference on Empirical Methods in Natural Language Processing*.

Owen Rambow, Srinivas Bangalore, and Marilyn Walker. 2001. Natural language generation in dialog systems. In *Proceedings of the First International Conference on Human Language Technology Research*.

Adwait Ratnaparkhi. 2002. Trainable approaches to surface natural language generation and their application to conversational dialog systems. *Computer Speech & Language*, 16(3):435–455. Spoken Language Generation.

Siva Reddy, Danqi Chen, and Christopher D Manning. 2019. CoQA: A conversational question answering challenge. *Transactions of the Association of Computational Linguistics (TACL)*.

Andreas Rücklé, Gregor Geigle, Max Glockner, Tilman Beck, Jonas Pfeiffer, Nils Reimers, and Iryna Gurevych. 2020. Adapterdrop: On the efficiency of adapters in transformers. *arXiv preprint arXiv:2010.11918*.

Minjoon Seo, Aniruddha Kembhavi, Ali Farhadi, and Hannaneh Hajishirzi. 2016. Bidirectional attention flow for machine comprehension. *arXiv preprint arXiv:1611.01603*.

Svitlana Vakulenko, Kate Revoredo, Claudio Di Ciccio, and Maarten de Rijke. 2019. QRFA: A data-driven model of information-seeking dialogues. In *ECIR 2019: 41st European Conference on Information Retrieval*, pages 541–557. Springer.

Tsung-Hsien Wen, Milica Gašić, Nikola Mrkšić, Pei-Hao Su, David Vandyke, and Steve Young. 2015. Semantically conditioned LSTM-based natural language generation for spoken dialogue systems. In *Proceedings of the 2015 Conference on Empirical Methods in Natural Language Processing*, pages 1711–1721. Association for Computational Linguistics.

Jun Yin, Xin Jiang, Zhengdong Lu, Lifeng Shang, Hang Li, and Xiaoming Li. 2016. Neural generative question answering. *Proceedings of the Workshop on Human-Computer Question Answering*.

Pengcheng Yin, Graham Neubig, Wen-tau Yih, and Sebastian Riedel. 2020. Tabert: Pretraining for joint understanding of textual and tabular data. *Proceedings of the 58th Annual Meeting of the Association for Computational Linguistics*.

Shuo Zhang, Zhuyun Dai, Krisztian Balog, and Jamie Callan. 2020. Summarizing and exploring tabular data in conversational search. In *Proceedings of the 43rd International ACM SIGIR Conference on Research and Development in Information Retrieval*.

Fengbin Zhu, Wenqiang Lei, Youcheng Huang, Chao Wang, Shuo Zhang, Jiancheng Lv, Fuli Feng, and Tat-Seng Chua. 2021. TAT-QA: A question answering benchmark on a hybrid of tabular and textual content in finance. *arXiv preprint arXiv:2105.07624*.

APPENDICES

We provide further details on statistics of the datasets used (Appendix A) and on the Rouge-2 scores for an encoder-decoder adapter layer ablation study (Appendix B).

A Dataset Statistics

Statistics of the three datasets, i.e., Tablesum, FeTaQA and NarrativeQA are listed in Table 6. Tablesum has the longest answer length. The answers are summary-like, often, describing aspects of the table contents. The FeTaQA dataset contains answers of mostly single sentences and targeted towards specific facts asked in the question. The NarrativeQA dataset focuses on questions from stories. The answer lengths vary from single words to long sentences. For the tabularQA dataset, Tablesum contains larger tables than the FeTaQA dataset even though it is limited to 200 unique tables over which questions are asked. The FeTaQA dataset's tables contain more columns on average than Tablesum.

Tablesum	
Domain	Open
Modality	Table
Table-type	Regular
Training samples	798
Validation samples	200
Test samples	–
Max question length	114
Max target length	1,579
Max table row	155
Max table column	8
FeTaQA	
Domain	Open
Modality	Table
Table-type	Hybrid
Training samples	7,326
Validation samples	1,001
Test samples	2,003
Train max question length	165
Train max target length	338
Train max table rows	34
Train max table columns	30
Val max question length	182
Val target length	325
Val max table rows	34
Val max table columns	22
Test max question length	193
Test max target length	295
Test max table lows	34
Test max table columns	22
NarrativeQA	
Domain	Stories
Modality	Text
Training samples	65,494
Validation samples	6,922
Test samples	21,114
Train max question length	175
Train max target length	171
Train max context length	6,045
Val max question length	158
Val target length	187
Val max context length	6,033
Test max question length	1,220
Test target length	224
Test max context length	6,090

Table 6: Dataset Statistics

B Encoder-Decoder Adapter Layer Ablation Rouge-2 Scores

Ablation results (Rouge-2 F-scores) of 36 configurations of adapter layers deleted from the later half of the encoder and decoder. Deleting the last encoder adapter layers leads to massive drop in performance as observed in the last three columns of Figures 7a, 7b and 7c. However, deleting the last decoder adapter layers results in better performance in comparison to the encoder layers at the same level as observed from the top 3 rows.

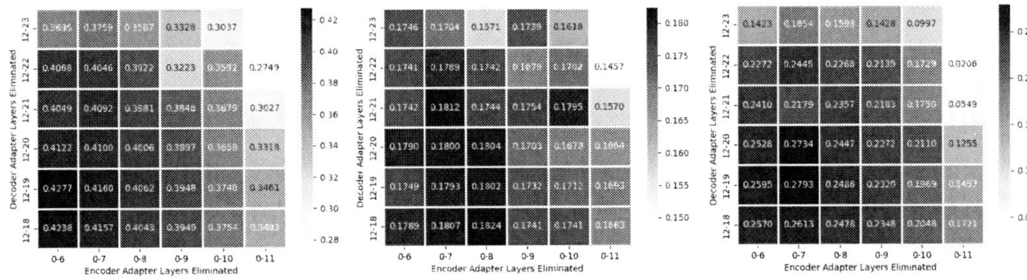

(a) FeTaQA Rouge-L scores (b) Tablesum Rouge-L scores (c) NarrativeQA Rouge-L scores

Figure 7: Adapter layer Rouge-2 ablation scores. The X-axis represents range of encoder adapter layers deleted, the Y-Axis represents range of decoder adapter layers deleted. x-y implies all adapter layers from x to y inclusive. There are 36 model ablation configurations displayed. The ablation starts from 0 to 6 encoder adapter layers removal and 12 to 18 decoder adapter layer removal represented by the bottom left cell ((0–6), (12–18)) and progressively increases deletion of encoder adapter layers along the X-axis and decoder adapter layers along the Y-axis.

Conversation- and Tree-Structure Losses for Dialogue Disentanglement

Tianda Li[1], **Jia-Chen Gu**[2], **Zhen-Hua Ling**[2], **Quan Liu**[3]
[1]Nankai University, Tianjin, China
[2]National Engineering Research Center for Speech and Language Information Processing, University of Science and Technology of China, Hefei, China
[3]State Key Laboratory of Cognitive Intelligence, iFLYTEK Research, Hefei, China
focuslee1214@gmail.com, gujc@mail.ustc.edu.cn
zhling@ustc.edu.cn, quanliu@iflytek.com

Abstract

When multiple conversations occur simultaneously, a listener must decide which conversation each utterance is part of in order to interpret and respond to it appropriately. This task is referred as *dialogue disentanglement*. A significant drawback of previous studies on disentanglement lies in that they only focus on pair-wise relationships between utterances while neglecting the conversation structure which is important for conversation structure modeling. In this paper, we propose a hierarchical model, named Dialogue BERT (DIALBERT), which integrates the local and global semantics in the context range by using BERT to encode each message-pair and using BiLSTM to aggregate the chronological context information into the output of BERT. In order to integrate the conversation structure information into the model, two types of loss of conversation-structure loss and tree-structure loss are designed. In this way, our model can implicitly learn and leverage the conversation structures without being restricted to the lack of explicit access to such structures during the inference stage. Experimental results on two large datasets show that our method outperforms previous methods by substantial margins, achieving great performance on dialogue disentanglement.

1 Introduction

In a multi-party chat stream (Traum, 2004; Uthus and Aha, 2013; Ouchi and Tsuboi, 2016; Gu et al., 2021), messages related to different topics are entangled with each other, which makes it difficult for a new user to understand the context of the discussion in the chat room. Dialogue disentanglement (Kummerfeld et al., 2019; Gu et al., 2020b; Yu and Joty, 2020; Liu et al., 2021a,b) aims at disentangling a whole conversation into several threads from a data stream so that each thread is about a specific topic. Early research either did not release their datasets (Adams and Martell, 2008; Wang et al., 2008) or used small datasets (Elsner and Charniak, 2008; Elsner and Schudy, 2009; Wang and Oard, 2009; Elsner and Charniak, 2010, 2011; Jiang et al., 2018). Kummerfeld et al. (2019) released a new large-scale dataset that made it possible to train a more complex model and to fairly compare different models. Figure 1 shows an example of dialogue disentanglement in this dataset.

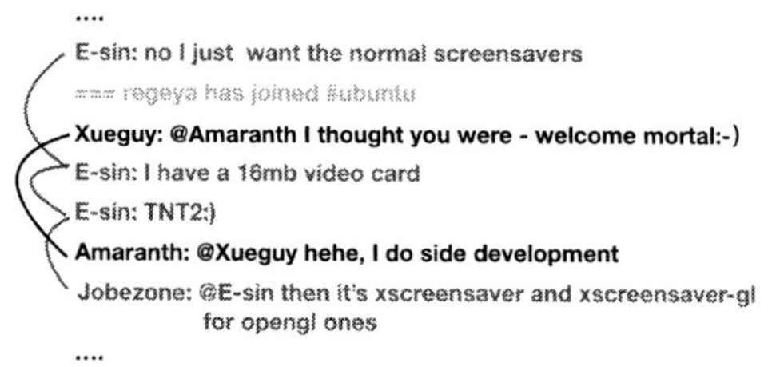

Figure 1: An example of dialogue disentanglement. In this example, conversations marked with different colours are entangled together. This task aims to separate this chat stream by conversations.

Currently, most of the existing methods for dialogue disentanglement employ a two-step approach framework. Firstly, a model is employed to determine the relation between two messages. Then a clustering algorithm is employed to separate these messages into different conversation clusters. Following this framework, Zhu et al. (2020) proposed a BERT-based model named Masked Hierarchical Transformer (MHT), which aims at making use of the conversation structures. This method uses a mask mechanism to explicitly build connections between context messages and their corresponding ancestors in a conversation. However, the main drawback of their approach is that the designed mask is computed based on the parents' relation of each message given the whole conversation, which is only available during the training stage. In order to deal with the lack of masks during the inference stage, they construct the

Proceedings of the Second DialDoc Workshop on Document-grounded Dialogue and Conversational Question Answering, pages 54 - 64
May 26, 2022 ©2022 Association for Computational Linguistics

pseudo mask label based on the predicted relations between any message-pair. However, the pseudo mask label cannot introduce reliable conversation structure information, especially when models cannot achieve a perfect prediction performance on relevant datasets.

In this work, we follow this two-step approach framework and propose a hierarchical BERT-based model, named Dialogue BERT (DIALBERT) for dialogue disentanglement. DIALBERT first use BERT (Devlin et al., 2019) to capture the matching information in each message pair. Then, a context-level BiLSTM is employed to aggregate and incorporate the context information. The semantics similarity of each message pair is measured by calculating their matching scores, and the message that has the highest matching score with the target message is regarded as the parent message of it. In addition, we aim at introducing and making use of conversation structures to help DIALBERT to make decision by training DIALBERT with two extra types of loss of conversation-structure loss and tree-structure loss. In this way, the model can implicitly learn and leverage conversation structures without being restricted to the lack of explicit access to such structures during inference.

We evaluate our method on two large datasets releasaed by Kummerfeld et al. (2019) and Zhu et al. (2020) respectively. Experimental results show our proposed method outperforms previous methods in terms of various evaluation metrics.

In summary, our contributions in this paper are three-fold: (1) A hierarchical model named DIALBERT is proposed for dialogue disentanglement. (2) Two losses of conversation- and tree-structure losses are introduced to make use of the structures of the conversation history. (3) The performance of the proposed method is evaluated on two large datasets, and the ablation studies further verified the effectiveness.

2 Related Work

The research for dialogue disentanglement dates back to Aoki et al. (2003) which conducted a study of voice conversations among 8-10 people with an average of 1.76 activate conversations at any given time. In recent studies, the mainstream method for dialogue disentanglement is the two-step approach: firstly, a neural network is used to determine the relation between two messages. Then a clustering algorithm is adopted to separate messages into different conversations. In the first step, Mehri and Carenini (2017) used recurrent neural networks(RNNs) to model adjacent messages. Jiang et al. (2018) was the first work that used convolutional neural networks to estimate the conversation-level similarity between closely posted messages. Zhu et al. (2020) proposed a Masked Hierarchical Transformer based on BERT to calculate the matching score by using conversation structures. In addition to neural networks, statistical (Du et al., 2017) and linguistic features (Elsner and Charniak, 2008, 2010, 2011; Mayfield et al., 2012) have also been used in the existing research. In the clustering stage, some research proposed the clustering algorithm by using threshold such as Jiang et al. (2018). Most studies grouped two messages with the highest matching score into the same conversation. In our study, we follow this mainstream setting.

3 Problem Formulation

Given a dataset $\mathcal{D}$, $\{M^{(1)}, M^{(2)}, ..., M^{(N)}\}$ represents a list of messages and each message belongs to a specific conversation. Following the setting of previous studies (Elsner and Charniak, 2008, 2010, 2011; Mayfield et al., 2012; Jiang et al., 2018), in order to find the parent message of a target message, $T-1$ messages occurring before this target message and itself form the context message set of this target message. The target message is a word sequence that can be represented by $M^T = \{m_1^T, m_2^T, ..., m_{n_T}^T\}$, and each context message is a word sequence that can be represented by $M^i = \{m_1^i, m_2^i, ..., m_{n_i}^i\}$, where n_T and n_i are the sequence length of messages and $i \in \{1, 2, ..., T\}$. Every target message has a label $Y \in \{1, 2, ..., T\}$ indicating which message in context range is the parent message of the target message (each message has and only has one parent message). Our goal is to learn a prediction model to predict which message in $\{M^1, M^2, ..., M^T\}$ is the parent message of the target message M^T for $T \in \{1, 2, .., N\}$. Note that if the target message is the first message of a conversation, the parent of the target message is itself.

4 Methodology

4.1 DIALBERT

DIALBERT calculates the matching scores between the target message and its context messages. The overall architecture is shown in Figure 2. The

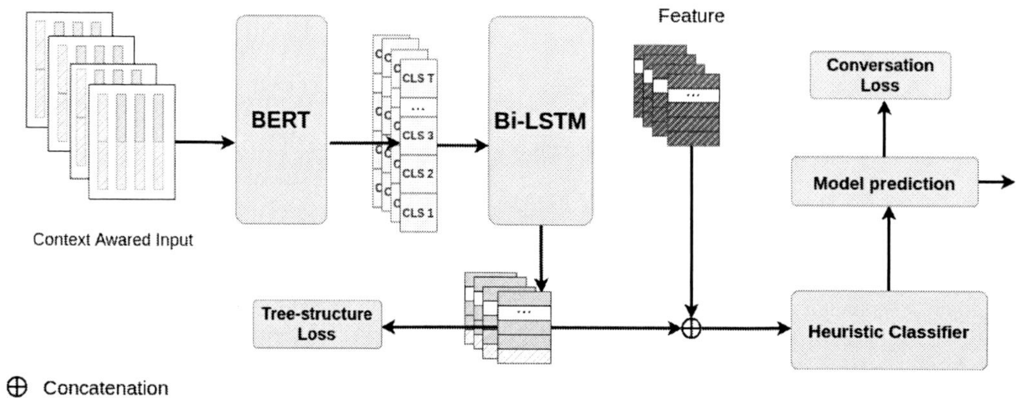

Figure 2: The overall architecture of DIALBERT. `CLS T` is the `[CLS]` hidden state of the T-th message pair. Note that the hand-craft features designed before the heuristic classifier is introduced in Kummerfeld et al. (2019). These features are not used on the Reddit dataset.

context message that has the largest matching score with the target message will be regarded as the parent message. For the second step, after we get the parent message of each target message, we group messages into different conversations based on the parental relations.

4.1.1 Context-Aware Input

In order to take context semantics in a chat into consideration, $T-1$ preceding messages of the target message are used along with the target message to form the context message set. Specifically, every context message will be concatenated with the target message to form a message pair. Then, all the message pairs will be combined together as a single input to predict the parent message of each target message. The input $\mathbf{u}_i$ can be formulated as: $\mathbf{u}_i = [cls, m_1^T, ..., m_{n_T}^T, sep, m_1^i, ..., m_{n_i}^i, sep]$, where $\mathbf{U} = \{\mathbf{u}_i\}_{i=1}^T$. $i \in [1, 2, ..., T]$ is the index of the context message. cls and sep are the start and separation tokens predefined in BERT, respectively. Note that $\mathbf{u}_T$ is composed of two target messages.

4.1.2 Context BERT Module

A strategy to consider context is to concatenate the context messages with the target message. But this strategy weakens the relationships between each context message as they are organized in chronological order in the chat stream.

In order to better consider the chronological order information of context messages, we propose a context BERT module to encode the history context by using both BERT and a BiLSTM model. Specifically, we encode input $\mathbf{U}$ by adopting BERT, and the output of the reserved cls will be used as feature vectors $\mathbf{E} = \{\mathbf{e}_i\}_{i=1}^T$. Each feature vector $\mathbf{e}_i$ contains the semantics in its corresponding message pair. In addition, we further encode the feature vectors $\mathbf{E}$ with a single layer Bi-LSTM to obtain the high-order feature vectors $\mathbf{F}$, which have captured the semantics of history context and can be represented as $\{\mathbf{f}_i\}_{i=1}^T$. The formulae of the calculation are as follows:

$$\mathbf{e}_i = \mathrm{BERT}(\mathbf{u}_i), \forall i \in [1, 2, ..., T], \quad (1)$$

$$\mathbf{f}_i = \mathrm{BiLSTM}(\mathbf{e}_i), \forall i \in [1, 2, ..., T], \quad (2)$$

$$\mathbf{m} = \mathrm{Softmax}(\mathrm{Linear}(\mathbf{F})), \quad (3)$$

where the dimension of the hidden units in a BiLSTM layer is k. $\mathbf{m} = \{m_i\}_{i=1}^T$ are matching degrees that will be used to calculate the tree-structure loss in Section 4.2.

4.1.3 Heuristic Classifier

To model the higher-order interaction between the target message and its context messages, a heuristic classifier which has proved to be effective in different studies (Yoon et al., 2018; Chen et al., 2017, 2018), is employed. Specifically, the interaction vectors $\mathbf{G} = \{\mathbf{g}_i\}_{i=1}^T$ will be fed into a single layer classifier to get matching scores, with the following formulae:

$$\mathbf{g}_i = [\mathbf{f}_i, \mathbf{f}_T, \mathbf{f}_i \circ \mathbf{f}_T, \mathbf{f}_i - \mathbf{f}_T], \quad (4)$$

$$\mathbf{p} = \mathrm{Softmax}(\mathrm{Linear}(\mathbf{tanh}(\mathbf{G}\mathbf{W}_3^{\mathrm{T}} + \mathbf{b}_3))), \quad (5)$$

where $\mathbf{W}_3 \in \mathbb{R}^{4k \times 8k}$ is weight matrix and $\mathbf{b}_3 \in \mathbb{R}^{4k}$ is the bias. $\circ$ is element-wise product and $-$ is element-wise subtraction. $\mathbf{p} = \{p_i\}_{i=1}^T$ are the matching scores, and will be used to calculate cross-entropy loss $\mathcal{L}_{CE}$ (shown below) and conversation-structure loss $\mathcal{L}_{CV}$.

$$\mathcal{L}_{CE} = -\frac{1}{T}\sum_{i=1}^{T} y_i \log(p_i), \quad (6)$$

where $\{y_i\}_{i=1}^{T}$ is the one-hot embedding of golden label Y. T is the context range. The overall loss for DIALBERT model can be formalized as :

$$\mathcal{L}_{overall} = \mathcal{L}_{CE} + \alpha\mathcal{L}_{CV} + \beta\mathcal{L}_{TS}, \quad (7)$$

where α and β are hyperparameters. The conversation-structure loss $\mathcal{L}_{CV}$ and tree-structure loss $\mathcal{L}_{TS}$ will be introduced in Section 4.2. Finally, the context message with the largest matching score is regarded as the parent message of target message, and we group these two messages into the same conversation.

4.2 Conversation- and Tree-Structure Loss

In the list of messages, different conversations are entangled together, and each conversation has its own semantic coherence and cohesion. Most previous studies failed to use the structure of each conversation when the parent message of a target message in the context is determined. In order to encourage our model to find the parent message of the target message based on the context coherence of the conversation, we introduce conversation-structure loss and tree-structure loss in addition to the cross-entropy loss. In this way, our model can learn and leverage the structure of the conversation implicitly and will not suffer from a lack of conversation structure information during the inference/testing stage. Intuitively, both conversation-structure loss and tree-structure loss can encourage the model to select most relevant message as the parent message.

4.2.1 Conversation-Structure Loss

The conversation-structure loss is computed based on the matching score:

$$\mathcal{L}_{CV} = -\frac{1}{T}\sum_{i=1}^{T} y_i^c \log(p_i), \quad (8)$$

where $\{y_i^c\}_{i=1}^{T}$ are the conversation labels and each y_i^c is a binary label indicating whether the i-th context message is in the conversation same as the target message. $\{p_i\}_{i=1}^{T}$ are matching scores of message pairs. T is context range. The intention of the conversation-structure loss is to encourage the model to choose the parent message for a target message from the messages in the same conversation.

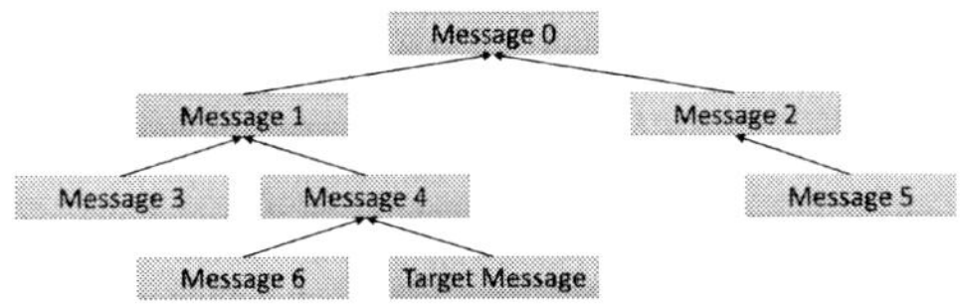

Figure 3: An example of the conversation structure. A chat stream consists of multiple these structures. Conversation-structure loss will help the model distinguish which conversation structure does target message belong to and Tree-Structure loss will help the model further distinguish ancestor messages of target message in the structure.

4.2.2 Tree-Structure Loss

In order to further make use of the structure of conversation, we propose tree-structure loss. Intuitively, in a structure of a conversation (shown in Figure 3), ancestors of the target message (i.e., message 0, message 1 and message 4) are most relevant to the target message. Because the target message can be regarded as the response to its ancestor messages or as an extension of the topic discussed in the ancestor messages, the intention of the tree-structure loss is to help the model further narrow down the candidates. The tree-structure loss encourages the model to choose the parent message for a target message from all ancestor messages in the same conversation. The tree-structure loss has two terms that are designed for ancestor nodes and other nodes, respectively. The first term of the tree-structure loss can be computed with the following formulae:

$$y_i^a = \begin{cases} 0.5 & if \quad d = 0, \\ 1.2\text{-}0.2{*}d & if \quad 0 < d \leq 5, \\ 0.1 & if \quad 5 < d, \end{cases} \quad (9)$$

$$\mathcal{L}_{FirstTerm} = -\frac{1}{T}\sum_{i=1}^{T} y_i^a log(m_i), \quad (10)$$

where d is the distance between the specific context message and target message in the structure of a conversation. For example, in Figure 3, d of *message 1* and the *target message* is 2. Note that $d = 0$ is the distance for the special message pair in which the target message is paired with itself. Because our target is to find the parent message.

In order to add the penalty to the model, if non-ancestor messages in the conversation are selected as the parent of the target message, we designed three strategies for calculating the second term of the tree-structure loss: *uniform-penalty*, *penalty-by-distance*, and *penalty-by-layer-difference*. For *uniform strategy*, $y_i^b = 0.1$ if the i-th context message is not an ancestor message of the target message. For *penalty-by-distance*, the strategy is formalized as follows:

$$y_i^b = \begin{cases} 1\text{-}\dfrac{d}{20} & if \quad 0 \leq d < 20 \\ 0.1 & if \quad 20 \leq d \end{cases}, \tag{11}$$

where d is the distance between the target message and the corresponding message in the structure of the conversation; e.g., in Figure 3, d between *message 3* and *target message* is 3. For *penalty-by-layer-difference*, the strategy can be formalized as:

$$y_i^b = \begin{cases} 1\text{-}\dfrac{l_i}{10} & if \quad 0 \leq l_i < 10 \\ 0.1 & if \quad 10 \leq l_i \end{cases}, \tag{12}$$

$$l_i = \mid layer_{target} - layer_i \mid, \tag{13}$$

where $layer_{target}$ is the layer number of the target message in the structure of the conversation. $layer_i$ is the layer number of message i; e.g., the layer difference between *message 2* and *target message* is $\mid 4 - 2 \mid = 2$. The tree-structure loss $\mathcal{L}_{TS}$ can be formulated as:

$$\mathcal{L}_{SecondTerm} = -\frac{1}{T}\sum_{i=1}^{T} y_i^b \log(m_i), \tag{14}$$

$$\mathcal{L}_{TS} = \mathcal{L}_{FirstTerm} - \mathcal{L}_{SecondTerm}. \tag{15}$$

Note that if the i-th context message is not in the same conversation as the target message, then $y_i^a = 0$, $y_i^b = 0$.

5 Experiments

5.1 Datasets

Our proposed method was evaluated on the Ubuntu IRC dataset (Kummerfeld et al., 2019), which is manually annotated with reply-to relationship between messages. The statistics of distances between the target and its parent message is shown in Figure 4. In addition, we also evaluated our proposed method on the Reddit-large dataset

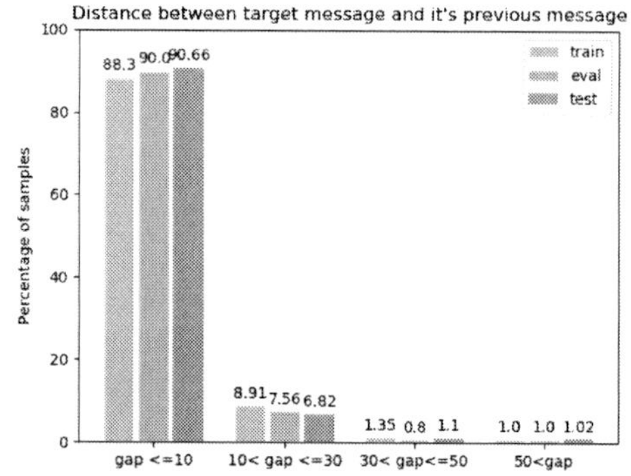

Figure 4: The percentage of distances between the target message and its parent message in the Ubuntu IRC dataset.

	Message	Conversation	Avg. Distance
	Ubuntu IRC		
Train	67463	3825	6.55
Validation	2500	250	6.87
Testing	5000	280	6.16
	Reddit		
Train	468679	20178	5.53
Validation	37300	2098	5.97
Testing	72933	4133	5.95

Table 1: Statistics of the Ubuntu IRC and the Reddit datasets. The last column denoted the averaged distance between a target message and its parent message.

proposed in Zhu et al. (2020).[1] We followed the settings in Zhu et al. (2020) to further filter the Reddit-large dataset: if a comment or the user who posted the comment is deleted, the comment itself and all its descendants are not included in the dataset. These conversations were splitted into train/validation/testing sets in a ratio of 8:1:1. The overall statistics of the two datasets are shown in Table 1 and data examples from these two datasets are shown in Table 2.

5.2 Evaluation Metrics

For the Ubuntu IRC dataset, we follow the setting in Kummerfeld et al. (2019). The evaluation metrics used in our experiments include: the modified Variation of Information (VI) (Kummerfeld

[1] Zhu et al. (2020) only provide the comment IDs and crawling scripts. The data collected in our paper is crawled on March 23, 2020 using the provided scripts and IDs.

Parent	Index	Message
...	...	...
996	1000	[03:04] Amaranth: @cliche American
992	1001	[03:04] Xenguy: @Amaranth I thought you were – welcome mortal ;-)
1000	1002	[03:04] cliche: @ Amaranth, hahahaha
1003	1003	=== welshbyte has joined #ubuntu
997	1004	[03:04] e-sin: no i just want the normal screensavers
995	1005	[03:04] Amaranth: @benoy Do you have cygwinx installed and running?
1006	1006	[03:04] babelfishi: can anyone help me install my Netgear MA111 USB adapter?
1004	1007	[03:04] e-sin: i have a 16mb video card
1008	1008	=== regeya has joined #ubuntu
1007	1009	[03:04] e-sin: TNT2 :)
1001	1010	[03:05] Amaranth: @Xenguy hehe, i do side development
1007	1011	[03:05] jobezone: @e-sin then it's xscreensaver and xscreensave-gl for opengl ones.
1005	1012	[03:05] benoy: how do i install that? I couldn't find that in the list of things
1010	1013	[03:05] Amaranth: @Xenguy things like alacarte and easyubuntu
...	...	...
1	1	DeathisLaughing: HP forgot to print the label for this ink cartridge...that's mildly ironic...
1	2	BitJit: @ DeathisLaughing Mystery ink box! Will it fit in your printer?! no.
1	3	andrewsmith1986: @ DeathisLaughingI love this subreddit.
1	4	myfutureperfect: @ DeathisLaughing They ran out of ink. So, what?
1	5	sageDieu: @ DeathisLaughing They probably couldn't afford it
1	6	dsbaciga: @ DeathisLaughing I like that they ignore the low ink cartridge notifications just like I do.

Table 2: Data examples of the Ubuntu IRC dataset (upper) and the Reddit dataset (lower).

et al., 2019), Adjusted Rand Index (ARI), One-to-One Overlap (1-1) of the cluster (Elsner and Charniak, 2008), as well as the precision, recall, and F1 score between the cluster prediction and ground truth. Note that the precision, recall, and F1 score are calculated using the number of perfectly matching conversations, excluding conversations that have only one message (mostly system messages). We take VI as the main metric. For the Reddit dataset, we follow the setting of Zhu et al. (2020). Specifically, the graph accuracy and the conversation accuracy are adopted. The graph accuracy is used to measure the average agreement between the ground truth and predicted parent for each utterance. The conversation accuracy is used to measure the average agreement between conversation structures and predicted structures. Specifically, only if all messages in a conversation are predicted correctly, the predicted structure is regarded as correct. We take graph accuracy as the main metric.

5.3 Implementation Details

The base version of BERT was used in our experiments. The initial learning rate was set to 2e-5. The maximum sequence length was set to 100. The number of hidden unit k was 384. For the two extra losses, $\alpha = 0.15$ and $\beta = 1$ achieved the best performance. The value of α was selected from $[0.1, 0.15, 0.2]$, and that of β was selected from $[0.5, 1]$. Dropout was applied on the output layer of the *ConBERT* and heuristic classifier with a ratio of 0.1. For the IRC dataset, batch size was set to 4 and the context range T was set to 50. For the Reddit dataset, batch size was set to 3 and the context range T was set to 16. All experiments were conducted on a 24G RTX TITAN GPU. All codes were implemented in the TensorFlow framework (Abadi et al., 2016) and are published to help replicate our results. [2]

5.4 Comparison Baselines

We compare our models with those reported in Kummerfeld et al. (2019) and Zhu et al. (2020), which are shown in the Table 3. Below we list variants of our models, which are also shown in the bottom part of Table 3.

DIALBERT: Domain adaptation has shown great effectiveness to improve dialogue performance (Gu et al., 2020a; Whang et al., 2020) .In this setting, DIALBERT with adaptation [3] will be used to find parent message according to the ranking scores.

[2] https://github.com/TeddLi/Disentangle

[3] The Ubuntu forum data published in Dialog System Technology Challenges 8 (DSTC 8) - Track 2 as external data was adopted to perform domain adaptation. The input was constructed as {`[CLS]`, `title`, `question`, `[SEP]`, `answer`, `[SEP]`}. Both tasks of masked language model (MLM) and next sentence prediction (NSP) were employed during domain adaptation. Note that domain adaptation was only employed in Ubuntu IRC dataset.

	VI	ARI	1-1	F1	P	R
Linear+ feature *	88.9	-	69.5	21.8	19.3	24.9
Feedforward + feature *	91.3	-	75.6	36.2	34.6	38.0
× 10 union*	86.2	-	62.5	33.4	40.4	28.5
× 10 vote*	91.5	-	76.0	38.0	36.3	39.7
× 10 intersect*	69.3	-	26.6	32.1	67.0	21.1
Elsner(2008)*	82.1	-	51.4	15.5	12.1	21.5
Lowe(2017)*	80.6	-	53.7	8.9	10.8	7.6
Dec. Att. (dev)*	70.3	-	39.8	0.6	0.9	0.7
Dec. Att. + feature (dev)*	87.4	-	66.6	21.1	18.2	25.2
ESIM (dev)*	72.1	-	44.0	1.4	2.2	1.8
ESIM + feature (dev)*	87.7	-	65.8	22.6	18.9	28.3
BERT (dev)*	74.7	-	45.4	2.2	2.6	2.7
BERT + feature (dev)*	89.5	-	71.7	21.4	30.0	25.0
MHT (dev)*	82.1	-	59.6	8.7	12.6	10.3
MHT +feature (dev)*	89.8	-	75.4	35.8	32.7	34.2
DIALBERT w/o. adapt (dev)	93.4	79.2	83.1	44.4	48.4	41.1
DIALBERT (dev)	**94.1**	**81.1**	**85.6**	**48.0**	**49.5**	**46.6**
Structural Characterization (dev)	94.4	81.8	86.1	52.6	51.0	54.3
DIALBERT w/o. adapt	92.5	63.5	76.5	39.8	36.4	43.8
DIALBERT	92.6	69.6	78.5	44.1	42.3	46.2
DIALBERT + feature	92.4	64.6	77.6	42.2	38.8	46.3
DIALBERT + ensemble	93.3	75.2	-	**46.8**	**44.3**	49.6
DIALBERT + cov	93.2	72.8	79.7	44.8	42.1	47.9
DIALBERT + cov + uni	93.1	68.2	78.2	43.8	40.0	48.2
DIALBERT + cov + dis	**93.9**	**76.3**	**81.2**	46.5	43.3	**50.1**
DIALBERT + cov + layer	93.2	72.0	79.5	43.1	40.0	46.8
Ptr-Net	92.3	70.2	-	36.0	33.0	38.9
Ptr-Net + Joint train&Self-link	94.2	80.1	-	44.5	44.9	44.2
Structural Characterization	94.6	76.8	84.2	51.7	51.8	51.7

Table 3: Results on the Ubuntu IRC development and test sets. Note that feature was introduced along with the original dataset (Kummerfeld et al., 2019), so the "feature" used with different models was the same. The results marked with * were copied from their corresponding publications. Dec. Att. denoted the decomposable attention model (Parikh et al., 2016), ESIM denoted the enhanced sequential inference model (Chen et al., 2017), and MHT denoted masked hierarchical Transformer (Zhu et al., 2020). Numbers in bold denoted the best performance without comparing with Ptr-Net (Yu and Joty, 2020) and structural characterization(Ma et al., 2022), which are the latest proposed methods for dialogue disentanglement and are included for reference.

DIALBERT + feature: The same setting as DIALBERT, but also combined with the features used in Kummerfeld et al. (2019). The features consist of three parts: (1) Global-level features, including year and frequency of the conversation. (2) Utterance level features, including types of message, targeted or not, time difference between the last message, etc. (3) Utterance pair features including how far apart in position and the time between the messages, whether one message targets another, etc. Specifically, we concatenate these external features with high-order feature vectors **F** in our model. These features are same as those used in other baseline models.

DIALBERT + ensemble: In this setting, the weights of the model prediction probability were averaged for each sample across 8 DIALBERT models.

Model	Graph	Conversation
ESIM	23.2	0
Decomposable Attention	16.4	0
BERT	29.6	0.24
DIALBERT	33.7	0.36
DIALBERT + cov	34.5	0.31
DIALBERT + cov + uni	**36.1**	0.38
DIALBERT + cov + dis	34.4	**0.41**
DIALBERT + cov + layer	33.1	0.29

Table 4: Results of different models on the Reddit test set in terms of the accuracy (%).

	VI	ARI	1-1	F1	P	R
Our model	**93.9**	**76.3**	**81.2**	**46.5**	**43.3**	**50.1**
- extra losses	92.7	69.2	78.5	44.3	42.1	46.7
- adaptation	92.5	67.8	78.6	41.0	37.6	45.1
- BiLSTM	90.8	62.9	75.0	32.5	29.3	36.6

Table 5: Ablation analysis on different components using the Ubuntu IRC dataset.

DIALBERT w/o. adaptation: In this setting, the adaptation process was ablated. DIALBERT was finetuned on the IRC dataset directly.

DIALBERT + cov: The conversation-structure loss was employed in addition to the cross-entropy loss.

DIALBERT + cov + (uni or dis or layer): Three results of using different tree-structure losses were reported.

5.5 Experimental Results

The performances of different models on the IRC test set are shown in Table 3. Our model outperforms all of the previous models in all evaluation metrics. Specifically, on the test set, the previous work using an ensemble of 10 feedforward models obtained through a vote is capable of reaching the previous best performance. We can see that our best model (DIALBERT+cov+dis) achieves better performance by a large margin. To compare our results with those reported in Zhu et al. (2020), we report the performances of DIALBERT and DIALBERT *w/o. adaptation* on the development set as well. [4] We can see even without domain

[4] Zhu et al. (2020) did not include results on the test set.

Parent	DialBERT	DialBERT extra losses	Index	Message
...	...	...		
1232	1232	1232	1232	[19:15] franendar: how can I install a specific glibc version?
1226	1226	1226	1233	[19:15] EriC: paste grep Prompt /etc/update-manager/release-upgrades
1232	1232	1232	1234	[19:15] franendar: im getting this: sudo apt-get install build-essential
1233	1233	1233	1235	[19:15] EriC: empty
1232	1236	**1232**	1236	[19:15] MonkeyDust: many glibc questions these days, i wonder how come
1234	1234	1234	1237	[19:15] franendar: im getting this: version 'GLIBCXX_3.4.21' not found
1235	1235	1235	1238	[19:15] EriC: cat /etc/update-manager/release-upgrades
1223	1231	1231	1239	[19:15] nick420: Unable to locate package java8-installer
1238	1238	1238	1240	[19:16] EriC: prompt=never
1240	1240	1240	1241	[19:16] EriC: So, prompt=lts?
1241	1240	**1241**	1242	[19:16] EriC: yeah
1242	1242	1242	1243	[19:16] EriC: Thanks
...	...	...		

Table 6: An example that DialBERT cannot predict correctly, but DialBERT + *extra losses* does. In this table, Parent is the golden label; DialBERT and DialBERT + *extra losses* is the the perdiction of different models; Index is the message index.

adaptation and extra losses, DialBERT already outperforms *MHT+feature*. All our other models perform even better on the development set, but due to the space limit, we only report the above two models on the development set.

The same observation can be seen on the Reddit dataset as shown in Table 4. Note that the values of conversation accuracy (*Conv. Acc.*) are small, due to the definition of the metric itself.

Different from other NLP tasks, according to the results, BERT does not have much advantages over other models, which indicates semantic knowledge learned from pre-training is not a direct indicator of improvement for disentanglement. The result that DialBERT outperforms BERT on all six evaluation metrics could be explained by the vital importance of context in conversations disentanglement, and DialBERT makes better use of pre-trained knowledge. The substantial margin between DialBERT and DialBERT *w/o. adaptation* demonstrates adaptation does give further improvement of DialBERT. It is also notable that DialBERT+*feature* does not have much performance improvement compared with DialBERT, which means the information contained in feature has been implicitly learned during the domain adaptation process. As the result, we further report the ensemble results and external loss results based on DialBERT with adaptation.

The results that DialBERT+*cov* outperforms DialBERT shows that the conversation-structure loss does help. Among the three strategies of tree-structure losses, only the *penalty-by-distance* strategy can further improve the performance of DialBERT+*cov*. The reason might be both *uniform-penalty* strategy and *penalty-by-layer-difference* strategy ignore the distance between each message and target message in tree structures, and distance information is of vital importance to understand the conversation structures. That explains why *penalty-by-distance* strategy can further improve the result in both the IRC test set and in Reddit test set.

It can be seen that the results of DialBERT and DialBERT with conversation-structure loss doesn't show a substantial margin in the Reddit test set. The reason might be the differences in data collection. For the IRC dataset, data are collected from *Linux IRC channel* which means different conversations can happen at the same time and messages in context range are not necessary within the same conversation with the target message. But for the Reddit dataset, data are crawled by a list of all posts in a conversation which means messages of each conversation are together in the dataset. As a result, the conversation information can not give as much improvement as in IRC dataset.

5.6 The Value Design for Tree-Structure Loss

The selection of d and l is based on the statistic of both datasets that we used. For equation 9, $d = 5$ will cover most of samples. Because our target is to find the parent message of target message. So we set $d = 0$ a smaller value to give the "real" parent message more "credit". For the same reason, we set threshold d and l to be 20 and 10 in equation 11 and equation 12 respectively. Please note that the d in equation 9 is designed for ancestor messages. The d in equation 11, however, is designed for non-ancestor messages which are generally further away from the target message. The d in equation 11 will not be 0. As the result, we set different threshold d value. The intention that we designed descending y_i^b based on distance (or layer-difference) is the assumption that the nearer a message and the target message is the more semantic relevant it could be. We designed the *uniform-penalty* strategy to verify the correctness of the assumption (as shown in Table 3), and results show that *penalty-by-distance* and *penalty-by-layer-difference* do reach better performance.

5.7 Ablation

To find out how each component contributes to the final results, we display the ablation analysis of different component based on our best system DIALBERT+*cov*+*dis* (as shown in Table 5). The performance of the model drops in all of 6 evaluation metrics after the removal of extra losses, which demonstrates the effectiveness of integrating conversation structure information into the losses.

Moreover, the performance of the model drops in 5 out of 6 evaluation metrics after the removal of adaptation process, which indicates adaptation learns useful semantic information, especially under the condition that the dataset is in a specific domain. After the removal of BiLSTM, in which the model has to make a prediction without any context consideration, results fall remarkably according to all evaluation metrics. As we discussed before, context is very important for disentangling a conversation. We can see from the ablation results, every component added on BERT in our model contributes to the final result.

Our model can not only introduce global and local conversation semantics but also introduce the conversation structures implicitly, resulting in achieving a new state-of-the-art results by outperforming other models substantially.

5.8 Case Study

As shown in Table 6, there are three conversations involve in this example, i.e., {1232, 1234, 1236, 1237 }, {1233, 1235, 1238, 1240, 1241, 1242, 1243} and {1249}, where these numbers denote the index for each message. For the messages 1236 and 1242, DIALBERT + *extra losses* can find the correct parent message, which indicates that extra losses do help the DIALBERT in dialogue disentanglement. Specifically, for the message 1236, conversation-structure loss plays a more important role, because the preceding messages after parent message are from two conversation. For the message 1242, tree-structure loss plays a more important role, because the preceding messages after parent message are from the same conversation. For message 1239, both DIALBERT and DIALBERT + *extra losses* cannot predict correctly, the reason might be that the distance from parent message is too far in this case, which demonstrates that dialogue disentanglement is still hard and extra losses can not handle all the cases.

6 Conclusions

In this paper, we propose a novel framework for dialogue disentanglement. Different from previous work, we integrate both local and global semantics by proposing an adapted hierarchical BERT-based model (DIALBERT) to disentangle conversations. Moreover, in order to make use of conversation structures, we finetune our model with two losses (i.e., conversation-structure loss and tree-structure loss). We evaluate our method on two large datasets. Results show that our method achieves a new state-of-the-art performances on both datasets and outperforms models from previous work with a substantial margin. In the future, we will design non-heuristic methods for modeling the conversation structure with less hyperparameters which is a challenge worth exploring.

Acknowledgements

We thank anonymous reviewers for their valuable comments.

References

Martín Abadi, Paul Barham, Jianmin Chen, Zhifeng Chen, Andy Davis, Jeffrey Dean, Matthieu Devin, Sanjay Ghemawat, Geoffrey Irving, Michael Isard, et al. 2016. Tensorflow: A system for large-scale machine learning. In *12th {USENIX} Symposium on Operating Systems Design and Implementation ({OSDI} 16)*, pages 265–283.

Paige H Adams and Craig H Martell. 2008. Topic detection and extraction in chat. In *2008 IEEE international conference on Semantic computing*, pages 581–588. IEEE.

Paul M Aoki, Matthew Romaine, Margaret H Szymanski, James D Thornton, Daniel Wilson, and Allison Woodruff. 2003. The mad hatter's cocktail party: a social mobile audio space supporting multiple simultaneous conversations. In *Proceedings of the SIGCHI conference on human factors in computing systems*, pages 425–432. ACM.

Qian Chen, Zhen-Hua Ling, and Xiaodan Zhu. 2018. Enhancing sentence embedding with generalized pooling. In *Proceedings of the 27th International Conference on Computational Linguistics*, pages 1815–1826.

Qian Chen, Xiaodan Zhu, Zhen-Hua Ling, Si Wei, Hui Jiang, and Diana Inkpen. 2017. Enhanced lstm for natural language inference. In *Proceedings of the 55th Annual Meeting of the Association for Computational Linguistics (Volume 1: Long Papers)*, pages 1657–1668.

Jacob Devlin, Ming-Wei Chang, Kenton Lee, and Kristina Toutanova. 2019. BERT: Pre-training of deep bidirectional transformers for language understanding. In *Proceedings of the 2019 Conference of the North American Chapter of the Association for Computational Linguistics: Human Language Technologies, Volume 1 (Long and Short Papers)*, pages 4171–4186.

Wenchao Du, Pascal Poupart, and Wei Xu. 2017. Discovering conversational dependencies between messages in dialogs. In *Thirty-First AAAI Conference on Artificial Intelligence*.

Micha Elsner and Eugene Charniak. 2008. You talking to me? a corpus and algorithm for conversation disentanglement. In *Proceedings of ACL-08: HLT*, pages 834–842.

Micha Elsner and Eugene Charniak. 2010. Disentangling chat. *Computational Linguistics*, 36(3):389–409.

Micha Elsner and Eugene Charniak. 2011. Disentangling chat with local coherence models. In *Proceedings of the 49th Annual Meeting of the Association for Computational Linguistics: Human Language Technologies*, pages 1179–1189.

Micha Elsner and Warren Schudy. 2009. Bounding and comparing methods for correlation clustering beyond ilp. In *Proceedings of the Workshop on Integer Linear Programming for Natural Language Processing*, pages 19–27.

Jia-Chen Gu, Tianda Li, Quan Liu, Zhen-Hua Ling, Zhiming Su, Si Wei, and Xiaodan Zhu. 2020a. Speaker-aware BERT for multi-turn response selection in retrieval-based chatbots. In *Proceedings of the 29th ACM International Conference on Information & Knowledge Management*, pages 2041–2044.

Jia-Chen Gu, Tianda Li, Quan Liu, Xiaodan Zhu, Zhen-Hua Ling, and Yu-Ping Ruan. 2020b. Pre-trained and attention based neural networks for building noetic task-oriented dialogue systems. In *Proceedings of the Thirty-Fourth AAAI Conference on Artificial Intelligence, AAAI 2020, Workshop on the Eighth Dialog System Technology Challenge, DSTC8, New York, NY, USA, February 7-12, 2020*.

Jia-Chen Gu, Chongyang Tao, Zhenhua Ling, Can Xu, Xiubo Geng, and Daxin Jiang. 2021. MPC-BERT: A pre-trained language model for multi-party conversation understanding. In *Proceedings of the 59th Annual Meeting of the Association for Computational Linguistics and the 11th International Joint Conference on Natural Language Processing (Volume 1: Long Papers)*, pages 3682–3692.

Jyun-Yu Jiang, Francine Chen, Yan-Ying Chen, and Wei Wang. 2018. Learning to disentangle interleaved conversational threads with a siamese hierarchical network and similarity ranking. In *Proceedings of the 2018 Conference of the North American Chapter of the Association for Computational Linguistics: Human Language Technologies, Volume 1 (Long Papers)*, pages 1812–1822.

Jonathan K Kummerfeld, Sai R Gouravajhala, Joseph J Peper, Vignesh Athreya, Chulaka Gunasekara, Jatin Ganhotra, Siva Sankalp Patel, Lazaros C Polymenakos, and Walter Lasecki. 2019. A large-scale corpus for conversation disentanglement. In *Proceedings of the 57th Annual Meeting of the Association for Computational Linguistics*, pages 3846–3856.

Hui Liu, Zhan Shi, Jia-Chen Gu, Quan Liu, Si Wei, and Xiaodan Zhu. 2021a. End-to-end transition-based online dialogue disentanglement. In *Proceedings of the Twenty-Ninth International Conference on International Joint Conferences on Artificial Intelligence*, pages 3868–3874.

Hui Liu, Zhan Shi, and Xiaodan Zhu. 2021b. Unsupervised conversation disentanglement through co-training. In *Proceedings of the 2021 Conference on Empirical Methods in Natural Language Processing*, pages 2345 2356.

Xinbei Ma, Zhuosheng Zhang, and Hai Zhao. 2022. Structural characterization for dialogue disentanglement. In *Proceedings of the 60th Annual Meeting of the Association for Computational Linguistics*.

Elijah Mayfield, David Adamson, and Carolyn Rose. 2012. Hierarchical conversation structure prediction in multi-party chat. In *Proceedings of the 13th Annual Meeting of the Special Interest Group on Discourse and Dialogue*, pages 60–69.

Shikib Mehri and Giuseppe Carenini. 2017. Chat disentanglement: Identifying semantic reply relationships with random forests and recurrent neural networks. In *Proceedings of the Eighth International Joint Conference on Natural Language Processing (Volume 1: Long Papers)*, pages 615–623.

Hiroki Ouchi and Yuta Tsuboi. 2016. Addressee and response selection for multi-party conversation. In *Proceedings of the 2016 Conference on Empirical Methods in Natural Language Processing*, pages 2133–2143.

Ankur Parikh, Oscar Täckström, Dipanjan Das, and Jakob Uszkoreit. 2016. A decomposable attention model for natural language inference. In *Proceedings of the 2016 Conference on Empirical Methods in Natural Language Processing*, pages 2249–2255.

David Traum. 2004. Issues in multiparty dialogues. In *Workshop on Agent Communication Languages*, pages 201–211. Springer.

David C Uthus and David W Aha. 2013. Multiparticipant chat analysis: A survey. *Artificial Intelligence*, 199:106–121.

Lidan Wang and Douglas W Oard. 2009. Context-based message expansion for disentanglement of interleaved text conversations. In *Proceedings of human language technologies: The 2009 annual conference of the North American chapter of the association for computational linguistics*, pages 200–208.

Yi-Chia Wang, Mahesh Joshi, William W Cohen, and Carolyn Penstein Rosé. 2008. Recovering implicit thread structure in newsgroup style conversations. In *Proceedings of the Second International Conference on Weblogs and Social Media, ICWSM 2008.*

Taesun Whang, Dongyub Lee, Chanhee Lee, Kisu Yang, Dongsuk Oh, and Heuiseok Lim. 2020. An effective domain adaptive post-training method for BERT in response selection. In *Proceedings of the Annual Conference of the International Speech Communication Association, INTERSPEECH*, volume 2020, pages 1585–1589.

Deunsol Yoon, Dongbok Lee, and SangKeun Lee. 2018. Dynamic self-attention: Computing attention over words dynamically for sentence embedding. *arXiv preprint arXiv:1808.07383.*

Tao Yu and Shafiq Joty. 2020. Online conversation disentanglement with pointer networks. In *Proceedings of the 2020 Conference on Empirical Methods in Natural Language Processing (EMNLP)*, pages 6321–6330.

Henghui Zhu, Feng Nan, Zhiguo Wang, Ramesh Nallapati, and Bing Xiang. 2020. Who did they respond to? conversation structure modeling using masked hierarchical transformer. In *Proceedings of the AAAI Conference on Artificial Intelligence*, volume 34, pages 9741–9748.

Conversational Search with Mixed-Initiative - Asking Good Clarification Questions backed-up by Passage Retrieval

Yosi Mass, Doron Cohen, Asaf Yehudai and David Konopnicki
IBM Research AI
Haifa University, Mount Carmel, Haifa, HA 31905, Israel
{yosimass,doronc,davidko}@il.ibm.com
Asaf.Yehudai@ibm.com

Abstract

We deal with the scenario of conversational search, where user queries are under-specified or ambiguous. This calls for a mixed-initiative setup. User-asks (queries) and system-answers, as well as system-asks (clarification questions) and user response, in order to clarify her information needs. We focus on the task of selecting the next clarification question, given the conversation context. Our method leverages passage retrieval from a background content to fine-tune two deep-learning models for ranking candidate clarification questions. We evaluated our method on two different use-cases. The first is an open domain conversational search in a large web collection. The second is a task-oriented customer-support setup. We show that our method performs well on both use-cases.

1 Introduction

A key task in information and knowledge discovery is the retrieval of relevant information given the user's information need (usually expressed by a query). With the abundance of textual knowledge sources and their diversity, it becomes more and more difficult for users, even expert ones, to query such sources and obtain valuable insights.

Thus, users need to go beyond the traditional ad-hoc (one-shot) retrieval paradigm. This requires to support the new paradigm of conversational search – a sophisticated combination of various mechanisms for exploratory search, interactive IR, and response generation. In particular, the conversational paradigm can support mixed-initiative: namely, the traditional user asks - system answers interaction in addition to system-asks (clarification questions) and user-answers, to better guide the system and reach the information needed (Krasakis et al., 2020).

Existing approaches for asking clarification questions include *selection* or *generation*. In the selection approach, the system selects clarification questions from a pool of pre-determined questions (Aliannejadi et al., 2019). In the generation approach, the system generates clarification questions using rules or using neural generative models (Zamani et al., 2020).

In this work we focus on the selection task. While the latter (i.e., generation) may represent a more realistic use-case, still there is an interest in the former (i.e., selection) as evident by the Clarifying Questions for Open-Domain Dialogue Systems (ClariQ) challenge (Aliannejadi et al., 2020). Moreover, the selection task represents a controlled and less noisy scenario, where the pool of clarifications can be mined from e.g., query logs.

In this paper we deal with content-grounded conversations. Thus, a conversation starts with an initial user query, continues with several rounds of conversation utterances (0 or more), and finally ends with one or more documents being returned to the user. Some of the agent utterances are marked as clarification questions.

The task at hand is defined as follows. Given a conversation context up to (and not including) a clarification-question utterance, predict the next clarification question. A more formal definition is given in Section 3.2 below.

Intuitively, clarification questions should be used to distinguish between several possible intents of the user. We approximate those possible intents through passages that are retrieved from a given corpus of documents. A motivating example from the (Aliannejadi et al., 2020) challenge is given in Figure 1. The user wants to get information about the topic *all men are created equal.* Through the retrieved passage, the system can ask the mentioned clarification questions.

We use two deep-learning models. The first one learns an association between conversation context and clarification questions. The second learns an association between conversation context, candidate passages and clarification questions.

Proceedings of the Second DialDoc Workshop on Document-grounded Dialogue and Conversational Question Answering, pages 65 - 71
May 26, 2022 ©2022 Association for Computational Linguistics

Evaluation was done on two different use-cases. The first one is an open domain search in a large web corpus (Aliannejadi et al., 2020). The second is an internal task-oriented customer-support setup, where users ask technical questions. We show that our method performs well on both use-cases.

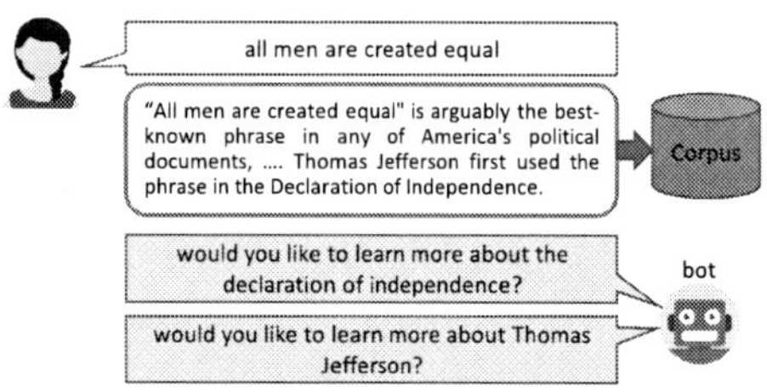

Figure 1: A motivating example

2 Related work

We focus on works that deal with clarification-questions selection. Aliannejadi et al. (2019) describes a setup very similar to ours for the aforementioned task. They apply a two-step process. In the first step, they use BERT (Devlin et al., 2019) to retrieve candidate clarification questions and, in the second step, they re-rank the candidates using multiple sources of information. Among them are the scores of retrieved documents using the clarification questions. However, they do not look at passage content as we do.

The ClariQ[1] challenge organized a competition for selecting the best clarification questions in an open-domain conversational search. The system by NTES_ALONG (Ou and Lin, 2020) was ranked first. They first retrieve candidate clarification questions and then re-rank them using a ROBERTA (Liu et al., 2019) model, that is fine-tuned on the relation between a query and a clarification question. Unlike our method, they do not exploit passage content.

In Rao and Daumé III (2018), they select clarification questions using the expected value of perfect information, namely a good question is one whose expected answer will be useful. They do not assume a background corpus of documents.

3 Clarification-questions Selection

3.1 Problem definition

A conversation C is a list of utterances, $C = \{c_0, ..., c_n\}$ where c_0 is the initial user query. Each utterance has a speaker which is either a user or an agent.[2] Since we deal with content-grounded conversations, the last utterance is an agent utterance, that points to a document.

We further assume that agent utterances are tagged with a *clarification flag* where a value of 1 indicates that the utterance is a clarification question. This flag is either given as part of the dataset (e.g., in the open domain dataset, ClariQ) or is derived automatically by using a rule-based model or a classifier. We discuss such rules for the second task-oriented customer-support dataset (see Section 4.1 below).

The **Clarification-questions Selection** task is defined as follows. Given a conversation context $C^j = \{c_0, ..., c_{j-1}\}$, predict a clarification question at the next utterance of the conversation.[3]

3.2 Method

The proposed run-time architecture is depicted in Figure 2. It contains two indices and two fine-tuned BERT models. The *Documents index* contains the corpus of documents (recall that we deal with conversations that end with a document(s) being retrieved). This index supports passage retrieval. The *Clarification-questions index* contains the pool of clarification questions. The two BERT models are used for re-ranking of candidate clarification questions as described below.

Given a conversation context C^j, we first retrieve top-k passages from the Document index (See Section 3.3 below). We then use those passages, to retrieve candidate clarification questions from the Clarification-questions index (See Section 3.4 below). We thus have, for each passage, a list of candidate clarification questions.

The next step re-ranks those candidate clarification questions. Re-ranking is done by the fusion of ranking obtain through two BERT models. Each model re-ranks the clarification questions by their relevance to the given conversation context and the retrieved passages (see Section 3.5 below). The components of the architecture are described next in more details.

3.3 Conversation-based passage retrieval

Documents in the document index are represented using two fields. The first field contains the actual document content. The second field augments the

[1] http://convai.io

[2] An agent can be either a human agent or a bot.

[3] We always return clarification questions. We leave it for future work to decide whether a clarification is required.

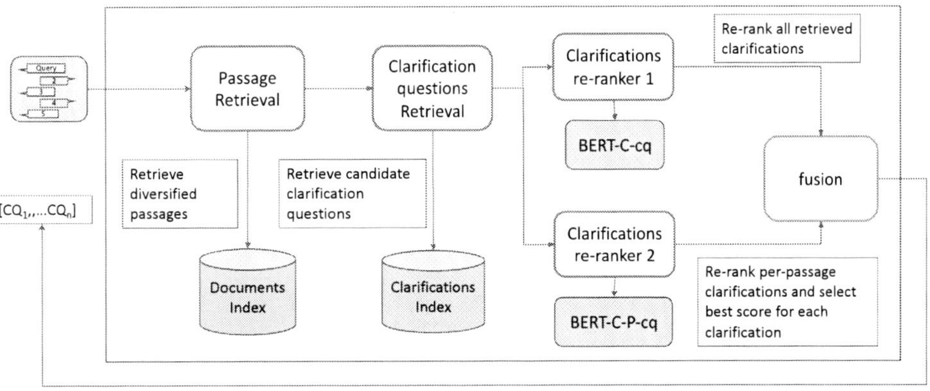

Figure 2: Clarification-questions selection run-time architecture

document's representation with the text of all dialogs that link to it in the train-set (Amitay et al., 2005). We refer to these two fields as `text` and `anchor` respectively. We also keep a third field `anchor_and_text` that contain the concatenation of the above two fields.

Given a conversation context C^j, Passage retrieval is performed in two steps. First, top-k documents are retrieved from the `anchor_and_text` field. using a disjunctive query over all words in the conversation C^j. Following (Ganhotra et al., 2020), we treat the dialog query as a verbose query and apply the Fixed-Point (FP) method (Paik and Oard, 2014) for weighting its words. Yet, compared to "traditional" verbose queries, dialogs are further segmented into distinct utterances. Using this observation, we implement an *utterance-biased* extension for enhanced word-weighting. To this end, we first score the various utterances based on the initial FP weights of words they contain. We then propagate utterance scores back to their associated words.

In the second step, candidate passages are extracted from those top-k documents using a sliding window of fixed size with some overlap. Each candidate passage p is assigned an initial score based on the coverage of terms in C^j by p. The coverage is defined as the sum over all terms in each utterance, using terms' global *idf* (inverse document frequency) and their (scaled) tf (term frequency). The final passage score is a linear combinations of its initial score and the score of the document it is extracted from. Details are given in appendix A.1

3.4 Clarification-questions retrieval

The pool of clarification questions is indexed into a Clarification index. We use the passages returned for a given conversation context C^j, to extract an initial set of candidate clarification questions as follows. For each passage P, we concatenate its content to the text of all utterances in C^j, and use it as a query to the Clarification index.

We thus have, for each passage, a list of candidate clarification questions.

3.5 Clarification-questions re-ranking

The input to this step is a conversation context C^j, a list of candidate passages, and a list of candidate clarification questions for each passage. We use two BERT (Devlin et al., 2019) models to re-rank the candidate clarification questions. The first model, *BERT-C-cq* learns an association between conversation contexts and clarification questions. The second model, *BERT-C-P-cq* learns an association between conversation contexts, passages and clarification questions. Training and using the two models is described below.

Fine-tuning of the models. The first model, BERT-C-cq, is fine-tuned through a triplet network (Hoffer and Ailon, 2015) that is adopted for BERT fine-tuning (Mass et al., 2019). It uses triplets (C^j, cq^+, cq^-), where cq^+ is the clarification question of conversation C at utterance c_j (as given in the conversations of the training set). Negative examples (cq^-) are randomly selected from the pool of clarification questions (not associated with C).

For fine-tuning the second model, BERT-C-P-cq, we need to retrieve relevant passages. We use a weak-supervision assumption that all passages in a relevant document (i.e., a document returned for

C), are relevant as well. A triplet for the second BERT model is thus $(C^j\ [SEP]\ P, cq^+, cq^-)$, where P is a passage retrieved for C^j, $[SEP]$ is BERT's separator token, cq^+ and cq^- are positive and negative clarification questions selected as described above for the first model.

Due to the BERT limitation on max number of tokens (512), we represent a conversation context C^j using the last m utterances whose total length is less than 512 characters. We also take the passage window size to be 512 characters.[4]

Re-ranking with the models. Each candidate clarification question cq_i is fed to the first model with the conversation context as (C^j, cq_i), and to the second model as $(C^j\ [SEP]\ P, cq_i)$, where P is the passage that was used to retrieve cq_i. Final scores of the candidates is set by simple CombSUM (Wu, 2012) fusion of their scores from the two BERT models.

4 Experiments

4.1 Datasets

We evaluated our method on two datasets. The first, **ClariQ** (Aliannejadi et al., 2020) represents an information-seeking use-case. The second, **Support** contains conversations and technical documents of an internal customer support site. Statistics on the two datasets are given in Table 1.

The **ClariQ** dataset was built by crowd sourcing for the task of clarification-questions selection, thus it has high quality clarification questions. Each conversation has exactly three turns. Initial user query, an agent clarification question and the user response to the clarification question. The agent utterance is always a clarification question.

The **Support** dataset contains noisy logs of human-to-human conversations, that contain a lot of chit-chat utterances such as *Thanks for your help* or *Are you still there?* We thus applied the following rules to identify agent clarification questions. i) We consider only sentences in agent utterances that contain a question mark. ii) We look for question words in the text (e.g., *what, how, where, did, etc.*) and consider only the text between such a word and the question mark. iii) If no question words were found, we run the sentences with the question mark through Allennlp's constituency parser (Joshi et al., 2018), and keep sentences with a Penn-Treebank clause type of *SQ* or *SBARQ*[5].

The above rules can be used to detect question-type sentences. However, we are interested in clarification questions that are related to the background collection of documents and not in chit-chat questions (such as e.g., *how are you today?*). To filter out such chit-chat question types, we apply a 4th rule as follows. iv) Recall that each conversation ends with a document answer. We send the detected question and its answer (the next user's utterance), as a passage retrieval query (see Section 3.1 above) to the Documents index and keep only those questions that returned in their top-3 results, a passage from the document of the conversation.

Table 1: Datasets statistics

	ClariQ	Support
#docs	2.7M	520
#conversations (train/dev/test)	187/50/60	500/39/43
#total clarifications	3940	704
#avg/max turns per C	3/3	8.2/80.5
#avg/max clarifications per C	14/18	1.27/5

4.2 Setup of the experiments

We use Apache Lucene[6] for indexing the documents. We use English language analyzer and default BM25 similarity (Robertson and Zaragoza, 2009).

For the customer support dataset (**Support**) we used the `anchor_and_text` field for initial document retrieval, since most documents in the dataset do have training conversations.

The open-domain dataset (**ClariQ**) contains a large number of documents (2.7M), but only a small portion of them do have training conversations. Using the `anchor_and_text` field for retrieval will prefer that small subset of documents (since only they have anchor text). Thus for this dataset, we used the `text` field for retrieval.

For passage retrieval, we used a sliding window of 512 characters on retrieved documents' content. We used common values for the hyper parameters, with $\lambda = 0.5$ to combine document and passage scores, and $\mu = 2000$ for the dirichlet smoothing of the documents LM used in the FixedPoint re-ranking. Details of the passage retrieval are given in Apendix A.1.

The full conversations were used to retrieve passages. For feeding to the BERT models, we concatenated the last m utterances whose total length

[4]note that BERT uses tokens while for the passages and representation of conversation we use characters

[5]`https://gist.github.com/nlothian/9240750`

[6]https://lucene.apache.org/

was less than 512 characters (we take full utterances that fit the above size. We do not cut utterances).

We used the pytorch huggingface implementation of BERT[7]. For the two BERT models we used bert-base-uncased (12-layers, 768-hidden, 12-heads, 110M parameters). Fine-tuning was done with the following default hyper parameters. max_seq_len of 256 tokens[8] for the BERT-C-cq model and 384 for the BERT-C-P-cq model, learning rate of 2e-5 and 3 training epochs.

We retrieved at most 1000 initial candidate clarifications for each passage. All experiments were run on a 32GB V100 GPUs. The re-ranking times of 1000 clarification questions for each conversation took about $1-2$ sec. For evaluation metrics we followed the ClariQ leaderboard [9] and used the Recall@30 as the main metrics.

4.3 Results

Table 2 reports the results on the dev sets of the two datasets.[10] On both datasets, each of the BERT re-rankers showed a significant improvement over the initial retrieval from the Clarification-questions index (denoted by **IR-Base**). For example on **Support**, **BERT-C-cq** achieved $R@30$=0.538 compared to $R@30$=0.294 of **IR-Base** (an improvement of 82%).

We can further see that the two BERT models (**BERT-C-cq** and **BERT-C-P-cq**), yield quite similar results on both datasets, but, when fusing their scores (**BERT-fusion**), there is another improvement of about 2.5% over each of the rankers separately. For example on **ClariQ**, **BERT-fusion** achieved $R@30$=0.791, compared to $R@30$=0.77 of **BERT-C-cq**.

This improvement can be attributed to complementary matching that each of the two BERT models learns. The second model learns latent features that are revealed only through the retrieved passages, while the first model works better for cases where the retrieved passages are noisy. For example for query 133 in **Clariq**, *all men are created equal* (see Figure 1 above), **BERT-C-P-cq** could find nine correct clarification questions out of 14 in its top-30 (including those two in the Figure), while **BERT-C-cq** found only three of them.

Table 3 shows the official Clariq leaderboard result on the test set. We can see that our method **BERT-fusion**[11] was ranked forth but was the second best as a team. We note that the top performing system (NTES_ALONG) gave preferences to clarification questions from the test data, capitalizing the specific **Clariq** properties that test topics came from different domain than the train topics. This is not a valid assumption in general. In contrast, we treat all clarification questions equally in the given pool of clarification questions.

Table 2: Retrieval quality on the dev set of the two datasets

ClariQ	R@5	R@10	R@20	R@30
IR-Base	.327	.575	.669	.706
BERT-C-cq	.352	.631	.743	.770
BERT-C-P-cq	.344	.615	.750	.774
BERT-fusion	**.353**	**.639**	**.758**	**.791**
Support				
IR-Base	.102	.153	.269	.294
BERT-C-cq	**.358**	**.410**	.487	.538
BERT-C-P-cq	.217	.294	.487	.538
BERT-fusion	.294	**.410**	**.500**	**.551**

Table 3: Retrieval quality on the test set of the ClariQ dataset

ClariQ	R@5	R@10	R@20	R@30
NTES_ALONG	.340	.632	.833	.874
NTES_ALONG	.341	.635	.831	.872
NTES_ALONG	.338	.624	.817	.868
BERT-fusion	.338	.631	.807	.857
TAL-ML	.339	.625	.817	.856
Karl	.335	.623	.799	.849
Soda	.327	.606	.801	.843

5 Conclusions

We presented a method for clarification-questions selection in conversational-search scenarios that end with documents as answers.

We showed that using passages, combined with deep-learning models, improves the quality of the selected clarification questions. We evaluated our method on two diversified dataset. On both datasets, the usage of passages for clarification-questions re-ranking achieved improvement of $12\% - 87\%$ over base IR retrieval.

[7] https://bit.ly/2Me0Gk1

[8] note that here we use tokens while for the passages and representation of conversation we use characters

[9] https://convai.io

[10] We compare our methods on the dev sets since in **Clariq** we had access only to the dev set. We note that in both datasets, the dev sets wer not used during the training, thus they can be regarded as an held-out test set

[11] Our run was labeled CogIR in the official leaderboard

References

Mohammad Aliannejadi, Julia Kiseleva, Aleksandr Chuklin, Jeff Dalton, and Mikhail Burtsev. 2020. Convai3: Generating clarifying questions for open-domain dialogue systems (clariq).

Mohammad Aliannejadi, Hamed Zamani, Fabio Crestani, and W. Bruce Croft. 2019. Asking clarifying questions in open-domain information-seeking conversations. In *Proceedings of the 42nd International ACM SIGIR Conference on Research and Development in Information Retrieval*, SIGIR'19, page 475–484, New York, NY, USA. Association for Computing Machinery.

Einat Amitay, Adam Darlow, David Konopnicki, and Uri Weiss. 2005. Queries as anchors: selection by association. In *Proceedings of the 16th ACM Conference on Hypertext and Hypermedia*, pages 193–201.

Jacob Devlin, Ming-Wei Chang, Kenton Lee, and Kristina Toutanova. 2019. BERT: Pre-training of deep bidirectional transformers for language understanding. In *Proceedings of the 2019 Conference of the North American Chapter of the Association for Computational Linguistics: Human Language Technologies, Volume 1 (Long and Short Papers)*, pages 4171–4186, Minneapolis, Minnesota. Association for Computational Linguistics.

Jatin Ganhotra, Haggai Roitman, Doron Cohen, Nathaniel Mills, R. Chulaka Gunasekara, Yosi Mass, Sachindra Joshi, Luis A. Lastras, and David Konopnicki. 2020. Conversational document prediction to assist customer care agents. In *Proceedings of the 2020 Conference on Empirical Methods in Natural Language Processing, EMNLP 2020, Online, November 16-20, 2020*, pages 349–356. Association for Computational Linguistics.

Elad Hoffer and Nir Ailon. 2015. Deep metric learning using triplet network. In *3rd International Conference on Learning Representations, ICLR 2015, San Diego, CA, USA, May 7-9, 2015, Workshop Track Proceedings*.

Vidur Joshi, Matthew Peters, and Mark Hopkins. 2018. Extending a parser to distant domains using a few dozen partially annotated examples.

Antonios Minas Krasakis, Mohammad Aliannejadi, Nikos Voskarides, and Evangelos Kanoulas. 2020. Analysing the effect of clarifying questions on document ranking in conversational search. *Proceedings of the 2020 ACM SIGIR on International Conference on Theory of Information Retrieval*.

Yinhan Liu, Myle Ott, Naman Goyal, Jingfei Du, Mandar Joshi, Danqi Chen, Omer Levy, Mike Lewis, Luke Zettlemoyer, and Veselin Stoyanov. 2019. Roberta: A robustly optimized BERT pretraining approach. *CoRR*, abs/1907.11692.

Yosi Mass, Haggai Roitman, Shai Erera, Or Rivlin, Bar Weiner, and David Konopnicki. 2019. A study of bert for non-factoid question-answering under passage length constraints. *CoRR*, abs/1908.06780.

Wenjie Ou and Yue Lin. 2020. A clarifying question selection system from ntes_along in convai3 challenge. *CoRR*, abs/2010.14202.

Jiaul H. Paik and Douglas W. Oard. 2014. A fixed-point method for weighting terms in verbose informational queries. In *Proceedings of the 23rd ACM International Conference on Conference on Information and Knowledge Management*, CIKM '14, page 131–140, New York, NY, USA. Association for Computing Machinery.

Sudha Rao and Hal Daumé III. 2018. Learning to ask good questions: Ranking clarification questions using neural expected value of perfect information. In *Proceedings of the 56th Annual Meeting of the Association for Computational Linguistics (Volume 1: Long Papers)*, pages 2737–2746, Melbourne, Australia. Association for Computational Linguistics.

Stephen Robertson and Hugo Zaragoza. 2009. The probabilistic relevance framework: Bm25 and beyond. *Found. Trends Inf. Retr.*, 3(4):333—389.

Shengli Wu. 2012. *Data Fusion in Information Retrieval*, volume 13.

Hamed Zamani, Susan Dumais, Nick Craswell, Paul Bennett, and Gord Lueck. 2020. Generating clarifying questions for information retrieval. In *Proceedings of The Web Conference 2020*, WWW '20, page 418–428, New York, NY, USA. Association for Computing Machinery.

A Appendix

A.1 Passage Retrieval details

We use Apache Lucene for indexing the documents, configured with English language analyzer and default BM25 similarity (Robertson and Zaragoza, 2009).

After retrieving top-k documents, candidate passages are extracted from those documents using a sliding window of fixed size with some overlap. Each retrieved passage p is assigned an initial score based on the coverage of terms in C^j by p. The coverage is defined as the sum over all terms in each utterance, using terms' global idf (inverse document frequency) and their (scaled) tf (term frequency). Let c be a conversation with n utterances $c = u_1, ...u_n$. Passage score is computed as a linear combination of its initial score $score_{init}(p, c)$ and the score of its enclosing document. Both scores are normalized.

$$score(p, c) = \lambda * score(d) + (1 - \lambda) * score_{init}(p, c) \quad (1)$$

We used lambda=0.5, i.e., fixed equal weights for the document and the passage scores.

The initial passage score $score_{init}(p, c)$ is computed as a weighted sum over its utterances scores $score_{ut}(p, u_i)$. Utterance scores are discounted such that later utterances have greater effect on the passage score.

$$\begin{aligned} score_{init}(p, c) &= \sum_{i=1}^{n} weight_{ut}(i) * score_{ut}(p, u_i) \\ weight_{ut}(i) &= discount\_factor^{(n-i)} \\ discount\_factor &= 0.85 \end{aligned} \tag{2}$$

Utterance score $score_{ut}(p, u)$ reflects utterance's terms coverage by the passage, considering terms' global *idf* (inverse document frequency) and their (scaled) tf (term frequency). Multiple coverage scorers are applied, which differ by their term frequency scaling schemes. Finally, the utterance score is a product of these coverage scores $score_{cov}(p, u)$.

$$\begin{aligned} score_{ut}(p, u) &= \Pi_{j=1}^{m} \, score_{cov_j}(p, u) \\ m &= 2 \quad \text{(two scaling schemes are employed)} \\ score_{cov_j}(p, u) &= \sum_{t \in t^{pu}} idf(t) * scale_j(t, p) \\ t^{pu} &= t^u \bigcap t^p \quad \text{(terms appearing in both)} \\ t^p, t^u &= \quad \text{(passage terms, utterance terms)} \end{aligned} \tag{3}$$

Different scaling schemes provide different interpretations of terms' importance. We combine two tf scaling methods, one that scales by a BM25 term score, and another that scales by the minimum of $tf(t)$ in the utterance and passage.

$$\begin{aligned} scale_1 &= BM25(t, p) \\ scale_2 &= min(tf(t, p), tf(t, c)) \end{aligned} \tag{4}$$

The final passage score is a linear combinations of its initial score and the score of the document it is extracted from. Candidate passage ranking exploits a cascade of scorers.

Graph-combined Coreference Resolution Methods on Conversational Machine Reading Comprehension with Pre-trained Language Model

Zhaodong Wang   Kazunori Komatani
SANKEN, Osaka University

Abstract

Coreference resolution such as for anaphora has been an essential challenge that is commonly found in conversational machine reading comprehension (CMRC). This task aims to determine the referential entity to which a pronoun refers on the basis of contextual information. Existing approaches based on pre-trained language models (PLMs) mainly rely on an end-to-end method, which still has limitations in clarifying referential dependency. In this study, a novel graph-based approach is proposed to integrate the coreference of given text into graph structures (called coreference graphs), which can pinpoint a pronoun's referential entity. We propose two graph-combined methods, evidence-enhanced and the fusion model, for CMRC to integrate coreference graphs from different levels of the PLM architecture. Evidence-enhanced refers to textual level methods that include an evidence generator (for generating new text to elaborate a pronoun) and enhanced question (for rewriting a pronoun in a question) as PLM input. The fusion model is a structural level method that combines the PLM with a graph neural network. We evaluated these approaches on a CoQA pronoun-containing dataset and the whole CoQA dataset. The result showed that our methods can outperform baseline PLM methods with BERT and RoBERTa.

1 Introduction

In recent years, using a large-scale pre-trained language model (PLM) as a backbone for various challenging machine comprehension tasks (Devlin et al., 2019) has become fundamental, especially in conversational machine reading comprehension (CMRC) (Liu et al., 2019a). CMRC tasks not only require a model to fully understand the given articles but also propose to mimic the way humans seek information in conversations through question-answering. Most PLM utilize attention mechanism and achieve positive results on a broad range of CMRC datasets (Choi et al., 2018; Reddy et al., 2019). PLMs generally use an end-to-end approach trained from questions to answers. However, the explainability of the answers generated through the intrinsic multi-head self-attention mechanism remains insufficient. Although these PLMs have demonstrated great advantages in terms of solving questions that simply need semantic matching, limitations in logical comprehension (Ding et al., 2019) such as in coreference resolution still exist.

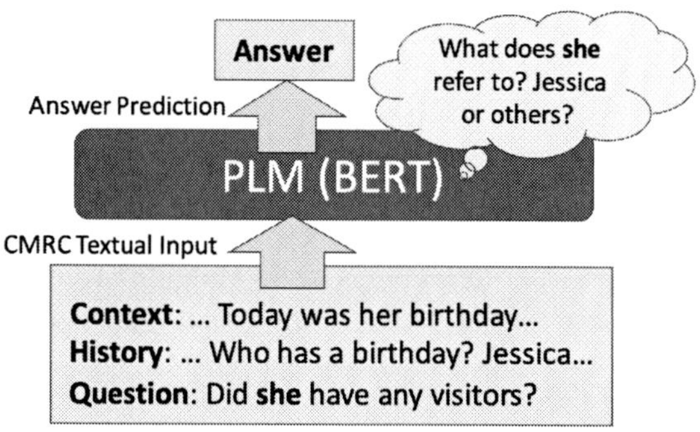

Figure 1: Coreference resolution is required for end-to-end PLM in CMRC task.

Coreference resolution such as for anaphora (von Heusinger and Egli, 2012) is commonly found in CMRC tasks. Anaphora can be described as a pronoun word (anaphor) contained in a current question, in which its referential entity (antecedent) has already been introduced earlier in the conversation history or article context. As shown in Figure 1, to answer the current question "*Did she have any visitors?*", the model requires that the pronoun "*she*" be resolved as an anaphor referring to the entity "*Jessica*" as its antecedent, on the basis of the given context and conversation history. Therefore, CMRC models require mechanisms that can resolve referential dependencies to properly understand the intent of current questions.

Considering the shortcomings of the PLM approach in logical comprehension such as in coref-

Proceedings of the Second DialDoc Workshop on Document-grounded Dialogue and Conversational Question Answering, pages 72 - 82
May 26, 2022 ©2022 Association for Computational Linguistics

erence resolution, research on how to better adapt models to learn reasoning is gradually gaining attention (Yeh and Chen, 2019; Qu et al., 2019; Song et al., 2018). FlowQA (Huang et al., 2019) was proposed to add a reasoning layer between questions and answers to incorporate intermediate representations of a conversation history. The question rewriting (QR) model (Vakulenko et al., 2021; Lin et al., 2020) was proposed to rewrite current questions on the basis of a conversation history. Specifically, the QR model simplifies complex multi-turn question-answering (QA) tasks into single-turn QA tasks, which can solve a current question without a conversation history.

However, because these models are built through the embeddings of a conversation history (Qu et al., 2019), they generally suffer from two drawbacks in coreference reasoning for CMRC tasks. (1) Since the input length of a conversation history is limited by the PLM's structure, the current question sometimes contains pronouns whose referential entity does not appear in the conversation history, so the model cannot accordingly resolve referential dependencies. (2) To achieve coreference reasoning, a CMRC model also needs to seek information from the context of articles. Due to the sequence nature of the PLM and the multiple referential dependencies in the context of an article, these models cannot handle each referential dependency precisely, as shown in Figure 2's context part in different colors.

In this paper, we propose solving the coreference of a target pronoun through additional mined information to enhance PLMs' coreference reasoning ability for CMRC. A novel graph approach is proposed that integrates the coreferences of given text into graph structures, which we call the coreference graph. The coreference graph is constructed separately by using the conversation history and article context as text information. Each entity in the graph holds a unique place label in accordance with the text information, which can be used to pinpoint every pronoun's referential dependency precisely. To better implement the coreference graph as an enhanced component into PLMs, we propose two graph-combined methods: the evidence-enhanced method and the fusion model method. These two methods integrate graph information from the textual and structural levels of the PLM architecture, respectively.

The **evidence-enhanced** method involves two textual level methods that enrich the PLM's input information for coreference reasoning: an **evidence** generator (EG) generates new text to elaborate pronouns, and an **enhanced** question (EQ) rewrites a pronoun into a referential entity in a question.

The **fusion model** is a structural level method that combines the PLM with a graph neural network. This model treats the PLM as an encoder to extract sequence features of pronouns and referential words from input. After that, the graph features of the corresponding words are computed by graph neural networks on the basis of the connectivity of the coreference graph. These two features are integrated using learnable weights to enhance the PLM's coreference reasoning ability.

For the experiments, we used questions from CoQA (Reddy et al., 2019) that contained pronouns to compose a new dataset (pronoun-containing dataset) specialized for the coreference reasoning ability of the CMRC model. We evaluated various combinations of our proposed methods on different PLMs, and we also compared them with the existing QR approach. The results showed that our methods can greatly outperform in terms of F1 score on the CoQA pronoun-containing dataset, 2.6 on BERT (Devlin et al., 2019) and 0.7 on RoBERTa (Liu et al., 2019b). We also used the whole CoQA dataset to evaluate the fusion model, which achieved the best performance in our methods, to compare its overall performance with RoBERTa. The contributions of this paper are as follows.

- We propose a novel graph approach for coreference resolution. This approach can establish referential dependency that appears not only in a conversation history but also in an article context.

- We show that both our evidence-enhanced and fusion model methods boost the performance of different PLMs in CMRC coreference resolution. Therefore, we prove that the introduction of additional information can further leverage the performance of PLMs in complex reasoning such as in coreference resolution.

- Our approaches provide a precise reasoning route for CMRC's coreference resolution and overcome the PLM model's weakness of interpretability.

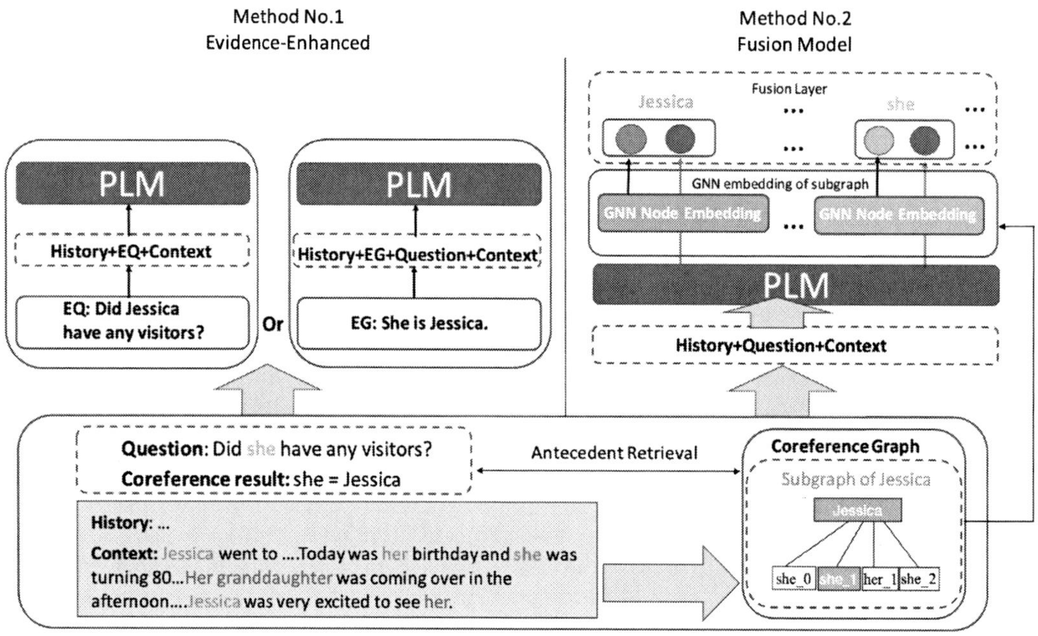

Figure 2: Overview of evidence-enhanced and fusion model. To answer current question, model should determine pronoun's referential entity through context or conversation history; graph-based coreference resolution can precisely determine dependency and add additional information to current question. Left part denotes textual level method of evidence-enhanced method. Right part denotes fusion model and fusion of PLM and graph embedding.

2 Background

2.1 Pre-trained Language Model

In recent years, the emergence of pre-trained language models (PLMs), including BERT (Devlin et al., 2019), GPT-2 (Radford et al., 2019), XLNET (Yang et al., 2019), and RoBERTa (Liu et al., 2019b), has refreshed the performance of various NLP tasks with advanced comprehension abilities. BERT is a representative model that is based on a multi-layer transformer (Vaswani et al., 2017). It is trained by using a massive amount of text data through a masked language model and next sentence prediction. There have been several improvements to the BERT model (Qiu et al., 2020), such as ConvBERT (Jiang et al., 2020), which specifically improves its performance in MRC. These PLM-based models mostly increase the scale of model parameters or improve the attention mechanism through their structure, but they still lack reasoning-level analysis and evidence support due to them using end-to-end learning methods (Chen and Yih, 2020).

2.2 Coreference Resolution

Coreference resolution is the task of retrieving all references in text that refer to the same entity. With the development of deep learning, the neural network has been gradually used to solve coreferencing, such as CoNLL-2012 (Pradhan et al., 2012), in recent years (Xu and Choi, 2020; Kirstain et al., 2021). Lee et al. (Lee et al., 2017) first applied the LSTM (Sak et al., 2014) network to coreference resolution; it can extract referential dependencies directly from text. Joshi (Joshi et al., 2019) provided a PLM baseline for coreference resolution through BERT. Joshi also provided SpanBERT Joshi et al. (2020), which enhanced the PLM's performance, especially in coreference extraction.

In this paper, we use AllenNLP Gardner et al. (2018)'s framework as an implementation of the approach by Lee et al.(Lee et al., 2017) with spanBERT for textual word embedding, and we achieve high-precision coreference extraction from a conversation history and article context.

2.3 Machine Reading Comprehension

Current machine reading comprehension (MRC) tasks can be classified into single-turn and multi-turn types, depending on whether the question-answering relies on the conversation history. To tackle single-turn MRC such as SQuAD (Rajpurkar et al., 2018), many models based on semantic matching have been proposed, such as BiDAF (Seo et al., 2017), DrQA (Chen et al., 2017), (Lin et al., 2018), QANet (Yu et al., 2018), and BERT (Devlin et al., 2019), for MRC.

However, for multi-turn MRC like CoQA (Reddy et al., 2019) and QuAC (Choi et al., 2018), conversation-based questions and answers are introduced to enhance the connection between questions (known as CMRC (Liu et al., 2019a)). The ambiguity of a question increases (Min et al., 2020) due to the addition of a conversation history. Thus, to predict the answer $\hat{A}_i$ for the current question Q_i, the model should not only have to comprehend the article context C but also the conversation history H_i from the beginning (Q_1, A_1) to the previous turn (Q_{i-1}, A_{i-1}) for integration.

$$H_i = \{Q_1, A_1, ..., Q_{i-1}, A_{i-1}\} \quad (1)$$

$$\hat{A}_i = argmax(P(A_i|Q_i, C, H_i)) \quad (2)$$

For multi-turn MRC, several works (Huang et al., 2019; Yeh and Chen, 2019; Qu et al., 2019; Song et al., 2018) have incorporated reasoning representation to capture a conversation history's embedding. In comparison, approaches like question rewriting (QR) (Papakonstantinou and Vassalos, 1999) aim to break down multi-turn MRC into single-turn subtasks to minimize the complexity of multi-turn MRC (Vakulenko et al., 2021). CANARD (Elgohary et al., 2019) rewrites QuAC's questions and introduces this rewriting to the QR task. QR models (Vakulenko et al., 2021; Lin et al., 2020) rewrite current questions to incorporate a conversation history. However, due to the variable length of a conversation history, such models still have limitations in precisely resolving the coreference in questions.

3 Propsed Methods

In this section, we describe the architecture of our methods as an enhanced PLM component, as illustrated in Figure 2. The model contains two stages. (1) We construct a coreference graph from textural information towards solving the pronoun's referential entity in a question. (2) We use our two methods, evidence-enhanced and the fusion model, to integrate a referential entity's information into PLMs using textual and structural levels, respectively.

3.1 Coreference Graph

Inspired by the previous works (Song et al., 2018; Bastings et al., 2017; Dhingra et al., 2018), we introduce graph structures for the anaphora in questions. Specifically, our method uses the approach by Lee et al. (Lee et al., 2017) with SpanBERT word embedding to precisely extract all coreferences in text and organize them into graph structures. Additionally, we propose modeling the conversation history and article context separately in structures to fully use the graph information.

In the article context part, because there may be multi-identical pronouns referring to different entities in a context (e.g., "he" could refer to two males in the same article context), the current sentence number (order number) is kept after entities to ensure their uniqueness. As shown in Figure 3 with different numbers. To organize the entities into a graph, all of the anaphors (pronouns) are connected to the initially-occurring antecedent (referential entity). In this way, the entire context can be processed into a graph with multiple clusters, and each cluster holds a unique referential entity, as illustrated in Figure 3 in different colors.

In the conversation history part, to avoid multi-identical pronouns, the Q_i label for the i-th question and A_i label for the i-th answer are added behind an entity in a conversation history. In the construction part, considering the time-sequence nature of a conversation history, we use a conversation history's order sequences $(Q_1, A_1, Q_2, A_2, ...)$ to connect these entities into a queue structure.

3.1.1 Coreference Graph Construction

As illustrated in Figure 3, this procedure can extract the coreference information from text into a coreference graph. First, we extract reference words with relevant number labels as referential entities. In this way, each reference word can be classified into various clusters (shown in different colors in the top half of Figure 3). In the graph construction of the article context part, we use the first referential entity in one cluster and the initially-occurring antecedent as the head node. We connect all the remaining referential entities in the cluster to the head node. For the conversation history part, we connect the referential entities in the cluster in a queue in the order sequence $(Q_1, A_1, Q_2, A_2, ...)$. Accordingly, this step is repeated for every cluster until each reference word has been processed into a graph structure as a unique entity.

3.1.2 Antecedent Retrieval

Antecedent retrieval is a process of querying the referential entity of a target pronoun through a coreference graph. For retrieval from an article context, the target pronoun and the sentence's order index are considered to form a query entity. When the node of the query entity is found, it is used as the starting node for a graph search until a non-pronoun entity is found as a referential entity for the result.

3.2 Method No.1: Evidence-Enhanced

We learned from previous studies (Zhou et al., 2019; Ding et al., 2019) that additional evidence is essential for a PLM's logical comprehension. Therefore, we present textual reformulation methods for resolving the referential dependency of current pronouns. As shown in Figure 2, after retrieving the referential entity ("she" refers to "Jessica"), the model needs to obtain this information for the current question Q_i. In PLMs like BERT (Devlin et al., 2019), the CMRC typically defines the model's input as the concatenation of three segments. Specifically, given a context C, the input for BERT is "**[CLS]**H_i**[SEP]**Qi**[SEP]**C." To ensure that new information is introduced with as little impact as possible for the PLM input, we propose two textual-level methods:

- **Evidence Generator (EG):** Generating inferential sentences to solve coreference on the basis of textual rules (like *"She" is "Jessica"*) and then adding the inferential sentence as evidence before the question. The input structure is "**[CLS]**H_i**[SEP]**EG_{Q_i}**[SEP]**Q_i**[SEP]**C."

- **Enhanced Question (EQ):** Reformulating a question by replacing the pronouns in the question with referential entities to create an enhanced question and replacing the enhanced question with the original one as input. The input structure is "**[CLS]**H_i**[SEP]**EQ_{Qi}**[SEP]**C."

3.3 Method No.2: Fusion Model

Inspired by Qiu et al. Qiu et al. (2019), we propose using the graph neural network to extract a coreference graph's features. We fuse these graph features with sequence features from the PLM to enhance the PLM's coreference reasoning ability.

3.3.1 Embeding Fusing

We want the model to learn both the graph and sequence features of an entity during computation. Additionally, we hope that the model can balance the two kinds of features by using learnable weights. Therefore, the final embedding $FinalEmb_k$ of all entities k in a coreference graph is calculated as follows ($[A:B]$ means to concatenate the two vectors A and B in a row, and $\odot$ means the Hadamard product).

$$w_k = ReLU(W \times [PLM_k : GNN_k]) \quad (3)$$

$$FinalEmb_k = w_k \odot PLM_k + (1 - w_k) \odot GNN_k \quad (4)$$

The computed final embedding is passed through the fully connection layer to compute the answer prediction for the current question.

4 Experiment Setup

4.1 Datasets Description

CoQA (Reddy et al., 2019) consists of 127K questions and answers from documents in 5 domains (Children, Literature, Middle& High School English Exams, CNN News, Wikipedia). The question-answering can be divided into extractive and non-extractive types (Niu et al., 2020). Similar to SQuAD, the extractive type selects a span from the context for the final answer to the question. The non-extractive type is defined as choices from Yes/No/Unknown for answering. We used two datasets to perform this experiment:

- **CoQA all:** The complete CoQA dataset.

- **CoQA pronoun-containing (38% of CoQA all):** Used to evaluate the model's performance in coreference resolution for anaphora. Samples in which questions contained pronouns from CoQA were extracted to form a partial dataset.

Compared with the evidence-enhanced method, the fusion model does not need the input of the model to be changed for learning. Therefore, we additionally used the CoQA-all dataset to evaluate the overall performance of the model.

All evaluations were conducted using the overall F1 score by using CoQA's official evaluation script[1].

[1] https://stanfordnlp.github.io/coqa/

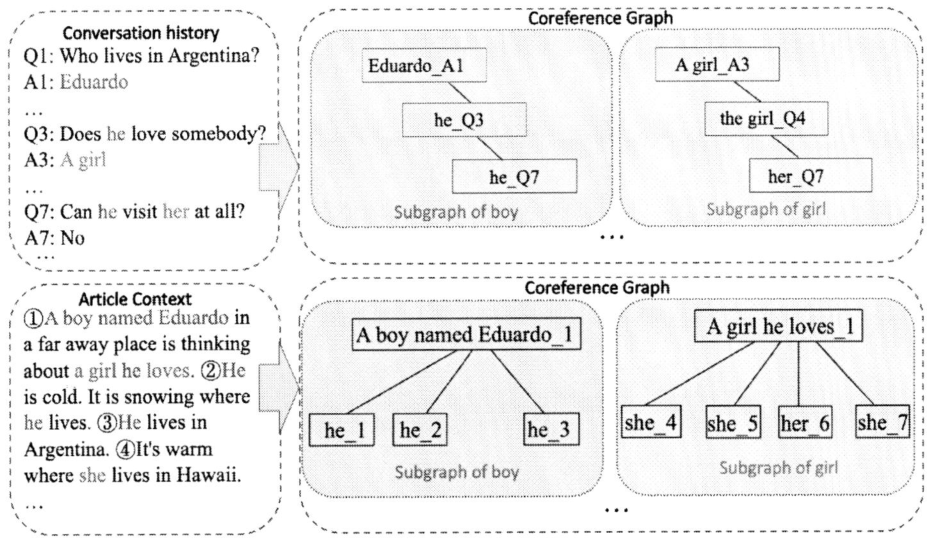

Figure 3: An example of converting conversation history and article context into the coreference graph. The same color represent entities has same referring entity, also in the same cluster as graph.

4.2 SpanBERT-based Coreference Extraction

We applied the coreference resolution model from AllenNLP[2]. This model adopts Lee et al. (Lee et al., 2017)'s approach to extracting the coreferences in clusters. Rather than using GloVe's word embedding in the initial model, SpanBERT (Joshi et al., 2020) for word embedding was used due to its superiority on the task of extraction.

4.3 Baseline of PLMs

4.3.1 BERT

Due to the multi-turn characteristic that CMRC retains compared with MRC tasks, the conversation history before Q_i should be considered as input into the model. In this experiment, a BERT-base-uncased (Devlin et al., 2019) fine-tuned by using all CoQA was used as our baseline model. It takes a concatenation of three segments as input (length of conversation history is 2). Specifically, given a context C, the input for BERT is [CLS]$(Q_{i-2}, A_{i-2}), (Q_{i-1}, A_{i-1})$[SEP]$Qi$[SEP]$C$, in which "[CLS]" is a classifier for "Yes/No/Unknown/Span" for CoQA's non-extractive questions.

4.3.2 RoBERTa

On the basis of BERT model's architecture, RoBERTa (Liu et al., 2019b) removes next sentence prediction and possesses better robustness through modifications and pre-training with larger data. RoBERTa can exceed almost all performances compared with the BERT model. In the experiment, we adopted a RoBERTa-base-uncased with the same training configuration as BERT. We found that RoBERTa achieves remarkable scores on the CoQA pronoun-containing dataset, which means that the capability RoBERTa holds towards coreference resolution is comparably higher than BERT accordingly.

4.4 GNN Embedding Algorithms

4.4.1 Graph Attention Networks

The graph attention network (GAT) (Velickovic et al., 2017) learns the structural features of graphs from the spatial domain through a multi-headed attention mechanism. In this experiment, we used PyTorch Geometric[3] as the implementation of GAT graph embedding, and the number of multi-heads was set to 8.

4.4.2 Graph Convolutional Network

The graph convolutional network (GCN) (Kipf and Welling, 2017) learns the structural features of graphs from convolution layers. It can be used to study the properties of a graph from the eigenvalues and eigenvectors of a Laplacian matrix. GCN has been successful in processing graph data by extracting structure-aware features. In this experiment, we

[2]https://demo.allennlp.org/coreference-resolution

[3]https://pytorch-geometric.readthedocs.io/en/latest/

Model	Approach	Child.	Liter.	M&H.	News	Wiki	Overall
		CoQA pronoun-containing dataset					
BERT-base	baseline	76.0	70.0	72.9	73.8	77.7	73.9
	+QR	60.7	66.1	69.0	70.2	73.6	69.7
	+Hist.+EG	75.2	72.0	75.4	76.2	**81.1**	75.7
	+Hist.+EQ	76.1	74.0	**76.2**	**76.9**	80.0	**76.5**
	+Cont.+EG	**77.8**	72.6	**76.2**	76.1	80.3	76.4
	+Cont.+EQ	75.8	72.7	74.2	75.3	80.7	75.5
	+Hist.&Cont.+EG	77.1	**74.8**	75.0	76.0	81.0	**76.5**
	+Hist.&Cont.+EQ	76.8	72.4	75.2	75.3	79.2	75.6
RoBERTa-base	baseline	82.5	80.0	81.6	83.1	84.1	82.1
	+Hist.+EQ	80.9	77.9	81.2	80.5	84.7	80.8
	+Hist.&Cont.+EG	82.4	**80.4**	81.1	83.4	84.4	82.2
	+Hist.&Cont.+GCN	**83.5**	**80.4**	81.5	**83.7**	**85.9**	**82.8**
	+Hist.&Cont.+GAT	83.0	79.7	**82.6**	82.9	85.4	82.6
		CoQA all					
RoBERTa-base	baseline	81.1	79.3	80.4	82.8	83.9	81.5
	+Hist.&Cont.+GCN	**82.3**	**80.0**	80.4	**84.2**	**84.6**	**82.3**
	+Hist.&Cont.+GAT	81.0	79.2	**80.7**	82.9	84.5	81.7

Table 1: Comparison of baseline method with QR model, evidence-enhanced method and fusion model for CoQA. "EG" and "EQ" denote evidence generator and enhanced question, respectively. For coreference graph in antecedent retrieval, "Hist." denotes using conversation history part, "Cont." denotes using article content part, "Hist.&Cont." denotes using both. "GCN" and "GAT" denote fusion model using graph embedding algorithms of GCN and GAT, respectively.

used PyTorch Geometric as the implementation of GCN graph embedding.

4.4.3 Initialization

For all nodes contained in the coreference graph, we initialize the node features using embeddings at the token level E_i generated through PLM. Here, we compute the average value for each node feature F_i for initialization. e.g.. the node "the girl" is composed of two tokens, "the" and "girl," and node feature $F_{the:girl}$ for initialization can be calculated as follows.

$$F_{the:girl} = \frac{1}{2}(E_{the} + E_{girl}) \tag{5}$$

4.5 Details

All experiments were implemented on PyTorch [4]. BERT and RoBERTa were implemented by using the Huggingface Transformers library [5]. The approach by Lee et al. (Lee et al., 2017) was implemented through the pre-trained model "coref-spanbert-large" from AllenNLP. We used three 11-GB GPUs (GTX 1080Ti), a batch size of 24 for BERT, and a batch size of 10 for RoBERTa in all experiments.

BERT and RoBERTa were utilized as our baseline, represent the basic and advanced PLMs respectively. To compare our approaches with others, we applied Question Rewriting (QR) model (Lin et al., 2020) using T5 (Raffel et al., 2020), trained on CANARD (Elgohary et al., 2019). To identify the effectiveness of coreference graph, we proposed to use information from different parts of coreference graph as comparisons.

5 Results & Analysis

The results are shown in Table 1, which presents a performance comparison of the baseline approaches, end-to-end QR, and our proposed methods integrated with different parts of the coreference graph. We can see that compared with the baselines, both the evidence-enhanced method and fusion model method improved the model's performance in different categories (Child., Liter., M&H., News, Wiki, and Overall).

Specifically, the combination of the EG with the coreference graph (Hist.& Cont.) improved the overall F1 score by 2.6 on the BERT baseline and

[4]https://pytorch.org/

[5]https://huggingface.co/docs/transformers/index

BERT-base				
Baseline	Our EG	F1>0	F1 ≥0.5	F1=1
False	False	342	503	997
True	False	145	175	180
False	True	219	263	244
True	True	2356	2121	1641
Total: 3062				

Table 2: Analysis of results for all answers for CoQA pronoun-containing test dataset (3062 samples in total). Comparison of baseline BERT with our best EG method "BERT+ EG + Hist.&Cont." "True" and "False" indicate whether each answer produced by QA model was correct or incorrect, respectively, in accordance with F1 thresholds provided in right-side columns.

by 0.1 on the RoBERTa baseline. Therefore, we concluded that while dealing with anaphora's coreference resolution, both the EG and EQ were effective as enhanced components of the PLM baseline model with BERT.

Comparing EG and EQ approaches comprehensively for BERT and RoBERTa, the EG one had generally higher scores. One possible reason is that generating additional evidence behind a question as input maintains the integrity of the original question. Although the EQ approach also achieved relevant performance, the textual substitution of pronouns may alter the intention of the question and mislead the model to make erroneous answer predictions.

To measure the effectiveness of the evidence-enhanced approach for each question, we compared the F1 scores of the answers produced by the baseline (BERT) and our evidence-enhanced model with the best performance ("EG+hist.&cont.," as shown in Table 2). "True" and "False" indicate whether the answer predicted by the model was correct or incorrect, in accordance with the F1 thresholds provided in the right-side columns. As shown in Table 2, the second row reflects the case where our model got an erroneous answer when the baseline's answer was correct, which can be interpreted as getting an erroneous referential entity of the target pronoun, thus leading to an erroneous prediction. The third row indicates that the answer of our model was correct and that of the baseline's was wrong. Compared with the second row, the third row shows the effectiveness of our model: introducing the correct referential entity and enhancing the model to output the correct answer. Additionally, in the third row, with the rise of the F1 threshold, the number increased from F1 >0 to F1 ≥ 0.5, which means that our model slightly corrected the baseline's answer from completely wrong into closer to correct. However, from the decline from F1 ≥ 0.5 to F1 $=1$, we can infer that our model still has limitations in making fully correct answer predictions.

From the results for the fusion model, we found that the fusion model achieved a further improvement (by up to 0.7 on RoBERTa) compared with the baseline and evidence-enhanced methods. This model also showed improvement on the CoQA-all dataset, which contains samples that are not needed for coreference resolution (without pronouns in questions), compared with the baseline. This indicates that the fusion model can effectively use coreference graph information. It can solve coreference resolution and maintain the ability to solve no-coreference questions. Therefore, compared with the evidence-enhanced approach, the fusion model has higher robustness.

Through comparing the two different graph embedding methods, GAT and GCN, we found that GCN generally outperformed GAT in terms of score in each category. We assume one reason is that the processed graphs always hold the same structure (a vertex containing multiple one-hop neighbor nodes), and such a simple structure is not adequately learned by GAT's multi-head attention, which is suitable for capturing features from the spatial domain. In contrast, GCN captures the graph features of each neighbor by using convolution layers, so it performed better in this experiment.

6 Case Study

We investigated how our approaches improve the coreference reasoning ability of the RoBERTa baseline approach. To compare the differences in answer prediction, we used RoBERTa-base as the baseline. RoBERTa-base + Hist.&Cont. + EG had the best performance in Table 1 as the evidence generator (EG), and RoBERTa-base + FusionMd.(+GCN) had the best performance as the fusion model. We selected several specific cases from CoQA for elaboration.

An example is shown in Figure 4. In this example, the coreference graph resolves that "he" refers to "Joseph Aloisius Ratzinger." Because of the absence of coreference resolution, the baseline incorrectly predicted the answer at the wrong place.

#Example
Article context C:
...Ratzinger established himself as a highly regarded university theologian by the late 1950s and was appointed a full professor in 1958...
Conversation History H_i:
...
Q_{i-1}: Did he have a lot of experience as a pastor?
A_{i-1}: No.
Current Question Q_i: What was his occupation immediately preceding his papacy?
Resolution in coreference graph:
his = Joseph Aloisius Ratzinger
Answer prediction:
Fusion model: Theologian.
Evidence-Enhanced: Academic and professor of theology.
Baseline: A major figure on the Vatican stage.
Gold answer: Theologian.

Figure 4: Answer predictions from different CMRC models.

EG resolved the referential dependencies, so the prediction's meaning was close to the correct answer. However, the fusion model could integrate the coreference information and predict the answer span accurately.

7 Conclusion

In this paper, we proposed the coreference graph, which can integrate coreferences from text into a graph structure. To use the information retrieved from a coreference graph, we introduced the evidence-enhanced method, which comprises two textual-level coreference resolution approaches to leverage BERT's performance on CMRC. However, the results showed that the improvement for RoBERTa is still limited. Therefore, we proposed the fusion model, using graph neural networks to incorporate the coreference graph into PLM structure. In comparison with the baseline and evidence-enhanced methods, the fusion model showed further improvement on RoBERTa, maintaining relatively higher robustness when learning coreference resolution. We confirmed that in conversational reading comprehension, a graph-structured representation of the article context and conversational history can both be an information supplement for answering a current question, especially with different PLMs. Rather than the end-to-end method in PLMs, our approaches can generate readable text as evidence when answering a question, which strengthens the interpretability of PLMs.

References

Jasmijn Bastings, Ivan Titov, Wilker Aziz, Diego Marcheggiani, and Khalil Sima'an. 2017. Graph convolutional encoders for syntax-aware neural machine translation. In *Proceedings of the 2017 Conference on Empirical Methods in Natural Language Processing, EMNLP 2017, Copenhagen, Denmark, September 9-11, 2017*, pages 1957–1967. Association for Computational Linguistics.

Danqi Chen, Adam Fisch, Jason Weston, and Antoine Bordes. 2017. Reading Wikipedia to answer open-domain questions. In *Proceedings of the 55th Annual Meeting of the Association for Computational Linguistics (Volume 1: Long Papers)*, pages 1870–1879, Vancouver, Canada. Association for Computational Linguistics.

Danqi Chen and Wen-tau Yih. 2020. Open-domain question answering. In *Proceedings of the 58th Annual Meeting of the Association for Computational Linguistics: Tutorial Abstracts*, pages 34–37, Online. Association for Computational Linguistics.

Eunsol Choi, He He, Mohit Iyyer, Mark Yatskar, Wen-tau Yih, Yejin Choi, Percy Liang, and Luke Zettlemoyer. 2018. QuAC: Question answering in context. In *Proceedings of the 2018 Conference on Empirical Methods in Natural Language Processing*, pages 2174–2184, Brussels, Belgium. Association for Computational Linguistics.

Jacob Devlin, Ming-Wei Chang, Kenton Lee, and Kristina Toutanova. 2019. BERT: Pre-training of deep bidirectional transformers for language understanding. In *Proceedings of the 2019 Conference of the North American Chapter of the Association for Computational Linguistics: Human Language Technologies, Volume 1 (Long and Short Papers)*, pages 4171–4186, Minneapolis, Minnesota. Association for Computational Linguistics.

Bhuwan Dhingra, Qiao Jin, Zhilin Yang, William W. Cohen, and Ruslan Salakhutdinov. 2018. Neural models for reasoning over multiple mentions using coreference. In *Proceedings of the 2018 Conference of the North American Chapter of the Association for Computational Linguistics: Human Language Technologies, NAACL-HLT, New Orleans, Louisiana, USA, June 1-6, 2018, Volume 2 (Short Papers)*, pages 42–48. Association for Computational Linguistics.

Ming Ding, Chang Zhou, Qibin Chen, Hongxia Yang, and Jie Tang. 2019. Cognitive graph for multi-hop reading comprehension at scale. In *Proceedings of the 57th Annual Meeting of the Association for Computational Linguistics*, pages 2694–2703, Florence, Italy. Association for Computational Linguistics.

Ahmed Elgohary, Denis Peskov, and Jordan L. Boyd-Graber. 2019. Can you unpack that? learning to rewrite questions-in-context. In *Proceedings of the 2019 Conference on Empirical Methods in Natural Language Processing and the 9th International Joint Conference on Natural Language Processing, EMNLP-IJCNLP 2019, Hong Kong, China, November 3-7, 2019*, pages 5917–5923. Association for Computational Linguistics.

Matt Gardner, Joel Grus, Mark Neumann, Oyvind Tafjord, Pradeep Dasigi, Nelson F. Liu, Matthew Peters, Michael Schmitz, and Luke Zettlemoyer. 2018. AllenNLP: A deep semantic natural language processing platform. In *Proceedings of Workshop for NLP Open Source Software (NLP-OSS)*, pages 1–6, Melbourne, Australia. Association for Computational Linguistics.

Hsin-Yuan Huang, Eunsol Choi, and Wen-tau Yih. 2019. Flowqa: Grasping flow in history for conversational machine comprehension. In *7th International Conference on Learning Representations, ICLR 2019, New Orleans, LA, USA, May 6-9, 2019*. OpenReview.net.

Zihang Jiang, Weihao Yu, Daquan Zhou, Yunpeng Chen, Jiashi Feng, and Shuicheng Yan. 2020. Convbert: Improving bert with span-based dynamic convolution. In *Advances in Neural Information Processing Systems 33: Annual Conference on Neural Information Processing Systems 2020, NeurIPS 2020, December 6-12, 2020, virtual*.

Mandar Joshi, Danqi Chen, Yinhan Liu, Daniel S. Weld, Luke Zettlemoyer, and Omer Levy. 2020. SpanBERT: Improving pre-training by representing and predicting spans. *Transactions of the Association for Computational Linguistics*, 8:64–77.

Mandar Joshi, Omer Levy, Luke Zettlemoyer, and Daniel S. Weld. 2019. BERT for coreference resolution: Baselines and analysis. In *Proceedings of the 2019 Conference on Empirical Methods in Natural Language Processing and the 9th International Joint Conference on Natural Language Processing, EMNLP-IJCNLP 2019, Hong Kong, China, November 3-7, 2019*, pages 5802–5807. Association for Computational Linguistics.

Thomas N. Kipf and Max Welling. 2017. Semi-supervised classification with graph convolutional networks. In *5th International Conference on Learning Representations, ICLR 2017, Toulon, France, April 24-26, 2017, Conference Track Proceedings*. OpenReview.net.

Yuval Kirstain, Ori Ram, and Omer Levy. 2021. Coreference resolution without span representations. In *Proceedings of the 59th Annual Meeting of the Association for Computational Linguistics and the 11th International Joint Conference on Natural Language Processing, ACL/IJCNLP 2021, (Volume 2: Short Papers), Virtual Event, August 1-6, 2021*, pages 14–19. Association for Computational Linguistics.

Kenton Lee, Luheng He, Mike Lewis, and Luke Zettlemoyer. 2017. End-to-end neural coreference resolution. In *Proceedings of the 2017 Conference on Empirical Methods in Natural Language Processing, EMNLP 2017, Copenhagen, Denmark, September 9-11, 2017*, pages 188–197. Association for Computational Linguistics.

Sheng-Chieh Lin, Jheng-Hong Yang, Rodrigo Nogueira, Ming-Feng Tsai, Chuan-Ju Wang, and Jimmy Lin. 2020. Conversational question reformulation via sequence-to-sequence architectures and pretrained language models. *CoRR*, abs/2004.01909.

Yankai Lin, Haozhe Ji, Zhiyuan Liu, and Maosong Sun. 2018. Denoising distantly supervised open-domain question answering. In *Proceedings of the 56th Annual Meeting of the Association for Computational Linguistics (Volume 1: Long Papers)*, pages 1736–1745.

Shanshan Liu, Xin Zhang, Sheng Zhang, Hui Wang, and Weiming Zhang. 2019a. Neural machine reading comprehension: Methods and trends. *Applied Sciences*, 9(18):3698.

Yinhan Liu, Myle Ott, Naman Goyal, Jingfei Du, Mandar Joshi, Danqi Chen, Omer Levy, Mike Lewis, Luke Zettlemoyer, and Veselin Stoyanov. 2019b. Roberta: A robustly optimized BERT pretraining approach. *CoRR*, abs/1907.11692.

Sewon Min, Julian Michael, Hannaneh Hajishirzi, and Luke Zettlemoyer. 2020. Ambigqa: Answering ambiguous open-domain questions. In *Proceedings of the 2020 Conference on Empirical Methods in Natural Language Processing, EMNLP 2020, Online, November 16-20, 2020*, pages 5783–5797. Association for Computational Linguistics.

Yilin Niu, Fangkai Jiao, Mantong Zhou, Ting Yao, Jingfang Xu, and Minlie Huang. 2020. A self-training method for machine reading comprehension with soft evidence extraction. In *Proceedings of the 58th Annual Meeting of the Association for Computational Linguistics*, pages 3916–3927. Association for Computational Linguistics.

Yannis Papakonstantinou and Vasilis Vassalos. 1999. Query rewriting for semistructured data. *ACM SIGMOD Record*, 28(2):455–466.

Sameer Pradhan, Alessandro Moschitti, Nianwen Xue, Olga Uryupina, and Yuchen Zhang. 2012. CoNLL-2012 shared task: Modeling multilingual unrestricted coreference in OntoNotes. In *Joint Conference on EMNLP and CoNLL - Shared Task*, pages 1–40, Jeju Island, Korea. Association for Computational Linguistics.

Delai Qiu, Yuanzhe Zhang, Xinwei Feng, Xiangwen Liao, Wenbin Jiang, Yajuan Lyu, Kang Liu, and Jun Zhao. 2019. Machine reading comprehension using structural knowledge graph-aware network. In *Proceedings of the 2019 Conference on Empirical Methods in Natural Language Processing and the 9th International Joint Conference on Natural Language Processing (EMNLP-IJCNLP)*, pages 5896–5901, Hong Kong, China. Association for Computational Linguistics.

XiPeng Qiu, TianXiang Sun, YiGe Xu, YunFan Shao, Ning Dai, and XuanJing Huang. 2020. Pre-trained models for natural language processing: A survey. *Science China Technological Sciences*, 63(10):1872–1897.

Chen Qu, Liu Yang, Minghui Qiu, W Bruce Croft, Yongfeng Zhang, and Mohit Iyyer. 2019. Bert with history answer embedding for conversational question answering. In *Proceedings of the 42nd international ACM SIGIR conference on research and development in information retrieval*, pages 1133–1136.

Alec Radford, Jeffrey Wu, Rewon Child, David Luan, Dario Amodei, Ilya Sutskever, et al. 2019. Language models are unsupervised multitask learners. *OpenAI blog*, 1(8):9.

Colin Raffel, Noam Shazeer, Adam Roberts, Katherine Lee, Sharan Narang, Michael Matena, Yanqi Zhou, Wei Li, and Peter J. Liu. 2020. Exploring the limits of transfer learning with a unified text-to-text transformer. *J. Mach. Learn. Res.*, 21:140:1–140:67.

Pranav Rajpurkar, Robin Jia, and Percy Liang. 2018. Know what you don't know: Unanswerable questions for SQuAD. In *Proceedings of the 56th Annual Meeting of the Association for Computational Linguistics (Volume 2: Short Papers)*, pages 784–789, Melbourne, Australia. Association for Computational Linguistics.

Siva Reddy, Danqi Chen, and Christopher D. Manning. 2019. Coqa: A conversational question answering challenge. *Transactions of the Association for Computational Linguistics*, 7:249–266.

Hasim Sak, Andrew W. Senior, and Françoise Beaufays. 2014. Long short-term memory recurrent neural network architectures for large scale acoustic modeling. In *INTERSPEECH 2014, 15th Annual Conference of the International Speech Communication Association, Singapore, September 14-18, 2014*, pages 338–342. ISCA.

Min Joon Seo, Aniruddha Kembhavi, Ali Farhadi, and Hannaneh Hajishirzi. 2017. Bidirectional attention flow for machine comprehension. In *5th International Conference on Learning Representations, ICLR 2017, Toulon, France, April 24-26, 2017, Conference Track Proceedings*. OpenReview.net.

Linfeng Song, Zhiguo Wang, Mo Yu, Yue Zhang, Radu Florian, and Daniel Gildea. 2018. Exploring graph-structured passage representation for multihop reading comprehension with graph neural networks. *CoRR*, abs/1809.02040.

Svitlana Vakulenko, Shayne Longpre, Zhucheng Tu, and Raviteja Anantha. 2021. Question rewriting for conversational question answering. In *Proceedings of the 14th ACM International Conference on Web Search and Data Mining*, pages 355–363.

Ashish Vaswani, Noam Shazeer, Niki Parmar, Jakob Uszkoreit, Llion Jones, Aidan N Gomez, Łukasz Kaiser, and Illia Polosukhin. 2017. Attention is all you need. In *Advances in neural information processing systems*, pages 5998–6008.

Petar Velickovic, Guillem Cucurull, Arantxa Casanova, Adriana Romero, Pietro Lio, and Yoshua Bengio. 2017. Graph attention networks. *stat*, 1050:20.

HK von Heusinger and Urs Egli. 2012. *Reference and anaphoric relations*, volume 72. Springer Science & Business Media.

Liyan Xu and Jinho D. Choi. 2020. Revealing the myth of higher-order inference in coreference resolution. In *Proceedings of the 2020 Conference on Empirical Methods in Natural Language Processing, EMNLP 2020, Online, November 16-20, 2020*, pages 8527–8533. Association for Computational Linguistics.

Zhilin Yang, Zihang Dai, Yiming Yang, Jaime Carbonell, Russ R Salakhutdinov, and Quoc V Le. 2019. Xlnet: Generalized autoregressive pretraining for language understanding. *Advances in neural information processing systems*, 32.

Yi-Ting Yeh and Yun-Nung Chen. 2019. Flowdelta: Modeling flow information gain in reasoning for conversational machine comprehension. In *Proceedings of the 2nd Workshop on Machine Reading for Question Answering, MRQA@EMNLP 2019, Hong Kong, China, November 4, 2019*, pages 86–90. Association for Computational Linguistics.

Adams Wei Yu, David Dohan, Minh-Thang Luong, Rui Zhao, Kai Chen, Mohammad Norouzi, and Quoc V. Le. 2018. Qanet: Combining local convolution with global self-attention for reading comprehension. In *6th International Conference on Learning Representations, ICLR 2018, Vancouver, BC, Canada, April 30 - May 3, 2018, Conference Track Proceedings*. OpenReview.net.

Jie Zhou, Xu Han, Cheng Yang, Zhiyuan Liu, Lifeng Wang, Changcheng Li, and Maosong Sun. 2019. GEAR: graph-based evidence aggregating and reasoning for fact verification. In *Proceedings of the 57th Conference of the Association for Computational Linguistics, ACL 2019, Florence, Italy, July 28- August 2, 2019, Volume 1: Long Papers*, pages 892–901. Association for Computational Linguistics.

Construction of Hierarchical Structured Knowledge-based Recommendation Dialogue Dataset and Dialogue System

Takashi Kodama, Ribeka Tanaka,* Sadao Kurohashi
Graduate School of Informatics, Kyoto University
Yoshida-honmachi, Sakyo-ku, Kyoto, 606-8501, Japan
{kodama, kuro}@nlp.ist.i.kyoto-u.ac.jp

Abstract

We work on a recommendation dialogue system to help a user understand the appealing points of some target (e.g., a movie). In such dialogues, the recommendation system needs to utilize structured external knowledge to make informative and detailed recommendations. However, there is no dialogue dataset with structured external knowledge designed to make detailed recommendations for the target. Therefore, we construct a dialogue dataset, Japanese Movie Recommendation Dialogue (JMRD), in which the recommender recommends one movie in a long dialogue (23 turns on average). The external knowledge used in this dataset is hierarchically structured, including title, casts, reviews, and plots. Every recommender's utterance is associated with the external knowledge related to the utterance. We then create a movie recommendation dialogue system that considers the structure of the external knowledge and the history of the knowledge used. Experimental results show that the proposed model is superior in knowledge selection to the baseline models.

1 Introduction

In recent years, research on recommendation dialogue systems, which systems recommend something to users through dialogues, has attracted much attention. Here, we focus on movie recommendations. A recommendation dialogue consists of two phases: (1) the user's preferences are elicited, and a movie is selected from several candidates, and (2) in-depth information is provided for the selected movie. We focus on the latter phase in this study.

To provide in-depth information, the use of external knowledge is crucial. There has been much research on incorporating external knowledge in dialogue, and many kinds of knowledge-grounded dialogue datasets have been proposed (Dinan et al., 2019; Liu et al., 2020). These datasets often use plain texts or knowledge graphs as external knowledge. If the hierarchically structured knowledge is available in recommendation dialogues, it allows for more appropriate knowledge selection and informative response generation. However, there is no dialogue dataset with hierarchically structured knowledge to provide rich information for a single target (e.g., a movie).

To address the aforementioned problem, we propose a dialogue dataset, Japanese Movie Recommendation Dialogue (**JMRD**), in which recommendation dialogues are paired with the corresponding external knowledge. This dialogue dataset consists of about 5,200 dialogues between crowd workers. Each dialogue has 23 turns on average. We can say that our dataset provides in-depth movie recommendations utilizing various knowledge about a movie, with relatively a large number of dialogue turns. Specifically, as shown in Figure 1, one speaker (recommender) recommends a movie to the other speaker (seeker). Only the recommenders can have access to the knowledge about the movie, and they should use the external knowledge as much as possible in their utterances. The recommenders are asked to annotate the knowledge they used when sending their utterance. This procedure enables us to associate every recommenders' utterances with the corresponding external knowledge. The external knowledge is hierarchically structured into knowledge types common to all movies (e.g., "Title", "Released Year") and giving knowledge contents for each movie (e.g., "Rise of Planet of the Apes", "August 5, 2011").

We also propose a strong baseline model for the constructed dataset. This model considers the history of knowledge types/contents, noting that the order in which each piece of knowledge is used is essential in recommendation dialogues. The exper-

*Currently affiliated with Ochanomizu University, 2-1-1 Otsuka, Bunkyo-ku, Tokyo, 112-8610, Japan (E-mail: tanaka.ribeka@is.ocha.ac.jp).

Proceedings of the Second DialDoc Workshop on Document-grounded Dialogue and Conversational Question Answering, pages 83 - 92
May 26, 2022 ©2022 Association for Computational Linguistics

imental results show that our proposed model can select appropriate knowledge with higher accuracy than the baseline method.

Our contributions are three-fold.

- We construct a movie recommendation dialogue dataset associated with hierarchically structured external knowledge.
- We propose a strong baseline model, which selects knowledge based on hierarchically structured knowledge, for our dataset.
- To the best of our knowledge, we are the first to construct a human-to-human dialogue dataset based on external knowledge in Japanese.

2 Related Work

Recommendation dialogue has long attracted attention. However, most of them are goal-oriented dialogues in which the user's preferences are elicited from multiple recommendation candidates, and a recommendation target is decided according to that preferences (Bordes et al., 2017; Li et al., 2018). Li et al. (2018) propose REDIAL, a human-to-human movie recommendation dialogue dataset. The recommender presents several movies in one dialogue while inquiring about the seeker's preferences. Kang et al. (2019) collect GoRecDial dataset in a gamified setting where experts decide on a movie similar to the seekers' preference among a small set of movies (= five movies) in a minimal number of turns. OpenDialKG (Moon et al., 2019) is a recommendation and chit-chat dataset linking open-ended dialogues to knowledge graphs. In this study, we focus on the recommendation dialogue, which provides in-depth information about a movie rather than deciding which movie to recommend.

Research on the knowledge-grounded dialogue has also been growing in the last few years. Zhou et al. (2018) collect a human-to-human chit-chat dialogue dataset by utilizing Wikipedia articles of 30 famous movies. This dataset is unique in that it has two dialogue settings: either only one of the participants can see the knowledge, or both of them can see it. Moghe et al. (2018) also collect chit-chat dialogues about movies based on multiple types of knowledge: plot, review, Reddit comments, and fact table. Wizard of Wikipedia (Dinan et al., 2019) is an open-domain chit-chat dialogue dataset based on Wikipedia articles on 1,365 topics. It has become a standard benchmark in this research field. Su et al. (2020) collect a large Chinese chit-chat dialogue dataset (246,141 dialogues with 3,010,650 turns) about movies. Other dialogue datasets with external knowledge in Chinese are DuConv (Wu et al., 2019), KdConv (Zhou et al., 2020), and DuRecDial (Liu et al., 2020). DuConv (Wu et al., 2019) combines dialogues with knowledge graphs to track the progress of the dialogue topic. KdConv (Zhou et al., 2020) is also a chit-chat dialogue corpus that consists of relatively long dialogues to allow deep discussions in multiple domains (movies, music, and travel). Liu et al. (2020) focus on multiple dialogue types (e.g., QA, chit-chat, recommendation) and collect a multi-domain dialogue dataset associated with a knowledge graph. Compared to these studies, our work differs in that it uses hierarchically structured knowledge that contains both factoid (e.g., title) and non-factoid (e.g., review) information to make recommendations.

3 Japanese Movie Recommendation Dialogue

We choose movies as the domain for the recommendation dialogue because movies are interesting to everyone and facilitate smooth dialogue. In addition, movie recommendation dialogue is open-domain in nature according to the variety of movie topics, and it is a preferable property for NLP research. In this section, we explain the construction method of the JMRD.

3.1 External Knowledge Collection

The external knowledge is mainly collected from web texts such as Wikipedia. First, we select 261 movies based on the box-office revenue ranking. [1] For each of these movies, we collect movie information as external knowledge.

The external knowledge consists of seven knowledge types: title, released year, director, cast, genre, review, and plot, as shown in Figure 1. The title, released year, director, cast, and plot are extracted from the Wikipedia article of each movie (we allow at most one director and two casts). For the director and the casts, a brief description is also extracted from the first paragraph of each person's Wikipedia article. For the genre, we use the genre classification of Yahoo! Movies. [2] Reviews are collected

[1] http://www.eiren.org/toukei/index.html

[2] https://movies.yahoo.co.jp/

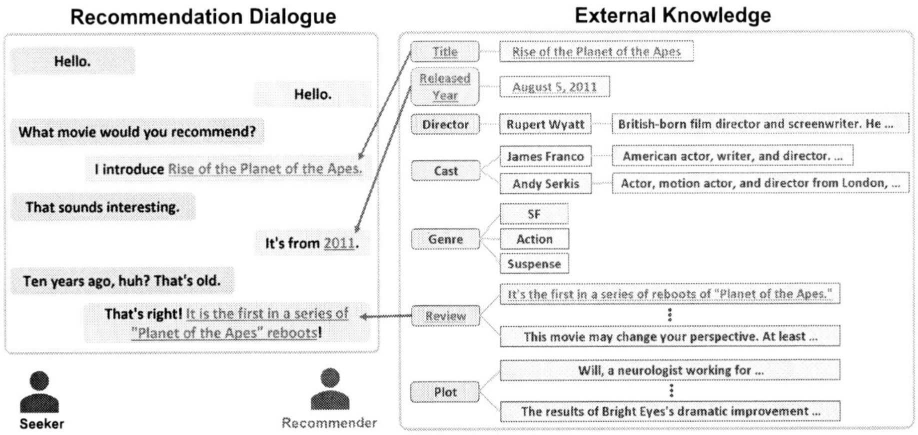

Figure 1: An example of JMRD dataset. The underlined parts of the external knowledge indicate the knowledge items used in the dialogue.

by crowdsourcing using Yahoo! Crowdsourcing. [3] Each worker selects a movie that he or she has seen from a list of 261 movies and writes down three recommendations for the selected movie. As a result, we collected an average of 16.5 reviews per movie.

We split the plot into sentences and present only the first ten sentences (or all sentences if fewer than ten) to reduce the burden of the recommender. Besides, we use the reviews written by the workers as it is, without splitting the sentences. We randomly selected five reviews between 15 and 80 characters long for each movie from the collected reviews. Those five reviews are used as the reviews for that movie.

3.2 Dialogue Collection

3.2.1 Settings

The two workers engaging in the movie recommendation dialogue have different roles: one is the **recommender**, and the other is the **seeker**. The flow of the dialogue takes place as follows:

1. Either the recommender or seeker can initialize the conversation.

2. The recommender decides which movie to recommend from the movie list. The recommender can choose a movie he or she wants to recommend or a movie that matches the seeker's preference obtained from a few message exchanges. The recommender can access the movie knowledge after deciding the movie to recommend. On the other hand, the seeker is only shown the chat screen and cannot access knowledge about the movie.

3. The recommender is instructed to use the presented knowledge as much as possible to recommend the movie. When the recommender sends their utterance, they must select the knowledge referred to by the utterance (multiple selection is allowed). For the utterance that does not use any knowledge, such as greetings, the recommender can select the "no knowledge" option.

4. The seeker is only instructed to enjoy and learn more about the recommended movie, and they can talk freely. This instruction refers to that of Wizard of Wikipedia (Dinan et al., 2019).

5. The dialogue lasts at least 20 turns after the movie is selected and can be terminated after 20 turns.

3.2.2 Dialogue Collection System

ParlAI (Miller et al., 2017) is a framework for collecting real-time chats in crowdsourcing. However, it is not easy to perform Japanese tasks with the Amazon Mechanical Turk used in ParlAI. Therefore, we build a new framework for dialogue collection, which incorporates crowdsourcing services where more native Japanese speakers can be gathered. In our framework, when workers access the specified URL for dialogue collection, pair match-

[3]https://crowdsourcing.yahoo.co.jp/

# dialogues	5,166
# utterances (R)	57,714
# utterances (S)	59,160
# movies	261
# workers	322
Avg. # turns per dialogue	22.6
Avg. # words per utterance (R)	23.8
Avg. # words per utterance (S)	6.9
Avg. # knowledge used per utterance	1.3
Avg. # knowledge used per dialogue	10.8

Table 1: Statistics of JMRD. R and S denote recommender and seeker respectively. We use Juman++ (Tolmachev et al., 2020) for word segmentation.

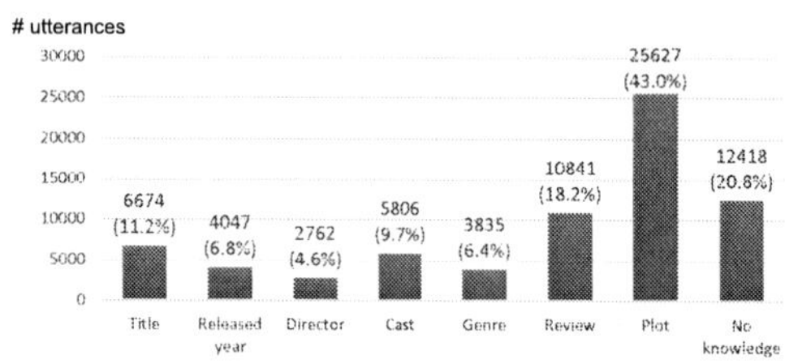

Figure 2: Distribution of external knowledge used.

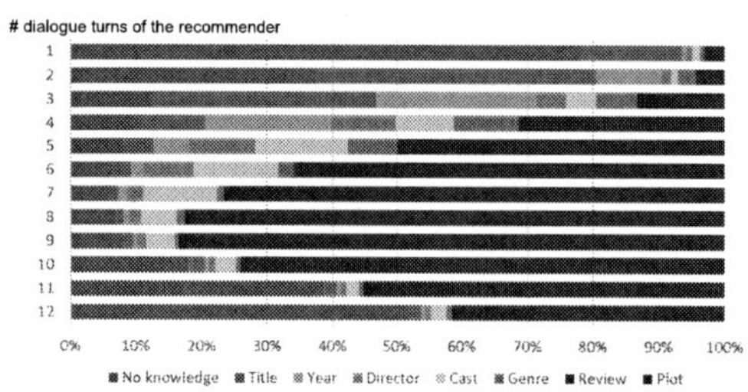

Figure 3: Distribution of external knowledge used in each dialogue turn of the recommender. The information up to turn 12 is shown here.

ing is performed, and a chat room is created for the worker to interact in real-time.

3.2.3 Statistics

The statistics are shown in Table 1. Our dataset consists of 5,166 dialogues with 116,874 turns. The average number of words per utterance of the recommender is more than three times larger than that of the seeker. It is probably because the recommender needs to talk more than the seeker to provide information to recommend a movie. The average number of knowledge items per utterance is 1.3, and the recommender tends to mention each knowledge item separately. There were on average 10.8 different types of knowledge used per dialogue, indicating that we could collect dialogues with various types of external knowledge.

	Q1	Q2	Q3	Q4	Q5
Recommender	4.36	4.00	3.94	4.01	-
Seeker	4.26	3.83	2.72	-	3.82

Table 2: Results of the questionnaire.

Figure 2 shows the distribution of the knowledge types used. The number of utterances that did not use any knowledge was only about 20% of the total, indicating that most utterances use some kind of external knowledge. In addition, non-factoid texts such as reviews and plots tend to be used more frequently.

Furthermore, Figure 3 shows the distribution of the knowledge used in each dialogue turn of the recommender. In the early part of the dialogue, there are many utterances without knowledge, such as greetings or utterances that mention the title. The recommenders often use factoid information such as released year, director, and cast in the middle of the dialogue. In the later part, non-factoid information such as reviews and plots are often used to convey specific content. In addition, after ten turns, the percentage of "No knowledge" increased again, as more generic recommendations such as "please check it out" are used. As can be seen from this analysis, our dataset is capable of analyzing human recommendation strategies.

3.2.4 Post-task Questionnaire

We ask the dialogue participants to answer the following post-task questionnaire in some of the collected dialogues (= 4,410 dialogues).

Q1: Do you like movies?

Q2: Did you enjoy the dialogue?

Q3: Do you know the movie you recommended (or that was recommended to you)?

Q4: Do you think you have recommended the movie well?

Q5: Do you want to watch the recommended movie?

All questions are answered on a 5-point Likert scale, with five being the best and one being the worse. The choices for Q1, Q2, Q4, and Q5 are [agree/somewhat agree/neutral/somewhat disagree/disagree]. The choices for Q3 are [have seen the movie and remember the contents well/have seen the movie and remember some the contents/have never seen the movie but know the plot/have never seen the movie but know only the title/do not know at all]. Q4 is for recommenders only, and Q5 is for seekers only.

Table 2 shows the results of the questionnaire. We found that most of the workers were highly interested in the topic of movies (Q1), and both recommenders and seekers enjoyed the dialogue, although it was relatively long, more than 20 turns (Q2). In addition, from Q3, we can see that the recommenders recommended movies they knew, while the seekers were often recommended movies they did not know. Finally, from Q4 and Q5, it was confirmed that the collected dialogues sufficiently achieved the purpose of movie recommendation.

4 Proposed Model

4.1 Outline

Each dialogue $\mathcal{D} = \{(x^l, y^l)\}_{l=1}^{L}$ in the dataset is paired with a knowledge pool $\mathcal{K} = (\mathbf{k_t}, \mathbf{k_c})$ about the movie recommended in that dialogue, where x^l, y^l is the utterance of the seeker and recommender at turn l and L is the number of turns in $\mathcal{D}$. In addition, $\mathbf{k_t}$ $(= \{k_{t,1}, \dots, k_{t,m}, \dots, k_{t,M}\})$ are the knowledge types, $\mathbf{k_c}$ $(= \{k_{c,1}, \dots, k_{c,n}, \dots, k_{c,N}\})$ are knowledge contents, and M, N are the number of knowledge types and knowledge contents contained in $\mathcal{K}$, respectively. At turn l, given the dialogue context (= the current seeker's utterance x^l and the last recommender's utterance y^{l-1}), the previously selected knowledge types $\{\hat{k}_t^1, \dots, \hat{k}_t^{l-1}\}$, and previously selected knowledge contents $\{\hat{k}_c^1, \dots, \hat{k}_c^{l-1}\}$, our target is to select a piece of knowledge $\hat{k}_c^l$ from $\mathbf{k_c}$ and generate response y^l utilizing $\hat{k}_c^l$. We call the previously selected knowledge types the "knowledge type history" and the previously selected knowledge contents the "knowledge content history" in this paper.

Figure 4 shows the overview of the proposed model. The proposed model mainly consists of the Encoding Layer, the Knowledge Selection Layer, and the Decoding Layer. We describe each of the components in the following sections.

4.2 Encoding Layer

The encoding layer is used to obtain the following representations: dialogue context, knowledge types, knowledge contents, knowledge type history, and knowledge content history. We use BERT (Devlin et al., 2019) as the encoder. For encoding the dialogue context, we obtain the hidden state $H^{x^l y^{l-1}}$ via BERT, and then perform average pooling to obtain $h^{x^l y^{l-1}}$ (Cer et al., 2018):

$$H^{x^l y^{l-1}} = BERT(x^l, y^{l-1}) \tag{1}$$

$$h^{x^l y^{l-1}} = avgpool(H^{x^l y^{l-1}}) \in \mathbb{R}^d \tag{2}$$

where d is the hidden size. We insert [SEP] between x^l and y^{l-1}, and insert [CLS] and [SEP] at the beginning and the end of the entire input string, respectively.

In the case of knowledge types, we insert [CLS] and [SEP] at the beginning and the end of the input string, respectively. After that, we get $\{h^{k_{t,m}}\}_{m=1}^{M}$ by feeding it to BERT in the same way. For the knowledge contents, we input the knowledge type in addition to the knowledge contents, following the method of Dinan et al. (2019). We insert a new special token [KNOW SEP] between the knowledge type and the knowledge content and further insert [CLS] and [SEP] at the beginning and the end of the input string, respectively. The resulting string is input to BERT to obtain $\{h^{k_{c,n}}\}_{n=1}^{N}$ likewise. We also compute the representations of knowledge type history $\{h^{\hat{k}_t^i}\}_{i=1}^{l-1}$ and that of knowledge content history $\{h^{\hat{k}_c^i}\}_{i=1}^{l-1}$.

4.3 Knowledge Selection Layer

We encode the knowledge type history via the transformer encoder (Vaswani et al., 2017). This transformer encoder (we call this "knowledge type encoder") adds a positional embedding for each turn (= turn embedding) to the input so that the model reflects in which turn each knowledge type was used (Meng et al., 2021). We concatenate the last output of this encoder $h_{trans}^{\hat{k}_t^{l-1}}$ with the hidden state of the dialogue context $h^{x^l y^{l-1}}$ as the query, and regard $\{h^{k_{t,m}}\}_{m=1}^{M}$ as the key. The attention over knowledge types $a_t \in \mathbb{R}^M$ is calculated as follows:

$$\begin{aligned} a_t &= [a_{t,1}, \dots, a_{t,m}, \dots, a_{t,M}] \\ &= softmax(Q_t {K_t}^\top) \\ Q_t &= MLP([h_{trans}^{\hat{k}_t^{l-1}}; h^{x^l y^{l-1}}]) \\ K_t &= MLP([h^{k_{t,1}}, \dots, h^{k_{t,M}}]) \\ [h_{trans}^{\hat{k}_t^1}, \dots, h_{trans}^{\hat{k}_t^{l-1}}] &= KTE([h^{\hat{k}_t^1}, \dots, h^{\hat{k}_t^{l-1}}]) \end{aligned} \tag{3}$$

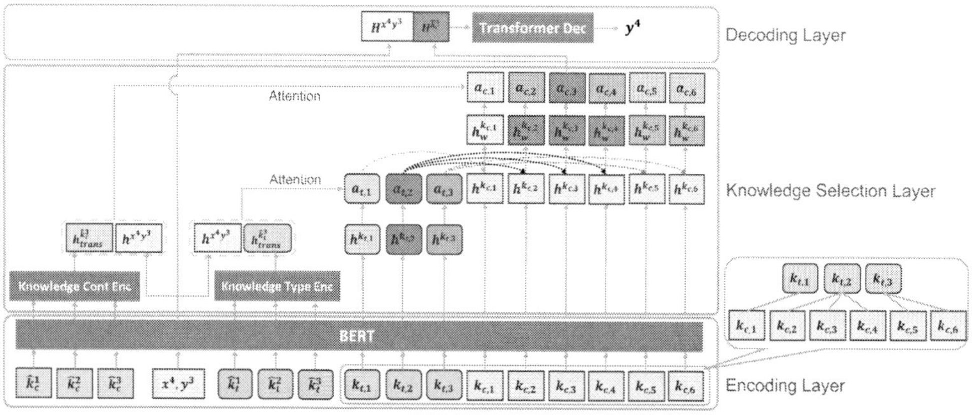

Figure 4: Overview of the proposed model. In this figure, the model generates the response y^4 at time $l = 4$. Knowledge Cont Enc, Knowledge Type Enc, and Transformer Dec denote the knowledge content encoder, the knowledge type encoder, and the transformer decoder, respectively.

where $MLP(\cdot)$ is a multilayer perceptron, KTE is the knowledge type encoder, and $[\cdot;\cdot]$ is the vector concatenation operation.

We compute the weighted hidden state of the knowledge contents $\{h_w^{k_{c,n}}\}_{n=1}^N$ based on the calculated attention a_t. This weighted hidden state is used to calculate the attention over the knowledge contents. Suppose the number of knowledge contents belonging to the m-th knowledge type is N_m, and the same weight $a_{t,m} \in a_t$ is given to all of them. In that case, the M-dimensional a_t can be extended to the N-dimensional $a'_t \in \mathbb{R}^N$ as follows, because N_m satisfies $\sum_{m=1}^M N_m = N$:

$$a'_t = [a_{t,1}, \ldots, \underbrace{a_{t,m}, \ldots, a_{t,m}}_{N_m}, \ldots, a_{t,M}] \quad (4)$$

Using a'_t, the weighted hidden states of the knowledge contents $\{h_w^{k_{c,n}}\}_{n=1}^N$ can be obtained as follows:

$$[h_w^{k_{c,1}}, \ldots, h_w^{k_{c,N}}] = a'_t[h^{k_{c,1}}, \ldots, h^{k_{c,N}}] \quad (5)$$

The knowledge content history is encoded by the transformer encoder as well. This transformer encoder, which we call "knowledge content encoder", has the same setting as the knowledge type encoder, but they do not share any parameters. We concatenate the last output of the encoder $h_{trans}^{\hat{k}_c^{l-1}}$ with $h^{x^l y^{l-1}}$ as the query, and regard the weighted hidden states of knowledge contents $\{h_w^{k_{c,n}}\}_{n=1}^N$ as the key. We can calculate the attention over the knowledge contents $a_c \in \mathbb{R}^N$ as follows:

$$\begin{aligned} a_c &= softmax(Q_c {K_c}^\top) \\ Q_c &= MLP([h_{trans}^{\hat{k}_c^{l-1}}; h^{x^l y^{l-1}}]) \\ K_c &= MLP([h_w^{k_{c,1}}, \ldots, h_w^{k_{c,N}}]) \\ [h_{trans}^{\hat{k}_c^1}, \ldots, h_{trans}^{\hat{k}_c^{l-1}}] &= KCE([h^{\hat{k}_c^1}, \ldots, h^{\hat{k}_c^{l-1}}]) \end{aligned} \quad (6)$$

where KCE is the knowledge content encoder. Finally, we select a knowledge content $\hat{k}_c^l$ at time l from the probability distribution of a_c.

4.4 Decoding Layer

At time l, the dialogue context x^l, y^{l-1} and the knowledge content $\hat{k}_c^l$ selected by the knowledge selection layer, are input to the transformer decoder to generate the response y^l. Specifically, we feed the concatenated embedding $H^{x^l y^{l-1} \hat{k}_c^l} = [H^{x^l y^{l-1}}; H^{\hat{k}_c^l}]$ to the decoder. The word generation probability $p(y_j^l)$ over the vocabulary V when the decoder generates the j-th word can be written as follows:

$$\begin{aligned} p(y_j^l) &= softmax(MLP(h_{dec}^{l,j})) \in \mathbb{R}^{1\times|V|} \\ h_{dec}^{l,j} &= TD(H^{x^l y^{l-1} \hat{k}_c^l}, emb(y_{<j}^l))) \in \mathbb{R}^{1\times d} \end{aligned} \quad (7)$$

where TD is the transformer decoder, $y_{<j}^l$ are the words generated up to the j-th word, $emb(y_{<j}^l)$ are the word embeddings of $y_{<j}^l$, which is initialized with the word embedding of BERT.

We use copy mechanism (Gu et al., 2016; See et al., 2017) to make it easier to generate knowledge words and follow the method used in Meng et al. (2021).

4.5 Learning Objective

Similar to Dinan et al. (2019), we combine the negative log-likelihood loss for the generated response $\mathcal{L}_{nll}$ with the cross-entropy loss for knowledge selection $\mathcal{L}_{knowledge}$ modulated by a weight λ, which is the hyperparameter. The final loss function $\mathcal{L}$ is as:

$$\mathcal{L} = (1 - \lambda)\mathcal{L}_{nll} + \lambda\mathcal{L}_{knowledge} \quad (8)$$

5 Experiments

5.1 Settings

We randomly split the dialogues into the train (90%), validation (5%), and test sets (5%). Input texts are truncated to the maximum input length of 64 tokens for dialogue contexts and knowledge contents and 5 tokens for knowledge types. In addition, a maximum of 20 turns of knowledge history can be entered for both knowledge types and knowledge contents. Our proposed dataset may have multiple pieces of knowledge associated with a recommender's utterance, but we use only one of them in this study for simplicity. In the case of an utterance with multiple knowledge items, we select the one with the highest Jaccard coefficient in the word set of the recommender's utterance and each knowledge as the correct knowledge. To input "No knowledge," we use the special token [NO KNOW] in place of knowledge type and content.

5.2 Baseline

We use an end-to-end Transformer Memory Network (TMN) (Dinan et al., 2019) as baseline. This model encodes the dialogue context and each knowledge respectively and selects knowledge by calculating the dot-product attention between them. It also performs end-to-end response generation using the selected knowledge. To make a fair comparison with our proposed model, we have replaced the original transformer encoder with a BERT encoder. We call this model TMN BERT.

As a baseline to consider knowledge history, we add the knowledge content encoder to TMN BERT and concatenate its output with the hidden states of the dialogue context. We call this model TMN BERT+KH. Knowledge selection is made by calculating the attention between the knowledge candidates and the concatenated hidden states. Other conditions are the same as in TMN BERT.

In addition, we use Random baseline that selects knowledge randomly.

5.3 Implementation Details

We use the NICT BERT Japanese pre-trained model (with BPE) [4] as the encoder. This BERT is also used to initialize the word embedding in the transformer decoder. The transformer encoders for knowledge type and knowledge content, and the transformer decoder have the same architecture, consisting of 2 attention heads, 5 layers, and the size of the hidden layer is 768 and the filter size is 3072. We train the models for 100 epochs with a batch size of 512 and 0.1 gradient clipping. We do early stopping if no improvement of the validation loss is observed for five consecutive epochs. All models are learned with Adam optimizer (Kingma and Ba, 2015) with $\beta_1 = 0.9$, $\beta_2 = 0.999$ and an initial learning rate = 0.00005. We use an inverse square root learning rate scheduler with the first 1,000 steps allocated for warmup. In addition, we set the hyperparameter λ to 0.95. At decoding, we use beam search with a beam of size 3. We add a restriction to prevent the same bigram from being generated multiple times.

5.4 Evaluation Metrics

We evaluate the models with automatic evaluation metrics. For knowledge selection, we use accuracy (**Acc**). For response reproducibility, we measure **BLEU$_{tgt}$-4** (Papineni et al., 2002), which is the 4-gram overlap between a generated response and a target response. We also use unigram F1 (**F1**) following the evaluation setting in Dinan et al. (2019). Additionally, we use **Jaccard** and **BLEU$_{know}$-4** to evaluate whether the knowledge is reflected in the generated response. **Jaccard** is the Jaccard coefficient of the set of words in the generated response and the set of words in the selected knowledge content. **BLEU$_{know}$-4** is the BLEU-4 computed between the generated response and the selected knowledge content.

5.5 Results and Analysis

The results of knowledge selection are shown in Table 3. The results show that our proposed method outperformed the baselines. TMN BERT+KH, which adds a mechanism to consider knowledge history to the baseline TMN BERT, is almost the same as TMN BERT in Acc. On the other hand,

[4] `https://alaginrc.nict.go.jp/nict-bert/index.html`

	knowledge selection	response reproducibility		knowledge reflection	
	Acc	F1	BLEU$_{tgt}$-4	Jaccard	BLEU$_{know}$-4
Random	4.18 (0.15)	24.05 (0.26)	4.63 (0.16)	5.87 (0.18)	0.47 (0.07)
TMN BERT	48.81 (0.25)	**42.97** (0.16)	**21.03** (0.70)	38.36 (0.81)	24.94 (1.36)
TMN BERT+KH	48.66 (0.06)	42.74 (0.46)	20.68 (0.56)	38.23 (0.94)	25.08 (1.29)
Ours	**49.72** (0.44)	42.92 (0.71)	20.78 (0.69)	**39.35** (1.41)	**25.88** (1.35)

Table 3: The evaluation results. Scores are the mean of three runs of the experiment with different random seeds, and standard deviations are shown in parentheses. The bold scores indicate the best ones over models.

	Dialogue	Knowledge
Recommender$_1$:	Nice to meet you.	No knowledge
Seeker$_1$:	Hello.	-
Recommender$_2$:	I am pleased to meet you.	No knowledge
Seeker$_2$:	What movies do you recommend?	-
TMN BERT	I will introduce a movie called Do You Like Disney Movies?	Danny Ocean immediately breaks his parole rules (no interstate movement) and reunites with his partner Rusty Ryan in Los Angeles. He confides in Ryan about a new theft scheme he had hatched while in prison. (Plot)
Ours:	Today I will introduce Ocean's Eleven.	Ocean's Eleven (Title)
Gold:	How about Ocean's Eleven?	Ocean's Eleven (Title)

Table 4: Examples of generated responses by our model and the baseline model. Subscript numbers indicate the number of turns in the dialogue. The knowledge type is indicated in parentheses in the knowledge column.

our proposed method improves Acc, suggesting the importance of considering knowledge structurally.

The results of response generation are also shown in Table 3. The proposed method did not perform well in terms of reproducibility for target responses. However, this should not be a major problem because it is known that it is inappropriate to measure reproducibility in dialogue evaluation (Liu et al., 2016). On the other hand, the proposed model performed the best for knowledge reflection. We believe this improvement is due to selecting knowledge more correctly according to the dialogue context and knowledge history.

5.6 Case Study

Table 4 shows an example of knowledge selection and response generation. TMN BERT, which does not consider knowledge history, selects the plot even though it is at the beginning of the dialogue. Moreover, the generated utterance does not reflect the selected knowledge. On the other hand, our proposed model introduces the movie title that has not yet been mentioned in this dialogue by considering the knowledge history.

As illustrated by the generated response of TMN BERT, the generated utterances may not reflect the selected knowledge or may contain words inconsistent with the selected knowledge. This problem is known as the hallucination problem (Roller et al., 2020; Shuster et al., 2021), and we leave the solution to this problem as future work.

6 Conclusion

We proposed JMRD, a hierarchically structured knowledge-based movie recommendation dialogue dataset. We also proposed an end-to-end dialogue system that utilizes the hierarchically structured knowledge of knowledge types and contents to perform knowledge selection and generate responses as a strong baseline for our dataset. The experimental results show that our model can select more appropriate knowledge than baselines.

As far as we know, this is the first Japanese dialogue dataset associated with external knowledge. We hope our dataset facilitates further research on movie recommendation dialogue based on structured external knowledge (especially in Japanese dialogue research).

In response generation, we can observe that the utterances do not reflect the knowledge in some cases, even when the knowledge is selected correctly. There is still much room for improvement in knowledge reflection, and we leave this as future work.

7 Acknowledgments

This work was supported by NII CRIS collaborative research program operated by NII CRIS and LINE Corporation. This work was also supported by JST, CREST Grant Number JPMJCR20D2, Japan.

References

Antoine Bordes, Y-Lan Boureau, and Jason Weston. 2017. Learning end-to-end goal-oriented dialog. In *ICLR*.

Daniel Cer, Yinfei Yang, Sheng-yi Kong, Nan Hua, Nicole Limtiaco, Rhomni St. John, Noah Constant, Mario Guajardo-Cespedes, Steve Yuan, Chris Tar, Brian Strope, and Ray Kurzweil. 2018. Universal sentence encoder for English. In *Proceedings of the 2018 Conference on Empirical Methods in Natural Language Processing: System Demonstrations*, pages 169–174, Brussels, Belgium. Association for Computational Linguistics.

Jacob Devlin, Ming-Wei Chang, Kenton Lee, and Kristina Toutanova. 2019. BERT: Pre-training of deep bidirectional transformers for language understanding. In *Proceedings of the 2019 Conference of the North American Chapter of the Association for Computational Linguistics: Human Language Technologies, Volume 1 (Long and Short Papers)*, pages 4171–4186, Minneapolis, Minnesota. Association for Computational Linguistics.

Emily Dinan, Stephen Roller, Kurt Shuster, Angela Fan, Michael Auli, and Jason Weston. 2019. Wizard of wikipedia: Knowledge-powered conversational agents. In *International Conference on Learning Representations*.

Jiatao Gu, Zhengdong Lu, Hang Li, and Victor O.K. Li. 2016. Incorporating copying mechanism in sequence-to-sequence learning. In *Proceedings of the 54th Annual Meeting of the Association for Computational Linguistics (Volume 1: Long Papers)*, pages 1631–1640, Berlin, Germany. Association for Computational Linguistics.

Dongyeop Kang, Anusha Balakrishnan, Pararth Shah, Paul Crook, Y-Lan Boureau, and Jason Weston. 2019. Recommendation as a communication game: Self-supervised bot-play for goal-oriented dialogue. In *Proceedings of the 2019 Conference on Empirical Methods in Natural Language Processing and the 9th International Joint Conference on Natural Language Processing (EMNLP-IJCNLP)*, pages 1951–1961, Hong Kong, China. Association for Computational Linguistics.

Diederick P Kingma and Jimmy Ba. 2015. Adam: A method for stochastic optimization. In *International Conference on Learning Representations (ICLR)*.

Raymond Li, Samira Kahou, Hannes Schulz, Vincent Michalski, Laurent Charlin, and Chris Pal. 2018. Towards deep conversational recommendations. In *Proceedings of the 32nd International Conference on Neural Information Processing Systems*, NIPS'18, pages 9748–9758, Red Hook, NY, USA. Curran Associates Inc.

Chia-Wei Liu, Ryan Lowe, Iulian Serban, Mike Noseworthy, Laurent Charlin, and Joelle Pineau. 2016. How NOT to evaluate your dialogue system: An empirical study of unsupervised evaluation metrics for dialogue response generation. In *Proceedings of the 2016 Conference on Empirical Methods in Natural Language Processing*, pages 2122–2132, Austin, Texas. Association for Computational Linguistics.

Zeming Liu, Haifeng Wang, Zheng-Yu Niu, Hua Wu, Wanxiang Che, and Ting Liu. 2020. Towards conversational recommendation over multi-type dialogs. In *Proceedings of the 58th Annual Meeting of the Association for Computational Linguistics*, pages 1036–1049, Online. Association for Computational Linguistics.

Chuan Meng, Pengjie Ren, Zhumin Chen, Zhaochun Ren, Tengxiao Xi, and Maarten de Rijke. 2021. Initiative-aware self-supervised learning for knowledge-grounded conversations. In *SIGIR*, pages 522–532.

Alexander Miller, Will Feng, Dhruv Batra, Antoine Bordes, Adam Fisch, Jiasen Lu, Devi Parikh, and Jason Weston. 2017. ParlAI: A dialog research software platform. In *Proceedings of the 2017 Conference on Empirical Methods in Natural Language Processing: System Demonstrations*, pages 79–84, Copenhagen, Denmark. Association for Computational Linguistics.

Nikita Moghe, Siddhartha Arora, Suman Banerjee, and Mitesh M. Khapra. 2018. Towards exploiting background knowledge for building conversation systems. In *Proceedings of the 2018 Conference on Empirical Methods in Natural Language Processing*, pages 2322–2332, Brussels, Belgium. Association for Computational Linguistics.

Seungwhan Moon, Pararth Shah, Anuj Kumar, and Rajen Subba. 2019. OpenDialKG: Explainable conversational reasoning with attention-based walks over knowledge graphs. In *Proceedings of the 57th Annual Meeting of the Association for Computational Linguistics*, pages 845–854, Florence, Italy. Association for Computational Linguistics.

Kishore Papineni, Salim Roukos, Todd Ward, and Wei-Jing Zhu. 2002. Bleu: a method for automatic evaluation of machine translation. In *Proceedings of the 40th Annual Meeting of the Association for Computational Linguistics*, pages 311–318, Philadelphia, Pennsylvania, USA. Association for Computational Linguistics.

Stephen Roller, Emily Dinan, Naman Goyal, Da Ju, Mary Williamson, Yinhan Liu, Jing Xu, Myle Ott,

Kurt Shuster, Eric Michael Smith, Y-Lan Boureau, and Jason Weston. 2020. Recipes for building an open-domain chatbot. abs/2004.13637.

Abigail See, Peter J. Liu, and Christopher D. Manning. 2017. Get to the point: Summarization with pointer-generator networks. In *Proceedings of the 55th Annual Meeting of the Association for Computational Linguistics (Volume 1: Long Papers)*, pages 1073–1083, Vancouver, Canada. Association for Computational Linguistics.

Kurt Shuster, Spencer Poff, Moya Chen, Douwe Kiela, and Jason Weston. 2021. Retrieval augmentation reduces hallucination in conversation. abs/2104.07567.

Hui Su, Xiaoyu Shen, Zhou Xiao, Zheng Zhang, Ernie Chang, Cheng Zhang, Cheng Niu, and Jie Zhou. 2020. MovieChats: Chat like humans in a closed domain. In *Proceedings of the 2020 Conference on Empirical Methods in Natural Language Processing (EMNLP)*, pages 6605–6619, Online. Association for Computational Linguistics.

Arseny Tolmachev, Daisuke Kawahara, and Sadao Kurohashi. 2020. Design and structure of the Juman++ morphological analyzer toolkit. *Journal of Natural Language Processing*, 27(1):89–132.

Ashish Vaswani, Noam Shazeer, Niki Parmar, Jakob Uszkoreit, Llion Jones, Aidan N. Gomez, Łukasz Kaiser, and Illia Polosukhin. 2017. Attention is all you need. In *NeurIPS*, pages 5998–6008. Curran Associates Inc.

Wenquan Wu, Zhen Guo, Xiangyang Zhou, Hua Wu, Xiyuan Zhang, Rongzhong Lian, and Haifeng Wang. 2019. Proactive human-machine conversation with explicit conversation goal. In *Proceedings of the 57th Annual Meeting of the Association for Computational Linguistics*, pages 3794–3804, Florence, Italy. Association for Computational Linguistics.

Hao Zhou, Chujie Zheng, Kaili Huang, Minlie Huang, and Xiaoyan Zhu. 2020. KdConv: A Chinese multi-domain dialogue dataset towards multi-turn knowledge-driven conversation. In *Proceedings of the 58th Annual Meeting of the Association for Computational Linguistics*, pages 7098–7108, Online. Association for Computational Linguistics.

Kangyan Zhou, Shrimai Prabhumoye, and Alan W Black. 2018. A dataset for document grounded conversations. In *Proceedings of the 2018 Conference on Empirical Methods in Natural Language Processing*, pages 708–713, Brussels, Belgium. Association for Computational Linguistics.

Retrieval-Free Knowledge-Grounded Dialogue Response Generation with Adapters

Yan Xu*, Etsuko Ishii*, Samuel Cahyawijaya, Zihan Liu, Genta Indra Winata, Andrea Madotto, Dan Su, Pascale Fung
Center for Artificial Intelligence Research (CAiRE)
The Hong Kong University of Science and Technology, Clear Water Bay, Hong Kong
{yxucb,eishii}@connect.ust.hk, pascale@ece.ust.hk

Abstract

To diversify and enrich generated dialogue responses, knowledge-grounded dialogue has been investigated in recent years. The existing methods tackle the knowledge grounding challenge by retrieving the relevant sentences over a large corpus and augmenting the dialogues with explicit extra information. Despite their success, however, the existing works have drawbacks on the inference efficiency. This paper proposes `KnowExpert`, an end-to-end framework to bypass the explicit retrieval process and inject knowledge into the pre-trained language models with lightweight adapters and adapt to the knowledge-grounded dialogue task. To the best of our knowledge, this is the first attempt to tackle this challenge without retrieval in this task under an open-domain chit-chat scenario. The experimental results show that `KnowExpert` performs comparably with some retrieval-based baselines while being time-efficient in inference, demonstrating the effectiveness of our proposed method.[1]

1 Introduction

Numerous studies in recent years have established sophisticated techniques to build open-domain dialogue systems. Although such systems can generate fluent and grammatically correct responses based on the dialogue history, they are unsatisfactory compared to human-to-human conversations. One primary reason is that existing dialogue systems are incapable of understanding and leveraging relevant knowledge, resulting in superficial and unintelligent responses when they dive into a specific topic (Li et al., 2020). To overcome this limitation, many research works have focused on developing knowledge-grounded dialogue (KGD) systems (Dinan et al., 2019; Chen et al., 2020; Zhao et al., 2020).

To equip the ability to incorporate knowledge, many recently proposed KGD systems (Lian et al., 2019; Kim et al., 2019; Roller et al., 2020; Chen et al., 2020; Zhao et al., 2020) comprise the following modules: (1) Knowledge Retrieval, for retrieving the related knowledge sentences from a large corpus (e.g., Wikipedia); (2) Knowledge Selection, for selecting the most relevant knowledge sentences for generation; and (3) Knowledge-augmented Generation, for augmenting the retrieved knowledge and conversation history to generate more knowledgeable responses. The key to this approach is the explicit retrieval phase to enhance the quality of generated responses.

Despite demonstrating remarkable progress and promising performance on the KGD task, the retrieval-based approaches have drawbacks in their efficiency. First, knowledge retrieval in corpora requires a model to search over a large amount of data, consuming considerable memory resources to store the whole knowledge corpus. It also takes additional processing time to retrieve knowledge and conduct further knowledge selection. Second, adding knowledge as additional context to the language generation model also causes significant computation overhead, which slows the language generation process. Efficiency plays an essential role in the practical use of dialogue systems, and it is necessary to limit resource requirements so as to generate responses faster and support more active users.

Recently, large pre-trained language models (LMs) have been shown to have the capability to carry implicit knowledge (Wang et al., 2020; Lauscher et al., 2020), which can be further applied to downstream classification tasks (Shwartz et al., 2020). Many existing works have proved that the "knowledge" can be embedded in the pretraining process (Brown et al., 2020). The explorations on the closed-book question answering (QA) task (Petroni et al., 2019; Roberts et al., 2020;

* These two authors contributed equally.

[1]Our code and models are available at https://github.com/HLTCHKUST/KnowExpert.

Proceedings of the Second DialDoc Workshop on Document-grounded Dialogue and Conversational Question Answering, pages 93 - 107
May 26, 2022 ©2022 Association for Computational Linguistics

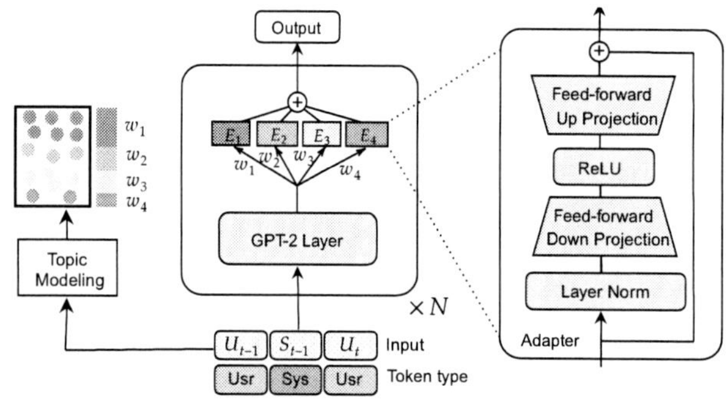

Figure 1: High-level architecture of the model. Taking a dialogue history as an input, the adapters are inserted upon the GPT-2 layers, acting as the knowledge experts, to enhance the response generation with the help from a topic model which assigns weights over the knowledge experts.

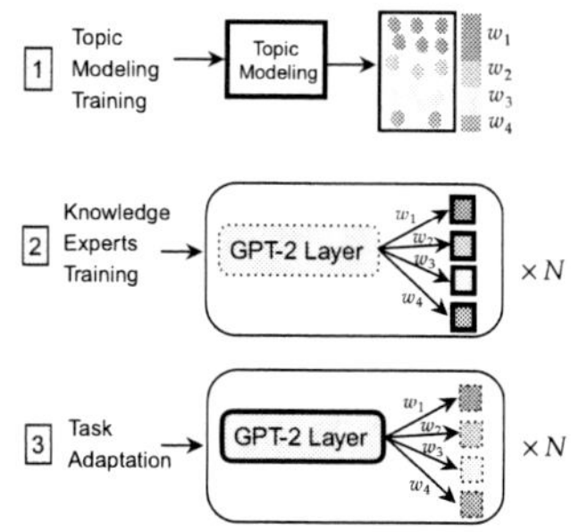

Figure 2: Illustration of the training procedure, where the thick lined modules are trained while the rest (dash lined) kept frozen in each training step.

Wang et al., 2021) with large pre-trained LMs also indicates the potential of leveraging the knowledge embedded inside LMs. For task-oriented dialogue systems, Madotto et al. (2020) store knowledge bases (KBs) of different sizes directly into the model parameters by aligning auto-extracted dialogue templates with the corresponding KBs for each data sample. Based on their success in other tasks, LMs have potential to apply their implicit knowledge for open-domain KGD tasks. However, our scenario is different from both the closed-book QA and task-oriented dialogue tasks, where given a question or user query, relevant knowledge choices are highly constrained by the inputs. In contrast, open-domain chit-chat suffers much from the one-to-many issue between the inputs and possible outputs. In other words, given the inputs on a specific topic, the choice of knowledge candidates is varying, which brings new challenges to embedding knowledge in this task.

Inspired by the previous explorations on other tasks, we propose to tackle the KGD challenge by using the implicit knowledge in LMs under the open-domain chit-chat scenario. In contrast to existing KGD systems, we bypass the retrieval step and propose an end-to-end framework, `KnowExpert`, to learn the knowledge corpus with the parameters of pre-trained LMs and incorporate the acquired knowledge for KGD generation. In the model, lightweight adapters (Bapna and Firat, 2019) are inserted into the pre-trained GPT-2 (Radford et al., 2019), acting as knowledge experts. Taking advantage of latent topics, the knowledge sentences are embedded into different knowledge experts by pseudo-conversation style training, while the latent topics measure the relevance between the dialogue samples and the clusters. We thus fine-tune LM layers where frozen pre-trained adapters are inserted for task adaptation. Experimental results show that `KnowExpert`performs comparably with some strong retrieval-based baselines, while its inference process is much more efficient since extra knowledge sentences are not required as a component of the inputs.

Our contributions are three-fold: (1) to the best of our knowledge, we are the first to explore learning prior knowledge with generative models for KGD tasks under open-domain chit-chat scenario; (2) our model bypass an explicit knowledge retrieval process, and has constant inference time regardless of the size of the knowledge corpus; and (3) our model performs comparably with some strong baselines and shows that a purely generation-based method for the KGD task is promising.

2 Related Work

2.1 Knowledge-Grounded Dialogue

The KGD task requires models to identify relevant knowledge sentences from a large corpus for grounding the response generation. Information retrieval (IR) systems, such as TF-IDF, can quickly retrieve related knowledge over a large corpus. However, the effectiveness is limited as they can only be leveraged to coarsely retrieve several relevant documents. However, providing the models with more documents may not improve the system since it will bring more noise into the inputs. What is more, the length of the packed inputs could exceed the length limitation of the LMs. Thus, the existing works still conduct further fine-grained

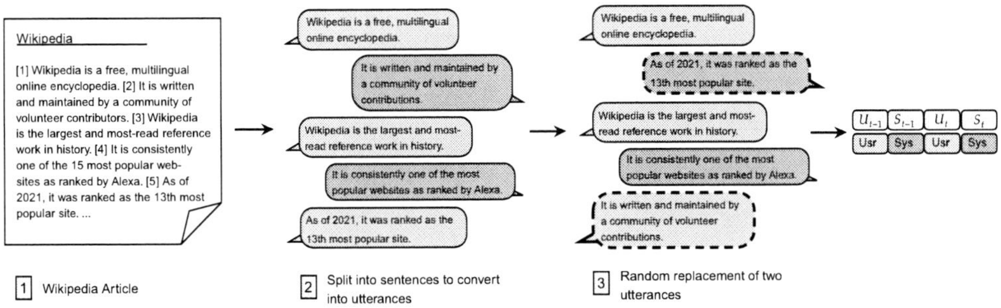

Figure 3: The demonstration of the procedure of converting a document in the knowledge corpus (e.g., a Wikipedia article) into the pseudo-conversation style. First, the article is split into sentences so that each to represent one utterance. Then, random two utterances are permuted to avoid over-fitting (presented with dashed lines).

knowledge selection to improve the accuracy of the knowledge retrieval process, which is one of the critical problems in the KGD task. Motivated by this, latent variables have been introduced to minimize the gap between prior and the posterior knowledge selection (Zhao et al., 2019; Kim et al., 2019; Lian et al., 2019; Chen et al., 2020). Zhao et al. (2020) explores the strategy to better rank the knowledge sentences, avoiding the most relevant candidates becoming truncated in the input sequences. Some existing KGD systems generate the knowledge first for further response generation. (Zhou et al., 2021) train the model to generate implicit knowledge sentences for open-domain dialogue response generation. Instead of training the large pre-trained LMs, (Liu et al., 2022) leverage prompts for knowledge and response generation. Cui et al. (2021) proposes the knowledge-enhanced fine-tuning for better handling the unseen entities in the conversation history. They also evaluate the model when there is no knowledge sentence as inputs during inference. However their proposed method only focus on the problem of unseen entities, whereas it is less helpful on the seen domain. In this paper, we propose a new promising direction to bypass the retrieval step and better leverage power of the pretrained LMs for knowledge-grounded diaogue generation.

2.2 Knowledge Retrieval in LMs

The concept of *knowledge retrieval in LMs* started with the proposal of the LAMA benchmark (Petroni et al., 2019), which heavily relies on prompts. By constructing the prompts as "fill-in-the-blank" cloze statements, pre-trained LMs can predict the factual knowledge (Petroni et al., 2019; Shin et al., 2020). The application of the idea of knowledge retrieval in LMs also appears in closed-book QA tasks. Roberts et al. (2020) investigates a simple fine-tuning technique on multiple QA datasets and proves that T5 (Raffel et al., 2019) can pack Wikipedia knowledge into its parameters.

2.3 Inference Efficiency in Language Model

Recent progress in natural language processing, including dialogue systems, has been benefited by Transformer-based large pre-trained LMs, yet current "best performing" models tend to have a more complex architecture with more parameters, which is not ideal considering inference in practical application. Many modified Transformer architectures have been explored to speed up inference latency while maintaining performance, for example, by leveraging knowledge distillation to compress or reduce the number of parameters (Tang et al., 2019; Sanh et al., 2019; Jiao et al., 2020; Sun et al., 2020), by performing a simple decomposition in lower layers (Cao et al., 2020), or by converting a structured decoder into a non-autoregressive module (Sun et al., 2019). Contrasting previous works, we emphasize the inference efficiency of our proposed framework in shortening the input sequences by removing the external knowledge components and reducing the storage resources needed, and we provide a faster inference process when scaling up the knowledge corpus.

3 Methodology

In this section, we present the framework and learning algorithm of `KnowExpert`. First, we offer several preliminary definitions used throughout the paper. Second, we explain the architecture of `KnowExpert`. Finally, we describe the strategy to train the framework.

3.1 Preliminary Definition

We denote a dialogue dataset as $\{\mathcal{D}^n\}_{n=1}^N$, and the dialogue history at turn t as $\mathcal{D}_t = \{(U_i, S_i)\}_{i=1}^t$, where U_t is the user utterance and S_t the system response. Along with the dialogue dataset, suppose we have a knowledge corpus $\{K_m\}_{m=1}^M$, where K_m refers to a piece of knowledge (e.g., a sentence from Wikipedia).

Given an input $X_t = (\mathcal{D}_{t-1}, U_t)$, we aim to learn a model f_Θ to generate a knowledgeable response $\tilde{S}_t$. Existing works frame this task as retrieving related knowledge K_t for augmented input: $\tilde{S}_t = f_\Theta(X_t, K_t)$. Here, we propose to bypass the retrieval process by adding knowledge into the model parameters Θ to generate a response solely based on dialogue history: $\tilde{S}_t = f_\Theta(X_t)$.

3.2 `KnowExpert` Architecture

`KnowExpert` is composed of two components: a GPT-2 with lightweight adapters and a contextual topic model, as depicted in Figure 1. Inspired by Peinelt et al. (2020), the topic model is introduced to evoke knowledge stored in the GPT-2 guided by the topic information during response generation.

GPT-2 with Adapters To incorporate knowledge, we insert lightweight adapters (Bapna and Firat, 2019) into each GPT-2 layer. The adapter has a two-linear-layer structure, which enables fast adaptation to targets. Given the hidden representation of the GPT-2 layer i, denoted as $H_i \in \mathbb{R}^{j \times h}$, where h and j are the hidden dimension and the current generation step, respectively, the adapter can be formulated as

$$\mathtt{A}_\theta(H_i) = \mathtt{ReLU}(\mathtt{LN}(H_i) W_i^{hd}) W_i^{dh} + H_i,$$

where $W_i^{hd} \in \mathbb{R}^{h \times d}$ and $W_i^{dh} \in \mathbb{R}^{d \times h}$ stand for the trainable parameters in θ, $\mathtt{LN}(\cdot)$ is layer normalization (Ba et al., 2016), and d is the bottleneck dimension. Here, we insert L knowledge adapters parameterized as $\{\theta_{E_l}\}_{l=1}^L$ where each serves as a knowledge expert in a certain topic domain.

Topic Modeling In `KnowExpert`, a topic model is used to inform GPT-2 with more relevant "topics" during response generation so as to induce more context-appropriate knowledge. The topic model is trained to cluster the training knowledge corpus into a pre-defined number (L) of topic clusters. While any sort of topic model can be used, we adopt a contextual topic model (CTM) which outperforms traditional topic models (Bianchi et al., 2021). The CTM combines pre-trained Sentence-Transformers embedding representations (Reimers and Gurevych, 2019) with a neural topic model, Neural-ProdLDA (Srivastava and Sutton, 2017), which takes advantage of Bag of Words (BoW) for more coherent representation.

Once trained, given an input sequence, the topic model outputs a L-dimension vector, which is its probability distribution of the pre-clustered topics. By taking the dialogue history as inputs, these probabilities are utilized as the similarity weights $\mathbf{w} = (w_1, w_2, ..., w_L)$ over the knowledge experts to compute the weighted sum of their hidden states, as shown in Figure 1. We utilize $\mathbf{w}$ under two different settings: (i) the **W**eighted-sum setting where we weighted-sum the outputs from each knowledge expert when passing the hidden state to the next GPT-2 layer, and (ii) the **O**ne-hot setting where we only consider the output of the knowledge expert with the largest weight. The models trained under these two settings are denoted as **KnowExpert**$_{\text{w}}$ and **KnowExpert**$_{\text{o}}$, respectively.

3.3 Learning Procedure

Our training follows a three-step paradigm (Figure 2). In each step, each component of `KnowExpert` is trained separately, which mimics human behavior during conversations referring to knowledge learned previously(Tuckute et al., 2021).

(i) Topic Modeling Training. We use knowledge sentences of the knowledge corpus in plain text format to train the CTM, with the pre-trained Sentence-Transformers frozen. For better guidance during training, we predict the topic distribution $\mathbf{w}$ using a concatenation of the dialogue history and the response. (We also tried other input combinations, but we achieve the best performance with the current one.) During inference, however, this scheme cannot be applied due to the absence of responses. Thus, we further fine-tune the Sentence-Transformer inside the CTM to deal with the absence of responses. In other words, we fine-tune the Sentence-Transformer model to produce the sentence embedding of the given dialogue history as similar to the sentence embedding of the concatenation mentioned above. We leverage the mean squared error (MSE) loss to evaluate the difference between two sentence embeddings and provide the model with supervison signals.

(ii) Knowledge Expert Training. We train a set of L topic-specific knowledge adapters inserted into the frozen backbone GPT-2 with the knowledge corpus to generate a knowledge sentence. The adapters are independently trained to minimize the negative log-likelihood over the knowledge corpus of the corresponding topic:

$$\mathcal{L}_{\mathcal{K}^l} = -\sum_{k \in \mathcal{K}^l} \sum_{1 \leq i \leq |k|} \log p(k_i | k_{<i}),$$

where k_i is the ith token of a knowledge sentence in topic $\mathcal{K}^l$.

Differently to general pre-training, we expect to leverage the pretraining process on the knowledge experts to benefit the KGD task. Under this case, dialogue-oriented training is required (Xu and Zhao, 2021). Motivated by this, we convert the format of knowledge sentences from plain text to a pseudo-conversational style to reduce the gap between knowledge expert training and task adaptation. The procedure of conversion is depicted in Figure 3.

First, we split a document of the knowledge corpus (e.g., a Wikipedia article) into sentences, and make each sentence a single utterance. Then, we randomly select 20% of utterances and replace them with the nearest selected utterance in each dialogue to avoid the adapters over-fitting to a specific order of the knowledge sentences. The replacement is done dynamically for every epochs. Adding the token type embeddings and special tokens between knowledge sentences, we treat the knowledge sentences for knowledge expert training in the same way as the dialogues for task adaptation. Note that we make each knowledge sentence act as a system utterance and a user utterance respectively so as to ensure that each is trained as a system utterance.

(iii) Task Adaptation. In the task adaptation step using the dialogue dataset, the whole GPT-2 model, except the inserted knowledge experts, is fine-tuned to generate a knowledgeable response:

$$\mathcal{L}_{\text{Task}} = -\sum_{1 \leq n \leq N} \sum_{1 \leq i \leq j} \log p(s_i^n | s_{<i}^n, X_t^n),$$

where each response is denoted as $\tilde{S}_t^n = \{s_i^n\}_{i=0}^j$. In this process, the number of trainable parameters is the same as that of the original GPT-2 model.

4 Experiments

4.1 Datasets

We conduct experiments on two datasets: Wizard of Wikipedia (WoW) (Dinan et al., 2019) and CMU Document Grounded Conversations (CMU_DoG) (Zhou et al., 2018). In the training process, we collect all the knowledge sentences provided by the WoW and CMU_DoG datasets to build a knowledge corpus with 117,495 articles.

4.2 Training Details

Topic Modeling. For preprocessing, we limit the vocaburary size for BoW to 20000. The number of topic clusters L is set as 4. We use the frozen RoBERTa (125M) model pre-trained with the NLI datasets (Conneau et al., 2017) and STS Benchmark (Cer et al., 2017) provided by Wolf et al. (2020) as the Sentence-Transformer inside the CTM. The CTM is trained with the Adam optimizer (Kingma and Ba, 2015) with $\beta_1 = 0.9, \beta_2 = 0.999$, and a learning rate of $2\text{e}{-3}$. For further fine-tuning of RoBERTA, we apply the Adam optimizer with the same β_1, β_2 and a learning rate of $1\text{e}{-6}$ with a linear scheduler.

Knowledge Expert Training. We utilize the CTM model to split the knowledge corpus mentioned above into $\mathcal{L}$ clusters for training the corresponding $\mathcal{L}$ knowledge experts. In the experiments, we utilize the pre-trained GPT-2 (117M) model provided by Wolf et al. (2020). The adapter bottleneck dimension d is set to be 768 for the knowledge adapters. All the adapters are learned with the Adam optimizer with $\beta_1 = 0.9, \beta_2 = 0.999$. The learning rate is set to be $1\text{e}{-4}$ for knowledge expert training with a linear scheduler, and the knowledge experts are trained with 50 epochs.

Task Adaptation. For task adaptation, we keep the same hyper-parameter setting as in knowledge expert training, while the learning rate is set as $1\text{e}{-5}$. The maximum number of training epochs is set as 50 with a linear learning rate scheduler and the patience for early stopping as 5. We employ a greedy search in decoding responses. Also noted that, each experiment mentioned above is conducted on a single RTX 2080 Ti GPU.

4.3 Baselines

We selected baseline models which follow the retrieval-encode schema, based on the relevance to our experimental settings: (i) **DRD** (Zhao et al.,

Model		WoW Seen				WoW Unseen				CMU_DoG	
		PPL↓	F1↑	Dist-1↑	Dist-2↑	PPL↓	F1↑	Dist-1↑	Dist-2↑	PPL↓	F1↑
Retrieval-based Approach	DRD	23.0	18.0	-	-	25.6	16.5	-	-	54.4	10.7
	ZRGKG	40.4	18.7	5.4	22.5	41.5	18.6	3.4	15.6	53.5	12.5
	GPT-2_{trunc}	14.6	18.7	-	-	16.9	18.3	-	-	18.6	10.8
	KnowledGPT	19.2	**22.0**	8.9	36.2	22.3	**20.5**	6.0	23.8	20.6	**13.5**
Retrieval-free Approach	GPT-2_f	18.8	17.0	4.9	21.1	21.0	16.3	3.9	16.8	17.8	11.8
	KE-Blender†	15.5	17.0	-	-	18.4	**16.7**	-	-	-	-
	KnowExpert$_w$+causal	15.2	18.4	6.4	26.4	20.0	16.6	4.9	20.4	16.8	12.1
	KnowExpert$_o$ (ours)	16.0	18.4	6.6	27.2	21.2	16.6	**5.2**	**21.6**	17.8	12.1
	KnowExpert$_w$ (ours)	15.3	**18.7**	**6.8**	**27.9**	20.1	**16.7**	**5.2**	21.2	17.2	**12.5**

Table 1: Automatic evaluation results ($L = 4$). PPL is short for Perplexity; F1 refers to the unigram-F1 score between the generated and gold responses; Dist-1/2 denotes uni-gram and bi-gram distinct metrics. We highlight the best results for each group in **bold**. We also underline the cases when our proposed `KnowExpert` outperforms the retrieval-based models. †Although KE-Blender is not a retrieval-free model, we present its reported inference performance without the knowledge inputs.

Winning Rate (%)	WoW Seen		WoW Unseen	
Models	Info.	Human.	Info.	Human.
KnowExpert$_w$ vs. GPT-2_f	**57.68**	48.69	**59.26**	**56.13**
KnowExpert$_o$ vs. GPT-2_f	**64.46**	**54.42**	**55.88**	**53.67**

Table 2: Human evaluation results in terms of the winning rate of our model over the GPT-2_f baseline for *Informativeness* and *Humanness*. A significance pairwise t-test is conducted and the results in bold are significantly better than those from the baseline model ($p < 0.05$).

# of Clus.	WoW Seen		WoW Unseen		Average
	PPL↓	F1↑	PPL↓	F1↑	F1↑
4	**15.95**	**18.41**	21.18	16.61	**17.51**
8	16.22	18.14	21.21	16.58	17.36
16	16.43	18.05	**21.12**	**16.76**	17.41

Table 3: Effects of the number of topic clusters. We present the results when setting the number of predefined topic clusters as 4, 8 and 16 while utilizing one-hot knowledge adapters (KE_o) to keep the same number of parameters in the models.

2019) intends to combat low-resource settings with pre-training techniques; (ii) **ZRGKG** (Li et al., 2020) explores the response generation problem without leveraging the matching annotations between the context-response and the knowledge sentences during training; (iii) **GPT-2_{trunc}** (Zhao et al., 2020) randomly ranks the provided knowledge sentences and directly concatenates them with the dialogue context as inputs, while truncating the part exceeding the maximum input length; (iv) **KnowledGPT** (Zhao et al., 2020) exploits pre-trained LMs as both a knowledge selection module and a response generation module which are optimized jointly; (v) **KE-Blender** (Cui et al., 2021) proposes knowledge-enhanced finetuning during training to better handle the unseen entities in the dialogue history. KE-Blender is not a retrieval-free model, but we focus on the case of no knowledge inputs during inference for KE-Blender, which is similar to our settings.

As an additional baseline for comparison among the solely generation-based approaches, we finetune the whole GPT-2 model to generate responses given dialogue contexts, without accessing an explicit knowledge corpus (**GPT-2_f**). To evaluate the effect of dialogue-oriented training for knowledge experts, we train the knowledge adapters with GPT-2-style causal pre-training and keep the other settings unchanged. The corresponding model is denoted as **KnowExpert$_w$+causal**.

4.4 Evaluation and Model Selection

Automatic Metrics Following Dinan et al. (2019), we present the perplexity (PPL) of generating the gold responses and uni-gram F1 as automatic evaluation metrics. The uni-gram F1 metric is implemented with the ParlAI [2] package. In addition, we also evaluate the uni-gram and bi-gram diversity of the generated response with the corpus-level DISTINCT (Li et al., 2016) metric.

Human Evaluation In addition to the automatic evaluation, we conduct human evaluation over the generated responses from two aspects: *Informativeness (Info.)* and *Humanness (Human.)*. "Info."

[2] https://github.com/facebookresearch/ParlAI

Context		User: Orc. System: Orcs are cool fictional humanoid beings. User: Yeah, I've seen them in a lot of things like magic and dnd.	
Generated responses with single knowledge expert in KnowExpert$_w$ ($L = 4$)	Expert 1	Do you know about the orcs? They are native to the Italian peninsula. ***Topics of Cluster 1****: east, river, south, state, city, area, island, ...*	✗
	Expert 2	They are a subgenre of "art games" that are a subgenre of video games. ***Topics of Cluster 2****: rock, band, music, album, football, single, ...*	✗
	Expert 3	Orcs are cool, they are a subspecies of elves in the warcraft universe. ***Topics of Cluster 3****: fiction, story, characters, novel, film, stars, ...*	✓
	Expert 4	They are a legendary race that are native to the americas. ***Topics of Cluster 4****: bon, bucks, rutgers, canberra, ivy, nets, ...*	✗
KnowExpert$_w$		They are a fictional humanoid creature from the "dungeons & dragons" fantasy roleplaying game.	

Table 4: Case study on the effect of different knowledge experts in KnowExpert$_w$ ($L = 4$). *Expert 1/2/3/4* denotes the generated responses with the same context with KnowExpert$_w$ using different knowledge experts separately on the WoW test seen set. Along with the generated responses, we also show the topic keywords of each cluster extracted with the topic model in § 3.2. In this example, Expert 3 is more related to the topic of the dialogue context.

evaluates how knowledgeable the generated responses are, based on the amount of new information introduced into the conversations and the factuality of the responses, while "Human." is used for evaluating the fluency and the coherence of the generated responses.

A/B testing is utilized to compare our proposed framework, KnowExpert$_w$ and KnowExpert$_o$, with the GPT-2$_f$ baseline on the WoW dataset. For each comparison, the same context and two options generated by the models in comparison are shown to the annotators. Each comparison requires three judgments, and 100 data samples are randomly selected from each domain. We conduct a human evaluation using a crowd-sourcing platform offered by Amazon Mechanical Turk.[3] We ensure that each sample is evaluated by three annotators. Further details and annotator instructions are included in Appendix B.

Model Selection In the training procedure, we have different criteria for selecting models for the three training steps: In (i) and (ii), we train the corresponding model for a specific number of epochs; in (iii), the model is selected according to the sum of the PPLs on the seen and unseen validation sets.

4.5 Results

Table 1 reports the automatic evaluation results. The improvements over the baseline model GPT-2$_f$ demonstrate the effectiveness of our proposed framework. In this task, KnowExpert$_w$ performs comparably with the retrieval-based baselines, especially on the seen domain, without using either retrieval or any explicit extra knowledge input in the inference process. Compared with the KE-Blender model under the retrieval-free setting, KnowExpertshows a significant advantage on the WoW seen and CMU_DoG datasets. In addition, KnowExpert$_w$ also shows consistently better performance over KnowExpert$_o$. Without dialogue-oriented training, the performance of the proposed model (KnowExpert$_w$+causal) drops even below tha of the model with the one-hot setting, which shows the importance of dialogue-oriented training. Despite the improvements over the baseline model, we also observe a performance gap between the seen and unseen domains, which requires future work.

Table 2 shows the human evaluation results in terms of the winning rate for Info. and Human. The results indicate that the introduction of the knowledge experts brings the GPT-2 model a significant improvement in generating a more informative response, without hurting the fluency and coherence of the generation under the weighted-sum setting. However, when using the knowledge experts under a one-hot setting, the improvement is not as large as that of the weighted-sum one on the unseen domain, which follows the results of the automatic metrics.

[3]https://www.mturk.com

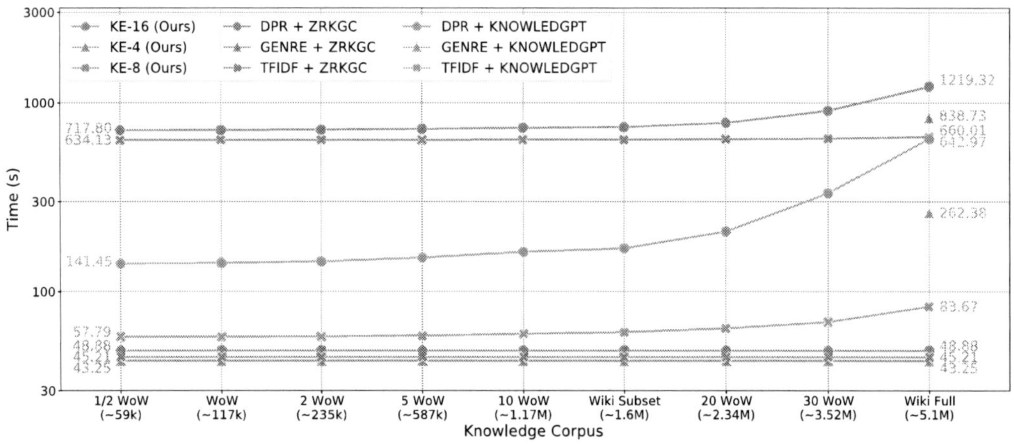

Figure 4: Inference efficiency of our approach generating 100 samples. We show the time on a logarithmic scale and the knowledge corpus sizes in ascending order. In the figure above, we demonstrate the overall end-to-end inference time of our method with the generation length of 23 (average response length in WoW dataset).

4.6 Effects of Number of Topic Clusters

The number of topic clusters is an important hyperparameter since it crucially impacts the quality of topic modeling and knowledge expert training. Because of the nature of the WoW and CMU_DoG datasets, we conduct experiments with $L = 4, 8, 16$. In Table A1 in the Appendix, we show in detail the most frequent words for each topic cluster with different numbers of topic clusters. For example, Cluster 2 when $L = 8$ is strongly related to the movie domain. As shown in Table 3, we select $L = 4$ since it achieves the best average F1 on two WoW test sets.

4.7 Case Study

We leverage different knowledge experts in a one-hot manner, generating responses with only one knowledge expert and the same dialogue history to study what each knowledge expert captures. As shown in Table 4, the responses generated with different knowledge experts tend to lean into different cluster topics with the same context. We also provide another example in Table A2. Some selected keywords are shown below, and more topic keywords are listed in Table A1 in the Appendix. Comparing the responses with the listed topic keywords, our knowledge experts tend to focus on the topics to which the knowledge documents they are trained on belong. For example, with the same context, Expert 2 is leaning into the music domain as Cluster 2 is strongly related to music, while Expert 3 relates more to the fiction topics, which align with the topic in Cluster 3. In addition, the shown cases also support the observation from Table 1 that the mixture-of-experts approach ensures a better model performance. The generated response of $\text{KnowExpert}_\text{w}$ is more on-topic and accurate thanks to leveraging the weighted sum of the experts. The above findings indicate that the proper ensemble of experts also helps the response generation.

Although the generated responses appear to be knowledgeable and fluent, they frequently raise an issue of factual correctness; for example, "Orcs" are not directly related to the "Italian peninsula". We also observe that a knowledge expert whose topics are more similar to the topic of the dialogue tends to generate more factual responses.

4.8 Inference Efficiency

We evaluate the response generation inference time of `KnowExpert` and two other retrieval-based baselines: ZRGKG and KnowledGPT. In addition to the time to generate responses, we also consider the time required for retrieving knowledge candidates from knowledge corpora of different sizes against the time required for topic modeling in `KnowExpert`. We take the retrieval methods TF-IDF, DPR (Karpukhin et al., 2020), and GENRE (Cao et al., 2021) for comparison. To have a fair comparison with our approach, we measure the end-to-end inference time by summing the time for retrieval and response generation. The generation length is pre-defined as the average response length in the WoW dataset. We randomly sample 100 instances from WoW seen and unseen test set and average the inference time of 10 trials. The detailed configuration is listed in Table C1 in the Appendix.

As shown in Figure 4, `KnowExpert` requires the least computing time and keeps a constant computational cost, regardless of the size of the knowledge corpus. This is because our topic modeling requires a constant computational cost, while that of TF-IDF or DPR incurs an increasing cost as the size of the knowledge corpus increases. Additionally, our model does not require a large external corpus during the inference time. These results suggest that our model is suitable for deployment in resource-limited platforms, such as in the on-device setting.

5 Conclusion

We propose `KnowExpert`, a retrieval-free framework for the KGD task. `KnowExpert`is the first attempt to tackle the challenge of injecting knowledge into the model parameters and leveraging it for the KGD task. We leverage light-weight adapters as knowledge experts, then train the backbone model to take advantage of them for response generation. By these means, our method can generate more knowledgeable responses without an explicit retrieval step compared to our baseline model. By bypassing the retrieval step over the knowledge corpus, the inference efficiency of the model is improved. Experimental results show that `KnowExpert` performs comparably with some retrieval-based models, demonstrating the promise of our proposed research direction.

Acknowledgement

We would thank Zhaojiang Lin, Peng Xu for discussing the project and the anonymous reviewers for the insightful reviews and constructive feedback. This work has been partially supported by the HKJCCT21EG01 of the Hong Kong Jockey Club, and School of Engineering Ph.D. Fellowship Award, the Hong Kong University of Science and Technology.

References

Lei Jimmy Ba, Jamie Ryan Kiros, and Geoffrey E. Hinton. 2016. Layer normalization. *CoRR*, abs/1607.06450.

Ankur Bapna and Orhan Firat. 2019. Simple, scalable adaptation for neural machine translation. In *Proceedings of the 2019 Conference on Empirical Methods in Natural Language Processing and the 9th International Joint Conference on Natural Language Processing (EMNLP-IJCNLP)*, pages 1538–1548.

Federico Bianchi, Silvia Terragni, and Dirk Hovy. 2021. Pre-training is a hot topic: Contextualized document embeddings improve topic coherence. In *ACL*.

Tom B Brown, Benjamin Mann, Nick Ryder, Melanie Subbiah, Jared Kaplan, Prafulla Dhariwal, Arvind Neelakantan, Pranav Shyam, Girish Sastry, Amanda Askell, et al. 2020. Language models are few-shot learners. *arXiv preprint arXiv:2005.14165*.

Nicola De Cao, Gautier Izacard, Sebastian Riedel, and Fabio Petroni. 2021. Autoregressive entity retrieval. In *International Conference on Learning Representations*.

Qingqing Cao, Harsh Trivedi, Aruna Balasubramanian, and Niranjan Balasubramanian. 2020. DeFormer: Decomposing pre-trained transformers for faster question answering. In *Proceedings of the 58th Annual Meeting of the Association for Computational Linguistics*, pages 4487–4497, Online. Association for Computational Linguistics.

Daniel Cer, Mona Diab, Eneko Agirre, Iñigo Lopez-Gazpio, and Lucia Specia. 2017. SemEval-2017 task 1: Semantic textual similarity multilingual and crosslingual focused evaluation. In *Proceedings of the 11th International Workshop on Semantic Evaluation (SemEval-2017)*, pages 1–14, Vancouver, Canada. Association for Computational Linguistics.

Xiuyi Chen, Fandong Meng, Peng Li, Feilong Chen, Shuang Xu, Bo Xu, and Jie Zhou. 2020. Bridging the gap between prior and posterior knowledge selection for knowledge-grounded dialogue generation. In *Proceedings of the 2020 Conference on Empirical Methods in Natural Language Processing (EMNLP)*, pages 3426–3437.

Alexis Conneau, Douwe Kiela, Holger Schwenk, Loïc Barrault, and Antoine Bordes. 2017. Supervised learning of universal sentence representations from natural language inference data. In *Proceedings of the 2017 Conference on Empirical Methods in Natural Language Processing*, pages 670–680, Copenhagen, Denmark. Association for Computational Linguistics.

Leyang Cui, Yu Wu, Shujie Liu, and Yue Zhang. 2021. Knowledge enhanced fine-tuning for better handling unseen entities in dialogue generation. In *Proceedings of the 2021 Conference on Empirical Methods in Natural Language Processing*, pages 2328–2337.

Emily Dinan, Stephen Roller, Kurt Shuster, Angela Fan, Michael Auli, and Jason Weston. 2019. Wizard of wikipedia: Knowledge-powered conversational agents. In *International Conference on Learning Representations*.

Xiaoqi Jiao, Yichun Yin, Lifeng Shang, Xin Jiang, Xiao Chen, Linlin Li, Fang Wang, and Qun Liu. 2020. TinyBERT: Distilling BERT for natural language understanding. In *Findings of the Association for Computational Linguistics: EMNLP 2020*, pages 4163–4174, Online. Association for Computational Linguistics.

Vladimir Karpukhin, Barlas Oguz, Sewon Min, Patrick Lewis, Ledell Wu, Sergey Edunov, Danqi Chen, and Wen-tau Yih. 2020. Dense passage retrieval for open-domain question answering. In *Proceedings of the 2020 Conference on Empirical Methods in Natural Language Processing (EMNLP)*, pages 6769–6781.

Byeongchang Kim, Jaewoo Ahn, and Gunhee Kim. 2019. Sequential latent knowledge selection for knowledge-grounded dialogue. In *International Conference on Learning Representations*.

Diederik P. Kingma and Jimmy Ba. 2015. Adam: A method for stochastic optimization. In *3rd International Conference on Learning Representations, ICLR 2015, San Diego, CA, USA, May 7-9, 2015, Conference Track Proceedings*.

Anne Lauscher, Olga Majewska, Leonardo FR Ribeiro, Iryna Gurevych, Nikolai Rozanov, and Goran Glavaš. 2020. Common sense or world knowledge? investigating adapter-based knowledge injection into pretrained transformers. *arXiv preprint arXiv:2005.11787*.

Jiwei Li, Michel Galley, Chris Brockett, Jianfeng Gao, and William B Dolan. 2016. A diversity-promoting objective function for neural conversation models. In *Proceedings of the 2016 Conference of the North American Chapter of the Association for Computational Linguistics: Human Language Technologies*, pages 110–119.

Linxiao Li, Can Xu, Wei Wu, YUFAN ZHAO, Xueliang Zhao, and Chongyang Tao. 2020. Zero-resource knowledge-grounded dialogue generation. In *Advances in Neural Information Processing Systems*, volume 33, pages 8475–8485. Curran Associates, Inc.

Rongzhong Lian, Min Xie, Fan Wang, Jinhua Peng, and Hua Wu. 2019. Learning to select knowledge for response generation in dialog systems. In *Proceedings of the 28th International Joint Conference on Artificial Intelligence*, pages 5081–5087. AAAI Press.

Zihan Liu, Mostofa Patwary, Ryan Prenger, Shrimai Prabhumoye, Wei Ping, Mohammad Shoeybi, and Bryan Catanzaro. 2022. Multi-stage prompting for knowledgeable dialogue generation. *arXiv preprint arXiv:2203.08745*.

Andrea Madotto, Samuel Cahyawijaya, Genta Indra Winata, Yan Xu, Zihan Liu, Zhaojiang Lin, and Pascale Fung. 2020. Learning knowledge bases with parameters for task-oriented dialogue systems. In *Proceedings of the 2020 Conference on Empirical Methods in Natural Language Processing: Findings*, pages 2372–2394.

Nicole Peinelt, Dong Nguyen, and Maria Liakata. 2020. tBERT: Topic models and BERT joining forces for semantic similarity detection. In *Proceedings of the 58th Annual Meeting of the Association for Computational Linguistics*, pages 7047–7055, Online. Association for Computational Linguistics.

Fabio Petroni, Tim Rocktäschel, Sebastian Riedel, Patrick Lewis, Anton Bakhtin, Yuxiang Wu, and Alexander Miller. 2019. Language models as knowledge bases? In *Proceedings of the 2019 Conference on Empirical Methods in Natural Language Processing and the 9th International Joint Conference on Natural Language Processing (EMNLP-IJCNLP)*, pages 2463–2473.

Alec Radford, Jeffrey Wu, Rewon Child, David Luan, Dario Amodei, and Ilya Sutskever. 2019. Language models are unsupervised multitask learners. *OpenAI Blog, 1(8):9*.

Colin Raffel, Noam Shazeer, Adam Roberts, Katherine Lee, Sharan Narang, Michael Matena, Yanqi Zhou, Wei Li, and Peter J Liu. 2019. Exploring the limits of transfer learning with a unified text-to-text transformer. *arXiv preprint arXiv:1910.10683*.

Nils Reimers and Iryna Gurevych. 2019. Sentence-BERT: Sentence embeddings using Siamese BERT-networks. In *Proceedings of the 2019 Conference on Empirical Methods in Natural Language Processing and the 9th International Joint Conference on Natural Language Processing (EMNLP-IJCNLP)*, pages 3982–3992, Hong Kong, China. Association for Computational Linguistics.

Adam Roberts, Colin Raffel, and Noam Shazeer. 2020. How much knowledge can you pack into the parameters of a language model? In *Proceedings of the 2020 Conference on Empirical Methods in Natural Language Processing (EMNLP)*, pages 5418–5426.

Stephen Roller, Emily Dinan, Naman Goyal, Da Ju, Mary Williamson, Yinhan Liu, Jing Xu, Myle Ott, Kurt Shuster, Eric M Smith, et al. 2020. Recipes for building an open-domain chatbot. *arXiv preprint arXiv:2004.13637*.

Victor Sanh, Lysandre Debut, Julien Chaumond, and Thomas Wolf. 2019. Distilbert, a distilled version of BERT: smaller, faster, cheaper and lighter. *CoRR*, abs/1910.01108.

Taylor Shin, Yasaman Razeghi, Robert L Logan IV, Eric Wallace, and Sameer Singh. 2020. Autoprompt: Eliciting knowledge from language models with automatically generated prompts. *arXiv preprint arXiv:2010.15980*.

Vered Shwartz, Peter West, Ronan Le Bras, Chandra Bhagavatula, and Yejin Choi. 2020. Unsupervised commonsense question answering with self-talk. *arXiv preprint arXiv:2004.05483*.

Akash Srivastava and Charles Sutton. 2017. Autoencoding variational inference for topic models. In *ICLR*.

Zhiqing Sun, Zhuohan Li, Haoqing Wang, Di He, Zi Lin, and Zhihong Deng. 2019. Fast structured decoding for sequence models. In *Advances in Neural Information Processing Systems*, volume 32. Curran Associates, Inc.

Zhiqing Sun, Hongkun Yu, Xiaodan Song, Renjie Liu, Yiming Yang, and Denny Zhou. 2020. MobileBERT: a compact task-agnostic BERT for resource-limited devices. In *Proceedings of the 58th Annual Meeting of the Association for Computational Linguistics*, pages 2158–2170, Online. Association for Computational Linguistics.

Raphael Tang, Yao Lu, Linqing Liu, Lili Mou, Olga Vechtomova, and Jimmy Lin. 2019. Distilling task-specific knowledge from BERT into simple neural networks. *CoRR*, abs/1903.12136.

Greta Tuckute, Alexander Paunov, Hope Kean, Hannah Small, Zachary Mineroff, Idan Blank, and Evelina Fedorenko. 2021. Frontal language areas do not emerge in the absence of temporal language areas: A case study of an individual born without a left temporal lobe. *bioRxiv*.

Cunxiang Wang, Pai Liu, and Yue Zhang. 2021. Can generative pre-trained language models serve as knowledge bases for closed-book qa? *arXiv preprint arXiv:2106.01561*.

Ruize Wang, Duyu Tang, Nan Duan, Zhongyu Wei, Xuanjing Huang, Cuihong Cao, Daxin Jiang, Ming Zhou, et al. 2020. K-adapter: Infusing knowledge into pre-trained models with adapters. *arXiv preprint arXiv:2002.01808*.

Thomas Wolf, Lysandre Debut, Victor Sanh, Julien Chaumond, Clement Delangue, Anthony Moi, Pierric Cistac, Tim Rault, Rémi Louf, Morgan Funtowicz, Joe Davison, Sam Shleifer, Patrick von Platen, Clara Ma, Yacine Jernite, Julien Plu, Canwen Xu, Teven Le Scao, Sylvain Gugger, Mariama Drame, Quentin Lhoest, and Alexander M. Rush. 2020. Transformers: State-of-the-art natural language processing. In *Proceedings of the 2020 Conference on Empirical Methods in Natural Language Processing: System Demonstrations*, pages 38–45, Online. Association for Computational Linguistics.

Yi Xu and Hai Zhao. 2021. Dialogue-oriented pre-training. *arXiv preprint arXiv:2106.00420*.

Xueliang Zhao, Wei Wu, Chongyang Tao, Can Xu, Dongyan Zhao, and Rui Yan. 2019. Low-resource knowledge-grounded dialogue generation. In *International Conference on Learning Representations*.

Xueliang Zhao, Wei Wu, Can Xu, Chongyang Tao, Dongyan Zhao, and Rui Yan. 2020. Knowledge-grounded dialogue generation with pre-trained language models. In *Proceedings of the 2020 Conference on Empirical Methods in Natural Language Processing (EMNLP)*, pages 3377–3390.

Kangyan Zhou, Shrimai Prabhumoye, and Alan W Black. 2018. A dataset for document grounded conversations. In *Proceedings of the 2018 Conference on Empirical Methods in Natural Language Processing*.

Pei Zhou, Behnam Hedayatnia, Karthik Gopalakrishnan, Seokhwan Kim, Jay Pujara, Xiang Ren, Yang Liu, and Dilek Hakkani-Tur. 2021. Think before you speak: Learning to generate implicit knowledge for response generation by self-talk. In *Proceedings of the 3rd Workshop on Natural Language Processing for Conversational AI*, pages 251–253.

A Additional Cluster Analysis

We show in Table A1 the topic keywords list of each cluster when the pre-defined number of clusters $L = 4, 8, 16$ in our Contextualized Topic Model. An additional example for case study is presented in Table A2. Similar to the analysis in Section 4.7, the provided dialogue history is aligned with the topics of Cluster 3, so the model is able to generate factual correct informative response with solely Expert 3, whereas the other experts are not helpful for the given data sample.

In Figure A1, we present the ratio of each cluster when $L = 4, 8, 16$. From the cluster distribution, we can observe that there is a dominant cluster in the WoW training data across different numbers of clusters. This is because of the nature of the WoW dataset. While setting a larger number of clusters will help the cluster ratio over the training and test sets to be more equal distributed, it will also lead to the problem that there is insufficient training data for each cluster during task adaptation.

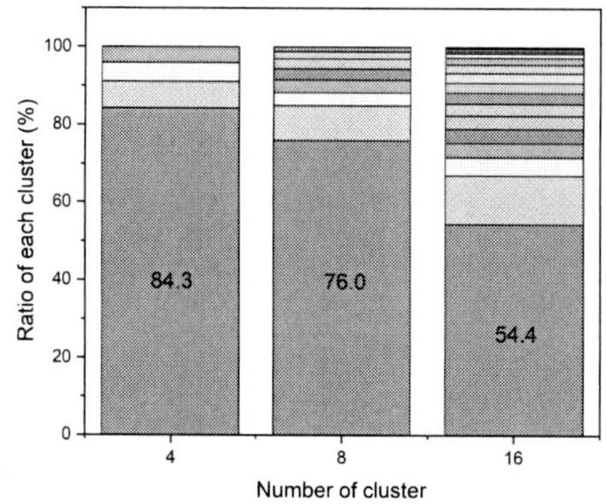

Figure A1: Ratio of the dialogue samples in WoW training set when $L = 4, 8, 16$. From the cluster distribution, we can observe a dominant cluster in the WoW training data.

B Additional Details on Human Evaluation

We collect human annotations for both humanness and informativeness via crowd-sourcing platform provided by Amazon Mechanical Turk.[4] For quality control, we limit the annotators' locations to be the United States, United Kingdom, Canada, or Australia to ensure English proficiency. Moreover, we qualify annotators with a HIT Approval rate larger than 95% and HIT Approved number greater than 5000. As the average time that annotators will spend per response comparison for informativeness is 168 seconds, we reject annotators who spend less than 10 seconds so as to maintain the quality. The annotator instructions for human evaluation are shown in Figure B2 and Figure B2. Each annotator is asked to judge either the humanness or informativeness of one dialogue. To get a consistent observation, we use the same 100 randomly selected prefixes of the dialogues across the comparisons.

C Configuration for Inference Efficiency

We randomly sample 100 data samples from the seen and unseen test set of WoW, respectively. The sampled data are leveraged for all the inference efficiency evaluation experiments. We set the batch size as 1, and repeat each evaluation five times respectively on samples from seen and unseen test set. The final value is the average of ten trials. The device configuration for inference efficiency evaluation is shown in Table C1 and Table C2. For the generation inference time evaluation, to have a fair comparison, the generation length is set as 23 for all the models, where 23 is the average response length in the WoW dataset.

Model	Device (CPU / GPU)	# of Device
TF-IDF	Intel Xeon E5-2620 V4 CPU	1
DPR	GeForce GTX 1080Ti	1
GENRE	GeForce GTX 1080Ti	1
CTM	Intel Xeon E5-2620 V4 CPU	1

Table C1: Device configuration for knowledge retrieval methods and CTM topic modeling.

Model	Device (CPU / GPU)	# of Device
ZRKGC	GeForce GTX 1080Ti	2
KnowledGPT	GeForce GTX 1080Ti	1
Ours	GeForce GTX 1080Ti	1

Table C2: Device configuration for response generation (with knowledge selection if applicable).

[4]https://www.mturk.com

$L=4$	
cluster 1	east, west, river, south, state, city, area, district, north, center, largest, island, park, states, county
cluster 2	rock, band, records, music, team, song, album, club, football, record, league, studio, single, released, professional
cluster 3	fiction, story, characters, book, disney, novel, episode, film, films, comic, stars, comics, opera, comedy, character
cluster 4	pain, bon, canberra, blocked, rutgers, khalil, edmonton, auckland, auburn, capitals, akron, karim, woodstock, cougars, euro
$L=8$	
cluster 1	systems, theory, data, software, computer, information, person, system, value, mobile, use, users, user, physical, devices
cluster 2	film, character, characters, episode, comic, television, comedy, fiction, story, comics, directed, novel, films, fictional, fantasy
cluster 3	company, school, university, students, education, founded, schools, institute, president, department, business, public, united, states, private
cluster 4	empire, roman, german, period, chinese, century, russian, soviet, religious, french, bc, king, war, battle, dynasty
cluster 5	area, south, city, north, west, ye, located, river, population, east, park, part, county, region, island
cluster 6	sugar, yellow, rice, tree, meat, cats, neck, pain, egg, sauce, corn, chicken, breed, hair, cheese
cluster 7	music, band, rock, song, album, records, studio, singer, pop, single, guitar, group, songs, recorded, released
cluster 8	league, team, football, club, sports, professional, championship, hockey, baseball, teams, cup, basketball, division, played, racing
$L=16$	
cluster 1	team, football, league, club, championship, cup, basketball, hockey, wrestling, professional, baseball, olympic, teams, race, rugby
cluster 2	company, brand, car, chain, ford, owned, cars, corporation, stores, inc, brands, sold, manufacturer, headquartered, restaurant
cluster 3	film, episode, directed, stars, fox, drama, comedy, cast, aired, episodes, soap, abc, show, opera, movie
cluster 4	light, used, water, surface, temperature, earth, power, energy, materials, chemical, space, speed, material, carbon, electric
cluster 5	album, records, song, studio, single, release, track, recorded, lead, songs, chart, recording, label, hot, hit
cluster 6	war, army, military, party, navy, ii, forces, election, force, battle, soviet, royal, corps, armed, campaign
cluster 7	care, organization, laws, act, tax, organizations, education, non, profit, policy, legal, law, health, rights, agency
cluster 8	brain, blood, normal, condition, cause, sleep, eye, causes, fever, heart, psychological, surgery, emotional, loss, drugs
cluster 9	ocean, mountain, region, land, coast, pacific, islands, sea, gulf, island, mountains, capital, rivers, km, river
cluster 10	computer, digital, data, software, internet, web, code, users, devices, value, mobile, application, device, systems, user
cluster 11	street, park, center, road, railway, station, historic, built, building, route, located, highway, opened, city, line
cluster 12	century, chinese, greek, christian, modern, medieval, ancient, period, middle, ad, roman, traditions, culture, bc, tradition
cluster 13	yellow, bird, tree, flowers, breed, meat, rice, dog, wild, white, sugar, leaf, colour, pepper, flower
cluster 14	professor, father, mother, worked, born, graduated, institute, degree, married, studied, bachelor, moved, mary, graduate, attended
cluster 15	bass, jazz, guitar, music, festival, stage, dance, theatre, artists, musical, bands, piano, hip, musician, blues
cluster 16	fantasy, comics, published, comic, game, fiction, book, universe, books, marvel, created, video, playstation, developed, dc

Table A1: Top 15 frequent words for each topic cluster of CTM with $L = 4, 8, 16$.

Context		User: Harry Potter.	
Case study with single knowledge expert in KnowExpert$_w$ ($L=4$)	Expert 1	Harry Potter is an American author, investor, philanthropist, and philanthropist. ***Topics of Cluster 1**: east, river, south, state, city, area, island, ...*	✗
	Expert 2	Harry Potter is an American musician, songwriter, record producer, and actor. ***Topics of Cluster 2**: rock, band, music, album, football, single, ...*	✗
	Expert 3	Harry Potter is a fantasy novel, written by J. K. Rowling. ***Topics of Cluster 3**: fiction, story, characters, novel, film, stars, ...*	✓
	Expert 4	I love Harry Potter, its a great American toy company ***Topics of Cluster 4**: bon, bucks, rutgers, canberra, ivy, nets, ...*	✗
KnowExpert$_w$		I love Harry Potter. It's a great American children's book series.	

Table A2: Case study on generated responses using the KnowExpert$_w$ model ($L = 4$) with the same context on the WoW test unseen set.

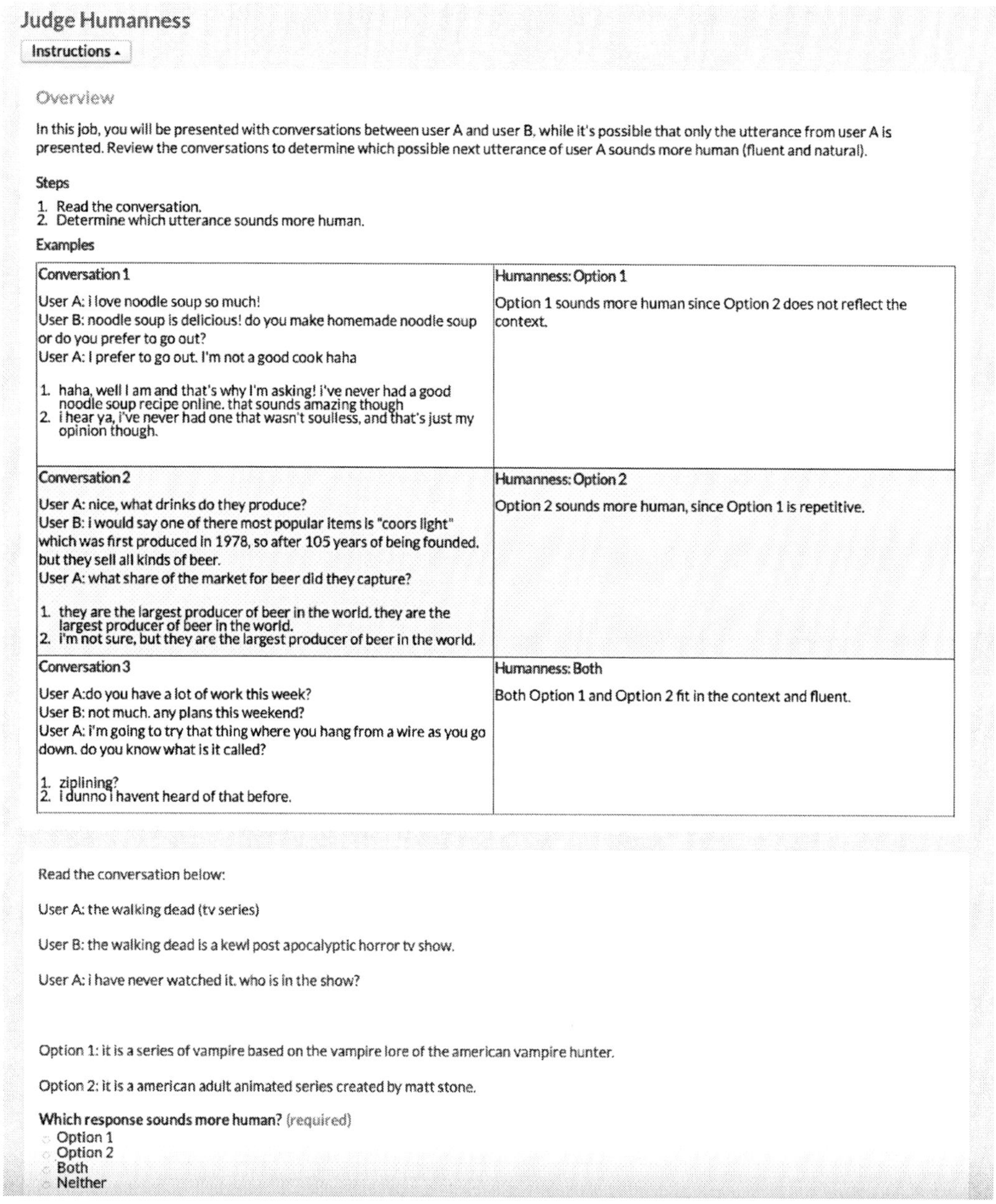

Judge Humanness

Instructions

Overview

In this job, you will be presented with conversations between user A and user B, while it's possible that only the utterance from user A is presented. Review the conversations to determine which possible next utterance of user A sounds more human (fluent and natural).

Steps

1. Read the conversation.
2. Determine which utterance sounds more human.

Examples

Conversation 1	Humanness: Option 1
User A: i love noodle soup so much! User B: noodle soup is delicious! do you make homemade noodle soup or do you prefer to go out? User A: I prefer to go out. I'm not a good cook haha 1. haha, well I am and that's why I'm asking! i've never had a good noodle soup recipe online. that sounds amazing though 2. i hear ya, i've never had one that wasn't soulless, and that's just my opinion though.	Option 1 sounds more human since Option 2 does not reflect the context.
Conversation 2	**Humanness: Option 2**
User A: nice, what drinks do they produce? User B: i would say one of there most popular items is "coors light" which was first produced in 1978, so after 105 years of being founded. but they sell all kinds of beer. User A: what share of the market for beer did they capture? 1. they are the largest producer of beer in the world. they are the largest producer of beer in the world. 2. i'm not sure, but they are the largest producer of beer in the world.	Option 2 sounds more human, since Option 1 is repetitive.
Conversation 3	**Humanness: Both**
User A:do you have a lot of work this week? User B: not much. any plans this weekend? User A: i'm going to try that thing where you hang from a wire as you go down. do you know what is it called? 1. ziplining? 2. i dunno i havent heard of that before.	Both Option 1 and Option 2 fit in the context and fluent.

Read the conversation below:

User A: the walking dead (tv series)

User B: the walking dead is a kewl post apocalyptic horror tv show.

User A: i have never watched it. who is in the show?

Option 1: it is a series of vampire based on the vampire lore of the american vampire hunter.

Option 2: it is a american adult animated series created by matt stone.

Which response sounds more human? (required)

- Option 1
- Option 2
- Both
- Neither

Figure B2: Human evaluation template for judging Humanness.

Judge Knowledgeable

Instructions

Overview

In this job, you will be presented with conversations between user A and user B, while it's possible that only the utterance from user A is presented. Review the conversations to determine which possible next utterance of user B sounds more knowledgeable, according to the amount of new information introduced to the conversation and the correctness of the utterance.

Steps

1. Read the conversation.
2. Determine which utterance sounds more knowledgeable.

Examples

Conversation 1	Knowledgeable: Option 1
User A: [enter the room] User B: [enter the room] User A: ever tried snapple? i'm not a huge fan of iced tea but it's really good. 1. i love snapple, it is a carbonated soft drink 2. i love snapple. it's a sweet, sweet, and sour apple.	Option 1 sounds more knowledgeable since Option 1 correctly mentioned that snapple is actually a type drinks, which Option 2 regarded it as an apple.
Conversation 2	**Knowledgeable: Option 2**
User A: i just got a husky puppy User B: it sounds cute! huskies are known amongst sled-dogs for their fast pulling style. User A: i guess in the north they are working dogs huh? 1. yes, they are also known as sled dogs. 2. yes, they are working dogs. they are also known for their ability to hear sounds that are too faint for humans.	Option 2 sounds more knowledgeable, since Option 1 does not really introduce new information into the conversation.
Conversation 3	**Knowledgeable: Both**
User A: what is another interesting fact about the color blue? User B: well with blue the eye perceives blue when observing light with a dominant wavelength between 450 and 495 nanpmetres. User A: wow, that is way above my head. when i think of colors, I basically just think of what i can see, but its crazy there are a lot more to it then " hey, there is the color blue" 1. yes, it is one of the three primary colors. 2. yes, it is a color that is associated with the sky and the earth.	Both Option 1 and Option 2 are correct and contains nearly the same amount of the new information into the conversation between A and B.

Read the conversation below:

User A: i guess in the north they are working dogs huh?

User B: sled dogs, including huskies, are used for transportation in arctic areas.

User A: that is so cool and probably helpful but mine is just a pet

Option 1: i'm not sure if they are used for hunting or for hunting dogs.

Option 2: they are also used for hunting and herding.

Which response sounds more knowledgeable? (according to the amount of new information introduced to the conversation and the correctness of the response.) (required)

- Option 1
- Option 2
- Both
- Neither

Figure B2: Human evaluation template for judging Informativeness.

G4: Grounding-guided Goal-oriented Dialogues Generation with Multiple Documents

Shiwei Zhang [†], **Yiyang Du**[‡], **Guanzhong Liu** [†§], **Zhao Yan**[†], **Yunbo Cao**[†]
[†]Tencent Cloud Xiaowei, [§]Tianjin University
[‡] State Key Lab of Software Development Environment, Beihang University
{zswzhang, zhaoyan, yunbocao}@tencent.com, duyiyang@buaa.edu.cn
rogerliu425@tju.edu.cn

Abstract

Goal-oriented dialogues generation grounded in multiple documents(MultiDoc2Dial) is a challenging and realistic task. Unlike previous works which treat document-grounded dialogue modeling as a machine reading comprehension task from single document, MultiDoc2Dial task faces challenges of both seeking information from multiple documents and generating conversation response simultaneously. This paper summarizes our entries to agent response generation subtask in MultiDoc2Dial dataset. We propose a three-stage solution, Grounding-guided goal-oriented dialogues generation(G4), which predicts groundings from retrieved passages to guide the generation of the final response. Our experiments show that G4 achieves SacreBLEU score of 31.24 and F1 score of 44.6 which is 60.7% higher than the baseline model.

1 Introduction

Conversational question answering techniques have attracted widespread attention as a fusion of document-based question answering and dialogue generation techniques. Most previous works have focused on single-document conversational question answering tasks, such as QuAC(Choi et al., 2018), CoQA(Reddy et al., 2019), Doc2Dial(Feng et al., 2020). As a more realistic task, goal-oriented dialogues generation is based on multiple documents as MultiDoc2Dial(Feng et al., 2021) faces challenges of identifying useful pieces of text from documents and generating response simultaneously.

Inspired by the method of Open-domain question answering (OpenQA), the MultiDoc2Dial task can be solved in a two-stage framework(Robertson et al., 1995; Lewis et al., 2020; Izacard and Grave, 2020a,b): (i) first to retrieve relevant passages from the knowledge source (the retriever)(Jones, 1972; Robertson et al., 1995; Karpukhin et al., 2020; Xiong et al., 2020; Brown et al., 2020); and (ii) second to produce an answer based on retrieved passages and the question (the generator)(Raffel et al., 2019; Lewis et al., 2019). what's more, the end-to-end methods which learn to retrieve and generate simultaneously(Lee et al., 2021; Singh et al., 2021) also achieves good results.

In MultiDoc2Dial task, as the dialogue flow shifts among the grounding documents through the conversation which makes the current session relevant to multiple documents, identifying the content that best matches the question from the relevant documents becomes the biggest challenge. After analysis, it is found that two-stage methods fail to locate the answer span position from multiple relevant documents and generate irrelevant responses to the query.

In this paper, we propose a grounding-guided three-stage framework(Retriever-Reader-Generator). The framework imitates the process of humans looking for answers from a browser: first read each relevant retrieved documents with question, and then combine the understanding of each document to generate a final answer. The generator of third stage can be guided by grounding spans, phrases in the retrieved document predicted by reader, mitigating the excessive deviation of the generated result from the correct response. Since the same corpus data is shared among reader and generator, data distribution of the input for generator are different in training and inference. We also propose a data augmentation approach to alleviate the discrepancy between training and inference. To conclude, our contributions are as follows:

- we propose a grounding-guided three-stage framework that mitigates the deviation of response from the question.
- we present a data augmentation approach which improves the diversity of groundings for generation thus further improving the robustness of the multi-stage framework.

Proceedings of the Second DialDoc Workshop on Document-grounded Dialogue and Conversational Question Answering, pages 108 - 114
May 26, 2022

2 Method

Our proposed model G4 is a three-stage framework: (i) retrieve relevant passages from the knowledge(retriever). (ii) predict groundings based on retrieved passages(reader). (iii)generate a response based on the groundings predicted by reader and relevant passages from retriever(generator).

2.1 Problem Definition

Given dialogue history $\{u_1, \ldots, u_{T-1}\}$ and current user's utterance u_T, MultiDoc2Dial task produces the response u_{T+1} based on knowledge from a set of relevant documents $D_0 \subseteq D$, where D denotes all knowledge documents. In particular, in the same dialogue session, different utterances might have different related documents. Depending on the form of the answer, two tasks are proposed in MultiDoc2Dial where the first is to identify the grounding document span and the second is to generate agent response. We focus on the second task in this paper.

2.2 Retriever

Given dialogue history $\{u_1, \ldots, u_{T-1}\}$, current user's utterance u_T and passages $P = \{p_0, p_1, \ldots, p_M\}$ which are splited from all knowledge documents. The retriever identify the top-k relevant passages $R = \{r_1, r_2, \ldots, r_k\} \subseteq P$, where P is the splited results of documents D. In order to distinguish the above D and P, we use "document" and "passage" respectively to denote the text of before and after segmentation. In the retrieval stage, we first split the documents into passages and then use dense-based retriever to identify relevant passages.

Retriever. We use the ANCE model (Xiong et al., 2020) to retrieve relevant passages from multi-documents. We finetune ANCE model with positive and negtive examples. We choose the golden passage which include the annotated grounding as positive examples. For initial negative examples, we use grounding and last utterance as query respectively to select top 2 retrieval passages except golden passage as hard negative examples, and use current response utterance with dialogue history as query to choose top 5 to 15 from retrieved results as negative examples based on BM25.

2.3 Reader

Taking current utterance u_T with dialogue history $\{u_1, \ldots, u_{T-1}\}$ and a retrieved passage p_i as input, the reader predicts grounding span in passage or reject to answer. Sliding window is applied to process long passage.

Span restrict. Unlike standard span-based question answering, possible start and end positions of grounding spans are restricted to phrases in the document. The phrase is consecutive sentences labeled in the original document with HTML tag, and the grounding span is one of the phrases in a document.For datasets without grounding labels, grounding span can be constructed according to final response with simple similarity algorithm. To reduce the difficulty of training, we only consider the start and end position of phrase for predict and apply softmax over tokens corresponding these position like previous work(Daheim et al., 2021). Start and end probability are calculated by a linear projection from the last hidden states of encoder:

$$\hat{\boldsymbol{p}}^{\text{ start}} = \sigma(\varphi(H)m_s) \quad \hat{\boldsymbol{p}}^{\text{ end}} = \sigma(\varphi(H)m_s)$$

where $\hat{\boldsymbol{p}}^{\text{ start}}$ and $\hat{\boldsymbol{p}}^{\text{ end}}$ is start and end probability distribution, H is the represation of encoder, m_s denote the mask vector that set to 1 if the start and end position of phrase else 0, σ is softmax function and $\varphi(\circ)$ is MLP. The cost function is defined as :

$$J(\boldsymbol{\theta}) = -\frac{1}{T}\sum_{t=1}^{T} \log\left(\hat{\boldsymbol{p}}_{y_t^s}^{\text{start}}\right) + \log\left(\hat{\boldsymbol{p}}_{y_t^e}^{\text{end}}\right)$$

where T is the number of training samples, y_t^s and y_t^e are the true start and end position of the t-th sample.

2.4 Grounding-guided generator

To fully leverage the multiple passages identified by the retriever, we adopt Fusion-in-Decoder(FiD) (Izacard and Grave, 2020b) as our response generation model. Based on seq2seq framework, FiD encodes every passage with query independently and decodes all encoded features jointly to generate response. As summed up in FiD, increasing the number of passages from 10 to 100 leads to significantly improvement on different OpenQA datasets. However, in the MultiDoc2Dial dataset, the current session is related to multiple documents, which makes it difficult for generator to identify grounding span for the current utterance. The above problem is exacerbated when the document is split into multi-passages so that the generated response might be irrelevant to grounding and simply increasing the number of passages yields only insignificant improvement.

Model	F1	SacreBLEU	METEOR	RougeL	total
DPR+RAG (Lewis et al., 2020)	34.25	19.44	33.30	31.85	118.84
EMDR (Singh et al., 2021)	43.33	24.82	41.81	41.83	151.79
DPR+FiD(Izacard and Grave, 2020b)	42.14	28.58	39.78	40.67	151.17
G4-base *(DPR+G^{org})*	43.65	30.33	41.38	41.64	157.00
G4-fin *(ANCE+G^{org})*	44.11	30.91	41.85	42.11	159.39
G4-aug *(DPR+$G^{augment}$)*	44.22	30.73	41.96	42.28	159.19
G4 *(ANCE+$G^{augment}$)*	44.60	31.24	42.41	42.68	160.93

Table 1: The results of Different models in MultiDoc2Dial dataset. DPR: DPR model officially released by MultiDoc2Dial. $\text{DPR}^{\text{optimized}}$: our fine-tuned ANCE model described in 2.2. G^{org}/G^{aug}: grounding-guided generator described in 2.4. G^{aug}: grounding-guided generation with data augmentation while G^{org} without augmentation.

Encode with grounding span and fusionly decode. Grounding-guided generator use the grounding span predicted by reader of second stage to guide the generator to produce agent response. Based on Fusion-in-Decoder model, we proposed two approach to introduce grounding span to guide generator:(i)The first way is to directly concatenate the grounding span to the front of the original passage. The input form of FiD encoder can be described as follows:

$$[\bar{S_u}, u_T, u_{T-1}...u_1; \bar{S_g}, g; \bar{S_p}, p]$$

where u_t, g, p is utterance of turn t, grounding span, original passage respectively and all parts start with special token: $\bar{S_u}$, $\bar{S_g}$,$\bar{S_p}$. In particular, g will be set to the empty string while reader reject to answer for current passage. (ii)The second way is to tag start and end position of grounding span in the passage. The input form listed as follows:

$$[\bar{S_u}, u_T, u_{T-1}...u_1; \bar{S_p}, p_i^0, p_i^1...\bar{S_g}, p_i^s, ...p_i^e, \bar{E_g}, p_i^n]$$

where $p_i = \{p_i^0, \ldots, p_i^n\}$ is the original retrieved passages, $\{p_i^s, \ldots, p_i^e\}$ is grounding span predicted by reader in the passage with the start and end position $\bar{S_g}$ $\bar{E_g}$ and $\bar{S_g}$ $\bar{E_g}$ will be deleted if reader reject to answer. In particular, when the length of the passage exceeds the maximum limit of the encoder, we also use dynamic truncate to ensure that the grounding spans are within the encoding window and are not truncated. If the length is greater than the maximum encoding window length, above (i) truncate from the tail, while (ii) truncate from head and tail to ensure that the grounding span is located in the middle of the window as much as possible. In the first method, if the length is greater than the maximum encoding window length in a conventional way, in the second method, the grounding span is truncated to ensure that the grounding span is located in the center of the window as much as possible.

Data augmentation. Since the generator and reader share the same corpus, the reader needs to predict on its training set. The F1 score of grounding prediction is 0.98 on the training set and 0.79 on the evaluation set, which would cause the generator to be overconfident in the given grounding and underperform on the evaluation set. To alleviate the above problem and enhance the robustness of the model, the reader accepts the top-k passages from retriever and finds evidence as "grounding span" for every passage include negative retrieved passage, then the generator produce the final response with evidence from reader. What's more, we adopt two methods of data augmentation for generator in training phase: (i) The first method replaces the groundings spans predicted randomly by the reader with another span of the same length with probability p. (ii) The second way replace the groundings spans predicted with one of the n best predicted spans predicted by reader with a probability p.

3 Experiments

Data We use the MultiDoc2Dial dataset(Feng et al., 2021) , a new task and dataset on modeling goal-oriented dialogues grounded in multiple documents, which contains 29748 queries in 4796 dialogues grounded in 488 documents.

Baseline Considering that MultiDoc2Dial is a relatively new benchmark, we tried several retriever-reader architecture models. We compare our model with the baseline model RAG(Lewis et al., 2020) in the MultiDoc2Dial paper. FiD(Izacard and Grave, 2020b) is a two-stage pipeline method which first retrieves passages and performs evidence fusion in the decoder based on multiple passage. EMDR(Singh et al., 2021) is the state-of-the-

Model Variant	F1	SacreBLEU	METEOR	RougeL	total
G4-base *(DPR+G^{org})*	43.65	30.33	41.38	41.64	157.00
w/o grounding	42.14	28.58	39.78	40.67	151.17
w grounding^{concat}	43.13	29.48	40.79	41.23	154.63
w grounding^{tag}	43.65	30.33	41.38	41.64	157.00
w augment^{nbest}	44.09	30.63	41.44	42.09	158.25
w augment^{random}	44.22	30.73	41.96	42.28	159.19

Table 2: The ablation results of G4 on MultiDoc2Dial validation dataset. *w/o* grounding: don't use the reader module, the generator directly accept the concatenation of the retrieved passages. grounding^{concat}: add grounding span with concatenate method. grounding^{tag}: add grounding span with tag method. augment^{nbest}: noise data with n-best predicted spans($n = 20$). augment^{random}: random noise data.

Model	R@1	R@5	R@10
BM25	17.26	37.80	46.49
DPR^{official}	38.40	65.90	75.20
DPR^{aug}	42.78	67.98	77.05
ANCE	39.54	68.46	77.27

Table 3: Performance of different retrieve methods on MultiDoc2Dial validation dataset. DPR^{official}: official DPR finetuned by (Feng et al., 2021). ANCE: ANCE model described in 2.4. DPR^{aug}: our DPR trained with better negative examples as ANCE.

art model for OpenQA task on the Natural Question dataset(Kwiatkowski et al., 2019) which apply an end-to-end training method for documents retrieval and answer generation.

Implementation In retriever, we choose the positive passage with 2 negative and 2 hard-negative examples to train ANCE model. We retrieve 50 passages for reader and generator and set batch size to 128. In reader, we initialize our span-based machine reading comprehension with RoBERT-based model and batch size is 32. In generator stage, we adopt the Fusion-in-Decoder model and follow it's architectural and basic experimental settings. We choose the T5-base as the initial weights and set the max source(dialogue+passage) length to 512 while max answer(response) length to 50. We use the probability of $p = 0.3$ to add noisy data mentioned in 2.4. Other experiment hyper-parameters can be seen in Appendix A.

Results. Table 1 reports the evaluation results on MultiDoc2Dial validation. We observe that our grounding-guided method (G4-base) clearly outperforms the MultiDoc2Dial baseline. Compared with the two-stage model FiD, the SacreBLEU score is significantly improved by 1.75 points, which fully proves that the grounding span predicted by the reader from second stage can effectively improve the generator's performance. Our grounding-guided generator with data augmentation and better retriever can even further improve by 2.66 SacreBLEU score than baseline. Combining Table 1 and Table 3, it can be concluded that improving the recall of retriever in the first stage can effectively improve the final generation. By choosing better negative examples, both our trained DPR and ANCE models achieve better results. At the same time, we also noticed that the end-to-end training method EMDR performs not very well on MultiDoc2Dial task.

Table 2 shows the effect of different methods of grounding-guided generation and data augmentation. Our two methods of introducing grounding span have significantly improved generation result, the first concatenation-based method by 0.99 points SacreBLEU and second tag-based by 1.51 points SacreBLEU. The tag-based method not only tells encoder the position of grounding span, but also dynamically adjusts the window according to the position of the grounding span to ensure that important part of passage wouldn't be truncated when the passage exceeds the maximum length of the encoder. Therefore, the tag-based method can achieve better results than concatenation-based method. In the training phase, adding noise data to grounding predicted by reader can improve the robustness of generator and avoid the generator over-reliance on the prediction results of the reader. Using the random selection for noise outperforms n-best data predicted by the model, probably because n-best answers are very similar to grounding spans.

What's more, since the retrieval stage may mistakenly recall irrelevant documents to the query, we also experimented with making the reader to identify negative retrieved passages. By randomly selecting retrieved passages that do not contain grounding span as negative samples, we train a binary classifier to enables the reader to identify irrelevant passages. In the inference phase, model will reject to predict grounding span when the binary classifier identifies a retrieved passage as negative, otherwise adopt the grounding span as final answer. The negative passages predicted by reader are also used as the input of generator, but without grounding span. The result shows that the reader model with the ability to identify negative passages has no gain or even worse for the final response generation. We believe that the reason may be that the reader and generator share the same training corpus, and training data with results predicted by reader makes the generator prone to overfitting.

4 Conclusion

In this paper, we propose a three-stage approach to the MultiDoc2Dial task, which adds readers to a two-stage framework based on retriever and generator. We show that the grounding predicted by the reader can effectively mitigate the deviation of the generated result from the grounding and correct response. In future work, we plan to introduce grounding information in a more efficient way based on end-to-end models.

References

Tom Brown, Benjamin Mann, Nick Ryder, Melanie Subbiah, Jared D Kaplan, Prafulla Dhariwal, Arvind Neelakantan, Pranav Shyam, Girish Sastry, Amanda Askell, et al. 2020. Language models are few-shot learners. *Advances in neural information processing systems*, 33:1877–1901.

Eunsol Choi, He He, Mohit Iyyer, Mark Yatskar, Wen-tau Yih, Yejin Choi, Percy Liang, and Luke Zettlemoyer. 2018. Quac: Question answering in context. *arXiv preprint arXiv:1808.07036*.

Nico Daheim, David Thulke, Christian Dugast, and Hermann Ney. 2021. Cascaded span extraction and response generation for document-grounded dialog. *arXiv preprint arXiv:2106.07275*.

Song Feng, Siva Sankalp Patel, Hui Wan, and Sachindra Joshi. 2021. Multidoc2dial: Modeling dialogues grounded in multiple documents. In *EMNLP*.

Song Feng, Hui Wan, Chulaka Gunasekara, Siva Sankalp Patel, Sachindra Joshi, and Luis A Lastras. 2020. doc2dial: A goal-oriented document-grounded dialogue dataset. *arXiv preprint arXiv:2011.06623*.

Gautier Izacard and Edouard Grave. 2020a. Distilling knowledge from reader to retriever for question answering. *arXiv preprint arXiv:2012.04584*.

Gautier Izacard and Edouard Grave. 2020b. Leveraging passage retrieval with generative models for open domain question answering. *arXiv preprint arXiv:2007.01282*.

Karen Sparck Jones. 1972. A statistical interpretation of term specificity and its application in retrieval. *Journal of documentation*.

Vladimir Karpukhin, Barlas Oğuz, Sewon Min, Patrick Lewis, Ledell Wu, Sergey Edunov, Danqi Chen, and Wen-tau Yih. 2020. Dense passage retrieval for open-domain question answering. *arXiv preprint arXiv:2004.04906*.

Tom Kwiatkowski, Jennimaria Palomaki, Olivia Redfield, Michael Collins, Ankur Parikh, Chris Alberti, Danielle Epstein, Illia Polosukhin, Jacob Devlin, Kenton Lee, et al. 2019. Natural questions: a benchmark for question answering research. *Transactions of the Association for Computational Linguistics*, 7:453–466.

Haejun Lee, Akhil Kedia, Jongwon Lee, Ashwin Paranjape, Christopher D Manning, and Kyoung-Gu Woo. 2021. You only need one model for open-domain question answering. *arXiv preprint arXiv:2112.07381*.

Mike Lewis, Yinhan Liu, Naman Goyal, Marjan Ghazvininejad, Abdelrahman Mohamed, Omer Levy, Ves Stoyanov, and Luke Zettlemoyer. 2019. Bart: Denoising sequence-to-sequence pre-training for natural language generation, translation, and comprehension. *arXiv preprint arXiv:1910.13461*.

Patrick Lewis, Ethan Perez, Aleksandra Piktus, Fabio Petroni, Vladimir Karpukhin, Naman Goyal, Heinrich Küttler, Mike Lewis, Wen-tau Yih, Tim Rocktäschel, et al. 2020. Retrieval-augmented generation for knowledge-intensive nlp tasks. *Advances in Neural Information Processing Systems*, 33:9459–9474.

Colin Raffel, Noam Shazeer, Adam Roberts, Katherine Lee, Sharan Narang, Michael Matena, Yanqi Zhou, Wei Li, and Peter J Liu. 2019. Exploring the limits of transfer learning with a unified text-to-text transformer. *arXiv preprint arXiv:1910.10683*.

Siva Reddy, Danqi Chen, and Christopher D Manning. 2019. Coqa: A conversational question answering challenge. *Transactions of the Association for Computational Linguistics*, 7:249–266.

Stephen E Robertson, Steve Walker, Susan Jones, Micheline M Hancock-Beaulieu, Mike Gatford, et al. 1995. Okapi at trec-3. *Nist Special Publication Sp*, 109:109.

Devendra Singh, Siva Reddy, Will Hamilton, Chris Dyer, and Dani Yogatama. 2021. End-to-end training of multi-document reader and retriever for open-domain question answering. *Advances in Neural Information Processing Systems*, 34.

Lee Xiong, Chenyan Xiong, Ye Li, Kwok-Fung Tang, Jialin Liu, Paul Bennett, Junaid Ahmed, and Arnold Overwijk. 2020. Approximate nearest neighbor negative contrastive learning for dense text retrieval. *arXiv preprint arXiv:2007.00808*.

A Experiment Hyper-parameters

A.1 Hyper-parameters for retriever

```
train_batch_size=128
num_negtive_examples=2
num_hard_negtive_examples=2
top_k=50
max_query_length=512
max_passage_length=512
dropout=0.1
attention_dropout=0.1
optim=adam
learning_rate=2e-05
```

A.2 Hyper-parameters for reader

```
train_batch_size=32
eval_batch_size=4
doc_stride=128
max_seq_length=512
max_ans_length=128
initial_weight=roberta-base
optim=adam
warmup_steps=1000
learning_rate=3e-5
```

A.3 Hyper-parameters for generator

```
train_batch_size=4
n_passages=50
max_source_length=512
max_target_length=50
dropout=0.1
attention_dropout=0.1
initial_weight=T5-base
learn_rate=1e-04
gradient_accumulation_steps=2
```

UGent-T2K at the 2nd DialDoc Shared Task: A Retrieval-Focused Dialog System Grounded in Multiple Documents

Yiwei Jiang*, Amir Hadifar*, Johannes Deleu, Thomas Demeester, Chris Develder
Ghent University – imec, IDLab
Ghent, Belgium
first_name.last_name@ugent.be

Abstract

This work presents the contribution from the Text-to-Knowledge team of Ghent University (UGent-T2K)[1] to the MultiDoc2Dial shared task on modeling dialogs grounded in multiple documents. We propose a pipeline system, comprising (1) document retrieval, (2) passage retrieval, and (3) response generation. We engineered these individual components mainly by, for (1)-(2), combining multiple ranking models and adding a final LambdaMART reranker, and, for (3), by adopting a Fusion-in-Decoder (FiD) model. We thus significantly boost the baseline system's performance (over +10 points for both F1 and SacreBLEU). Further, error analysis reveals two major failure cases, to be addressed in future work: (i) in case of topic shift within the dialog, retrieval often fails to select the correct grounding document(s), and (ii) generation sometimes fails to use the correctly retrieved grounding passage. Our code is released at this link.

1 Introduction

Most prior research on document-grounded dialog systems assumes a single document for each dialog (Choi et al., 2018; Reddy et al., 2019; Feng et al., 2020). There are relatively few works on Multi-Document Grounded (MDG) dialog modeling, which requires a dialog system to (i) retrieve grounded passages (or documents) given the user question, and then (ii) generate responses based on the retrieval results and dialog context. Real-world applications (e.g., administration question answering, travel booking assistance and procedural task guidance) for MDG are challenging because of more complex user behavior in such dialogs on diverse information sources. In particular, for (i) retrieval of grounding text passage(s) the challenges pertain to keeping track of dialog state, topic shift (e.g., switching from driving license requirements to car insurance), vocabulary mismatch, vague question formulation, etc. Furthermore, (ii) response generation needs to appropriately phrase the answer to fit in a human(-like) dialog rather than simply copying a source document snippet.

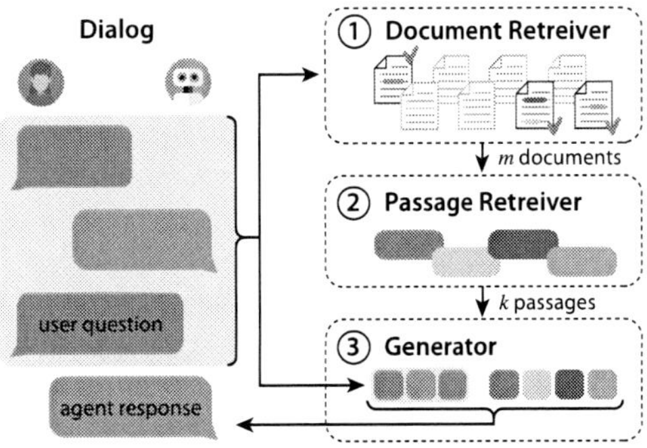

Figure 1: Our proposed pipeline dialog system.

We leverage the recently released dialog dataset, MultiDoc2Dial (Feng et al., 2021), to tackle aforementioned challenges. We build a pipeline system (Fig. 1) comprising (1) a document retriever, (2) a passage retriever, and (3) an answer generator fusing multiple grounding input passages. Given the dialog context (i.e., the dialog history and user question), a document retriever searches given supporting documents to select the top-m related ones. Subsequently, these full documents are segmented into shorter passages ranked by a passage retriever. For these retrieval components (1)-(2), we use an ensemble approach — combining BM25, cosine similarity, etc.; for passage retrieval, we included Dense Passage Retrieval (DPR; Karpukhin et al., 2020) — followed by a reranking step using LambaMART (Burges, 2010). The top-k passages are fused with the dialog context by a response generator to produce knowledge-grounded responses, based on Fusion in Decoder (FiD; Izacard and

* These authors contributed equally to this work.
[1]https://ugentt2k.gitlab.io

Proceedings of the Second DialDoc Workshop on Document-grounded Dialogue and Conversational Question Answering, pages 115 - 122
May 26, 2022 ©2022 Association for Computational Linguistics

Grave, 2021).

We contribute with: (i) a multi-stage pipeline system comprising first the grounding text retrieval stages, split further into document and subsequent passage retrieval components (both using a multi- feature ensemble system), and second an answer generation model fusing information from multiple passages; (ii) experiments demonstrating that our pipeline system outperforms the baseline method by a large margin (over +10 points for both F1 and SacreBLEU); (iii) insightful error analysis, suggesting that the main shortcomings of the current system include failures of (a) the *retrieval* stages in case of topic shifts by the user, and (b) the answer *generation* stage to identify the correct grounding passage among its inputs. Our codes are released at https://github.com/YiweiJiang2015/ugent-t2k-dialdoc

2 Task Definition

The MultiDoc2Dial shared task comprises two subtasks: in the *seen-domain* (referenced by subscript S), the system can rely on training data comprising both exemplary dialogs as well as the corresponding document set from the domains it will be tested on, whereas in the *unseen-domain* (referenced by U) no related dialogs nor documents have been seen by the system before.

In general, for both subtasks, a system first retrieves relevant documents from a document pool (D_S or D_U) given the dialog context, i.e., a user's question Q_i (i is the turn number) and the full conversation history $Q_{<i}$. Current state-of-the-art solutions split long documents into passages (P_S or P_U) to facilitate more fine-grained location of the grounding information. Second, the grounding information G (span(s) or passage(s)) for Q_i has to be identified within the passages of retrieved documents. The MultiDoc2Dial dataset was curated such that G for each question can be exactly found within one document, while the full dialog's answers jointly may span multiple documents, thus requiring a model to decide when to switch to a different document. (Note that, depending on how exactly a document is split into shorter passages, G may extend over more than one passage.) Third, a generation model takes as input G and $Q_{\leq i}$ to generate responses whose meaningfulness and coherence are rated using automatic metrics (i.e., F1_U, SacreBLEU, Rouge-L and Meteor).

3 Model

The next subsections detail the aforementioned components (1)-(3) of our pipeline system.

3.1 Document Retrieval

The input to our document retrieval model is a user's dialog question Q and the output is a set of m documents $\{d_1, d_2, \ldots, d_m\}$ selected from the document pool D. For each question, we rank all the documents by computing the similarity scores. We utilize various scoring modules as input to the LambdaMART reranker (Burges, 2010). Our scoring modules include: (i) different BM25 (Trotman et al., 2014) configurations, (ii) cosine similarity between dense representations on both word-level and passage-level, and (iii) off-the-shelf term-matching techniques provided by Terrier (Macdonald et al., 2012).

3.2 Passage Retrieval

Given the top-m documents returned by the document retriever, a passage retriever ranks passages belonging to these documents. More specifically, we follow the baseline's segmentation of a document into passages, ensuring a fair performance comparison between our passage retriever and the baseline. The same scoring modules for the document retrieval are applied on the passage level, with additional similarity features computed by DPR (Karpukhin et al., 2020)

3.3 Response Generation

We choose FiD (Izacard and Grave, 2021) as our generation model, which can be trained independently from the retrieval module. FiD was originally proposed for the open-book question answering problem (Kwiatkowski et al., 2019; Joshi et al., 2017) and showed great power in incorporating knowledge from multiple passages. It is built on top of a transformer-based seq2seq model. We employ BART (Lewis et al., 2020a) as the pretrained weights of FiD instead of T5 as in (Izacard and Grave, 2021), since fine-tuning BART is computationally more affordable in our case. The FiD's encoder takes as input a question and a list of top-k ranked passages formatted as $((Q, P_1), (Q, P_2)...(Q, P_k))$. Each pair (Q, P) is encoded individually. Concatenation of the k encodings is used as the memory accessed by the decoder for the cross-attention operation. The training objective is the cross-entropy loss between generated sequences and gold responses.

4 Experiments and Analysis

4.1 Dataset

We evaluate our pipeline system on the MultiDoc2Dial dataset, containing 4,796 conversations grounded in 488 documents. In the dialog data, each conversation covers at least one topic from four domains (see Appendix B.2). It is challenging to retrieve the grounding information when users shift their topic (i.e., implicitly referring to another document) during a dialog. In total, there are 61,078 turns, including 29,746 user questions that are split into 21,451, 4,201 and 4,094 for train, dev and test sets respectively.

4.2 Baseline System

The baseline system uses the Retrieval Augmented Generation (RAG; Lewis et al., 2020b) model composed of two neural modules: DPR for passage retrieval and BART for response generation. First, a pre-trained DPR is finetuned on the passage retrieval task built from MultiDoc2Dial dataset. Second, RAG is finetuned to generate responses for MultiDoc2Dial dialogs by inserting the finetuned DPR weights and freezing DPR's context encoder.

4.3 Retrieval and Generation Results

We present experiment results for the document retriever, passage retriever and generator separately. Ablation studies of the document retriever focus on analysing the contributions of different features. We validate the effectiveness of first using the document retriever, to boost the passage retriever's performance. Results of response generation experiments show that there is an optimal number of passages input to the FiD model. We also discuss FiD's inefficiency in recognizing grounding knowledge among multiple passage inputs.

4.3.1 Retriever

Document retrieval — Table 1 presents our results for the document retrieval. The first row shows a simple BM25 with the same configuration as official baseline but on document level. $BM25_{tuned}$ indicates BM25 with additional preprocessing and postprocessing over its input features and output rankings (see Section B.1 for details). $BM25_{title}$ is another BM25, solely trained on document titles and subtitles. The reason for this choice is to

Model	R@1	R@5	R@10	R@25
BM25 (baseline)	46.6	67.7	74.3	82.3
$BM25_{tuned}$	57.8	84.2	89.6	95.8
$BM25_{title}$	46.5	73.2	82.2	91.6
Word emb.	36.4	60.4	70.1	82.9
Passage emb.	34.9	61.9	71.3	84.5
DPH	49.3	77.2	85.9	94.1
$BM25_{tuned}$				
+ $BM25_{title}$	62.0	87.8	93.0	97.3
+ Terrier	62.5	88.9	93.5	97.5
+ embeddings	66.3	91.1	95.2	97.9
LambdaMART	65.9	92.3	96.1	98.7

Table 1: Recall scores for document retrieval on dev set.

distinguish the importance of the title words from other words, as the title provides a strong signal for document retrieval. In addition, to capture semantic relatedness and to address the word-mismatch problem between questions and documents, we compute word-level and passage-level embeddings to retrieve relevant documents. For word-level (denoted by 'Word emb.'), we simply average word vectors to obtain question and document representations, then using TF-IDF weighting and principal component removal (Arora et al., 2017) followed by cosine similarity. For passage-level (denoted by 'Passage emb.'), we use a pre-trained model[2] to embed a document's passages and use the highest passage score to rank the document. Macdonald et al. (2012) offer various term-matching approaches for text retrieval. The best performing model in our experiment is DPH (Amati, 2006).

In the second block of Table 1, we combine various ranking methods in an ensemble using rank fusion, simply summing the various scores.

We first aggregate scores from $BM25_{tuned}$ and $BM25_{title}$. The next row presents adding the combination of 13 term-matching techniques borrowed from the Terrier IR framework.[3] Finally, we add the embedding scores into the ensemble model, which significantly boosts the performance (increasing R@1 from 62.5 to 66.3), indicating the complementarity of the various ranking criteria. Finally, instead of naively summing all scores, we employ the LambdaMART algorithm, which yields the highest recall scores (except for R@1).

Passage retrieval — Table 2 compares our passage

[2] msmarco-bert-base-dot v5: available at https://bit.ly/3ID92fF

[3] http://terrier.org/ — Note that due to our limited time budget for the challenge, we did not properly analyze the contribution of the various Terrier features; therefore some of them may be unnecessary.

Model	m	R@1	R@5	R@10	R@15
BM25 (baseline)	488	19.6	41.9	50.8	-
DPR (baseline)	488	49.0	72.3	80.0	-
$\text{DPR}_{\text{top1 doc}}$	1	55.6	71.6	73.0	73.1
$\text{DPR}_{\text{top5 docs}}$	5	49.2	72.0	80.6	84.1
$\text{DPR}_{\text{top10 docs}}$	10	47.8	69.8	77.9	82.4
$\text{DPR}_{\text{top30 docs}}$	30	46.6	67.8	75.3	80.1
LambdaMART	30	57.0	82.1	88.3	91.4

Table 2: Recall scores for passage retrieval on dev set. Baseline scores come from (Feng et al., 2021). m denotes the number of top documents that are used for passage retrieval.

retrieval results to that of the baseline (Feng et al., 2021). To validate whether the document retrieval stage helps to limit the search space of passage retrieval, we perform a simple test that uses DPR to only rank passages from the top-m documents. Restricting the DPR to retrieve passages only from the top-1 document increases R@1 from 49.0 to 55.6 while it hurts R@10 (dropping from 80.0 to 73.0). By increasing m, R@10 improves at the cost of lowering R@1 as we expose the DPR to more passages that are similar to the dialog question. The maximum performance (R@15 = 91.4) is attained by LambdaMART on passages from the top-30 documents.[4]

Error analysis — We noted that the document retriever fails on 42 cases out of 4201 (i.e., R@30 = 99.0). We identified 4 major error types: (i) *topic shift* (22 cases), where grounding information hops from one document to another; (ii) *vague question* formulation (12 cases), where user questions are unclear and require the agent to ask follow-up questions for clarification; (iii) *annotation errors* (4 cases) due to some meaningless utterances; (iv) *hard examples* (4 cases) where our retriever totally failed.

4.3.2 Response Generator

Generation models are trained and evaluated on our LambdaMART retriever's output, ranking passages from the top-30 documents. The number of preceding dialog turns from the history (that are fed as input for the generator, see Fig. 1) is fixed at 5, which is the length leading to the best performance on the dev set in our preliminary experiments. Each turn is prefixed by a role indicator, i.e., ⟨AGENT⟩ and ⟨USER⟩. A separator ⟨CONTEXT⟩ is inserted between the question and passage text. See Appendix C for hyperparameter details. The evaluation metrics are calculated by the official shared task script. Our experiments study the impact of the number of passages in the generator's input and establish upper bounds of its performance. In addition, we introduce "knowledge misrecognition rate" to quantify limitations of our generation model (see further).

Upper-bound Tests — We perform three types of upper-bound tests as shown in Table 3: (i) only the grounding *passage* is provided to the FiD model (for both of train and dev sets) to generate a response (row 3); (ii) only the grounding *span* (phrases or sentences within the grounding passage) is input to the FiD model for generation (row 4); (iii) use the grounding span as the response to be evaluated against the gold one (row 5). Scores in Table 3 demonstrates a notable gap (78.33 w.r.t. total score) between the baseline (row 4) and an upper-bound model (row 1). It is noteworthy that directly using the grounding span as the response yields better performance (224.66) than inputting it to FiD (214.1), implying that a span-extraction model might get higher scores than the current generation one. However, while extracting correct spans provides users the needed information, it cannot satisfy the pragmatic requirements of a conversation (e.g., greetings at the beginning, yes/no prefix before giving the details). Thus, we choose a generation model as it has greater power in generating more coherent phrases at potential cost of losing partial information.

Impact of the Number of Passages $\mathbf{N_p}$ — Intuitively, the more passages are fed as input to FiD, the higher is the chance for FiD to capture the grounding information. Yet, it then also becomes harder to recognize the correct passage. We thus hypothesize that there should be an optimal number of passages N_p for which FiD to attains the best performance, without being distracted by too much information. Figure 2 shows that all performance metrics slightly drop when N_p exceeds 15 (even though they mostly recover once $N_p \geq 30$). The performance of the best model ($N_p = 15$) on the dev set is listed in row 5 of Table 3, with F1_U = 42.98 and SacreBLEU = 27.05.

Knowledge misrecognition — Comparing our system results to the upper bounds (see row 1 in Table 3), we note there is still considerable room for improvement. To identify where our generation model fails, we scrutinize generated responses sampled from inference results on dev set of our best

[4] We select 30 documents, because at the document level, we find R@30 = 99.

	Retriever	Model	F1_U	SacreBLEU	Meteor	ROUGE_L	Total
1	Perfect-	FiD + Grounding passage	51.99	37.97	47.60	50.20	187.76
2	Retriever	FiD + Grounding span	58.03	43.56	55.31	57.20	214.10
3		Grounding span as response	61.00	47.37	60.09	56.18	224.66
4	DPR	Baseline (RAG)	32.62	18.97	27.22	30.61	109.43
5	LambdaMART	FiD + LambdaMART	**42.89**	**27.05**	**42.69**	**40.51**	**153.15**

Table 3: Generation performance of the baseline and our FiD-BART-base model (*seen-domain* task; on dev set). Row 1-3 list the upper-bound performance. A perfect-retriever assumes that the grounding passage is always ranked as the top 1. Row 4-5 use realistic retrievers. The baseline scores are our reproduction results.

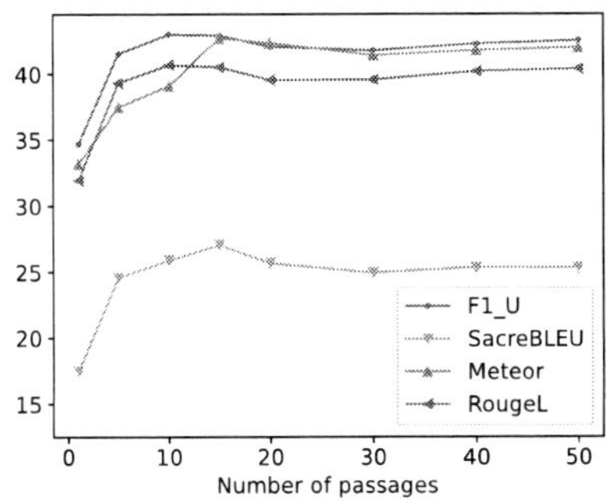

Figure 2: Impact of the number of passages ($N_p \geq 1$) on generation metrics. (*seen-domain* task; FiD-BART-base model; on dev set)

system ($N_p = 15$). An interesting observation is that the FiD model may behave poorly even when the grounding passage is retrieved among the top-15 results presented to the generator: FiD cannot always recognize the grounding passage among its multiple inputs. We propose to quantify this with "knowledge misrecognition rate" μ, calculated as the fraction of low-quality responses among all cases where the correct passage is included in the retrieved ones as fed as input to the generator. For example, using SacreBLEU, a low value thereof (e.g., <10) suggests that the model did not actually use elements from the ground truth passage in generating the response. Thus, using SacreBLEU < 10 as an indication of a "low-quality" response, we find that the misrecognition rate of our best system is $\mu = 50.3\%$ on the dev set. This means that over half of the correct retrieval results are lost in the generation phase. The high rate also implies that the FiD model alone lacks the necessary inductive bias to identify the grounded information among multiple passages. We consider this as a key element in designing future versions of the response generation component.

Leaderboard Submission — Our submission results on the test sets (including test-dev and test-test) are listed in Table 4. For the *unseen-domain* task, inference was performed by the model trained on *seen-domain* data as a test of our system's zero-shot ability. Besides the FiD-BART-base model, we also train a FiD-BART-large model, which achieves our best scores. For the *seen-domain* task, our best model outperforms the baseline by 11.05 and 10.07 for F1_U and SacreBLEU. For the *unseen-domain* task, these two metrics are improved by 14.10 and 14.88. As a result, our UGent-T2K team was ranked second and third for the *seen-domain* and *unseen-domain* tasks respectively.

5 Conclusion

We propose a pipeline system for dialogs grounded in multiple documents. Our system consists of a document retriever, a passage retriever and a multi-passage-fusing generator. The retriever is designed to limit the passage search space by first ranking documents, which proves to enhance the passage retrieval performance considerably for the Multi-Doc2Dial shared task. Compared to the baseline RAG model, our multi-passage-fusing generator achieves better knowledge-grounded answer generation. Based on error analysis of our current system, future work will focus on the topic shift issue for conversational retrieval and investigate the knowledge misrecognition problem for dialog generation.

Acknowledgements

This research received funding from the Flemish Government under the *"Onderzoeksprogramma Artificiële Intelligentie (AI) Vlaanderen"* programme. The first author was supported by *China Scholarship Council* (201806020194). We thank the anonymous reviewers whose comments helped to improve our work.

Task	Model	F1_U	SacreBLEU	Meteor	ROUGE_L	Total
seen-domain	Baseline	35.85	22.26	34.28	33.82	126.21
	FiD-BART-base	42.51	28.52	42.8	40.3	153.13
	FiD-BART-large	**46.90**	**32.23**	**47.96**	**44.89**	**171.98**
unseen-domain	Baseline	19.26	6.32	16.77	17.16	59.52
	FiD-BART-base	29.35	19.87	29.57	27.84	106.64
	FiD-BART-large	**33.36**	**21.20**	**33.57**	**31.47**	**119.60**

Table 4: Submission results on the leaderboard (on test-test set).

References

Giambattista Amati. 2006. Frequentist and bayesian approach to information retrieval. In *Proceedings of ECIR*.

Sanjeev Arora, Yingyu Liang, and Tengyu Ma. 2017. A simple but tough-to-beat baseline for sentence embeddings. In *Proceedings of ICLR*.

Christopher JC Burges. 2010. From ranknet to lambdarank to lambdamart: An overview. *Microsoft Research Technical Report*.

Eunsol Choi, He He, Mohit Iyyer, Mark Yatskar, Wen-tau Yih, Yejin Choi, Percy Liang, and Luke Zettlemoyer. 2018. QuAC: Question answering in context. In *Proceedings of EMNLP*.

Corinna Cortes and Vladimir Vapnik. 1995. Support-vector networks. *Machine Learning*.

Jacob Devlin, Ming-Wei Chang, Kenton Lee, and Kristina Toutanova. 2019. BERT: Pre-training of deep bidirectional transformers for language understanding. In *Proceedings of NAACL*.

Song Feng, Siva Sankalp Patel, Hui Wan, and Sachindra Joshi. 2021. MultiDoc2Dial: Modeling dialogues grounded in multiple documents. In *Proceedings of EMNLP*.

Song Feng, Hui Wan, Chulaka Gunasekara, Siva Patel, Sachindra Joshi, and Luis Lastras. 2020. doc2dial: A goal-oriented document-grounded dialogue dataset. In *Proceedings of EMNLP*.

Xiao Han, Yuqi Liu, and Jimmy Lin. 2021. The simplest thing that can possibly work: (pseudo-)relevance feedback via text classification. In *Proceedings of SIGIR-ICTIR*.

Gautier Izacard and Edouard Grave. 2021. Leveraging passage retrieval with generative models for open domain question answering. In *Proceedings of EACL*.

Mandar Joshi, Eunsol Choi, Daniel Weld, and Luke Zettlemoyer. 2017. TriviaQA: A large scale distantly supervised challenge dataset for reading comprehension. In *Proceedings of ACL*.

Vladimir Karpukhin, Barlas Oguz, Sewon Min, Patrick Lewis, Ledell Wu, Sergey Edunov, Danqi Chen, and Wen-tau Yih. 2020. Dense passage retrieval for open-domain question answering. In *Proceedings of EMNLP*.

Tom Kwiatkowski, Jennimaria Palomaki, Olivia Redfield, Michael Collins, Ankur Parikh, Chris Alberti, Danielle Epstein, Illia Polosukhin, Jacob Devlin, Kenton Lee, Kristina Toutanova, Llion Jones, Matthew Kelcey, Ming-Wei Chang, Andrew M. Dai, Jakob Uszkoreit, Quoc Le, and Slav Petrov. 2019. Natural Questions: A Benchmark for Question Answering Research. *Transactions of the Association for Computational Linguistics*.

Mike Lewis, Yinhan Liu, Naman Goyal, Marjan Ghazvininejad, Abdelrahman Mohamed, Omer Levy, Veselin Stoyanov, and Luke Zettlemoyer. 2020a. BART: Denoising sequence-to-sequence pre-training for natural language generation, translation, and comprehension. In *Proceedings of ACL*.

Patrick Lewis, Ethan Perez, Aleksandra Piktus, Fabio Petroni, Vladimir Karpukhin, Naman Goyal, Heinrich Küttler, Mike Lewis, Wen-tau Yih, Tim Rocktäschel, et al. 2020b. Retrieval-augmented generation for knowledge-intensive nlp tasks. In *Proceedings of NeurIPS*.

Yinhan Liu, Myle Ott, Naman Goyal, Jingfei Du, Mandar Joshi, Danqi Chen, Omer Levy, Mike Lewis, Luke Zettlemoyer, and Veselin Stoyanov. 2019. RoBERTa: A robustly optimized BERT pretraining approach. *arXiv preprint arXiv:1907.11692*.

Craig Macdonald, Richard McCreadie, Rodrygo LT Santos, and Iadh Ounis. 2012. From puppy to maturity: Experiences in developing Terrier. In *Proceedings of SIGIR-OSIR*.

Siva Reddy, Danqi Chen, and Christopher D. Manning. 2019. CoQA: A conversational question answering challenge. *Transactions of the Association for Computational Linguistics*.

Andrew Trotman, Antti Puurula, and Blake Burgess. 2014. Improvements to bm25 and language models examined. In *Proceedings of ADCS*.

Appendices

A Passage segmentation

The current version of the MultiDoc2Dial dataset provides 488 documents in which we found 56 duplicate documents[5]. The baseline relies on a

[5]The full list of duplicates can be found in https://bit.ly/376TxPX

structure-wise segmentation method. More specifically, in a document html file, a header tagged by <h1> or <h2> and its children nodes are treated as a passage prefixed by its hierarchical titles. We note that some passages produced in this way are too short (424 passages are shorter than 20 tokens, e.g., headers with empty content below) or too long (24 passages longer than 1,000 tokens) as shown in Fig. 3(a), not to mention those repetitive passages due to document duplicates. Given that common transformer-based generation models takes input up to 512 tokens, such length distribution either wastes a generation model's capacity when short passages are padded or loses a significant portion of information when long passages are truncated. To eliminate these extreme cases, three measures are taken based on our cleaned document set: (i) We remove the 56 duplicate documents. (ii) For each of the remaining documents, we first split it using the structure-wise method, calling the results "sections" to differentiate from the baseline's "passages". If a section has fewer than 150 tokens, it is directly added to the final passage list. If not, it will be further split into passages using a flexible sliding window which allows for a passage with tokens fewer than the window size in order to not break sentences.[6] (iii) Next, a passage with fewer than 60 tokens is merged with its following passage — except if it appears at the end of a section, in which case it will be appended to its preceding one. Figure 3(b) depicts the passage length distribution using our segmentation method. The long tail problem of the baseline is largely resolved. As Table 5 shows, our new segmentation method reduces the total number of passages from 4,110 to 3,734 while it increases the average passage length from 130.4 to 154.1.

Passage-Segmentation	#passages	avg length (tokenizer)	avg length (white space)
Baseline	4,110	130.4	105.4
Ours	3,734	154.1	132.5

Table 5: Total number of passages and average passage length produced by the baseline method and ours. "tokenizer" and "white space" denote using the BART tokenizer and splitting words by white space respectively.

[6]Window size $\leq$ 150, stride = 50. Since we rely on Spacy to extract sentences, some of them may be broken depending on Spacy model's decision.

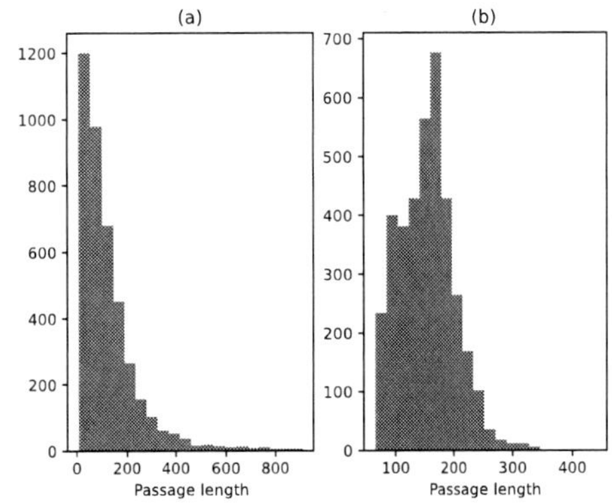

Figure 3: Passage length histograms of baseline and our passage segmentation. The length is the number of tokens processed by the BART tokenizer. (a) Baseline passages. The x-axis is truncated to 1,000 to make smaller value bins more clear. (b) Our passages after removing duplicate documents and merging short passages. No passage is omitted.

B Experiments

This section reports (i) the ablation study of BM25 for document retrieval revealing how different features affect the retrieval performance; (ii) domain classification that enhances document retrieval; (iii) passage retrieval experiments based on our new segmentation method.

B.1 Ablation study of BM25 for document retrieval

Table 6 presents our results for $\text{BM25}_{\text{tuned}}$ on document retrieval. The first row shows the simple BM25 model without any preprocessing on inputs (question and documents). The next four rows respectively represent: lower casing inputs, removing stop-words, removing punctuation, and stemming, which greatly improve the performance (over +10 points for R@25). We obtained slight improvement with a domain classifier that predicts the conversation domain (see Appendix B.2). We also observed that using n-grams ($n = 1,2,3$) features instead of unigrams brings a further improvement with additional 3.2 points of R@25.

B.2 Domain Classifier

In the training data of MultiDoc2Dial , the grounding documents were crawled from 4 U.S. government websites,[7] covering 4 domains: Social Security Administration, U.S. Department of Veterans

[7]ssa.gov, va.gov, dmv.ny.gov, studentaid.gov

Model	R@1	R@5	R@10	R@25
BM25	45.6	66.3	73.3	81.4
+ lowering	46.6	67.7	74.3	82.3
+ stop-removal	50.2	74.3	82.2	90.2
+ punk-removal	52.4	77.5	84.4	92.5
+ stemming	50.3	75.9	83.7	91.6
+ domain-scores	50.7	76.6	84.5	92.6
+ n-grams	57.8	84.2	89.6	95.8

Table 6: $BM25_{tuned}$ recall scores for document retrieval on dev set.

Affairs, Department of Motor Vehicles (New York State) and Federal Student Aid, which are respectively noted as `ssa`, `va`, `dmv` and `student`. We applied the idea proposed by Han et al. (2021) to further improve BM25 performance by training a domain classifier, i.e., finetuning the RoBERTa-large model (Liu et al., 2019) to predict a domain label for a given dialog. The domain scores are multiplied to BM25 after which a weighted combination between the initial BM25 and the new scores is used to create the final ranked list. In our experiments, we simply assume equal weights (0.5) for the two scores. Table 7 presents different classifiers' accuracy for *seen-domain* prediction.

Model	Accuracy
SVM (Cortes and Vapnik, 1995)	96.7
Bert-large (Devlin et al., 2019)	97.0
Roberta-large (Liu et al., 2019)	98.2

Table 7: Domain classifier accuracy on dev set.

B.3 Retrieval based on new segmentation

Table 8 presents the passage retrieval results based on our passage segmentation. We experiment with three models: DPR ranking all the passages, DPR ranking only the passages within top-m documents and the LambdaMART model based on top-30 documents. Restricting DPR's search space within the top-5 documents increases R@15 from 80.1 to 87.1, which further grows to 90.4 with the LambdaMART model.

C Hyperparameters

FiD was finetuned from pretrained BART weights with the following hyperparameter settings:

```
batch_size=4
total_epochs=15
max_source_length=400
max_target_length=64
```

Model	m	R@1	R@5	R@10	R@15
DPR	3,734	46.3	68.2	76.0	80.1
$DPR_{top1\ doc}$	1	52.9	70.8	73.2	73.6
$DPR_{top5\ docs}$	5	47.2	74.0	83.0	86.9
$DPR_{top10\ docs}$	10	45.9	71.8	81.0	85.3
$DPR_{top30\ docs}$	30	45.2	70.1	78.8	83.1
LambdaMART	30	48.0	80.0	87.4	90.4

Table 8: Recall scores for passage retrieval on dev set. The passage set is produced by the method described in Appendix A.

```
label_smoothing=0.1
optimizer=AdamW
weight_decay=0.1
adam_epsilon=1e-08
max_grad_norm=1.0
lr_scheduler=linear
learning_rate=5e-05
warmup_steps=500
gradient_accumulation_steps=2
```

Grounded Dialogue Generation with Cross-encoding Re-ranker, Grounding Span Prediction, and Passage Dropout

Kun Li[1]* **Tianhua Zhang**[2]* **Liping Tang**[2], **Junan Li**[2],
Hongyuan Lu[1], **Xixin Wu**[1], **Helen Meng**[1,2†]
[1]The Chinese University of Hong Kong, Hong Kong SAR, China
[2]Centre for Perceptual and Interactive Intelligence, Hong Kong SAR, China
{kunli, hylu, hmmeng}@se.cuhk.edu.hk
{thzhang, lptang, jali}@cpii.hk
xixinwu@cuhk.edu.hk

Abstract

MultiDoc2Dial presents an important challenge on modeling dialogues grounded with multiple documents. This paper proposes a pipeline system of "retrieve, re-rank, and generate", where each component is individually optimized. This enables the passage re-ranker and response generator to fully exploit training with ground-truth data. Furthermore, we use a deep cross-encoder trained with localized hard negative passages from the retriever. For the response generator, we use grounding span prediction as an auxiliary task to be jointly trained with the main task of response generation. We also adopt a passage dropout and regularization technique to improve response generation performance. Experimental results indicate that the system clearly surpasses the competitive baseline and our team CPII-NLP ranked 1st among the public submissions on ALL four leaderboards based on the sum of F1, SacreBLEU, METEOR and RougeL scores.

1 Introduction

The task of developing information-seeking dialogue systems has seen many recent research advancements. The goal is to answer users' questions grounded on documents in a conversational manner. MultiDoc2Dial[1] is a realistic task proposed by Feng et al. (2021) to model goal-oriented information-seeking dialogues that are grounded on multiple documents and participants are required to generate appropriate responses towards users' utterances according to the documents. To facilitate this task, the authors also propose a new dataset that contains dialogues grounded in multiple documents from four domains. Unlike previous work that mostly describe document-grounded dialogue modeling as a machine reading comprehension task based on one particular document or passage, the MultiDoc2Dial involves multiple topics within a conversation, hence it is grounded on different documents. The task contains two sub-tasks: Grounding Span Prediction aims to find the most relevant span from multiple documents for the next agent response, and Agent Response Generation generates the next agent response. This paper focuses on our work in to the second sub-task, and presents three major findings and contributions:

- In order to fully leverage the ground-truth training data, we propose to individually optimize the retriever, re-ranker, and response generator.
- We propose to adopt a deep cross-encoded re-ranker that is trained with localized hard negatives sampled from the retriever results.
- We propose to use grounding span prediction as an auxiliary task for the generator and use passage dropout as a regularization technique to improve the generation performance.

Experimental results indicate that our proposed system achieves a performance with marked improvement over the strong baseline.

2 Related Work

Open-domain Question Answering systems have evolved to adopt the popular "Retriever-Reader (Generator)" architecture since DrQA (Chen et al., 2017). Previous work (Lee et al., 2019, Guu et al., 2020) adopt end-to-end training strategy to jointly learn the retriever and reader with question-answer pairs. Retrieval-augmented Generation (RAG) (Lewis et al., 2020b) uses Dense Passage Retriever (DPR) (Karpukhin et al., 2020) as the retriever to extract multiple documents related to the query and feed them into a BART (Lewis et al., 2020a) generator for answer generation. Izacard and Grave (2021) proposed the Fusion-in-Decoder method

*Contributed equally.
†Corresponding author.
[1]https://doc2dial.github.io/multidoc2dial/

Proceedings of the Second DialDoc Workshop on Document-grounded Dialogue and Conversational Question Answering, pages 123 - 129
May 26, 2022 ©2022 Association for Computational Linguistics

which processes passages individually in the encoder but jointly in the decoder, surpassing the performance of RAG.

Other work like QuAC (Choi et al., 2018), ShARC (Saeidi et al., 2018) and CoQA (Reddy et al., 2019) focus on the machine reading comprehension task, which assumes that the associated document is given. In particular, Feng et al. (2020) proposed the Doc2Dial task ,which aims to extract the related span from the given documents for generating the corresponding answer.

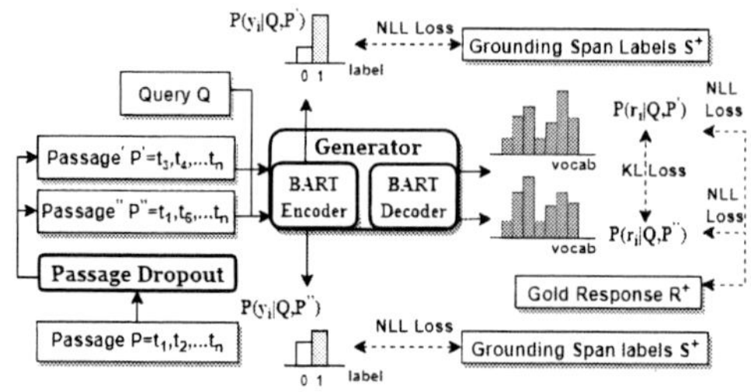

Figure 1: Training process of our generator.

3 Task Description

The MultiDoc2Dial task aims to generate an appropriate response $\mathcal{R}$ based on an input query $\mathcal{Q}$ (the current user turn u_T and the concatenated dialogue history $\{u_1^{T-1}\} := u_1, u_2, ..., u_{T-1}$) and a collection of passages $\{\mathcal{P}_i\}_{i=1}^M$. The passages are extracted from documents based on document structural information indicated by markup tags in the original HTML file. The organizer splits the MultiDoc2Dial data into train, validation, development and test set, and results on the latter two are evaluated through the leaderboard[2]. The validation, development and test set contain two settings: *seen* and *unseen*, which is categorized based on whether there are dialogues grounded on the documents seen/unseen during training. We leave detailed dataset description in Appendix A.

4 Methodology

We propose a pipeline system of "retrieve, re-rank, and generate". Following previous work in Lewis et al. (2020b); Feng et al. (2021), we adopt DPR (Karpukhin et al., 2020) as the retriever (§4.1) to efficiently filter out irrelevant passages and narrow the search space. We then refine the retrieval results with a deep cross-encoder (§4.2) trained with localized negatives (Gao et al., 2021). We introduce a passage dropout and regularization technique to enhance the robustness of the generator (§4.3) and use the grounding span prediction as an auxiliary task. Further more, pipeline training is adopted where each component is individually optimized to fully utilize the supervision. Experimental results (§5.3) also indicate the effectiveness and merits of the training strategy, which we observed to be a key factor for the performance gain.

[2]https://eval.ai/web/challenges/challenge-page/1437/leaderboard

4.1 Passage Retrieval

Following Feng et al. (2021), we adopt DPR (Karpukhin et al., 2020) as the retriever with a representation-based bi-encoder, that is, a dialogue query encoder $q(\cdot)$ and a passage context encoder $p(\cdot)$. Given an input query $\mathcal{Q}$ and a collection of passages $\{P_i\}_{i=1}^M$, we extract the query encoding as $q(\mathcal{Q})$ and the passage encoding as $p(\mathcal{P}_i)$. The similarity is defined as the dot product of the two vectors $\langle q(\mathcal{Q}), p(\mathcal{P}_i)\rangle$ and the model is trained to optimize the negative log likelihood of the positive passage among L in-batch and hard negatives. We then pre-compute the representations of all passages and index them offline. Maximum Inner Product Search (MIPS) with Faiss (Johnson et al., 2017) is adopted to retrieve the top-K passages during inference.

4.2 Passage Re-ranking

To re-rank the passages retrieved by DPR, we use a BERT-based cross-encoder that exploits localized negatives sampled from DPR results (Gao et al., 2021). This means that the construction of the training set for the re-ranker is based on the top negative passages retrieved by the DPR. Specifically, given a query $\mathcal{Q}$, its corresponding ground truth passage $\mathcal{P}^+$, and its top-N negative passages $\{\mathcal{P}_j^-\}_{j=1}^N$ retrieved by DPR, we first calculate a deep distance function for each positive and negative passage against the query:

$$\text{dist}(\mathcal{Q}, \mathcal{P}) = v^T \text{cls}(\text{BERT}(\text{concat}(\mathcal{Q}, \mathcal{P}))), \tag{1}$$

where v represents a trainable vector, cls extracts the [CLS] vector from BERT. Consequently, such a distance function is deeply cross-encoded, as we feed the concatenation of the query and the passage into the model instead of encoding them individually with a representation-based bi-encoder (Feng et al., 2021). We then apply a contrastive loss:

$$\mathcal{L}_c = -\log \frac{\exp(\text{dist}(\mathcal{Q}, \mathcal{P}^+))}{\sum_{\mathcal{P} \in \mathcal{P}_\pm} \exp(\text{dist}(\mathcal{Q}, \mathcal{P}))}, \quad (2)$$

where $\mathcal{P}_\pm$ represents $\mathcal{P}^+ \cup \{\mathcal{P}_i^-\}_{i=1}^N$. Here, it is important to condition the gradient on the negative passages to learn to recognize the positive passage from hard negatives retrieved by the DPR. [3]

Ensemble We create an ensemble of three pretrained models (Dietterich, 2000), namely, BERT (Devlin et al., 2019), RoBERTa (Liu et al., 2019), and ELECTRA (Clark et al., 2020) for re-ranking. We first calculate their distance function with Equation 1, with the output scores denoted as $\mathcal{O}_B$, $\mathcal{O}_R$, and $\mathcal{O}_E$. We define the final scores $\mathcal{O}$ as the weighted summation of the above three scores:

$$\mathcal{O} = \alpha \mathcal{O}_B + \beta \mathcal{O}_R + \gamma \mathcal{O}_E, \quad (3)$$

where α, β, and γ represent the weight hyperparameters for each model.

4.3 Response Generation

For response generation, we leverage the pretrained sequence-to-sequence model $\text{BART}_{\text{large}}$ (Lewis et al., 2020a), where the encoder is fed the concatenation of a query and a passage $[\mathcal{Q}, \mathcal{P}]$, and the decoder is then required to generate the corresponding response $\mathcal{R}$. We use the ground truth passage as $\mathcal{P}$ for training. The training process can be summarized as follows:

Joint Training with Grounding Prediction The grounding span in a passage is the supporting evidence for the response, which can provide helpful information for response generation. Therefore, we take grounding span prediction as the auxiliary task and apply multi-task learning for model training. Specifically, the passage is first encoded into a sequence of hidden representations $h_i = \text{Encoder}([\mathcal{Q}, \mathcal{P}]), i \in \{1, ..., |\mathcal{P}|\}$. Then a classifier outputs the probability of the i-th token of $\mathcal{P}$ to lie within the grounding span as $P(y_i|\mathcal{Q}, \mathcal{P}) = \text{sigmoid}(\text{MLP}(h_i))$. We define this task's training objective as:

$$\mathcal{L}_G = -\sum_{i=1}^{|\mathcal{P}|} \log P(y_i|\mathcal{Q}, \mathcal{P}). \quad (4)$$

Passage Dropout and Regularization Preliminary experiments indicate that the generator is prone to overfit to some passages quoted frequently in the train set, which may cause generalization errors when applied to previously unseen passages. Hence, we apply passage dropout to enhance the robustness of the generator. In details, for a training sample $([\mathcal{Q}, \mathcal{P}], \mathcal{R})$, a consecutive span with a specified length (of 25% in our experiments) in $\mathcal{P}$ is randomly selected and then dropped, which produces $\mathcal{P}'$. It is noteworthy that passage dropout is required to avoid truncating content of grounding spans.[4] Furthermore, we repeat passage dropout twice for each sample in a batch, and obtain $([\mathcal{Q}, \mathcal{P}'], \mathcal{R})$ as well as $([\mathcal{Q}, \mathcal{P}''], \mathcal{R})$. Since the grounding span in a passage serves as the oracle for response generation, the two modified inputs should have similar prediction distribution, denoted as $P(r_i|\mathcal{Q}, \mathcal{P}', r_{<i})$ and $P(r_i|\mathcal{Q}, \mathcal{P}'', r_{<i})$, where r_i is the i-th token of $\mathcal{R}$. Hence, inspired by Liang et al. (2021), we propose to regularize the predictions from different passage dropouts by minimizing the bidirectional Kullback-Leibler (KL) divergence between these two different output distributions as $\mathcal{L}_{KL}$:

$$\sum_i (\text{KL}(P(r_i|\mathcal{Q}, \mathcal{P}', r_{<i}) \| P(r_i|\mathcal{Q}, \mathcal{P}'', r_{<i})) + \text{KL}(P(r_i|\mathcal{Q}, \mathcal{P}'', r_{<i}) \| P(r_i|\mathcal{Q}, \mathcal{P}', r_{<i}))). \quad (5)$$

We define the training objective for response $\mathcal{R}$ as the basic negative log-likelihood:

$$\mathcal{L}_{NLL} = -\sum_i (\log P(r_i|\mathcal{Q}, \mathcal{P}', r_{<i}) + \log P(r_i|\mathcal{Q}, \mathcal{P}'', r_{<i})). \quad (6)$$

With passage dropout, the learning objective of grounding prediction (Eq.4) is updated for $\mathcal{P}'$ and $\mathcal{P}''$. Then we have the final training objective:

$$\mathcal{L} = \frac{1}{2}\mathcal{L}_{KL} + \mathcal{L}_{NLL} + \mathcal{L}_G. \quad (7)$$

4.4 Inference

After the re-ranker returns the top-5 passages corresponding to the query $\mathcal{Q}$, we filter out the passages with a low re-ranking score (Eq.3), namely, the ones that have a score gap of over 0.3 comparing to the top-1. Then the remaining passages are concatenated as a single passage $\mathcal{P}$. Finally the generator

[3] Feng et al. (2021) found that there exists passages that are similar to one another in the dataset. Therefore, it is intuitively important to distinguish these hard negative passages from the ground truth passage. Empirically, we also found that excluding hard negative passages from the training process hampers the re-ranking performance.

[4] If the selected span overlaps with a grounding span, this sampling is discarded and another span would be sampled.

seen	Val			Dev			Test		
	F1	**S-BLEU**	**ROUGE**	**F1**	**S-BLEU**	**ROUGE**	**F1**	**S-BLEU**	**ROUGE**
RAG	36.64	23.24	35.23	36.23*	21.41*	34.01*	35.85*	22.26*	33.82*
Ours	47.29	34.29	46.04	50.14	34.99	47.91	52.06	37.41	50.19
unseen	Val			Dev			Test		
	F1	**S-BLEU**	**ROUGE**	**F1**	**S-BLEU**	**ROUGE**	**F1**	**S-BLEU**	**ROUGE**
RAG	13.68	4.46	13.19	18.66*	5.99*	16.95*	19.26*	6.32*	17.16*
Ours	36.74	24.20	35.49	36.39	26.33	34.71	34.65	27.57	34.49

Table 1: Comparison between the baseline and the proposed framework on the validation, development and test set. The scores with * are cited from the leaderboard. **S-BLEU** represents SacreBLEU.

predicts a response $\mathcal{R}$ given the input $[\mathcal{Q}, \mathcal{P}]$.[5] We employ beam-search (beam width=5) during decoding.

5 Experiments and Results

We evaluate the passage retrieval results with recall (R) and mean reciprocal rank (MRR). We report response generation performance based on F1, Exact Match (EM) (Rajpurkar et al., 2016), SacreBLEU (S-BLEU; Post, 2018), and RougeL (Lin, 2004).

5.1 Main Results

Table 1 shows the results we obtain for each data split, each including the *seen* and *unseen* settings. RAG (Lewis et al., 2020b) is the baseline adopted by the organizer, and we reproduce it with a more aggressive setting (e.g., a greater input length and beam size), in order to have a fair comparison with the proposed approach. Our generator is a single model. Table 1 shows that the proposed approach consistently outperforms the baseline with significant gaps. We argue that the improvement is derived from (1) high-quality retrieval, (2) stronger generator and (3) pipeline-based training, which will be discussed in the following sections.

5.2 Retrieval Results

Since the passage supervision of the development and test data is unavailable and the leaderboards do not provide the retrieval scores, we analyze the passage retrieval performance on the validation set[6] as shown in Table 2. The baseline adopts DPR (Karpukhin et al., 2020) as retriever, and we evaluate both the official and our reproduced versions.

Method	*seen*			*unseen*		
	MRR@5	**R@1**	**R@5**	**MRR@5**	**R@1**	**R@5**
Official DPR*	0.487	0.379	0.656	0.277	0.207	0.405
Reproduced DPR	0.548	0.445	0.714	0.328	0.248	0.471
BERT B	0.719	0.643	0.834	0.615	0.529	0.752
ELECTRA E	0.719	0.640	0.837	0.582	0.521	0.694
RoBERTa R	0.748	0.683	0.849	0.641	0.562	0.760
$\mathcal{E}(B, R)$	0.754	0.689	0.855	0.664	0.603	**0.769**
$\mathcal{E}(E, R)$	0.756	0.689	**0.858**	0.643	0.595	0.719
$\mathcal{E}(B, E, R)$	**0.760**	**0.696**	**0.858**	**0.666**	**0.620**	0.744

Table 2: Retrieval performance on the MultiDoc2Dial validation set. All models are fine-tuned using the training set only. * indicates the model trained on the official pre-processed data; others are trained on our pre-processed version. $\mathcal{E}(\cdot)$ denotes ensemble.

Introducing the re-ranker gave marked improvement for all three pre-trained models, especially when applied to the *unseen* passages. In particular, RoBERTa achieves 53.5% and 126.6% improvement over the Reproduced DPR at R@1 on the *seen* and *unseen* settings respectively. The ensemble of different re-rankers brings further improvement – $\mathcal{E}(B, E, R)$ exceeds the best single re-ranker by around 0.01 across all metrics on the *seen* data. Furthermore, improved retrieval directly enhances the final task results. Besides a more powerful generator, the large gap between RAG and our approach on the *unseen* Val data in Table 1 may also be attributed to the great performance gain on passage retrieval, from 0.248 to 0.62 on R@1.

5.3 Ablation Study on the Generator

Table 3 shows that each component in our approach contributes to improvement. Passage dropout and regularization bring notable performance gains for the *unseen* setting. This demonstrates robustness in the generator, which is important in practical use.

To investigate the merits of pipeline training on generation, we separate the $\text{BART}_{\text{large}}$ generator from other parts in the reproduced RAG. We input queries combined with the passages returned by the re-reranker for inference. The first and sec-

[5] Grounding Prediction and passage dropout are not implemented in the inference phrase.

[6] We evaluate on a cleaned validation set where repeated queries are removed, resulting in 4181 unique instances (cf. 4201 originally) and 121 unique instances (cf. 121 originally) in the *seen* and *unseen* settings respectively.

Method	seen			unseen		
	F1	**EM**	**S-BLEU**	**F1**	**EM**	**S-BLEU**
BART in the RAG	43.77	6.36	30.91	31.92	2.48	21.25
BART	45.91	7.02	32.36	32.93	2.48	20.73
+ multi-task training	46.51	6.67	32.90	33.61	2.48	21.37
+ passage dropout	47.05	**7.38**	32.82	34.27	4.13	21.94
+ regularization	**47.29**	7.31	**34.29**	**36.74**	**4.96**	**24.20**

Table 3: Ablation analysis of the generators based on the validation set. *BART in the RAG* denotes the generator in the fully-trained RAG. The same retrieval is used in all cases. **S-BLEU** represents SacreBLEU.

ond rows of Table 3 show that the BART in the RAG gained some improvement through better retrieval, but remains inferior to the BART trained in a pipeline fashion. This is mainly attributed by the fact that under the end-to-end training framework of the RAG, the generator could receive some deteriorated query-passage pairs during training, if the retriever can not successfully return gold passages to the generator. Contrarily, pipeline training for the generator can make full use of training data.

6 Conclusion

This paper presents a pipeline system of "retrieve, re-rank, and generate" for the MultiDoc2Dial challenge. The advantage is that each of the three components can fully exploit the ground-truth training data. We apply a deep cross-encoder architecture where we create a training set using localized hard negatives sampled from the retriever results. We adopt grounding span prediction as an auxiliary task to be jointly trained with the response generator. We also apply passage dropout and regularization to improve response generation performance. Experimental results indicate that the proposed system improves over a strong, competitive baseline and our team got 1st place on ALL four leaderboards.

Acknowledgements

This work is partially supported by the Centre for Perceptual and Interactive Intelligence (CPII) Ltd., a CUHK-led under the InnoHK scheme of Innovation and Technology Commission; and in part by the HKSAR RGC GRF (Ref No. 14207619).

References

Danqi Chen, Adam Fisch, Jason Weston, and Antoine Bordes. 2017. Reading Wikipedia to answer open-domain questions. In *Proceedings of the 55th Annual Meeting of the Association for Computational Linguistics (Volume 1: Long Papers)*, pages 1870–1879, Vancouver, Canada. Association for Computational Linguistics.

Eunsol Choi, He He, Mohit Iyyer, Mark Yatskar, Wen-tau Yih, Yejin Choi, Percy Liang, and Luke Zettlemoyer. 2018. Quac: Question answering in context. In *Proceedings of the 2018 Conference on Empirical Methods in Natural Language Processing, Brussels, Belgium, October 31 - November 4, 2018*, pages 2174–2184. Association for Computational Linguistics.

Kevin Clark, Minh-Thang Luong, Quoc V. Le, and Christopher D. Manning. 2020. Pre-training transformers as energy-based cloze models. In *EMNLP*.

Jacob Devlin, Ming-Wei Chang, Kenton Lee, and Kristina Toutanova. 2019. BERT: Pre-training of deep bidirectional transformers for language understanding. In *Proceedings of the 2019 Conference of the North American Chapter of the Association for Computational Linguistics: Human Language Technologies, Volume 1 (Long and Short Papers)*, pages 4171–4186, Minneapolis, Minnesota. Association for Computational Linguistics.

Thomas G. Dietterich. 2000. Ensemble methods in machine learning. In *Multiple Classifier Systems*, pages 1–15, Berlin, Heidelberg. Springer Berlin Heidelberg.

Song Feng, Siva Sankalp Patel, Hui Wan, and Sachindra Joshi. 2021. MultiDoc2Dial: Modeling dialogues grounded in multiple documents. In *Proceedings of the 2021 Conference on Empirical Methods in Natural Language Processing*, pages 6162–6176, Online and Punta Cana, Dominican Republic. Association for Computational Linguistics.

Song Feng, Hui Wan, R. Chulaka Gunasekara, Siva Sankalp Patel, Sachindra Joshi, and Luis A. Lastras. 2020. doc2dial: A goal-oriented document-grounded dialogue dataset. In *Proceedings of the 2020 Conference on Empirical Methods in Natural Language Processing, EMNLP 2020, Online, November 16-20, 2020*, pages 8118–8128. Association for Computational Linguistics.

Luyu Gao, Zhuyun Dai, and Jamie Callan. 2021. Rethink training of BERT rerankers in multi-stage retrieval pipeline. In *Advances in Information Retrieval - 43rd European Conference on IR Research, ECIR 2021, Virtual Event, March 28 - April 1, 2021, Proceedings, Part II*, volume 12657 of *Lecture Notes in Computer Science*, pages 280–286. Springer.

Kelvin Guu, Kenton Lee, Zora Tung, Panupong Pasupat, and Ming-Wei Chang. 2020. REALM: retrieval-augmented language model pre-training. *CoRR*, abs/2002.08909.

Gautier Izacard and Edouard Grave. 2021. Leveraging passage retrieval with generative models for open domain question answering. In *Proceedings of the 16th*

Conference of the European Chapter of the Association for Computational Linguistics: Main Volume, EACL 2021, Online, April 19 - 23, 2021, pages 874–880. Association for Computational Linguistics.

Jeff Johnson, Matthijs Douze, and Hervé Jégou. 2017. Billion-scale similarity search with GPUs. *arXiv e-prints*, page arXiv:1702.08734.

Vladimir Karpukhin, Barlas Oguz, Sewon Min, Patrick Lewis, Ledell Wu, Sergey Edunov, Danqi Chen, and Wen-tau Yih. 2020. Dense passage retrieval for open-domain question answering. In *Proceedings of the 2020 Conference on Empirical Methods in Natural Language Processing (EMNLP)*, pages 6769–6781, Online. Association for Computational Linguistics.

Kenton Lee, Ming-Wei Chang, and Kristina Toutanova. 2019. Latent retrieval for weakly supervised open domain question answering. *CoRR*, abs/1906.00300.

Mike Lewis, Yinhan Liu, Naman Goyal, Marjan Ghazvininejad, Abdelrahman Mohamed, Omer Levy, Veselin Stoyanov, and Luke Zettlemoyer. 2020a. BART: denoising sequence-to-sequence pre-training for natural language generation, translation, and comprehension. In *Proceedings of the 58th Annual Meeting of the Association for Computational Linguistics, ACL 2020, Online, July 5-10, 2020*, pages 7871–7880. Association for Computational Linguistics.

Patrick S. H. Lewis, Ethan Perez, Aleksandra Piktus, Fabio Petroni, Vladimir Karpukhin, Naman Goyal, Heinrich Küttler, Mike Lewis, Wen-tau Yih, Tim Rocktäschel, Sebastian Riedel, and Douwe Kiela. 2020b. Retrieval-augmented generation for knowledge-intensive NLP tasks. In *Advances in Neural Information Processing Systems 33: Annual Conference on Neural Information Processing Systems 2020, NeurIPS 2020, December 6-12, 2020, virtual.*

Xiaobo Liang, Lijun Wu, Juntao Li, Yue Wang, Qi Meng, Tao Qin, Wei Chen, M. Zhang, and Tie-Yan Liu. 2021. R-drop: Regularized dropout for neural networks. In *Advances in Neural Information Processing Systems*.

Chin-Yew Lin. 2004. ROUGE: A package for automatic evaluation of summaries. In *Text Summarization Branches Out*, pages 74–81, Barcelona, Spain. Association for Computational Linguistics.

Yinhan Liu, Myle Ott, Naman Goyal, Jingfei Du, Mandar Joshi, Danqi Chen, Omer Levy, Mike Lewis, Luke Zettlemoyer, and Veselin Stoyanov. 2019. RoBERTa: A Robustly Optimized BERT Pretraining Approach. *arXiv e-prints*, page arXiv:1907.11692.

Matt Post. 2018. A call for clarity in reporting BLEU scores. In *Proceedings of the Third Conference on Machine Translation: Research Papers*, pages 186–191, Brussels, Belgium. Association for Computational Linguistics.

Pranav Rajpurkar, Jian Zhang, Konstantin Lopyrev, and Percy Liang. 2016. SQuAD: 100,000+ questions for machine comprehension of text. In *Proceedings of the 2016 Conference on Empirical Methods in Natural Language Processing*, pages 2383–2392, Austin, Texas. Association for Computational Linguistics.

Siva Reddy, Danqi Chen, and Christopher D. Manning. 2019. Coqa: A conversational question answering challenge. *Trans. Assoc. Comput. Linguistics*, 7:249–266.

Marzieh Saeidi, Max Bartolo, Patrick S. H. Lewis, Sameer Singh, Tim Rocktäschel, Mike Sheldon, Guillaume Bouchard, and Sebastian Riedel. 2018. Interpretation of natural language rules in conversational machine reading. In *Proceedings of the 2018 Conference on Empirical Methods in Natural Language Processing, Brussels, Belgium, October 31 - November 4, 2018*, pages 2087–2097. Association for Computational Linguistics.

Thomas Wolf, Lysandre Debut, Victor Sanh, Julien Chaumond, Clement Delangue, Anthony Moi, Pierric Cistac, Tim Rault, Rémi Louf, Morgan Funtowicz, and Jamie Brew. 2019. Huggingface's transformers: State-of-the-art natural language processing. *CoRR*, abs/1910.03771.

Split	Setting	Instance Num	Passage Num
Train	seen	21451	3820
Validation	*seen*	4201	3820
	unseen	121	963
Development	*seen*	199	3820
	unseen	417	963
Test	*seen*	661	3820
	unseen	126	963

Table 4: Data statistics of different splits. We split a single conversation into multiple instances of the train and validation set.

A Dataset Description

MultiDoc2Dial contains 4796 conversations with an average of 14 turns grounded in 488 documents from four domains. After splitting, the number of passages in the *seen* set is $M = 4110$ for the official data pre-processing and $M = 3820$ for our processed data to remove duplicate passages. Similarly, the number of passages in the *unseen* set is $M = 963$. Table 4 shows the statistics of dataset in different splits.

B Implementation Details

Our implementations of DPR, BERT, RoBERTa, ELECTRA, and BART are based on the Transformers library (Wolf et al., 2019). All the models are trained on an RTX 3090 GPU with 24GB VRAM.

Retriever We train the retriever on our pre-processed MultiDoc2Dial data with an effective batch size of 16 following Facebook DPR (Karpukhin et al., 2020) and the corresponding results are shown in Table 2 named as Reproduced DPR. The Official DPR in Table 2 is fine-tuned with a batch size 128 by the organizer.

Re-ranker Three public pre-trained language models are ensembled, namely, deepset/bert-large-uncased-whole-word-masking-squad2[7], deepset/roberta-large-squad2[8] and deepset/electra-base-squad2[9]. We train the models with a batch size 1 for LARGE (gradient accumulation=4) and 4 for BASE. We use 6 epochs, a learning rate of 1e-5 and weight decay of 0.01. The maximum length of query, i.e., the concatenated dialogue history $\{u_1^{T-1}\}$ and the current user turn u_T is set as 128. Following Feng et al. (2021), the query is constructed using reverse conversation order as $u^T[SEP]agent : u^{T-1}||user : u^{T-2}||...||user : u^1$ and truncated from the tail by the tokenizers. The number of localized negatives in training is 7, sampled from Top-N (N=50) returned negative passages from retriever. During inference, re-ranker re-scores Top-K (K=100) returned passage candidates from retriever and selects the Top-5 passages for generator.

[7]https://huggingface.co/deepset/bert-large-uncased-whole-word-masking-squad2

[8]https://huggingface.co/deepset/roberta-large-squad2

[9]https://huggingface.co/deepset/electra-base-squad2

A Knowledge Storage and Semantic Space Alignment Method for Multi-documents Dialogue Generation

Minjun Zhu[1,2], Bin Li[3], Fei Xia[1,2], Yixuan Weng[1*]
[1] National Laboratory of Pattern Recognition,, Institute of Automation, CAS
[2] School of Artificial Intelligence, University of Chinese Academy of Sciences
[3] College of Electrical and Information Engineering, Hunan University
{zhuminjun2020,xiafei2020}@ia.ac.cn, libincn@hnu.edu.cn, wengsyx@gmail.com

Abstract

Question Answering (QA) is a Natural Language Processing (NLP) task that can measure language and semantics understanding ability, it requires a system not only to retrieve relevant documents from a large number of articles but also to answer corresponding questions according to documents. However, various language styles and sources of human questions and evidence documents form the different embedding semantic spaces, which may bring some errors to the downstream QA task. To alleviate these problems, we propose a framework for enhancing downstream evidence retrieval by generating evidence, aiming at improving the performance of response generation. Specifically, we take the pre-training language model as a knowledge base, storing documents' information and knowledge into model parameters. With the Child-Tuning approach being designed, the knowledge storage and evidence generation avoid catastrophic forgetting for response generation. Extensive experiments carried out on the multi-documents dataset show that the proposed method can improve the final performance, which demonstrates the effectiveness of the proposed framework.

1 Introduction

With the rapid and vigorous development of the field of artificial intelligence and language intelligence, Question Answering (QA) systems has received more and more extensive attention. Specifically, the QA system aims to provide precise answers in response to the user's questions in natural language. An essential task in the QA system is conversational question answering and document-grounded dialogue modeling. The conversational question answering dialogue-like interface that enables interaction between human users and the documentation provides sufficient information. Prior work typically formulates the task as a machine reading comprehension task assuming the associated document or text snippet is given, such as QuAC (Choi et al., 2018), ShARC (Saeidi et al., 2018), CoQA (Reddy et al., 2019), OR-QuAC (Qu et al., 2020) and Doc2Dial (Feng et al., 2020).

One of the difficulties of conversational QA tasks is to model the historical information in the process of system retrieval and generation. The recently released conversational question answering datasets like CoQA (Reddy et al., 2019) and QuAC (Choi et al., 2018) aim to lead a reader to answer the latest question by comprehending the given context passage and the conversation history. As they provide context passages in their task setting, they omit the stage of document retrieval. While on the MultiDoc2Dial (Feng et al., 2021) dataset, retrieval is necessary. Recently, Qu et al. (2020) extend the QuAC dataset to a new OR-QuAC dataset by adapting to an open retrieval conversational question answering system (OpenConvQA), it can retrieve relevant passages from a large collection before inferring the answer, taking into account the conversation QA pairs, which is similar with the MultiDoc2Dial dataset.

To enhance the modeling of historical sessions and avoid the problem of weak semantic relatedness between problems and evidence in the retrieval stage. we propose a novel three-stage framework, which stores knowledge and makes alignment in semantic space. Specifically, we find that it is inconsistent to search for most question-related evidence only by the inner product of the question and long text of dialogue history. As stated by Feng et al. (2021) about task 2: Agent Response Generation is more difficult than task 1: Grounding Span Prediction, because agent utterance varies in style and is not directly extracted from document content. Different language styles and sources lead to different semantic spaces of question and evidence document embedding. As a result, it inspires us

*Corresponding author.

Proceedings of the Second DialDoc Workshop on Document-grounded Dialogue and Conversational Question Answering, pages 130 - 135
May 26, 2022 ©2022 Association for Computational Linguistics

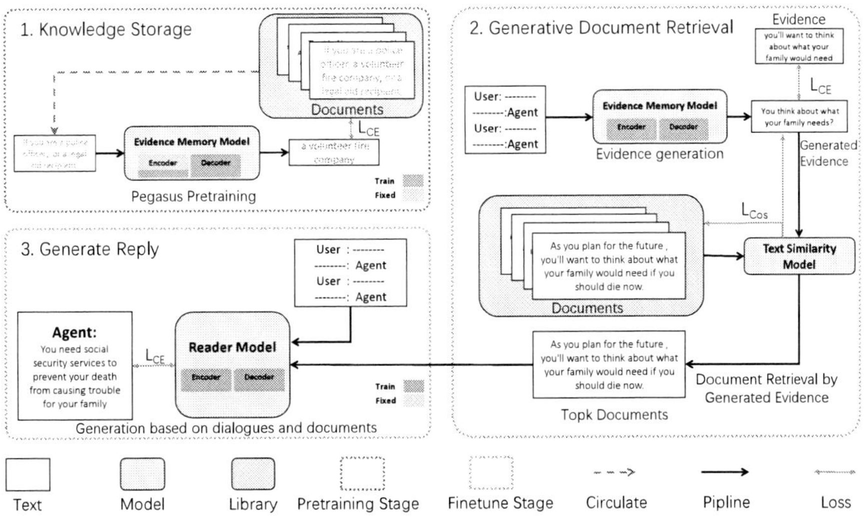

Figure 1: The overview of the proposed three-stage method, where the evidence memory model in the Knowledge Storage and the Generation Document retrieval module is the same T5.

to propose a framework that uses model-generated evidence to enhance question-related evidence. We summarize our contributions as follows:

- To address the inconsistency between the semantic space of questions and evidence documents, we propose a framework for enhancing downstream evidence retrieval by generating evidence and enhancing the performance of response generation.
- We take the pre-training language model as a knowledge base, and store documents' information and knowledge into model parameters through the Pegasus pre-training method (Zhang et al., 2019), which effectively improves the memory of the pre-trained language model for documents. This constitutes our knowledge storage stage.
- We applied the Child-Tuning approach in Xu et al. (2021) to knowledge storage and evidence generation to avoid catastrophic forgetting caused by two-stage training.

2 Main method

In this section, the overall framework is illustrated in Figure 1, where we will elaborate on the main method for the MultiDoc2Dial task. Based on the pre-trained language model, we design a three-stage semantic alignment method including the knowledge storage stage, generative document retrieval, and reply generation modules, which are described in turn as follows.

2.1 Knowledge storage

In this stage, we trained the pre-training language model for knowledge storage. Because the semantic space of the question embedding and the documents' embedding is inconsistent (Feng et al., 2021), we generate additional possible evidence as auxiliary features to increase the semantic alignment of embedding in downstream tasks. The traditional retrieval method (Qu et al., 2020) is designed to search related documents based on question embedding and documents embeddings. However, in this scenario, the genre, style, and size of questions and documents are different, which will lead to question and documents embeddings in different semantic spaces. To improve the accuracy of document retrieval, they should be searched in the same semantic space. we believe that the maximum inner product search of relevant evidence-based evidence can match with stronger semantic relevance. Before generating evidence, we use the pretraining method to make the model memory document knowledge more deeply. We pre-trained T5 (Raffel et al., 2019; Tay et al., 2021) with Pegasus (Zhang et al., 2019) method, randomly sampling 3/4 of the sentences of the document and training the model to generate the other 1/4 of the sentences. We think this way can enable the model to learn complete document information. In addition,

Model	Method	F1_U	sacreBLEU_U	Meteor_U	Rouge_U	All
T5 Model	Finetune with Utterance	28.090	12.386	25.627	26.199	92.302
	Zeroshot	10.485	1.144	8.723	10.267	41.104
Pegasus Pre-trained Model	Finetune with Utterance	28.556	13.062	26.429	26.434	94.481
	Finetune with Evidence	**35.672**	**16.171**	**34.318**	**34.013**	**130.174**

Table 1: Comparison results between different methods without using retrieval.

Following Xu et al. (2021), we use the child-tune method to perform Pegasus (Zhang et al., 2019) pre-training, only 25% of the parameters of the encoder and 100% of the parameters of the decoder are detected as the most important child network for the target task. Fisher information for the i-th parameter is as follows:

$$F_i = \frac{1}{n}\sum_{j=1}^{n}\left(\frac{\partial \log p\left(y_j \mid x_j; \theta\right)}{\partial \theta_i}\right)^2 \quad (1)$$

After this phase, we believe it will benefit the later evidence generation task.

2.2 Generate document retrieval

The goal of generating document retrieval is to obtain the most relevant evidence-based on the question and dialogue history. We formulate this problem in two steps. First, we use the evidence memory model to generate relevant evidence. The model trained from the knowledge storage can be considered evidence modeling. Second, the generated evidence is used to retrieve a shred of evidence from the document collections. We use SimCSE Model[1] (Gao et al., 2021) to obtain the embedding of the question and generated shreds of evidence, and use MIPS (Maximum Inner Product Search) to get the most relevant evidence from the evidence base. For top-k searching, we use the loss function based on the Cos function for training.

$$L_{\text{Cos}} = \log \frac{e^{\operatorname{sim}\left(h_i, h_i^{+}\right)/\ell}}{\sum_{j=1}^{N} e^{\operatorname{sim}\left(h_i, h_j^{+}\right)/\ell}} \quad (2)$$

2.3 Reply generation

In the reply generation module, the T5 model is used to generate the next sentence reply answer with the input obtained in the previous generate document retrieval module.

[1]https://huggingface.co/princeton-nlp/sup-simcse-roberta-large

Domain	# Doc	# Dial	Two-seg	>Two-seg	Single
Ssa	109	1191	701	188	302
Va	1398	1337	648	491	198
Dmv	149	1328	781	257	290
Student	92	940	508	274	158
Total	488	4796	2638	1210	948

Table 2: Statistics of the MultiDoc2Dial task dataset.

3 Experimental

3.1 Data description

MultiDoc2Dial (Feng et al., 2021) is a Multi-Document-Grounded Dialogue dataset, which is derived from Doc2Dial dataset (Feng et al., 2020) with changing a single document to multiple documents. The task is to generate grounded agent responses given dialogue queries and domain documents. Specifically, the system gets the latest user turn, dialogue history, and all domain documents as inputs, and requires the system to return agent responses in natural language. The specific distribution of the MultiDoc2Dial task data set is shown in Table 2.

3.2 Evaluation metrics

We follow the previous settings in Feng et al. (2020, 2021). In the retrieval task, we calculate recall (@1), which measures the number of correct documents found in the first prediction. We report token-level F1 scores, Exact Match (EM) (Rajpurkar et al., 2016) scores, and sacreBLEU (Post, 2018) scores for the generated text.

3.3 Implementation details

In these tasks, we are mainly based on the huggingface framework[2] (Wolf et al., 2020). We use the AdamW (Loshchilov and Hutter, 2018) optimizer. Linear decay of learning rate and gradient clipping of 1e-4. Dropout (Srivastava et al., 2014) of 0.1 is applied to prevent overfitting. We implemented the code of training and reasoning based on PyTorch[3] (Paszke et al., 2019) in one NVIDIA A100 GPU.

[2]https://github.com/huggingface/transformers

[3]https://pytorch.org

Method	D^{token}-bm25	D^{struct}-bm25	D^{token}-nq	D^{struct}-nq	D^{token}-ft	D^{token}-ft	$GDR^{w/o}$-ques.	GDR^{with}-ques.
Top-1 Acc	20.5	18.0	27.7	28.6	36.4	39.1	24.5	**42.5**

Table 3: Result of the TopK accuracy in the retrieval task between different baseline methods, where GDR means generate document retrieval, and with and w/o-ques. mean whether adding input question.

Model	Method	F1	Exact Match	sacreBLEU	All
Baseline	D^{struct}-bm25	27.9	2.0	12.5	42.4
	D^{struct}-nq	33.0	3.6	17.6	54.2
	D^{struct}-ft	36.0	4.1	21.9	62.0
Pegasus Pretrained Model	without retrieval	35.7	3.9	16.2	55.8
	with retrieval	34.4	3.0	20.6	58.0
T5 Model	without retrieval	28.1	2.9	15.6	46.6
	with retrieval	**43.4**	**5.1**	**24.8**	**73.3**

Table 4: Comparison with different methods for the final results on the Validation set. In the baseline, we follow the previous settings: Struct means the corresponding document index is based on structure-segmented passages, nq means using the original pre-trained bi-encoder from DPR, ft means fine-tune. We adopt underline to show the score of second place.

All experiments select the best parameters on the valid set and then report the score of the best model (valid set) on the test set.

Knowledge storage We use Google's open-source T5 large model[4] for pre-training. We use the AdamW (Loshchilov and Hutter, 2018; Xu et al., 2021) optimizer and the learning rate is set to $1e-4$ with the warm-up (He et al., 2016). We also fixed some parameters in the T5 model whose gradient change was less than 75% of all parameters in the first round of training. The batch size is 6. We set the maximum length of 350. We intercepted according to the document fragments, randomly selected $1/4$ of the subfragments as labels, and repeated 50 rounds as knowledge storage.

Generate document retrieval We fine-tune the Knowledge Storage Model with "context -> evidence", and then we use this model to generate the evidence of the dev set. After that, we use the Text Similarity Model[5] (Gao et al., 2021) to retrieve the top K documents from the document library. Here, we set $K = 1$. In detail, we input the final problem into the model together with the evidence generated by the previous model. Then use the same model to obtain the semantic vectors of all documents, and use cosine similarity to calculate the most similar documents.

Reply generation We re-use a new T5 model, which uses "the last question of the dialogue </s> dialogue history information </s> related documents" to fine-tune. We set the maximum length of 700 and batch size is set at 6. If the document content exceeds the limit, it will be deleted.

3.4 Experimental results

We conducted three comparative experiments as shown in Table 1, Table 3 , Table 4and Table 5 respectively, where the first is the non-retrieval experiment. When training with utterance as the label, compared with T5 original model, the model trained with Pegasus can obtain better performance. Even without training samples, it can achieve good results. It is worth noting that better performance can be achieved if the evidence is used as a training label. The reason may be that in this training scenario the output is relatively consistent with Pegasus training, which can stimulate the potential knowledge base features of the model. In the retrieval task shown in Table 3, we first use the context to generate possible evidence, then fine-tune it in Simcse, then find the most likely documents based on MIPS. We tested two cases, one in which the generated evidence is embedded into the semantic vector for retrieval, and the other in which the question and the generated evidence are co-embedded into the semantic vector for retrieval. The experimental results show that although the retrieval performance of single evidence is not good, it can achieve better results if it is used as input together with the problem as an additional auxiliary feature. After the retrieval performance is improved, we use the T5 model to take evidence and context for training. About all the evaluation metrics, on the validation set, we conduct an exhaustive comparison experiment among our Pega-

[4] google/t5-efficient-large-nl36

[5] https://huggingface.co/princeton-nlp/sup-simcse-roberta-large

Model	F1	sacreBLEU	METEOR	RougeL	Total
Baseline	35.85	22.26	34.28	33.82	126.21
Ours	**36.69**	**22.78**	**35.46**	**34.52**	**129.44**

Table 5: Comparison with different methods for the final results on the Test set.

sus Pre-trained Model, T5, and baselines in Table 4. And it can also be significantly improved compared with the baseline methods on the Test set, which is shown in Table 5.

4 Conclusion

In this paper, we propose a generative evidence retrieval method, which transforms the context and problems into possible evidence for further retrieval. Specifically, we first use Pegasus to completely save the knowledge base into the language model and use Child-tune to avoid the catastrophic forgetting problem for response generation. More precisely, it avoids the problem of weak semantic relatedness between the "question text" to be retrieved and the retrieved "answer text", and can effectively increase the accuracy of retrieval. In the future, we will study how to combine the evidence generation model with the utterance generation model to further improve the generation quality.

References

Eunsol Choi, He He, Mohit Iyyer, Mark Yatskar, Wen tau Yih, Yejin Choi, Percy Liang, and Luke Zettlemoyer. 2018. Quac: Question answering in context. In *Empirical Methods in Natural Language Processing*.

Song Feng, Kshitij P. Fadnis, Q. Vera Liao, and Luis A. Lastras. 2020. Doc2dial: A framework for dialogue composition grounded in documents. In *National Conference on Artificial Intelligence*.

Song Feng, Siva Sankalp Patel, Hui Wan, and Sachindra Joshi. 2021. Multidoc2dial: Modeling dialogues grounded in multiple documents. In *EMNLP*.

Tianyu Gao, Xingcheng Yao, and Danqi Chen. 2021. SimCSE: Simple contrastive learning of sentence embeddings. In *Empirical Methods in Natural Language Processing (EMNLP)*.

Kaiming He, Xiangyu Zhang, Shaoqing Ren, and Jian Sun. 2016. Deep residual learning for image recognition. In *2016 IEEE Conference on Computer Vision and Pattern Recognition (CVPR)*, pages 770–778.

Ilya Loshchilov and Frank Hutter. 2018. Decoupled weight decay regularization. In *International Conference on Learning Representations*.

Adam Paszke, Sam Gross, Francisco Massa, Adam Lerer, James Bradbury, Gregory Chanan, Trevor Killeen, Zeming Lin, Natalia Gimelshein, Luca Antiga, Alban Desmaison, Andreas Kopf, Edward Yang, Zachary DeVito, Martin Raison, Alykhan Tejani, Sasank Chilamkurthy, Benoit Steiner, Lu Fang, Junjie Bai, and Soumith Chintala. 2019. Pytorch: An imperative style, high-performance deep learning library. In *Advances in Neural Information Processing Systems*, volume 32. Curran Associates, Inc.

Matt Post. 2018. A call for clarity in reporting bleu scores.

Chen Qu, Liu Yang, Cen Chen, Minghui Qiu, W. Bruce Croft, and Mohit Iyyer. 2020. Open-retrieval conversational question answering. In *International ACM SIGIR Conference on Research and Development in Information Retrieval*.

Colin Raffel, Noam Shazeer, Adam Roberts, Katherine Lee, Sharan Narang, Michael Matena, Yanqi Zhou, Wei Li, and Peter J. Liu. 2019. Exploring the limits of transfer learning with a unified text-to-text transformer. *CoRR*, abs/1910.10683.

Pranav Rajpurkar, Jian Zhang, Konstantin Lopyrev, and Percy Liang. 2016. Squad: 100,000+ questions for machine comprehension of text. In *Empirical Methods in Natural Language Processing*.

Siva Reddy, Danqi Chen, and Christopher D. Manning. 2019. Coqa: A conversational question answering challenge. *Transactions of the Association for Computational Linguistics*, 7:249–266.

Marzieh Saeidi, Max Bartolo, Patrick S. H. Lewis, Sameer Singh, Tim Rocktäschel, Michael Sheldon, Guillaume Bouchard, and Sebastian Riedel. 2018. Interpretation of natural language rules in conversational machine reading. In *Empirical Methods in Natural Language Processing*.

Nitish Srivastava, Geoffrey E. Hinton, Alex Krizhevsky, Ilya Sutskever, and Ruslan Salakhutdinov. 2014. Dropout: a simple way to prevent neural networks from overfitting. *Journal of Machine Learning Research*, 15:1929–1958.

Yi Tay, Mostafa Dehghani, Jinfeng Rao, William Fedus, Samira Abnar, Hyung Won Chung, Sharan Narang, Dani Yogatama, Ashish Vaswani, and Donald Metzler. 2021. Scale efficiently: Insights from pre-training and fine-tuning transformers. *CoRR*, abs/2109.10686.

Thomas Wolf, Lysandre Debut, Victor Sanh, Julien Chaumond, Clement Delangue, Anthony Moi, Pierric Cistac, Tim Rault, Rémi Louf, Morgan Funtowicz,

Joe Davison, Sam Shleifer, Patrick von Platen, Clara Ma, Yacine Jernite, Julien Plu, Canwen Xu, Teven Le Scao, Sylvain Gugger, Mariama Drame, Quentin Lhoest, and Alexander M. Rush. 2020. Transformers: State-of-the-art natural language processing. In *Proceedings of the 2020 Conference on Empirical Methods in Natural Language Processing: System Demonstrations*, pages 38–45, Online. Association for Computational Linguistics.

Runxin Xu, Fuli Luo, Zhiyuan Zhang, Chuanqi Tan, Baobao Chang, Songfang Huang, and Fei Huang. 2021. Raise a child in large language model: Towards effective and generalizable fine-tuning. In *Proceedings of the 2021 Conference on Empirical Methods in Natural Language Processing (EMNLP)*. Association for Computational Linguistics.

Jingqing Zhang, Yao Zhao, Mohammad Saleh, and Peter J. Liu. 2019. Pegasus: Pre-training with extracted gap-sentences for abstractive summarization.

Improving Multiple Documents Grounded Goal-Oriented Dialog Systems via Diverse Knowledge Enhanced Pretrained Language Model

Yunah Jang[1] Dongryeol Lee[1] Hyungjoo Park[1] Taegwan Kang[1]
Hwanhee Lee[1] Hyunkyung Bae[1] Kyomin Jung[2]
[1]Department of Electrical and Computer Engineering, Seoul National University, Seoul, Korea
[2]Automation and Systems Research Institute, Seoul National University, Seoul, Korea
{vn2209, drl123, harry0816, zd9370, wanted1007, hkbae, kjung}@snu.ac.kr

Abstract

In this paper, we mainly discuss about our submission to MultiDoc2Dial task, which aims to model the goal-oriented dialogues grounded in multiple documents. The proposed task is split into grounding span prediction and agent response generation. The baseline for the task is the retrieval augmented generation model, which consists of a dense passage retrieval model for the retrieval part and the BART model for the generation part. The main challenge of this task is that the system requires a great amount of pre-trained knowledge to generate answers grounded in multiple documents. To overcome this challenge, we adopt multi-task learning, data augmentation, model pretraining and contrastive learning to enhance our model's coverage of pretrained knowledge. We experiment with various settings of our method to show the effectiveness of our approaches. Our final model achieved 37.78 F1 score, 22.94 SacreBLEU, 36.97 Meteor, 35.46 RougeL, a total of 133.15 on DialDoc Shared Task at ACL 2022 released test set.

1 Introduction

Recently, deep learning-based dialog systems have attracted much attention from academia and the industry. The main challenge of dialog systems is to generate fluent responses consistent with the users' text input. As Pre-trained Language Models (PLMs) (e.g., BART (Lewis et al., 2019) and GPT2 (Radford et al., 2019)) have emerged, dialog systems have taken advantage of PLMs (Zhao et al., 2020; Wu et al., 2019; Budzianowski and Vulic, 2019), which can enhance the quality of dialog response by applying implicit language knowledge.

However, these systems lack knowledge of specific topics and thus show weakness in conducting an in-depth conversation with humans. There have been various works for knowledge-grounded dialogue systems to address this problem. (Kim et al., 2020; Zhan et al., 2021) Knowledge grounded dialogue models are capable of generating precise responses based on both the dialogue context and external sources. Therefore, researchers have usually constructed dialogue flows grounded in related documents (Dinan et al., 2018; Zhou et al., 2018b) or knowledge graphs (Moon et al., 2019; Zhou et al., 2018a; Tuan et al., 2019). In particular, Feng et al. (2020) have introduced the Doc2Dial tasks for goal-oriented document-grounded dialog systems. Compared to previous works, Doc2dial has introduced a more challenging setting with multi-turn queries and aims to generate natural language responses from relevant grounding document. On top of that, they also propose the MultiDoc2Dial dataset (Feng et al., 2021) ,which is built upon the Doc2Dial dataset. MultiDoc2Dial dataset is more closely related to real-life scenarios than the prior work since the agent generates responses based on multiple documents as grounding knowledge. Due to its multi-document setting, utilizing knowledge has become more complex.

To utilize external knowledge in dialogue, knowledge grounded models generally consist of a retrieval model and a generative model. Recently, the Retrieval Augmented Generation (RAG) model (Lewis et al., 2020a) has been proposed to leverage both parametric (Raffel et al., 2019; Lewis et al., 2019) and non-parametric memory (Lewis et al., 2020b; Xiao et al., 2020) methods by combining pre-trained seq2seq models and the dense vector index of grounding documents. However, the RAG model lacks knowledge related to question answering and dialogue generation.

In this paper, our team JPL proposes four approaches to enhance RAG's diverse knowledge: multi-task learning, data augmentation, pretraining and contrastive learning. Multi-task learning, extra pretraining on conversational question answering datasets, and data augmentation enhance the model's task-oriented knowledge. Contrastive

Proceedings of the Second DialDoc Workshop on Document-grounded Dialogue and Conversational Question Answering, pages 136 - 141
May 26, 2022 ©2022 Association for Computational Linguistics

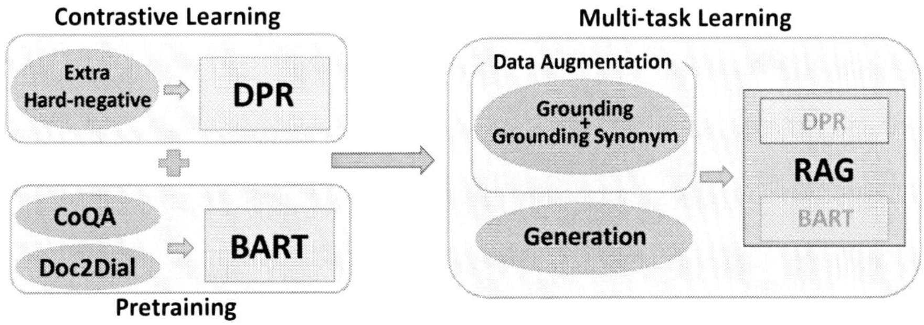

Figure 1: **Our training pipeline** We utilize four methods to cultivate the RAG model's diverse knowledge. To enhance model's task-agnositic knowledge, we add a hard negative sample for contrastive learning on the DPR retriever module. Pretraining BART with conversational QA datasets, data augmentation on grounding task, and multi-task learning improves task-specific knowledge for the final RAG model.

learning for the DPR retriever module strengthen task-agnostic knowledge. We participate in the second DialDoc shared task held by ACL, Multi-Doc2Dial: Modeling Dialogues Grounded in Multiple Documents (Feng et al., 2021). These methods cultivate the dialogue model's capability to use complex external knowledge on top of PLM's inherent power.

Splits	Train	Val	Test
Dialogues	3474	661	661
Queries	21453	4201	4094
Passages(struct)		4110	

Table 1: **Dataset Statistics** We split documents by using structural information from markup tags integrated in HTML files.

2 Shared Task

2.1 Dataset

In this shared task, we focus on the MultiDoc2Dial dataset (Feng et al., 2021), which contains conversations that are grounded in multiple documents. The dataset is constructed based on the Doc2Dial dataset, the dataset for the prior shared task at the DialDoc 2021 workshop. Unlike its predecessor, each dialogue in the MultiDoc2Dial dataset has multiple segments with different grounding documents for adjacent segments. The dataset consists of 4800 dialogues with an average of 14 turns that are grounded in 488 documents from four different domains (dmv, ssa, studentaid, va). Details of the MultiDoc2Dial dataset are given in Table 1.

2.2 Multidoc2dial

For the evaluations on MultiDoc2Dial dataset, two sub-tasks are proposed. Task 1 aims to predict the grounding span for the next agent response. For task 1, we get (1) current user turn, (2) dialogue history, (3) the entire set of documents from all domains as input. For the output, we aim to figure out the most relevant grounding text span from one document for the next agent response. Task 2 aims to generate agent response in natural language. For task 2, we get (1) current user turn, (2) dialogue history, (3) the entire set of documents from all domain as an input.

2.3 Baseline Model

In this shared task, the author proposed a baseline model based on the HuggingFace RAG. [1] For the retriever part, DPR (Karpukhin et al., 2020) was given in the form of both finetuned DPR encoders by author [2] and the original Facebook DPR. [3] The generator module of the baseline is BART-large from the HuggingFace.[4] Our final submission model is composed of our own fine-tuned DPR and Bart-large pretrained with conversational QA datasets.

3 Methodology

We use four methods to enhance the model's ability to efficiently utilize external grounding knowledge especially on dialogue modeling.

[1]https://huggingface.co/docs/transformers/master/model_doc/rag
[2]https://huggingface.co/sivasankalpp
[3]https://github.com/facebookresearch/DPR
[4]https://huggingface.co/facebook/bart-large

3.1 Multi-task Learning

Multi-task learning improves the model's performance when different tasks share information or semantics. If the tasks have a higher correlation, it is likely for the model to benefit more from multi-task learning. The final goal of the proposed task is to generate natural language responses, which corresponds to the generation task. Figure 2 presents the similarity between the ground truth of each task. From this statistic, it is clear that two tasks share much semantic information.

In order to implement multi-task learning, we first train the model on the grounding task with prefix "TASK1: " added to the input string for the generator. Then, using the last checkpoint, we continue training the model on the generation task with prefix "TASK2: " concatenated to each input string.

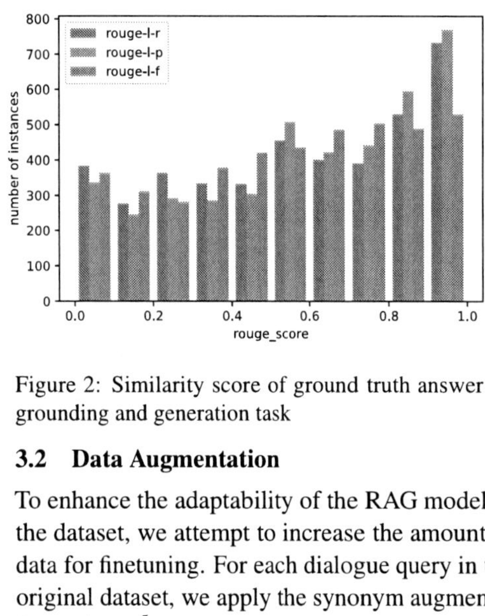

Figure 2: Similarity score of ground truth answer on grounding and generation task

3.2 Data Augmentation

To enhance the adaptability of the RAG model to the dataset, we attempt to increase the amount of data for finetuning. For each dialogue query in the original dataset, we apply the synonym augmenter from nlpaug[5]. The synonym augmenter randomly changes some words in the input to similar words based on WordNet[6]. We exclude '[SEP]', 'agent:' 'user:' since these words are special tokens for the task.

3.3 Pretraining on Conversational QA Datasets

To enhance the generative performance of the model, we pretrain the RAG generator on two datasets.

CoQA The first dataset is the CoQA dataset (Reddy et al., 2018), a conversational QA dataset grounded in a diverse range of documents. Because MultiDoc2Dial is not a large dataset, there is always a possibility of underfitting. CoQA, with its 127k questions, can provide us with much-needed extra data for our generator. As the format of the CoQA dataset (grounding document, then questions) is different from the input format of our BART model (query and dialogue context, followed by the grounding document), we reformat the dataset to fit our needs before training.

Doc2Dial The second dataset is the Doc2Dial dataset (Feng et al., 2020), a goal-oriented document-grounded dialogue dataset which is extremely similar to the MultiDoc2Dial dataset. As mentioned above, most of the instances in the MultiDoc2Dial dataset are formed by modifying Doc2Dial instances to fit a multi-document setting. Along with the existence of a single grounding document, this extreme similarity of content makes it an ideal candidate to train our generator without relying on the proper functioning of the retriever. Therefore, we can expect pretraining the generator on the Doc2Dial dataset to boost the generative capabilities of our model. As with CoQA, we reformat the dataset to fit the input of our BART model before training.

For both datasets, we do not cut down the grounding document to fit the maximum input length of our model. This may have resulted in truncation of the relevant span in some instances, and remains an area of possible improvement.

3.4 Contrastive Learning

To enhance the retrieval performance of the model, we adopt data augmentation to increase the number of hard negative contexts in the DPR training data. We apply the antonym augmenter from nlpaug[7]. The antonym augmenter takes positive contexts, which is the correct grounding document for the dialogue, as input. Based on WordNet antonym, the augmenter switches some words in the inputs to their respective antonyms and outputs the augmented sentences. We consider these outputs as the hard negative contexts and added them to the original dataset. We use the augmented dataset to finetune DPR.

[5]https://github.com/makcedward/nlpaug

[6]https://wordnet.princeton.edu/

[7]https://github.com/makcedward/nlpaug

4 Experiments

4.1 Training Details

We fine-tune RAG by following the default hyper-parameter settings from the baseline code.[8] Due to hardware shortage, there are minor modifications; we set the gradient accumulation step as 2 and reduce the training and evaluation batch size to 4 and 1, respectively. We only report results of utilizing document structural information for segmentation since it shows better results in our experimental settings. The retrieved documents are not re-ranked since this method doesn't benefit the model performance.

4.2 Results and Analysis

Model	F1	EM	S_Bleu
baseline	34.69	3.86	20.63
+Multi-task learning	34.85	3.98	19.86
+Data Augmentation	33.55	3.28	19.01

Table 2: **RAG Fine-tuning Methods Results** Models are evaluated with F1, Exact Match, and sacreBLEU scores. The baseline model is composed of the released version of finetuned DPR[9] and BART-large on the HuggingFace.

4.2.1 RAG Fine-tuning Methods

In this section, the Facebook released version of DPR and BART-large in the HuggingFace constitute the baseline model.

Multi-task Learning We sequentially fine-tune the model on the grounding and generation tasks. Table 2 shows the results for multi-task learning. There are improvements in the F1 and EM score using multi-task learning, even though considering the fact that the model was trained on the generation task for a much shorter time. We expect the model to show better results with more extended training.

Data Augmentation For data augmentation, we apply synonym transformation to the original dataset, attaining twice the baseline size. Table 2 presents the result for data augmentation on generation task. We have observed that applying data augmentation to the generation task degraded the performance. However, by utilizing augmented data on the grounding task, the model achieves a 40.55 F1 score and a 23.49 exact match score. Compared to our baseline model implementation trained with the original grounding task data, training with augmented data improved +0.5 F1 score and +0.64 exact match score. These results demonstrate that synonym data augmentation on the generation task's gold answers does not provide the model with any informative knowledge for the generation task. Therefore, we include augmented data only on grounding task during multi-task learning.

Model	F1	EM	S_Bleu
baseline	34.69	3.86	20.63
+CoQA	35.08	4.02	20.37
+CoQA&Doc2Dial	35.34	4.09	20.63
DPR(adv_nq)	34.05	3.57	19.76
+DPR(+hard neg)	35.09	3.83	20.87

Table 3: **Module Specific Methods Results** We evaluate models with F1, Exact Match, and sacreBLEU scores. **+CoQA&Doc2Dial** reports results for BART-large pretrained on CoQA and Doc2Dial dataset. **DPR(adv_nq)** is the RAG model composed of our own fine-tuned DPR using shared task configuration. **+DPR(+hard_negative)** corresponds to results for RAG with our fine-tuned DPR version with an extra hard negative sample.

4.2.2 Module Specific Methods

This section mainly discusses results for module-specific training methods. We fine-tune RAG's retriever and pretrain generator, DPR and BART, with contrastive learning and conversational QA datasets. We set the baseline model as the same configuration with section 4.2.1.

Pretraining We pretrain BART-large on CoQA and Doc2Dial before integrating it into RAG. We train 10 epochs for each dataset using hyperparameters suggested by the DialDoc2021 baseline code on subtask2.[10] Table 3 shows the result for pretraining. We report two results; pretrained on CoQA only and pretrained on both CoQA and Doc2Dial. Both datasets enhanced the model performance in terms of F1 and EM scores. There is extra room for improvement since we pretrain BART only for a few epochs due to long training time and limited resources.

Contrastive Learning We fine-tune DPR using the settings implemented by the shared task. We fine-tune the recently released version of DPR, `checkpoint.retriever.single-adv-hn.nq.bert-base-encoder`, for 50 epochs

[8]https://github.com/IBM/multidoc2dial

[10]https://github.com/doc2dial/sharedtask-dialdoc2021

on our new DPR dataset with one extra hard negative sample generated by antonym augmentation. Table 3 reports the results for contrastive learning. Despite using the same hyperparameters for DPR, there is degradation in the score for fine-tuning on our setting. However, after adding another hard negative sample, the model shows better performance on the shared task.

4.2.3 Leaderboard Submission

Our final model for DialDoc shared task at ACL 2022 utilizes all four suggested methods in this paper. We only participate in MultiDoc2Dial-seen-domain task which training data and test data share the same domains for the grounding documents. Our best performing model achieves 37.78 F1 score, 22.94 SacreBLEU, 36.97 Meteor, 35.46 RougeL, a total of 133.15 on the officially released test set (MDD-SEEN).

5 Conclusion

In this paper, we explain our submissions to the MultiDoc2Dial shared task. We utilize various conversational QA datasets and methods to improve the given baseline model. Our RAG model is composed of DPR for the retriever and BART for the generator. We train DPR with contrastive learning with an extra hard negative sample. BART is pre-trained on conversational QA datasets, CoQA and Doc2Dial. On the end-to-end level, we implement multi-task learning to utilize model knowledge obtained from the previous grounding task that is trained on augmented data. All of the mentioned techniques enhance the model performance compared to the suggested baseline model.

Acknowledgements

K. Jung is with ASRI, Seoul National University, Korea. This work was supported by the National Research Foundation of Korea (NRF) grant funded by the Korea government (No. 2021R1A2C2008855)

References

Pawel Budzianowski and Ivan Vulic. 2019. Hello, it's GPT-2 - how can I help you? towards the use of pretrained language models for task-oriented dialogue systems. *CoRR*, abs/1907.05774.

Emily Dinan, Stephen Roller, Kurt Shuster, Angela Fan, Michael Auli, and Jason Weston. 2018. Wizard of wikipedia: Knowledge-powered conversational agents. *arXiv preprint arXiv:1811.01241*.

Song Feng, Siva Sankalp Patel, Hui Wan, and Sachindra Joshi. 2021. Multidoc2dial: Modeling dialogues grounded in multiple documents. *CoRR*, abs/2109.12595.

Song Feng, Hui Wan, R. Chulaka Gunasekara, Siva Sankalp Patel, Sachindra Joshi, and Luis A. Lastras. 2020. doc2dial: A goal-oriented document-grounded dialogue dataset. *CoRR*, abs/2011.06623.

Vladimir Karpukhin, Barlas Oguz, Sewon Min, Patrick Lewis, Ledell Wu, Sergey Edunov, Danqi Chen, and Wen-tau Yih. 2020. Dense passage retrieval for open-domain question answering. In *Proceedings of the 2020 Conference on Empirical Methods in Natural Language Processing (EMNLP)*, pages 6769–6781, Online. Association for Computational Linguistics.

Byeongchang Kim, Jaewoo Ahn, and Gunhee Kim. 2020. Sequential latent knowledge selection for knowledge-grounded dialogue.

Mike Lewis, Yinhan Liu, Naman Goyal, Marjan Ghazvininejad, Abdelrahman Mohamed, Omer Levy, Veselin Stoyanov, and Luke Zettlemoyer. 2019. BART: denoising sequence-to-sequence pre-training for natural language generation, translation, and comprehension. *CoRR*, abs/1910.13461.

Patrick S. H. Lewis, Ethan Perez, Aleksandra Piktus, Fabio Petroni, Vladimir Karpukhin, Naman Goyal, Heinrich Küttler, Mike Lewis, Wen-tau Yih, Tim Rocktäschel, Sebastian Riedel, and Douwe Kiela. 2020a. Retrieval-augmented generation for knowledge-intensive NLP tasks. *CoRR*, abs/2005.11401.

Patrick S. H. Lewis, Pontus Stenetorp, and Sebastian Riedel. 2020b. Question and answer test-train overlap in open-domain question answering datasets. *CoRR*, abs/2008.02637.

Seungwhan Moon, Pararth Shah, Anuj Kumar, and Rajen Subba. 2019. OpenDialKG: Explainable conversational reasoning with attention-based walks over knowledge graphs. In *Proceedings of the 57th Annual Meeting of the Association for Computational Linguistics*, pages 845–854, Florence, Italy. Association for Computational Linguistics.

Alec Radford, Jeffrey Wu, Rewon Child, David Luan, Dario Amodei, Ilya Sutskever, et al. 2019. Language models are unsupervised multitask learners. *OpenAI blog*, 1(8):9.

Colin Raffel, Noam Shazeer, Adam Roberts, Katherine Lee, Sharan Narang, Michael Matena, Yanqi Zhou, Wei Li, and Peter J. Liu. 2019. Exploring the limits of transfer learning with a unified text-to-text transformer. *CoRR*, abs/1910.10683.

Siva Reddy, Danqi Chen, and Christopher D. Manning. 2018. Coqa: A conversational question answering challenge. *CoRR*, abs/1808.07042.

Yi-Lin Tuan, Yun-Nung Chen, and Hung-yi Lee. 2019. Dykgchat: Benchmarking dialogue generation grounding on dynamic knowledge graphs. *arXiv preprint arXiv:1910.00610*.

Qingyang Wu, Yichi Zhang, Yu Li, and Zhou Yu. 2019. Alternating recurrent dialog model with large-scale pre-trained language models. *CoRR*, abs/1910.03756.

Jinfeng Xiao, Lidan Wang, Franck Dernoncourt, Trung Bui, Tong Sun, and Jiawei Han. 2020. Open-domain question answering with pre-constructed question spaces. *CoRR*, abs/2006.08337.

Haolan Zhan, Lei Shen, Hongshen Chen, and Hainan Zhang. 2021. CoLV: A collaborative latent variable model for knowledge-grounded dialogue generation. In *Proceedings of the 2021 Conference on Empirical Methods in Natural Language Processing*, pages 2250–2261, Online and Punta Cana, Dominican Republic. Association for Computational Linguistics.

Xueliang Zhao, Wei Wu, Can Xu, Chongyang Tao, Dongyan Zhao, and Rui Yan. 2020. Knowledge-grounded dialogue generation with pre-trained language models. *CoRR*, abs/2010.08824.

Hao Zhou, Tom Young, Minlie Huang, Haizhou Zhao, Jingfang Xu, and Xiaoyan Zhu. 2018a. Commonsense knowledge aware conversation generation with graph attention. In *IJCAI*, pages 4623–4629.

Kangyan Zhou, Shrimai Prabhumoye, and Alan W Black. 2018b. A dataset for document grounded conversations. *arXiv preprint arXiv:1809.07358*.

Docalog: Multi-document Dialogue System using Transformer-based Span Retrieval

Sayed Hesam Alavian[†,*] **Ali Satvaty** [†*], **Sadra Sabouri** [◇*], **Ehsaneddin Asgari**[+§] **and Hossein Sameti** [†§]
[†] AI Group, Computer Engineering Department, Sharif University of Technology, Tehran, Iran
[◇] Electrical Engineering Department, Sharif University of Technology, Tehran, Iran
+ NLP Expert Center, Data:Lab, Volkswagen AG, Munich, Germany
{alavian, stvty}@ce.sharif.edu, sadra@ee.sharif.edu, [§]**asgari@berkeley.edu**, [§]**sameti@sharif.edu**

Abstract

Information-seeking dialogue systems, including knowledge identification and response generation, aim to respond to users with fluent, coherent, and informative answers based on users' needs. This paper discusses our proposed approach, *Docalog*, for the DialDoc-22 (MultiDoc2Dial) shared task. *Docalog* identifies the most relevant knowledge in the associated document, in a multi-document setting. *Docalog*, is a three-stage pipeline consisting of *(1) a document retriever model (DR. TEIT)*, *(2) an answer span prediction model*, and *(3) an ultimate span picker* deciding on the most likely answer span, out of all predicted spans. In the test phase of MultiDoc2Dial 2022, *Docalog* achieved f1-scores of 36.07% and 28.44% and SacreBLEU scores of 23.70% and 20.52%, respectively on the *MDD-SEEN* and *MDD-UNSEEN* folds.

1 Introduction

Introducing a machine-generated dialogue with a human level of intelligence has been consistently among dreams of artificial intelligence with a vast number of applications in different domains, ranging from entertainment (Baena-Perez et al., 2020) to healthcare systems (Montenegro et al., 2019; Bharti et al., 2020). In such a system, the machine has to (i) understand the flow of conversation, (ii) raise informative questions, and (iii) answer problems in different domains of interest, and in some cases it has to act as an all-knowing agent (Dazeley et al., 2021). Recent advances in NLP have made this dream closer to reality. In the last decade, the success of the neural language model in language understanding and generation has encouraged more and more contributions from both academia and industry in the area of conversational artificial intelligence (Fu et al., 2020).

The major efforts in conversational artificial intelligence can be categorized into three subareas (Zaib et al., 2021): **(i) chat-oriented systems**, where the aim is to engage the users through a natural and fluent conversation (Nio et al., 2014), the examples are Alexa[1], Siri[2], or Cortana[3]; **(ii) task-oriented systems**, which are designed for a particular action, such as reserving a restaurant or planning an event by understanding the conversation (Yan et al., 2017); and **(iii) QA dialog systems** attempting to answer the user exploiting information deducted from a collection of seen documents or a knowledge base, for instance CoQA (Reddy et al., 2019), QuAC (Choi et al., 2018). Our work in this paper also falls in the third category.

In this system paper, we present our work on the DialDoc Shared Task 2022 centered on developing a QA dialogue system. A common approach to this problem comprises two subtasks of **(i) knowledge identification (KI)** to retrieve the knowledge from the documents and **(ii) response generation (RG)** to generate an answer based on the retrieved knowledge (Feng et al., 2020b; Kim et al., 2021). The multi-document scenario, meaning that the related documents have to be retrieved before the answer generation, is the main distinction between the DialDoc Shared Tasks in 2021 and 2022. To tackle this problem, we propose a three-stage pipeline, called *Docalog*, consisting of *(1) document retriever model (DR. TEIT)*, *(2) an answer span prediction model*, a state-of-the-art transformer-based model taking single documents (DR. TEIT results) as input and outputting the answer span for every input document, and *(3) an ultimate span picker* deciding on the most likely answer span, out of all predicted spans in the

* Equal contribution
§ Corresponding authors

[1]https://developer.amazon.com/en-US/alexa
[2]https://www.apple.com/uk/siri/
[3]https://www.microsoft.com/en-us/cortana

Proceedings of the Second DialDoc Workshop on Document-grounded Dialogue and Conversational Question Answering, pages 142 - 147
May 26, 2022 ©2022 Association for Computational Linguistics

step (2). In Multidoc2dial 2022 challenge, during the test phase, $DocAlog$ achieved an f1-score of 36.07% and a SacreBLEU of 23.70% on the *MDD-SEEN*, and an f1-score of 28.44% and a SacreBLEU of 20.52% on the *MDD-UNSEEN*.

2 Related Work

The main focus of DialDoc shared tasks has been on developing task-oriented information-seeking dialogue systems, an important setting in the domain of conversational AI (Feng et al., 2021). Some of the performing models in this domain have been CAiRE (Xu et al., 2021), SCIRDT (Li et al., 2021), and RWTH (Daheim et al., 2021). The proposed approaches of CAiRE and SCIRDT utilize additional data for the augmentation of pre-trained language models in span detection, and RWTH (Daheim et al., 2021) model uses neural retrievers for obtaining the most relevant document passages.

In a broader context, the major work in document-grounded dialogue modeling can be divided into the following categories: (i) QA in an unstructured content, e.g., CoQA (Reddy et al., 2019), QuAC (Choi et al., 2018), ShARC (Saeidi et al., 2018), DoQA (Campos et al., 2020), and Doc2Dial (Feng et al., 2020b) (ii) QA in a semi-structured content, such as tables or lists, e.g., SQA (Iyyer et al., 2017), and HybridQA (Chen et al., 2020) and thirdly (iii) QA in a multimedia content (images and videos with associated textual descriptions), e.g., RecipeQA (Yagcioglu et al., 2018), PsTuts-VQA (Colas et al., 2020), and MIMOQA (Singh et al., 2021).

3 Materials and Models

3.1 MultiDoc2Dial Shared Task Dataset

Training material used in this shared task is derived from the MultiDoc2Dial, a new dataset constructed based on Doc2Dial dataset V1.0.1 (Feng et al., 2020b). It contains a collection of documents and conversations exchanged between the user(s) and an agent grounded in the associated documents.

3.2 Model

The three-stage workflow of *Docalog* is depicted in Figure 1. Firstly, *DR. TEIT* predicts the N best documents based on the user input (q_t), and a query history of the respective user ($q_{1:(t-1)}$). Afterward, the span prediction model finds matching spans for a given query for each of the N best documents in the step before. Eventually, the ultimate span picker selects the most related span among predicted spans using a combination of the cosine similarity between the query and the span embeddings, as well as char-level TF-IDF-based cosine similarity between the query and the span vectors.

3.2.1 Document Retriever

In our retrieval model to encode the texts, we use a pre-trained language-agnostic BERT sentence embedding (LaBSE) (Feng et al., 2020a). One of our contributions here is to include the dialogue history in our document retriever model. We also found that the title tokens and their synonyms are extremely useful in document-changing dialogues, i.e., questions changing the context document during the conversation.

Our document retriever model, Document Retriever with Title Embedding and IDF on Texts (DR. TEIT), uses two scoring measures and aggregates them through a hyper-parameter in a convex combination (Eq. 1).

$$\lambda S_{TE} + (1 - \lambda) S_{TI}, \tag{1}$$

where S_{TE} is the title embedding based on the similarity between the sequence of query and the history ($q_{1..t}$) and the document titles. S_{TI} is a character n-gram ($2 \leq n \leq 8$) similarity score calculated between the aggregation of the query and the history ($q_{1..t}$) and the document texts using TF-IDF-based cosine similarity (Figure 1-c).

3.2.2 Span Predictor

Our span predictor is a RoBERTa language model (Zhuang et al., 2021) fine-tuned to predict the start and the end positions of the answer span, similar to CAiRE (Xu et al., 2021), one of the best performing models in DialDoc-2021. To model the history of questions, we append the last two history turns to the current question, as also proposed in (Ohsugi et al., 2019), and feed it to the model as part of the current question.

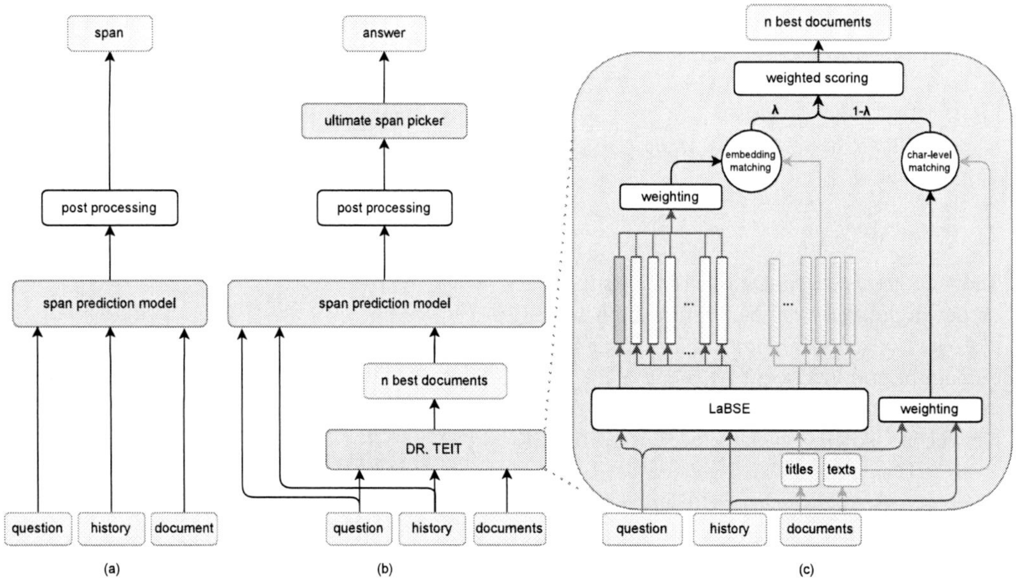

Figure 1: *Docalog* **model architecture and the overview diagram**: a) a standalone answer span prediction model. b) our three-stage model consists of (i) Dr. TEIT retriever model connected to the (ii) the span prediction model, and (iii) an aggregator which works as an ultimate span-picker deciding on the most likely span of the answer, out of all predicted spans. c) A detailed view of Dr. TEIT, the retriever architecture.

Prior to training our model on the DialDoc 2022 dataset, to gain more global knowledge in question answering, the span predictor of *Docalog* undergoes a pre-training phase on several CQA datasets such as CoQA (Reddy et al., 2019), QuAC (Choi et al., 2018), DoQA (Campos et al., 2020), and Doc2Dial (Feng et al., 2020b). Next, we fine-tune this model on the MultiDoc2Dial dataset using the grounding documents for each question. In this fine-tuning stage, we consider the task as a single-document question answering task. Therefore, at each training step, we only feed the model with the grounding document. The reason behind having a standalone span prediction model is to prevent the propagation of the retrieval error in the training phase.

3.2.3 Ultimate Span Picker

As discussed, the span detector provides the most-likely spans for each of the N best documents by the retriever. Since the answer-span probabilities are not comparable across documents, we need to rank the top-N identified spans searching for the ultimate answer. Therefore, similar to our document retriever, we use a convex combination between the embedding-based and character-level-based cosine similarities of the query and the detected spans through a hyper-parameter α that can be tuned on a validation set:

$$\alpha S_{SE} + (1 - \alpha) S_{SI}, \quad (2)$$

where S_{SE} is the span embedding similarity and S_{SI} is character-level *TF-IDF* similarity.

To summarize the workflow of *Docalog*, (1) a document retriever model using both embedding and character-level information retrieves the N most relevant documents to the current question. Based on the validation data we choose the hyper-parameter N in a way that we ensure selecting the answer document. (2) Using a trained span detector model, for each N document we detect the answer spans. (3) We use another document retriever model, this time to select the best-detected span, and the ultimate answer to the question is the post-processed version of this final span.

3.2.4 Experimental Settings

For the span prediction, we use a large RoBERTa language model [4] (Liu et al., 2019). During the training and the prediction phase, we feed the

[4]https://github.com/huggingface/transformers

Phase	Model	$F1_U$	SacreBLEU	METEOR	RougeL	$F1_G$	EM_G
MDD-SEEN (Dev)	baseline	36.23%	21.41%	34.16%	34.01%	44.90%	28.64%
	Docalog@1	**36.84%**	21.80%	**36.67%**	**34.44%**	**49.18%**	**36.18%**
	Docalog@2	34.99%	**23.30%**	33.81%	32.89%	46.62%	35.1%
	Docalog@3	35.19%	22.73 %	35.20%	33.56%	48.39%	35.67%
MDD-UNSEEN (Dev)	baseline	18.66%	5.99%	16.40%	16.95%	-	-
	Docalog@1	**26.12%**	**17.72%**	**25.52%**	**24.47%**	**33.36%**	**13.42%**
	Docalog@2	24.75%	15.07%	24.59%	22.76%	29.64%	9.59%
	Docalog@3	22.37%	14.21%	23.68%	21.02%	25.31%	7.75%
MDD-SEEN (Test)	baseline	35.85%	22.26%	34.28%	33.82%	-	-
	Docalog@1	**36.07%**	**23.70%**	**35.67%**	**34.44%**	**48.11%**	**34.19%**
	Docalog@2	33.41%	20.30%	33.52%	31.74%	44.11%	29.34%
	Docalog@3	29.90%	16.81%	30.25%	28.13%	39.33%	24.50%
MDD-UNSEEN (Test)	baseline	19.26%	6.32%	16.77%	17.16%	-	-
	Docalog@1	**28.44%**	**20.52%**	**27.54%**	**26.57%**	**35.41%**	**15.87%**
	Docalog@2	28.43%	20.51%	27.54%	26.57%	35.41%	15.87%
	Docalog@3	28.40%	20.51%	27.54%	26.57%	35.41%	15.87%

Table 1: *Docalog* **results on Multidoc2dial 2022 challenge.** Docalog@k indicates our method when working on the best k documents retrieved by the document retriever for the span detection and providing the final answer.

documents to the model with a stride size of 128 tokens. We pre-train our span-prediction model for 1 epoch on the CQA datasets and then fine-tuning was done on the MultiDoc2Dial dataset for 3 epochs. Our pre-training lasted around 13 hours and our fine-tuning step 15 hours, both of which were processed on a GeForce RTX 3070 GPU with 12GB memory.

Availablity: Our implementation of *Docalog* is available at github [5].

4 Results

Document Retriever: in our experiments, Dr. TEIT achieved a Precision@5 of 86% and a Mean Reciprocal Rank (MRR) of 0.72 indicating that on average, the hit is among the first two retrieved documents and it would be more than sufficient to take top-5 documents to the next step, i.e., span detection.

Docalog Results: In our final model, we combine DR. TEIT, as the retriever with our span predictor model. The comprehensive report of *Docalog* is provided in Table 1. We obtained the best F1 score of 36.07% with Docalog@1, suggesting that the ultimate span picker needs further improvements.

[5]https://github.com/Sharif-SLPL-NLP/Docalog-2022

5 Conclusions

We proposed Docalog, a solution for the DialDoc-22 challenge. *Docalog* is a three-stage pipeline consisting of *(1) a document retriever model (DR. TEIT)*, *(2) an answer span prediction model*, and *(3) an ultimate span picker* deciding on the most likely answer span, out of all predicted spans. Our experiments show that combining contextualized embedding information with character-level similarities between the answer and the question history can effectively help in the prediction of the ultimate answer. In the test phase of Multi-Doc2Dial 2022, *Docalog* achieved f1-scores of 36.07% and 28.44% and SacreBLEU scores of 23.70% and 20.52%, respectively on the *MDD-SEEN* and *MDD-UNSEEN* folds.

References

Rubén Baena-Perez, Iván Ruiz-Rube, Juan Manuel Dodero, and Miguel Angel Bolivar. 2020. A framework to create conversational agents for the development of video games by end-users. In *International Conference on Optimization and Learning*, pages 216–226. Springer.

Urmil Bharti, Deepali Bajaj, Hunar Batra, Shreya Lalit, Shweta Lalit, and Aayushi Gangwani. 2020. Medbot: Conversational artificial intelligence powered chatbot for delivering tele-health after covid-19. In *2020 5th international conference on communication and electronics systems (ICCES)*, pages 870–875. IEEE.

Jon Ander Campos, Arantxa Otegi, Aitor Soroa, Jan Deriu, Mark Cieliebak, and Eneko Agirre. 2020. DoQA

- accessing domain-specific FAQs via conversational QA. In *Proceedings of the 58th Annual Meeting of the Association for Computational Linguistics*, pages 7302–7314, Online. Association for Computational Linguistics.

Wenhu Chen, Hanwen Zha, Zhiyu Chen, Wenhan Xiong, Hong Wang, and William Yang Wang. 2020. HybridQA: A dataset of multi-hop question answering over tabular and textual data. In *Findings of the Association for Computational Linguistics: EMNLP 2020*, pages 1026–1036, Online. Association for Computational Linguistics.

Eunsol Choi, He He, Mohit Iyyer, Mark Yatskar, Wentau Yih, Yejin Choi, Percy Liang, and Luke Zettlemoyer. 2018. QuAC: Question answering in context. In *Proceedings of the 2018 Conference on Empirical Methods in Natural Language Processing*, pages 2174–2184, Brussels, Belgium. Association for Computational Linguistics.

Anthony Colas, Seokhwan Kim, Franck Dernoncourt, Siddhesh Gupte, Zhe Wang, and Doo Soon Kim. 2020. TutorialVQA: Question answering dataset for tutorial videos. In *Proceedings of the 12th Language Resources and Evaluation Conference*, pages 5450–5455, Marseille, France. European Language Resources Association.

Nico Daheim, David Thulke, Christian Dugast, and Hermann Ney. 2021. Cascaded span extraction and response generation for document-grounded dialog. In *Proceedings of the 1st Workshop on Document-grounded Dialogue and Conversational Question Answering (DialDoc 2021)*, pages 57–62, Online. Association for Computational Linguistics.

Richard Dazeley, Peter Vamplew, Cameron Foale, Charlotte Young, Sunil Aryal, and Francisco Cruz. 2021. Levels of explainable artificial intelligence for human-aligned conversational explanations. *Artificial Intelligence*, 299:103525.

Fangxiaoyu Feng, Yinfei Yang, Daniel Cer, Naveen Arivazhagan, and Wei Wang. 2020a. Language-agnostic bert sentence embedding. *arXiv preprint arXiv:2007.01852*.

Song Feng, Siva Sankalp Patel, Hui Wan, and Sachindra Joshi. 2021. MultiDoc2Dial: Modeling dialogues grounded in multiple documents. In *Proceedings of the 2021 Conference on Empirical Methods in Natural Language Processing*, pages 6162–6176, Online and Punta Cana, Dominican Republic. Association for Computational Linguistics.

Song Feng, Hui Wan, Chulaka Gunasekara, Siva Patel, Sachindra Joshi, and Luis Lastras. 2020b. doc2dial: A goal-oriented document-grounded dialogue dataset. In *Proceedings of the 2020 Conference on Empirical Methods in Natural Language Processing (EMNLP)*, pages 8118–8128, Online. Association for Computational Linguistics.

Zuohui Fu, Yikun Xian, Yongfeng Zhang, and Yi Zhang. 2020. Tutorial on conversational recommendation systems. In *Fourteenth ACM Conference on Recommender Systems*, pages 751–753.

Mohit Iyyer, Wen-tau Yih, and Ming-Wei Chang. 2017. Search-based neural structured learning for sequential question answering. In *Proceedings of the 55th Annual Meeting of the Association for Computational Linguistics (Volume 1: Long Papers)*, pages 1821–1831, Vancouver, Canada. Association for Computational Linguistics.

Boeun Kim, Dohaeng Lee, Sihyung Kim, Yejin Lee, Jin-Xia Huang, Oh-Woog Kwon, and Harksoo Kim. 2021. Document-grounded goal-oriented dialogue systems on pre-trained language model with diverse input representation. In *Proceedings of the 1st Workshop on Document-grounded Dialogue and Conversational Question Answering (DialDoc 2021)*, pages 98–102, Online. Association for Computational Linguistics.

Jiapeng Li, Mingda Li, Longxuan Ma, Wei-Nan Zhang, and Ting Liu. 2021. Technical report on shared task in DialDoc21. In *Proceedings of the 1st Workshop on Document-grounded Dialogue and Conversational Question Answering (DialDoc 2021)*, pages 52–56, Online. Association for Computational Linguistics.

Yinhan Liu, Myle Ott, Naman Goyal, Jingfei Du, Mandar Joshi, Danqi Chen, Omer Levy, Mike Lewis, Luke Zettlemoyer, and Veselin Stoyanov. 2019. Roberta: A robustly optimized bert pretraining approach. *arXiv preprint arXiv:1907.11692*.

Joao Luis Zeni Montenegro, Cristiano André da Costa, and Rodrigo da Rosa Righi. 2019. Survey of conversational agents in health. *Expert Systems with Applications*, 129:56–67.

Lasguido Nio, Sakriani Sakti, Graham Neubig, Tomoki Toda, and Satoshi Nakamura. 2014. Utilizing human-to-human conversation examples for a multi domain chat-oriented dialog system. *IEICE TRANSACTIONS on Information and Systems*, 97(6):1497–1505.

Yasuhito Ohsugi, Itsumi Saito, Kyosuke Nishida, Hisako Asano, and Junji Tomita. 2019. A simple but effective method to incorporate multi-turn context with BERT for conversational machine comprehension. In *Proceedings of the First Workshop on NLP for Conversational AI*, pages 11–17, Florence, Italy. Association for Computational Linguistics.

Siva Reddy, Danqi Chen, and Christopher D Manning. 2019. Coqa: A conversational question answering challenge. *Transactions of the Association for Computational Linguistics*, 7:249–266.

Marzieh Saeidi, Max Bartolo, Patrick Lewis, Sameer Singh, Tim Rocktäschel, Mike Sheldon, Guillaume Bouchard, and Sebastian Riedel. 2018. Interpretation of natural language rules in conversational machine reading. In *Proceedings of the 2018 Conference on Empirical Methods in Natural Language Processing*, pages 2087–2097, Brussels, Belgium. Association for Computational Linguistics.

Hrituraj Singh, Anshul Nasery, Denil Mehta, Aishwarya Agarwal, Jatin Lamba, and Balaji Vasan Srinivasan. 2021. MIMOQA: Multimodal input multimodal output question answering. In *Proceedings of the 2021 Conference of the North American Chapter of the Association for Computational Linguistics: Human Language Technologies*, pages 5317–5332, Online. Association for Computational Linguistics.

Yan Xu, Etsuko Ishii, Genta Indra Winata, Zhaojiang Lin, Andrea Madotto, Zihan Liu, Peng Xu, and Pascale Fung. 2021. CAiRE in DialDoc21: Data augmentation for information seeking dialogue system. In *Proceedings of the 1st Workshop on Document-grounded Dialogue and Conversational Question Answering (DialDoc 2021)*, pages 46–51, Online. Association for Computational Linguistics.

Semih Yagcioglu, Aykut Erdem, Erkut Erdem, and Nazli Ikizler-Cinbis. 2018. RecipeQA: A challenge dataset for multimodal comprehension of cooking recipes. In *Proceedings of the 2018 Conference on Empirical Methods in Natural Language Processing*, pages 1358–1368, Brussels, Belgium. Association for Computational Linguistics.

Zhao Yan, Nan Duan, Peng Chen, Ming Zhou, Jianshe Zhou, and Zhoujun Li. 2017. Building task-oriented dialogue systems for online shopping. In *Thirty-first AAAI conference on artificial intelligence*.

Munazza Zaib, Wei Emma Zhang, Quan Z Sheng, Adnan Mahmood, and Yang Zhang. 2021. Conversational question answering: A survey. *arXiv preprint arXiv:2106.00874*.

Liu Zhuang, Lin Wayne, Shi Ya, and Zhao Jun. 2021. A robustly optimized BERT pre-training approach with post-training. In *Proceedings of the 20th Chinese National Conference on Computational Linguistics*, pages 1218–1227, Huhhot, China. Chinese Information Processing Society of China.

R3 : Refined Retriever-Reader Pipeline for Multidoc2dial

Srijan Bansal* **Sumit Agarwal*** **Suraj Tripathi*** **Sireesh Gururaja***
Aditya Veerubhotla* **Ritam Dutt** **Teruko Mitamura** **Eric Nyberg**
{srijanb, sumita, surajt, sgururaj}@andrew.cmu.edu
{adityasv, rdutt, teruko}@andrew.cmu.edu, ehn@cs.cmu.edu
Language Technologies Institute, Carnegie Mellon University

Abstract

In this paper, we present our submission to the DialDoc shared task based on the MultiDoc2Dial dataset. MultiDoc2Dial is a conversational question answering dataset that grounds dialogues in multiple documents. The task involves grounding a user's query in a document followed by generating an appropriate response. We propose several improvements over the baseline's retriever-reader architecture to aid in modeling goal-oriented dialogues grounded in multiple documents. Our proposed approach employs sparse representations for passage retrieval, a passage re-ranker, the fusion-in-decoder architecture for generation, and a curriculum learning training paradigm. Our approach shows a 12 point improvement in BLEU score compared to the baseline RAG model.

1 Introduction

The task framework of document-grounded, conversational question answering unifies several closely related task frameworks, including open-domain question answering (QA), conversational QA, and knowledge-grounded generation. In open-domain question answering tasks, such as SQuAD (Rajpurkar et al., 2018), models are required to respond to a question with knowledge that may be located within a potentially large collection of documents. For conversational QA tasks like QuAC (Choi et al., 2018b), the queries posed to the model take the form of a dialogue, where previous dialogue turns contain necessary context to answer the current turn's question. Both of these task frameworks can be framed as either extractive QA or abstractive QA. Document-grounded conversational question answering tasks like CoQA (Reddy et al., 2019a) and Doc2Dial (Feng et al., 2020b) combine the above two frameworks. This setting requires models to understand user queries and their associated dialogue context, use them to find relevant grounding documents, and then generate coherent responses to user queries. This pipe-lined architecture forms the backbone of the baseline model, henceforth called retriever-reader.

In this paper, we present our approach to the MultiDoc2Dial (MDD) task (Feng et al., 2021), the successor to Doc2Dial, which complicates the Doc2Dial setting by constructing dialogues that are grounded in multiple documents. Each document is segmented into multiple passages, and thus document and passage are interchangeably used in this paper. As a result, models must retrieve the documents relevant to the current dialogue turn. These grounding documents could potentially be different from those grounded in previous dialogue turns.

We propose a model that improves over the baseline model by focusing on each component of its retriever-reader architecture. Firstly, we introduce sparse lexical representations in the retriever for matching, as outlined in Formal et al. (2021). Secondly, we rerank the retriever's results using techniques from Fajcik et al. (2021). Furthermore, we update the decoding process to incorporate the fusion-in-decoder (FiD) technique (Izacard and Grave, 2021). Finally, we use curriculum learning to train our models. We observe an improvement of 11.9 (BLEU) and 9.5 (F1) points on the validation; and an improvement of 9.5 (BLEU) and 10.3 (F1) points on test set in the MDD-SEEN setting compared to the baseline RAG model. We achieve 18.7 and 13.7 points improvement in the BLEU and F1 metric respectively on the MDD-UNSEEN test set compared to the baseline RAG model. Our submission (`CMU-QA`) stands 2nd and 3rd on the unseen and seen leaderboards [1] respectively.

*Equal contribution

[1] https://eval.ai/web/challenges/challenge-page/1437/leaderboard/3577

Proceedings of the Second DialDoc Workshop on Document-grounded Dialogue and Conversational Question Answering, pages 148 - 154
May 26, 2022 ©2022 Association for Computational Linguistics

2 Related Works

The MultiDoc2Dial setting draws on related tasks like open-domain QA and conversational QA. Consequently, we investigate techniques that have shown success on those tasks. Conversational QA tasks, which typically assume that the grounding document is provided, use transformer-based architectures; the leading submissions to the QuAC and CoQA leaderboards use RoBERTa (Liu et al., 2019) and DeBERTa (He et al., 2020), respectively. Retriever-reader architectures such as RAG (Lewis et al., 2020b) have become a popular choice for open-domain QA, increasingly using dense retrieval methods such as DPR (Karpukhin et al., 2020). We study works related to four areas for modeling improvement: retrieval, reranking, reader, and training.

Retriever : As the MultiDoc2Dial task is formulated in an open-domain setting, it requires the retrieval of relevant sources (passages) from a large pool of documents for generating the right output. Hence, we investigate the strides in information retrieval in recent years.

Recently, dense retrieval based approaches have shown competitive performance (Karpukhin et al., 2020; Xiong et al., 2020; Hofstätter et al., 2021) while also scaling to large corpora, like MS-MARCO dataset (Nguyen et al., 2016). They use a nearest neighbor index, such as FAISS (Johnson et al., 2019) to ensure scalability. Dense retrieval techniques aims to encode the query and passage into a shared semantic space where the relevance of a passage for a query can be computed by the inner product of their representations.

In contrast, sparse retrieval techniques perform exact token-level matching in the vocabulary space. There has been a growing interest in this field, with many advances achieving state-of-the-art results (Dai and Callan, 2020; Bai et al., 2020; Gao et al., 2021; Formal et al., 2021; MacAvaney et al., 2020). These models are advantageous due to their interpretable representations, efficient lookup, highly scalable inverted-list indexing, and excellent performance in exact term-based matching scenarios. Like dense retrieval based approaches, matches are computed via the dot product of the query and passage representations.

Reranking : While both dense and sparse retrieval methods have shown good progress, they must still embed the query and passage separately, because computing a match score between a query and every passage is computationally infeasible. As a compromise, re-ranking methods such as those in Fajcik et al. (2021) train a re-ranking module that can jointly embed the query and retrieved passages. Because the set of retrieved passages is significantly smaller than the whole corpus, re-ranking methods can model more complex relationships between the query and retrieved passages, and significantly boost retrieval performance.

Reader : Encoder-decoder based abstractive readers have been widely used in QA tasks. RAG (Lewis et al., 2020b) uses the BART-large model (Lewis et al., 2020a) which is pre-trained using a denoising objective and a variety of different noising functions. Moreover, RAG marginalizes output from each (query, passage) pair based on retrieval scores. It has obtained state-of-the-art results on a diverse set of generation tasks and outperforms comparably-sized T5 models.

Fusion in Decoder (FiD) (Izacard and Grave, 2021) performs well in extractive-based QA tasks like Natural Questions (Kwiatkowski et al., 2019). Unlike RAG model, the independent processing of the passages on the encoder side allows the FiD model to scale to a large number of passages, while the fusion in the decoder effectively combines evidence from multiple passages.

Training : Works such as Xu et al. (2020) have shown that fine-tuning a transformer model on examples, ordered on the basis of their difficulty, results in significant performance gains across different tasks. Kim et al. (2021) show more specifically that this type of curriculum design generalizes well to the document-grounded QA setting.

3 Task Description

MultiDoc2Dial is a conversational QA task that requires generating responses to user queries. In contrast to tasks like its predecessor, Doc2Dial (Feng et al., 2020a), and related tasks like QuAC (Choi et al., 2018a), ShARC (Saeidi et al.), and CoQA (Reddy et al., 2019b), which assume that the grounding document for the dialogue is given, MultiDoc2Dial constructs dialogues that are grounded in multiple documents. Each dialogue is constructed from a number of segments. Different segments are grounded in different documents; while all the dialogue turns within a segment are grounded in a single document. The dataset additionally marks the specific passage that is relevant to the current dialogue turn. However, the tran-

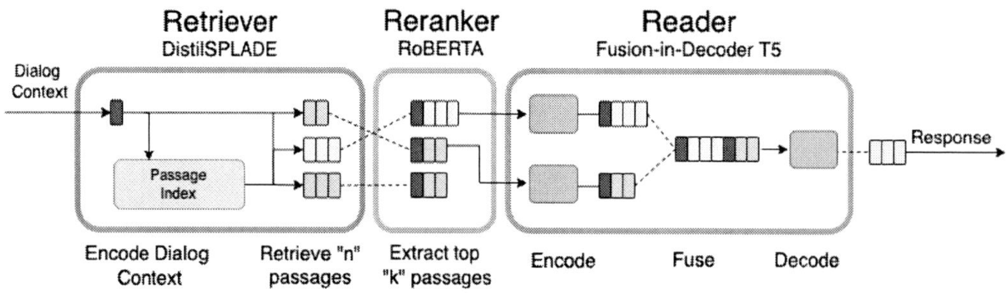

Figure 1: The proposed system architecture uses a bi-encoder (DistilSPLADE) retriever which fetches the top 100 relevant passages from the passage index, followed by a RoBERTA-based cross-encoder for reranking. The top 10 passages are passed to FiD with T5 to output the final response. This model is also used to perform curriculum learning as discussed in Section 4.

sitions between segments, which we refer to as topic shifts, are not marked. As a result, models are required not only to determine the grounding passages for each turn but also to determine which parts of the dialogue context continue to be relevant across topic shifts. The original dataset also presents several distinct domains of grounding documents from different public-facing websites that exhibit different writing styles. Each dialogue is grounded in documents drawn from the same domain.

The shared task defines two settings: one where all of the dialogues are grounded in documents from domains seen during training (MDD-SEEN), and another where the grounding domain is unseen (MDD-UNSEEN). Due to the open domain evidence retrieval and natural language response generation setting of the task, it lends itself well to a retriever-reader architecture. Broadly speaking, the MultiDoc2Dial task can be broken down into two distinct subtasks. Models must first retrieve the correct grounding passage from the provided corpora. They must then use the retrieved passages to generate a response to the user query in the most recent dialogue turn. While the MultiDoc2Dial paper defines both retrieval and a generation task, the shared task only evaluates reader outputs. Models are evaluated on the sum of different metrics: F1, BLEU (as implemented in Post 2018), METEOR (Banerjee and Lavie, 2005), and RougeL (Lin, 2004).

4 Methodology

For this task, we employ the standard retriever-reader architecture used in open-domain question answering. The model takes the user's current turn and dialogue context (previous turns) as the query. The query is then passed to the retriever which selects the top-n passages which are further passed to a reranker. The top-k (out of top-n) reranked passages are then fed to the reader along with the query to finally generate the agent's response.

In our experiments, we use DistilSPLADE (Formal et al., 2021) as our retriever, which augments the query and passages, subsequently projecting them to a sparse vector in the vocabulary space. Each coordinate in the projected vector represents the semantic importance of a term (also called "term impact" (Mallia et al., 2021)) for matching. The inputs are augmented by applying a sparsity-inducing activation function on the logits of a Masked Language Model such as BERT (Devlin et al., 2019), which selects the important words present in the passage and adds additional expansion to combat the vocabulary mismatch problem. The sparsity of the activation is complemented with the FLOPS regularizer (Paria et al., 2020) which minimizes the expected floating point operations required to perform matching. In addition to the training data provided in MS-MARCO (Campos et al., 2016), the model is trained using the pseudo-labels from a more expressive cross-encoder model, which improves the performance of the SPLADE model. This technique has shown state-of-the-art performance across several datasets and obtained the highest performance in our experiments.

The passages retrieved by the bi-encoder based retrieval are then passed through a RoBERTA (Liu et al., 2019) based cross-encoder. The RoBERTA model is trained to output a score that denotes the relevance of a passage to the given query. Due to the cross-attention between the query and the passage, the reranking proved to be effective by pulling up golden passages in the top-k documents that are passed on to the reader.

An abstractive reader is used to generate agent responses. We use a T5 based fusion in decoder (FiD) model which encodes all the top-k reranked passages one-by-one and concatenates them to form the input to the decoder. The decoder then learns to collect evidence from multiple passages to generate the response.

We also experiment with training our model using a curriculum learning approach originally proposed by Xu et al. (2020) and then implemented on Doc2Dial by Kim et al. (2021). To do so, we divide our training data randomly into 4 buckets, and train a teacher model on each bucket using FiD-T5. We then calculate each teacher model's performance (BLEU, RougeL and METEOR scores) on the other 3 buckets, which the teacher model has not seen during training. The training instances are then partitioned into "easy", "medium", and "hard" examples based on the scores chosen in Kim et al. (2021). We train in four phases, and each phase is trained until convergence. In the first phase, we train on a third of the easy examples; in the second, on a disjoint third of the easy examples, and a third of the medium examples; in the third phase, a disjoint third of all of the three partitions, and in the final phase, we train on the entire training set.

5 Experiments

Dataset : The MultiDoc2Dial dataset consists of 4796 dialogues, consisting 29,748 query turns and grounded in 4283 passages across 4 domains (Social Security Administration, Veteran Affairs, Student-Aid, and DMV). MDD-UNSEEN test corpus used in shared task is based on COVID domain.

5.1 Baseline

The proposed baseline for the MultiDoc2Dial shared task comprises a retrieval-augmented generator (RAG) model (Lewis et al., 2020b). The model uses a fine-tuned dense passage retrieval (DPR) model (Karpukhin et al., 2020) to find relevant passages and a pretrained sequence-to-sequence BART (Lewis et al., 2020a) to generate the response by marginalizing it according to document scores.

We use structure-based segmentation, with the original and reranking original scoring functions. We use DPR encoder finetuned on MultiDoc2Dial for retrieval, and a pretrained BART-large model.

5.2 Setup

Our experimental setup refines both the retriever and reader components of the existing architecture.

Retrieval We analyze the performance of different dense and sparse retrieval methods in a zero-shot setting on the MultiDoc2Dial dataset. For our dense retriever baselines, we conduct experiments with DPR, ANCE (Xiong et al., 2020) and TAS-B (Hofstätter et al., 2021). For sparse retrieval methods, we experiment with SPLADE-max and DistilSPLDAE (Formal et al., 2021). During training, we label the retrieved passages (excluding the golden passage) from BM25 as hard negatives. We also experiment with the finetuned DPR model to mine harder negatives.

Reranker Following (Fajcik et al., 2021), we select the top 100 passages from the DistilSPLADE retriever to be reranked using RoBERTA as a cross encoder. We use this reranking only during validation time. The top 10 reranked documents are passed to the reader.

Reader We experiment with both T5 and BART models as the reader. We use the T5 based reader model to circumvent the limited tokens used for BART along with the FiD model pretrained on natural questions [2]. We further experimented by placing the golden passage at the top-most position (Gold setting) in the retrieved passages before passing it to the reader during training. We also apply curriculum learning (CL) in the reader as per described in Section 4.

6 Results & Discussion

Table 1 shows our model's performance on the validation split. Applying DistilSPLADE as the retriever with FiD + T5 as the reader we saw a 10 point improvement in BLEU compared to the baseline. Reranking (RR) the retrieval outputs leads to further increase in the overall metrics. Additionally, curriculum learning (CL) boosts the model's performance. Setting M1 shows a BLEU score that is 1 point higher than the "DistillSplade + Fid + RR" model. We use the M1 setting for evaluation on the Test SEEN dataset. For the Gold setting, we saw a decrease in metrics for the RR and RR + CL settings.

6.1 Retrieval improvement

We present the results for different retriever configurations at Recall@10 and Recall@100 in Table

[2]https://github.com/facebookresearch/FiD

Model	Reader	EM	F1	BLEU	RougeL
Baseline	BART	3.6	33.8	19.2	31.4
DistilSPLADE + RAG	BART	4.8	38.5	23.7	36.2
DistilSPLADE + FiD	T5	5.1	42.3	29.7	40.2
DistilSPLADE + FiD + RR	T5	5.5	43.1	30.1	41.1
DistilSPLADE + FiD + RR + CL (**M1**)	T5	5.3	**43.3**	**31.1**	**41.4**
DistilSPLADE + FiD + Gold	T5	5.3	42.4	30.5	40.6
DistilSPLADE + FiD + Gold + RR	T5	5.5	42.5	30.4	40.7
DistilSPLADE + FiD + Gold + RR + CL (**M2**)	T5	**5.6**	43.0	30.5	41.0
M1 (on Shared Task MDD-SEEN test)	T5	-	46.2	31.8	44.2
M2 (on Shared Task MDD-UNSEEN test)	T5	-	33.0	25.0	32.0

Table 1: Model performance on the validation split for EM, F1, BLEU and RougeL. We see a consistent improvement across all metrics with DistilSPLADE as the retriever and FiD as the reader. Gold means the ground-truth passage was passed during training. Reranking (RR) and curriculum learning (CL) further boost performance on all metrics.

Model	R@10	R@100
DPR-PT	33.9	69.4
ANCE-PT	53.8	80.7
TAS-B-PT	53.9	85.0
SPLADE-max-PT	58.5	85.9
DistilSPLADE-PT	61.6	86.9
DPR-FT (Baseline)	73.2	92.8
SPLADE-max-FT	75.1	93.9
DistilSPLADE-FT	77.0	94.8
DistilSPLADE-FT+DPR-FT(Neg)	**78.6**	**94.9**
DistilSPLADE-FT+DPR-FT(Neg) + Reranker	**85.7**	**94.9**

Table 2: Performance of the retriever for different model configurations at Recall@10 and Recall@100. X-PT refers to the pretrained X model while X-FT implies that X was finetuned on MultiDoc2dial. DPR-FT was the retriever employed for the MultiDoc2Dial baseline.

2. It is evident that the pretrained sparse retrieval frameworks, Splade and DistilSPLADE, achieve better retrieval performance in comparison to the pretrained DPR model. This suggests that the exact matching over keywords and over the paraphrases generated for functional words achieves good retrieval performance. Unsurprisingly, the performance for all models improve significantly when they are fine-tuned on Multidoc2Dial dataset, with the sparse-retrievers still outperforming DPR. The performance shows a further boost when we use the fine-tuned DPR model to mine hard-negatives.

Reranking the validation passages increases the R@10 to 85% (Ref Table 2). This further leads to improvements in metrics in both the normal and the Gold setting.

6.2 Reader improvement

Our analysis, in Table 1, indicates that the FiD (T5-based) model outperforms the current BART-based baseline model on all the evaluation metrics. We observed an improvement of around 10 points in BLEU score in the FiD setting compared to the RAG model. FiD extracts relevant evidence from concatenated passages disregarding their retrieval scores, unlike RAG which uses them for marginalization. Reinforcing signals from the retriever for the reader component might be the cause of the dip in performance of RAG compared to FiD. We also observed that increasing the number of input tokens to the reader model helps capture dialogue and passage context relevant to the input query.

7 Conclusion

We introduced our submission (`CMU-QA`) for the Multidoc2Dial shared task. Our approach (R3) focuses on improving the overall retriever-reader pipeline using the sparse retriever DistilSPLADE and Fusion-in-decoder (FID) as the reader. We use a cross-attention based reranker to further boost recall scores. We refine the training process through curriculum learning to handle the diverse complexity of this dataset. For future work, we plan to improve results through better dialogue modelling and reducing noise or irrelevant information in the passages by taking top text spans. Further, we will aim to select the best of all candidate responses using a response re-ranker.

References

Yang Bai, Xiaoguang Li, Gang Wang, Chaoliang Zhang, Lifeng Shang, Jun Xu, Zhaowei Wang, Fangshan Wang, and Qun Liu. 2020. Sparterm: Learning term-based sparse representation for fast text retrieval. *ArXiv*, abs/2010.00768.

Satanjeev Banerjee and Alon Lavie. 2005. Meteor: An automatic metric for mt evaluation with improved correlation with human judgments. In *Proceedings of the acl workshop on intrinsic and extrinsic evaluation measures for machine translation and/or summarization*, pages 65–72.

Daniel Fernando Campos, Tri Nguyen, Mir Rosenberg, Xia Song, Jianfeng Gao, Saurabh Tiwary, Rangan Majumder, Li Deng, and Bhaskar Mitra. 2016. Ms marco: A human generated machine reading comprehension dataset. *ArXiv*, abs/1611.09268.

Eunsol Choi, He He, Mohit Iyyer, Mark Yatskar, Wen tau Yih, Yejin Choi, Percy Liang, and Luke Zettlemoyer. 2018a. Quac: Question answering in context. In *EMNLP*.

Eunsol Choi, He He, Mohit Iyyer, Mark Yatskar, Wen-tau Yih, Yejin Choi, Percy Liang, and Luke Zettlemoyer. 2018b. Quac: Question answering in context. In *Proceedings of the 2018 Conference on Empirical Methods in Natural Language Processing*, pages 2174–2184.

Zhuyun Dai and Jamie Callan. 2020. *Context-Aware Document Term Weighting for Ad-Hoc Search*, page 1897–1907. Association for Computing Machinery, New York, NY, USA.

Jacob Devlin, Ming-Wei Chang, Kenton Lee, and Kristina Toutanova. 2019. Bert: Pre-training of deep bidirectional transformers for language understanding. In *Proceedings of the 2019 Conference of the North American Chapter of the Association for Computational Linguistics: Human Language Technologies, Volume 1 (Long and Short Papers)*, pages 4171–4186.

Martin Fajcik, Martin Docekal, Karel Ondrej, and Pavel Smrz. 2021. R2-d2: A modular baseline for open-domain question answering. In *Findings of the Association for Computational Linguistics: EMNLP 2021*, pages 854–870.

Song Feng, Siva Sankalp Patel, Hui Wan, and Sachindra Joshi. 2021. MultiDoc2Dial: Modeling dialogues grounded in multiple documents. In *Proceedings of the 2021 Conference on Empirical Methods in Natural Language Processing*, pages 6162–6176, Online and Punta Cana, Dominican Republic. Association for Computational Linguistics.

Song Feng, Hui Wan, Chulaka Gunasekara, Siva Patel, Sachindra Joshi, and Luis Lastras. 2020a. doc2dial: A goal-oriented document-grounded dialogue dataset. In *Proceedings of the 2020 Conference on Empirical Methods in Natural Language Processing (EMNLP)*, pages 8118–8128, Online. Association for Computational Linguistics.

Song Feng, Hui Wan, Chulaka Gunasekara, Siva Sankalp Patel, Sachindra Joshi, and Luis A Lastras. 2020b. doc2dial: A goal-oriented document-grounded dialogue dataset. *arXiv preprint arXiv:2011.06623*.

Thibault Formal, Carlos Lassance, Benjamin Piwowarski, and Stéphane Clinchant. 2021. Splade v2: Sparse lexical and expansion model for information retrieval. *arXiv preprint arXiv:2109.10086*.

Luyu Gao, Zhuyun Dai, and Jamie Callan. 2021. Coil: Revisit exact lexical match in information retrieval with contextualized inverted list. In *NAACL*.

Pengcheng He, Xiaodong Liu, Jianfeng Gao, and Weizhu Chen. 2020. Deberta: Decoding-enhanced bert with disentangled attention. *arXiv preprint arXiv:2006.03654*.

Sebastian Hofstätter, Sheng-Chieh Lin, Jheng-Hong Yang, Jimmy Lin, and Allan Hanbury. 2021. Efficiently teaching an effective dense retriever with balanced topic aware sampling. In *Proceedings of the 44th International ACM SIGIR Conference on Research and Development in Information Retrieval*, pages 113–122.

Gautier Izacard and Edouard Grave. 2021. Leveraging passage retrieval with generative models for open domain question answering. In *EACL 2021-16th Conference of the European Chapter of the Association for Computational Linguistics*, pages 874–880. Association for Computational Linguistics.

Jeff Johnson, Matthijs Douze, and Hervé Jégou. 2019. Billion-scale similarity search with GPUs. *IEEE Transactions on Big Data*, 7(3):535–547.

Vladimir Karpukhin, Barlas Oguz, Sewon Min, Patrick Lewis, Ledell Wu, Sergey Edunov, Danqi Chen, and Wen-tau Yih. 2020. Dense passage retrieval for open-domain question answering. In *Proceedings of the 2020 Conference on Empirical Methods in Natural Language Processing (EMNLP)*, pages 6769–6781.

Boeun Kim, Dohaeng Lee, Sihyung Kim, Yejin Lee, Jin-Xia Huang, Oh-Woog Kwon, and Harksoo Kim. 2021. Document-grounded goal-oriented dialogue systems on pre-trained language model with diverse input representation. In *Proceedings of the 1st Workshop on Document-grounded Dialogue and Conversational Question Answering (DialDoc 2021)*, pages 98–102, Online. Association for Computational Linguistics.

Tom Kwiatkowski, Jennimaria Palomaki, Olivia Redfield, Michael Collins, Ankur Parikh, Chris Alberti, Danielle Epstein, Illia Polosukhin, Matthew Kelcey, Jacob Devlin, Kenton Lee, Kristina N. Toutanova, Llion Jones, Ming-Wei Chang, Andrew Dai, Jakob Uszkoreit, Quoc Le, and Slav Petrov. 2019. Natural questions: a benchmark for question answering research. *Transactions of the Association of Computational Linguistics*.

Mike Lewis, Yinhan Liu, Naman Goyal, Marjan Ghazvininejad, Abdelrahman Mohamed, Omer Levy, Veselin Stoyanov, and Luke Zettlemoyer. 2020a. Bart: Denoising sequence-to-sequence pre-training for natural language generation, translation, and comprehension. In *Proceedings of the 58th Annual Meeting of the Association for Computational Linguistics*, pages 7871–7880.

Patrick Lewis, Ethan Perez, Aleksandra Piktus, Fabio Petroni, Vladimir Karpukhin, Naman Goyal, Heinrich Küttler, Mike Lewis, Wen-tau Yih, Tim Rocktäschel, et al. 2020b. Retrieval-augmented generation for knowledge-intensive nlp tasks. *Advances in Neural Information Processing Systems*, 33:9459–9474.

Chin-Yew Lin. 2004. Looking for a few good metrics: Rouge and its evaluation.

Yinhan Liu, Myle Ott, Naman Goyal, Jingfei Du, Mandar Joshi, Danqi Chen, Omer Levy, Mike Lewis, Luke Zettlemoyer, and Veselin Stoyanov. 2019. Roberta: A robustly optimized bert pretraining approach. *arXiv preprint arXiv:1907.11692*.

Sean MacAvaney, Franco Maria Nardini, Raffaele Perego, Nicola Tonellotto, Nazli Goharian, and Ophir Frieder. 2020. Expansion via prediction of importance with contextualization. In *Proceedings of the 43rd International ACM SIGIR conference on research and development in Information Retrieval*, pages 1573–1576.

Antonio Mallia, O. Khattab, Nicola Tonellotto, and Torsten Suel. 2021. Learning passage impacts for inverted indexes. *Proceedings of the 44th International ACM SIGIR Conference on Research and Development in Information Retrieval*.

Tri Nguyen, Mir Rosenberg, Xia Song, Jianfeng Gao, Saurabh Tiwary, Rangan Majumder, and Li Deng. 2016. MS MARCO: A human generated machine reading comprehension dataset. *CoRR*, abs/1611.09268.

Biswajit Paria, Chih-Kuan Yeh, Ian En-Hsu Yen, Ning Xu, Pradeep Ravikumar, and Barnabás Póczos. 2020. Minimizing flops to learn efficient sparse representations. *CoRR*, abs/2004.05665.

Matt Post. 2018. A call for clarity in reporting BLEU scores. In *Proceedings of the Third Conference on Machine Translation: Research Papers*, pages 186–191, Belgium, Brussels. Association for Computational Linguistics.

Pranav Rajpurkar, Robin Jia, and Percy Liang. 2018. Know what you don't know: Unanswerable questions for squad. In *Proceedings of the 56th Annual Meeting of the Association for Computational Linguistics (Volume 2: Short Papers)*, pages 784–789.

Siva Reddy, Danqi Chen, and Christopher D Manning. 2019a. Coqa: A conversational question answering challenge. *Transactions of the Association for Computational Linguistics*, 7:249–266.

Siva Reddy, Danqi Chen, and Christopher D. Manning. 2019b. CoQA: A conversational question answering challenge. *Transactions of the Association for Computational Linguistics*, 7:249–266.

Marzieh Saeidi, Max Bartolo, Patrick Lewis, Sameer Singh, Tim Rocktäschel, Mike Sheldon, Guillaume Bouchard, and Sebastian Riedel. Interpretation of natural language rules in conversational machine reading.

Lee Xiong, Chenyan Xiong, Ye Li, Kwok-Fung Tang, Jialin Liu, Paul N. Bennett, Junaid Ahmed, and Arnold Overwijk. 2020. Approximate nearest neighbor negative contrastive learning for dense text retrieval. *CoRR*, abs/2007.00808.

Benfeng Xu, Licheng Zhang, Zhendong Mao, Quan Wang, Hongtao Xie, and Yongdong Zhang. 2020. Curriculum learning for natural language understanding. In *Proceedings of the 58th Annual Meeting of the Association for Computational Linguistics*, pages 6095–6104.

DialDoc 2022 Shared Task: Open-Book Document-grounded Dialogue Modeling

Song Feng*
Amazon AWS AI
sofeng@amazon.com

Siva Sankalp Patel
IBM Research
siva.sankalp.patel@ibm.com

Hui Wan
IBM Research
hwan@us.ibm.com

Abstract

The paper presents the results of the Shared Task hosted by the Second DialDoc Workshop on Document-grounded Dialogue and Conversational Question Answering co-located at ACL 2022. The primary goal of this Shared Task is to build goal-oriented information-seeking conversation systems that are grounded in the domain documents, where each dialogue could correspond to multiple sub-goals that are based on different documents. The task is to generate agent responses in natural language given the dialogue and document contexts. There are two task settings and leaderboards based on (1) the same sets of domains (*SEEN*) and (2) one unseen domain (*UNSEEN*). There are over 20 teams participating in Dev Phase and 8 teams participating in both Dev and Test Phases. There are multiple submissions that significantly outperform the baseline. The best-performing system achieves 52.06 F1 and the total of 191.30 on the *SEEN* task; and 34.65 F1 and the total of 130.79 on the *UNSEEN* task.

1 Introduction

Goal-oriented document-grounded dialogue systems enable end users to interactively query about domain-specific information based on the given documents. The tasks of querying document knowledge via conversational systems continue to attract a lot of attention from both research and industrial communities for various applications such as OR-ConvQA (Qu et al., 2020), MultiDoc2Dial (Feng et al., 2021), QReCC (Anantha et al., 2021), TopiOCQA (Adlakha et al., 2022) and Abg-CoQA (Guo et al., 2021). The previous Shared Task (Feng, 2021) by the First DialDoc Workshop addressed the task of goal-oriented information-seeking dialogue systems in the machine reading comprehension setting, where the dialogue is aiming at querying about the information provided in a given document (Feng et al., 2020). However, in real-life scenarios, for conversation in a given domain, the grounding document is often unknown, a dialogue turn could arbitrarily correspond to any document, hence each dialogue could be grounded in multiple documents. Thus, we propose to explore the open-book closed-domain setting for goal-oriented information-seeking dialogue systems that are grounded in the given domain documents.

We introduce the Shared Task at the Second DialDoc Workshop on Document-grounded Dialogue and Conversational Question Answering (DialDoc 2022 Shared Task). The Shared Task aims to deal with the information-seeking goal-oriented dialogues that have multiple sub-goals corresponding to different documents. The input includes the dialogue history, the current user turn, and a set of domain documents, the output is the agent's utterance in natural language. It comprises two tasks that address two different evaluation settings: (1) the *SEEN* task where the test data shares the same sets of domains as the training data; and (2) the *UNSEEN* task where the test data is all in one unseen domain different from the training data. We host the leaderboards for Dev and Test Phases for the *SEEN* and *UNSEEN* tasks respectively on `eval.ai`[1].

There are over 20 teams participating in Dev Phase and 8 teams participating in both Dev and Test Phases. Multiple submissions significantly outperform the baseline. The best-performing system achieves 52.06 F1 and the total of 191.30 on the *SEEN* task comparing to 35.85 and 126.21 by the baseline; and 34.65 F1 and the total of 130.79 on the *UNSEEN* task comparing to 19.26 and 59.52 by the baseline.

In this report, we first describe the dataset and the two task settings. Then, we summarize the approaches and evaluation results of several top participating teams.

* Work done while at IBM Research

[1] `https://eval.ai/`

Proceedings of the Second DialDoc Workshop on Document-grounded Dialogue and Conversational Question Answering, pages 155 - 160
May 26, 2022

domain	#doc	#dial	two-seg	>two-seg	single
ssa	109	1191	701	188	302
va	138	1337	648	491	198
dmv	149	1328	781	257	290
student	92	940	508	274	158
total	488	4796	2638	1210	948

Table 1: MultiDoc2Dial data statistics (Feng et al., 2021)

#	train	val	t-*SEEN*/*UNSEEN*
dials	3474	661	661 / —
predicts	21453	4201	661 / 126

Table 2: Statistics of dialogue data in train, dev and test splits for *SEEN* and *UNSEEN* task settings.

2 Dataset

In this Shared Task, the dataset is based on MultiDoc2Dial introduced by (Feng et al., 2021). It contains 4796 conversations with an average of 14 turns grounded in 488 documents from four domains including `va.org` and `studentaid.org`. For document data, each document includes a title, the body content with the span/section information as well as the HTML mark-ups such as `list` and `title`. For dialogue data, each turn in a dialogue contains: (1) the speaker role, (2) the dialogue act, (3) the grounding text span along with the title of the document, and (4) human generated utterance in natural language. Each dialogue contains one or multiple segments where each indicates that all turns within one segment are grounded in the same document. Table 1 shows the statistics of the dataset by domain, including the number of dialogues with two segments (two-seg), more than two segments (>two-seg), and no segmentations (single).

For model development, we provide the original split of training and validation data. For the leaderboard setup, we use a small portion (30%) of the test split based on the number of dialogues for Dev Phase and entire test split for the final Test Phase. For the *UNSEEN* task setting, the final test set includes the dialogue and document data all from an unseen domain *cdccovid* that is not in the original MultiDoc2Dial dataset. The dialogues from the unseen domain were collected in the same data collection process as MultiDoc2Dial dataset.

3 Task Description

Our Shares Task centers on building open-book goal-oriented dialogue systems, where an agent could provide an answer or ask follow-up questions for clarification or verification. The main goal is to generate grounded agent responses in natural language based on the dialogue context and domain knowledge in the documents. The provided training data is mainly based on MultiDoc2Dial dataset but the participants could utilize any public dataset without any additional human annotations on the MultiDoc2Dial dataset. It includes two task settings depending on whether the cases are from unseen domains (*SEEN* task) or one unseen domain (*UNSEEN* task) from training data. Here we only consider the cases where user queries are answerable. For test split, there is only one turn to predict per dialogue. Table 2 presents the number of dialogues ('dials') as well as the total turns for prediction ('predicts') in each data split, where the last column contains the numbers of examples for Test Phase evaluation for *SEEN* and *UNSEEN*, respectively.

4 Evaluation

The evaluation is focused on the groundedness and naturalness of the generated agent response. We consider the automatic metrics as intrinsic evaluation metrics, and human annotations for extrinsic evaluations.

4.1 Intrinsic Evaluation

We use the following metrics: F1 (Rajpurkar et al., 2016), SacreBLEU (Post, 2018), METEOR (Banerjee and Lavie, 2005) and RougeL (Lin, 2004). The rankings on the leaderboards are based on the sum of all four scores. For each leaderboard, we select the three top-ranked teams for further human evaluation.

4.2 Extrinsic Evaluation

We ask human annotators to rank three generated utterances, each from a different team, based on the relevance and fluency given the dialogue history and the grounding document passages as reference. *relevance* is used to measure how well the generated utterance is relevant to the grounding span as a response to the previous dialogue turn(s). *fluency* indicates whether the generated utterance is grammatically correct and generally fluent in English.

Rank	Participant Team	F1	SacreBLEU	METEOR	RougeL	Total
1	CPII-NLP	**52.06**	**37.41**	**51.64**	**50.19**	**191.30**
2	zsw_dyy_lgz	48.56	33.27	48.73	46.75	177.31
3	UGent-T2K	46.90	32.23	47.96	44.89	171.98
4	CMU_QA	46.22	31.82	46.02	44.19	168.24
5	JLP	37.78	22.94	36.97	35.46	133.15
6	Docalog	36.07	23.70	35.67	34.44	129.87
7	LingJing	36.69	22.78	35.46	34.52	129.44
-	Baseline	35.85	22.26	34.28	33.82	126.21

Table 3: The participating teams and the scores for Test Phase of *SEEN* leaderboard.

Rank	Participant Team	F1	SacreBLEU	METEOR	RougeL	Total
1	CPII-NLP	**34.65**	**27.57**	**34.08**	**34.49**	**130.79**
2	CMU_QA	33.01	25.04	32.92	31.95	122.91
3	UGent-T2K	33.36	21.20	33.57	31.47	119.60
4	zsw_dyy_lgz	32.78	21.32	32.74	31.44	118.28
5	Docalog	28.44	20.52	27.54	26.57	103.07
-	Baseline	19.26	6.32	16.77	17.16	59.52

Table 4: The participating teams and the scores for Test Phase of *UNSEEN* leaderboard.

For the *SEEN* task setting, we randomly select 100 generated turns where the normalized utterances are not all the same; for *UNSEEN*, we randomly select 80. We have three experts as annotators, with 10% overlap for the annotations.

5 Shared Task Submissions

We hosted the leaderboards[2] for Dev and Test Phases for the two task settings *SEEN* and *UNSEEN* on `eval.ai`. The Dev Phase lasted for three and a half months and the Test Phase lasted for a week. There are over 500 submissions by over 20 teams that participated in Dev Phase. For the final Test Phase, 8 teams submitted to the *SEEN* leaderboard, and 6 teams submitted to the *UNSEEN* leaderboard. Next, we summarize the approaches adopted by the top teams who submitted their technical papers.

The baseline approach for the Shared Task is based on RAG (Lewis et al., 2020b), where the DPR (Karpukhin et al., 2020) passage retriever is fine-tuned on MultiDoc2Dial dataset, as described in (Feng et al., 2021). Several teams significantly improved the results over the baseline as shown in Table 3 and 4. Team CPII-NLP achieved the highest scores on both *SEEN* and *UNSEEN* leaderboard.

[2]`https://eval.ai/web/challenges/challenge-page/1437/overview`

5.1 CPII-NLP

The team presents a pipeline system of retriever, re-ranker, and generator. The retriever adopts DPR (Karpukhin et al., 2020). The re-ranker is an ensemble of three cross-encoder models using BERT (Devlin et al., 2019), RoBERTa (Liu et al., 2019), and ELECTRA (Clark et al., 2020), respectively. The generator leverages the pre-trained sequence-to-sequence model BART$_{\texttt{large}}$ (Lewis et al., 2020a) jointly trained with a grounding span predictor. The three components are individually optimized, while passage dropout and regularization techniques are adopted to improve the response generation performance. CPII-NLP ranked 1st on both *SEEN* and *UNSEEN* leaderboards on F1, SacreBLEU, METEOR and RougeL scores.

5.2 zsw_dyy_lgz

The team presents their system named Grounding-Guided Goal-oriented dialogues Generation(G4), a three-stage approach composed of a retriever adopting ANCE(Xiong et al., 2021), a reader predicting grounding spans restricted to whole phrases, and a generator adopting FiD (Izacard and Grave, 2021) which leverages explicitly markings of grounding spans together with the original passages. Experiment results show that this approach effectively generates responses better grounded to text spans and closer to correct responses. To alleviate the issue of the reader accuracy being lower at inference than during training, they also present a data augmentation approach as regularization to account for more diverse groundings and improve the robustness.

5.3 CMU_QA

The team also follows the retriever-reader architecture and presents their system called Refined Retriever-Reader (R3). R3 includes several improvements over the baseline approach, including adopting a sparse retriever based on DistilSplade (Formal et al., 2021) instead of dense retriever, adding a RoBERTa-based cross-encoder passage reranker, using FiD (Izacard and Grave, 2021) as the generator, and a curriculum learning training paradigm. The experiment results show significant improvement over the baseline performance.

5.4 UGent-T2K

The team presents a cascade pipeline dialogue system for the task. The system consists of three modules: a document retriever, a passage retriever, and a response generator. The system uses DPR for the passage retrieval and FiD (Izacard and Grave, 2021) for the response generation. Then they use LambdaMART (Burges, 2010) for reranking. The experiment results show that document ranking could be helpful for passage retrieval and the multi-passage-fusing generator outperforms the RAG model.

5.5 Docalog

The team presents a three-stage pipeline consisting of (a) Document Retriever with Title Embedding and IDF on Texts (DR.TEIT); (2) a grounding span predictor; (3) an ultimate span picker. Their experiment results indicate that incorporating contextualized embedding information along with semantic similarity on the character level between the answer and question history can further improve the prediction of the ultimate answer.

5.6 JLP

The team explores various strategies for the dialogue task, including multi-task learning, tuning the generator BART (Lewis et al., 2020a) on additional QA datasets, data augmentation via synonym augmenter [3], and contrastive learning based on extra-hard negative examples. The experiment results indicate that all techniques help further improve the performance comparing to the baseline approach.

[3]https://github.com/makcedward/nlpaug

Team	Affiliation
CMU_QA	Carnegie Mellon University
CPII-NLP	The Chinese University of Hong Kong (CUHK) & Centre for Perceptual and Interactive Intelligence (CPII) Limited
Docalog	Sharif University of Technology & Volkswagen AG
JLP	Seoul National University
UGent-T2K	Ghent University
zsw_dyy_lgz	Tencent Cloud Xiaowei & Beihang University & Tianjin University

Table 5: Teams and their affiliations.

5.7 LingJing

The team presents a framework that most different than the baseline among the teams. It proposes to enhance downstream evidence retrieval by generating evidence into model parameters through pre-training. More specifically, it uses Pegasus (Zhang et al., 2020) to store document knowledge into a language model and then Child-Tuning (Xu et al., 2021) approach for evidence generation. The results are marginally better the baseline performance.

6 Conclusion

We present the results of DialDoc 2022 Shared Task. World-wide researchers and practitioners brought their individual perspectives on the task through this data competition. We received over 500 submissions during the Dev Phase by over 20 teams for both *SEEN* and *UNSEEN* leaderboards. For the final Test Phase, there were officially 8 teams submitted to the *SEEN* leaderboard and 6 teams submitted to the *UNSEEN* leaderboard. Most of the submissions during Test Phase beat the baseline performance by large margins.

Acknowledgements

We would like to thank IBM Research AI for sponsoring the Shared Task and competition prizes. We thank `eval.ai` for their help and support on hosting the leaderboards on their platform.

References

Vaibhav Adlakha, Shehzaad Dhuliawala, Kaheer Suleman, Harm de Vries, and Siva Reddy. 2022. Topiocqa: Open-domain conversational question answering with topic switching. *Transactions of the Association for Computational Linguistics*, 10:468–483.

Raviteja Anantha, Svitlana Vakulenko, Zhucheng Tu, Shayne Longpre, Stephen Pulman, and Srinivas Chappidi. 2021. Open-domain question answering goes conversational via question rewriting. In *Proceedings of the 2021 Conference of the North American Chapter of the Association for Computational Linguistics: Human Language Technologies*, pages 520–534, Online. Association for Computational Linguistics.

Satanjeev Banerjee and Alon Lavie. 2005. METEOR: An automatic metric for MT evaluation with improved correlation with human judgments. In *Proceedings of the ACL Workshop on Intrinsic and Extrinsic Evaluation Measures for Machine Translation and/or Summarization*, pages 65–72, Ann Arbor, Michigan. Association for Computational Linguistics.

Christopher JC Burges. 2010. From ranknet to lambdarank to lambdamart: An overview. *Learning*, 11(23-581):81.

Kevin Clark, Minh-Thang Luong, Quoc V. Le, and Christopher D. Manning. 2020. ELECTRA: Pre-training text encoders as discriminators rather than generators. In *ICLR*.

Jacob Devlin, Ming-Wei Chang, Kenton Lee, and Kristina Toutanova. 2019. BERT: Pre-training of deep bidirectional transformers for language understanding. In *Proceedings of the 2019 Conference of the North American Chapter of the Association for Computational Linguistics: Human Language Technologies, Volume 1 (Long and Short Papers)*, pages 4171–4186, Minneapolis, Minnesota. Association for Computational Linguistics.

Song Feng. 2021. DialDoc 2021 shared task: Goal-oriented document-grounded dialogue modeling. In *Proceedings of the 1st Workshop on Document-grounded Dialogue and Conversational Question Answering (DialDoc 2021)*, pages 1–7, Online. Association for Computational Linguistics.

Song Feng, Siva Sankalp Patel, Hui Wan, and Sachindra Joshi. 2021. MultiDoc2Dial: Modeling dialogues grounded in multiple documents. In *Proceedings of the 2021 Conference on Empirical Methods in Natural Language Processing*, pages 6162–6176, Online and Punta Cana, Dominican Republic. Association for Computational Linguistics.

Song Feng, Hui Wan, Chulaka Gunasekara, Siva Patel, Sachindra Joshi, and Luis Lastras. 2020. doc2dial: A goal-oriented document-grounded dialogue dataset. In *Proceedings of the 2020 Conference on Empirical Methods in Natural Language Processing (EMNLP)*, pages 8118–8128, Online. Association for Computational Linguistics.

Thibault Formal, Carlos Lassance, Benjamin Piwowarski, and Stéphane Clinchant. 2021. Splade v2: Sparse lexical and expansion model for information retrieval. *arXiv preprint arXiv:2109.10086*.

Meiqi Guo, Mingda Zhang, Siva Reddy, and Malihe Alikhani. 2021. Abg-coqa: Clarifying ambiguity in conversational question answering. In *3rd Conference on Automated Knowledge Base Construction*.

Gautier Izacard and Edouard Grave. 2021. Leveraging passage retrieval with generative models for open domain question answering. In *Proceedings of the 16th Conference of the European Chapter of the Association for Computational Linguistics: Main Volume*, pages 874–880, Online. Association for Computational Linguistics.

Vladimir Karpukhin, Barlas Oguz, Sewon Min, Patrick Lewis, Ledell Wu, Sergey Edunov, Danqi Chen, and Wen-tau Yih. 2020. Dense passage retrieval for open-domain question answering. In *Proceedings of the 2020 Conference on Empirical Methods in Natural Language Processing (EMNLP)*, pages 6769–6781, Online. Association for Computational Linguistics.

Mike Lewis, Yinhan Liu, Naman Goyal, Marjan Ghazvininejad, Abdelrahman Mohamed, Omer Levy, Veselin Stoyanov, and Luke Zettlemoyer. 2020a. BART: Denoising sequence-to-sequence pre-training for natural language generation, translation, and comprehension. In *Proceedings of the 58th Annual Meeting of the Association for Computational Linguistics*, pages 7871–7880, Online. Association for Computational Linguistics.

Patrick S. H. Lewis, Ethan Perez, Aleksandra Piktus, Fabio Petroni, Vladimir Karpukhin, Naman Goyal, Heinrich Küttler, Mike Lewis, Wen tau Yih, Tim Rocktäschel, Sebastian Riedel, and Douwe Kiela. 2020b. Retrieval-augmented generation for knowledge-intensive nlp tasks. In *NeurIPS*.

Chin-Yew Lin. 2004. ROUGE: A package for automatic evaluation of summaries. In *Text Summarization Branches Out*, pages 74–81, Barcelona, Spain. Association for Computational Linguistics.

Yinhan Liu, Myle Ott, Naman Goyal, Jingfei Du, Mandar Joshi, Danqi Chen, Omer Levy, Mike Lewis, Luke Zettlemoyer, and Veselin Stoyanov. 2019. Roberta: A robustly optimized BERT pretraining approach. *CoRR*, abs/1907.11692.

Matt Post. 2018. A call for clarity in reporting BLEU scores. In *Proceedings of the Third Conference on Machine Translation: Research Papers*, pages 186–191, Brussels, Belgium. Association for Computational Linguistics.

Chen Qu, Liu Yang, Cen Chen, Minghui Qiu, W. Bruce Croft, and Mohit Iyyer. 2020. *Open-Retrieval Conversational Question Answering*, page 539–548. Association for Computing Machinery, New York, NY, USA.

Pranav Rajpurkar, Jian Zhang, Konstantin Lopyrev, and Percy Liang. 2016. Squad: 100, 000+ questions for machine comprehension of text. In *EMNLP*.

Lee Xiong, Chenyan Xiong, Ye Li, Kwok-Fung Tang, Jialin Liu, Paul N. Bennett, Junaid Ahmed, and Arnold Overwijk. 2021. Approximate nearest neighbor negative contrastive learning for dense text retrieval. In *International Conference on Learning Representations*.

Runxin Xu, Fuli Luo, Zhiyuan Zhang, Chuanqi Tan, Baobao Chang, Songfang Huang, and Fei Huang. 2021. Raise a child in large language model: Towards effective and generalizable fine-tuning. In *Proceedings of the 2021 Conference on Empirical Methods in Natural Language Processing*, pages 9514–9528, Online and Punta Cana, Dominican Republic. Association for Computational Linguistics.

Jingqing Zhang, Yao Zhao, Mohammad Saleh, and Peter Liu. 2020. Pegasus: Pre-training with extracted gap-sentences for abstractive summarization. In *International Conference on Machine Learning*, pages 11328–11339. PMLR.

Author Index

Association for Computational Linguistics
209 N. Eighth Street
Stroudsburg, Pennsylvania 18360

ISBN 978-1-7138-6734-0

CURRAN ASSOCIATES INC.
proceedings.com